## Praise for *Designing Effective Teach*

“I am a believer that building oneself as an edu … environments. While reading *Designing Effective Teaching and Significant Learning* I could identify countless applicable connections with my leadership work as an engineering manager for a creative software company. This book comes at a pivotal moment in the evolution of learning: We have access to more information than ever, and technology is rapidly evolving. This means we need to be more strategic about what we learn and how transferable that is to the next task/job/industry. This book is both an invitation to reflect on our methods as educators and a practical guide for not only faculty members but also industry leaders on how to successfully prepare individuals for a future where their contributions are rewarding and impactful.”—***Manuel Castellanos Raboso****, Engineering Manager, Adobe Inc.*

“This book combines an action-oriented guide to effective teaching with a reflective workshop on significant learning. The authors blend personal stories, practical techniques, critical questions, and deep wisdom in ways that will resonate with busy faculty. I particularly appreciate the reminder to pay close attention to the students in our classes because, in the end, their learning is what makes our teaching meaningful.”—***Peter Felten****, Executive Director, Center for Engaged Learning, Elon University*

“Want to take your capabilities as a teacher from ‘Good’ to ‘Great’? This book can help you do that. It focuses on just the right range of topics and has a powerful blend of stories, examples of good course design, and substantive guidance.”—***L. Dee Fink****, former Founding Director, Instructional Development Program, University of Oklahoma*

“Well-organized and accessible, I appreciated how the book invites the reader to participate on the page in the enterprise of designing effective teaching and significant learning—two complementary aspects of effective instruction. This book will serve as a welcome refresher for seasoned educational developers and faculty and a friendly on-ramp for newcomers.”—***Hoag Holmgren****, Executive Director, Professional and Organizational Development Network in Higher Education*

“*Designing Effective Teaching and Significant Learning* is a uniquely comprehensive resource for post-secondary instructors. Building on a tried and true course design process, the authors augment their step-by-step guide with examples and in-depth explorations of important topics. I expect this volume will help guide faculty from the first course they teach through ongoing growth and development across their careers.”—***Cassandra Horii****; Founding Director; Center for Teaching, Learning, and Outreach; California Institute of Technology*

“The authors of *Designing Effective Teaching and Significant Learning* demonstrate a deep understanding of the subject of college teaching and learning at both the conceptual and pragmatic levels through stories, examples, and techniques. Developing a deeper understanding of teaching and learning helps both the student and teacher succeed.”—***John Mirocha****, Executive Coach and Consultant, John Mirocha & Associates; and former Professor of Management, St. Thomas University*

"Smartly anchored in L. Dee Fink's seminal work, *Creating Significant Learning Experiences*, this course design book extends the framework into topics typically not included in this type of book—instructional software, learning management system usage, cognitive science, course assessment rubrics, and program and institutional evaluation—in addition to the subjects you'd expect. It features plentiful examples; relatable cases; and, for each chapter, opening points-to-ponder and closing summary action checklists. It pays particular attention to the needs of community college faculty."—***Linda B. Nilson****, Director Emerita, Office of Teaching Effectiveness and Innovation, Clemson University*

"*Designing Effective Teaching and Significant Learning* builds on the work of L. Dee Fink by providing pragmatic advice to post-secondary faculty in the design of traditional, blended, and online courses. This book covers a broad range of topics, from basics in preparing or designing a course to more advanced concepts such as making courses accessible and assessing a program or institution. I found the chapter 'Communicating in Your Course' helpful in developing workshops for faculty on student engagement in online courses."—***Martin Springborg****, Director of Teaching and Learning, Inver Hills Community College and Dakota County Technical College*

"This book is a great resource for higher education instructors willing to challenge their traditional strategies and practices. . . . It promotes self-reflection on current teaching approaches and helps faculty understand, through illustrative examples, how the adoption of integrative strategies leads to significant learning experiences. In parallel, the reader is guided smoothly through the major steps of integrated course design: from using the taxonomy for significant learning to assessing and reflecting on the teaching and learning procedure, passing by defining and aligning the course outcomes with the learning and assessment activities, communicating effectively, making the course accessible and integrating learning technologies. It is undeniably an inspirational and enlightening work . . . not to be missed!"—***Faten el Hage Yahchouchi****; Deputy President for Teaching and Learning, Holy Spirit University of Kaslik (USEK); Beirut, Lebanon*

# DESIGNING EFFECTIVE TEACHING AND SIGNIFICANT LEARNING

**About the Cover:** The headwaters of the Mississippi River at Lake Itasca in Minnesota are symbolic of the mighty impact that quality course design and teaching can have on students' learning. What appears to start small gathers strength and power because the current, like learning, runs deep. The compass and blueprint reference course design excellence to guide our teaching and creation of significant learning experiences.

# DESIGNING EFFECTIVE TEACHING AND SIGNIFICANT LEARNING

*Zala Fashant, Stewart Ross, Linda Russell, Karen LaPlant, Jake Jacobson, and Sheri Hutchinson*

Foreword by L. Dee Fink

STERLING, VIRGINIA

Published by Stylus Publishing, LLC.
22883 Quicksilver Drive
Sterling, Virginia 20166-2019



Library of Congress Cataloging-in-Publication Data
The CIP for this text has been applied for.

13-digit ISBN: 978-1-64267-004-2 (cloth)
13-digit ISBN: 978-1-64267-005-9 (paperback)
13-digit ISBN: 978-1-64267-006-6 (library networkable e-edition)
13-digit ISBN: 978-1-64267-007-3 (consumer e-edition)

Printed in the United States of America

All first editions printed on acid-free paper
that meets the American National Standards Institute
Z39-48 Standard.



First Edition, 2020

*This book is dedicated to the students we have taught, the colleagues we have collaborated with, the mentors we have learned from, and our supportive families. Thank you all for helping us make this project a reality.*

# CONTENTS

# FOREWORD

When I finished writing the original edition of *Creating Significant Learning Experiences* in 2003, I thought the book had good ideas in it, but one never knows how others will receive it. However, the response to it has been far beyond anything I dared to hope for. As soon as the book came out, the requests for campus workshops on the ideas became so great that within two years I retired from my full-time job at the University of Oklahoma to do almost full-time consulting. In fact, my wife has often quipped (correctly) that "Dee didn't retire, he just changed jobs!"

One year after that, the demand for workshops continued to rise, so I contacted three fellow faculty developers whose workshops I admired and recruited them to lead my workshop too as members of Dee Fink & Associates. Coauthor Stewart Ross was one of these associates. My associates and I have now led hundreds of campus workshops in nearly every state in the United States and in more than 20 other countries in Latin America, Europe, the Middle East, Africa, Asia, and Oceania. The other exciting development has been hearing that the book has frequently been selected as one of the primary texts for courses on college teaching for graduate students and prospective college teachers.

What accounts for this response to the ideas in that book? When I asked people this question, they mention two parts of the book. First, they like the taxonomy of significant learning that builds on the famous taxonomy of desired kinds of learning created by Bloom, Engelhart, Furst, Hill, and Krathwohl (1956). Many mention that they especially like the new kinds of learning in my taxonomy, such as understanding oneself better, learning how to interact with others more effectively, embracing new values or interests and rethinking old values, and learning how to keep on learning after the course is over. These are the kinds of learning many teachers had intuitively felt were important but were not sure were legitimate learning goals for a college course. They said they were thrilled when the taxonomy gave them permission to include these new kinds of learning as explicit goals for their courses.

However, although the taxonomy prompts and inspires teachers to strive for a broader set of learning goals for their courses, it also challenges them with how to get these new kinds of learning to happen. This led to the second idea readers say they like in the book, the model of integrated course design. This model describes a step-by-step process that creates a high likelihood that a majority of students will actually achieve the desired kinds of learning because the teacher has the right learning and assessment activities for each kind of learning and has put these activities into a dynamic sequence.

The net effect of these ideas has been to give teachers a new sense of empowerment. Many of our workshop participants report they feel a new capacity for intentionality. The ideas take much of the mystery out of teaching because they have a fuller understanding of what teaching involves, and they have a new set of tools to get good teaching and good learning to happen for a greater proportion of their students.

However, even though the ideas of integrated course design seemed clear and relatively straightforward after people read the book or participated in a workshop, questions still arise when they start to perform each of the substeps involved. Questions included the following: Should I write the learning goals this way or that way? Are these learning and assessment activities appropriate for that learning goal? Is this a dynamic teaching strategy and sequence of activities, or is there a better sequence to use? And it is here where *Designing Effective Teaching and Significant Learning* comes in. This book offers readers two sets of helpful resources. First, this book draws on the extensive experiences of the contributors in working with and listening to teachers as they implement the ideas from Fink (2003). They note where teachers and instructional designers feel challenged and offer specific ideas, strategies, and tips on how to deal with questions like the following: How can I understand what challenges my students face in learning this material? How can I integrate technology to extend active learning through real-world and team-based experiences? How can I assess these new kinds of learning, the ones that go beyond purely cognitive learning? How can I better meet the learning needs of a greater diversity of learners? How can I be sure my course and its materials are accessible, meeting the Americans with Disabilities Act (1990) requirements so all learners can learn? And so forth.

Second, this book discusses several questions that go beyond course design per se, for example, How can I work with students more effectively? How can I assess my course in terms of its own stated learning goals and the degree to which it contributes to the institution's learning goals and mission? How can I reflect on my teaching to clearly identify my strengths and areas where change is needed? and How can I develop a plan for continuously expanding my teaching capabilities?

Teachers who learn how to implement the basic principles of learning-centered course design, and who learn how to address all the additional tasks related to teaching effectively, will greatly enhance the quantity and quality of student learning and their own joy in teaching.

L. Dee Fink
University of Oklahoma, Norman (retired)
September 2018

# PREFACE

Author Stewart Ross attended an integrated course design workshop in 2000 conducted by L. Dee Fink (2003) where he first learned about the taxonomy of significant learning, which changed his professional and personal life. This workshop helped him realize that his concern for adding value to college student lives was important and necessary. He had long felt that students' learning information and passing tests only to forget most of what was on the test was not good enough for college teaching and learning. Just as powerful, however, he was fortunate to meet and befriend Fink and soon became a presenter of the workshop.

To date, he has conducted more than 160 integrated course design workshops nationally and internationally along with teaching this design through online courses. He has worked with hundreds of faculty around the world who have taken the workshop or had him critique their completed course designs. He has now had the opportunity to contribute to the book you have in your hands or are reading electronically. In this book we provide examples of how faculty have taken theory into practice, creating rich, exciting courses for their college students that lead to engagement, motivation, and deep learning. Faculty who use the taxonomy for significant learning (Fink, 2003) to create courses that lead their students to lifelong learning, critical thinking, and the ability to learn how to learn after the course is over.

According to an anonymous workshop participant,

> The principles of Integrated Course Design have the potential to let students drive their own learning and generate their own momentum with my role to give oversight, coaching, and motivation. I plan to use principles such as backward design. I now realize that many of the principles are for life rather than just academic education.

Ross began his career teaching for 1 year at a high school then 2 years at a community college before moving to university teaching. During his first year at the university he wrote lectures; delivered them the next day; and gave high-stakes, 100-question, multiple-choice exams at midterm and at the final. If students did poorly, he never blamed himself and thought they hadn't studied enough. He did not think much about giving or receiving feedback or how he might improve student learning; he was too busy teaching. It was all about sharing information and expecting students to make it their own, somehow magically turning it into knowledge they could use.

When Ross reflected on those early days of his teaching, he realized that students were not learning well, mainly because of his lack of knowledge about, and alignment of, course outcomes, assessments, and learning activities. He had never thought much about what he really wanted students to learn and how they would learn. His goal had been to create mini music majors in an introductory music appreciation course. Over time, he became an award-winning instructor as he moved from a teacher-centered to a learner-centered paradigm.

Ross also learned much from the faculty participating in his course design workshops. Faculty are no longer content to share information with students hoping they will remember it long enough to pass tests. They are looking for powerful tools to use as they endeavor to increase student learning. Foundational knowledge is crucial to learning, but there is so much more. Students need to know how to use information. They need to see the connections among ideas in a course and from course to course and from courses to their own lives. Before graduating from college students should learn about themselves, develop confidence, and construct their own learning and a better understanding of who they are in their own ethical development. In today's world our students must be able to work using innovative thinking and with people from diverse backgrounds. They need to deliver information and ideas through a variety of technologies that best communicate with their audience; and the communication needs to be collaborative rather than one way.

## Setting the Tone: Good Teaching to Rich Learning

It is even more important for our students to find ways to learn how to learn on their own after their courses are completed and the degree is awarded. They need to learn about how they learn and how they plan to continue learning to advance in their career. This book is written for faculty who want to assist students in these pursuits, not so much with theory but with actual examples from experienced teachers and those who develop courses using significant student learning as their goal.

In the olden days, cars had hood ornaments that identified the designer of the car. When driving, no one focused on the hood ornament but looked farther down the road to see where they were going. Not taking current course design ideas into consideration is a lot like focusing our eyes on the hood ornament of the car instead of looking down the road. Course design can't just be about finishing the course. It needs to prepare students to look farther down the road. If your course design has been the same for a number of years, and it doesn't prepare students to perform the skills they need for success in work and life, then it is time for a redesign.

Today institutions struggle with how to retain students while preparing them for an ever-changing future society and workplace. Much more energy is being poured into showing students how a course is a part of a continuous curriculum that leads to the final goal of a certificate or degree. Support for student learning comes academically from learning centers that provide tutoring and advising help. We applaud this effort, but we can't stop there. We need to examine the core of learning, which is the course and the engagement the instructor has with the student. We need to show how the course is a part of a curriculum that leads to a successful life and career. As much as going to school is a great experience, success in the workplace is the goal. To paraphrase Shakespeare's Prince Hamlet, The work's the thing.

## Using This Book to Deliver Significant Learning

The purpose of the book is to provide you with the benefit of your knowledge and collective years of teaching in a variety of disciplines and of our faculty development experience. As in Ross's experience described earlier, we have been faculty and administrators at two- and four-year colleges and universities and have presented at many international disciplinary and teaching and learning conferences. This team has been recognized for its outstanding teaching and educational innovations.

In the field of faculty development we have directed teaching and learning centers on college and university campuses and led a campus network of leaders systemwide who have conducted more than 500 workshops, webinars, and conferences for more than 10,000 faculty members. We have learned that all full-time and part-time faculty members need to be at their best as everyone is on the starting lineup on the academic team. This content in this book is designed for all faculty, new and experienced, tenured and adjunct. You will learn about ideas that you can implement immediately and those that will need deeper planning.

The overarching content of this book considers all the elements of course design and its overall impact on student learning, effective teaching, and institutional mission. The design of the book provides you with the opportunity to start at the beginning and read to the end or examine individual chapters to gain more knowledge on a topic. It is meant to deliver just-in-time learning so you can benefit from the content of the chapter you need when you need it. Whether you are new, early, middle, or later-career faculty, you will be able to use the chapters as you need them for ideas and strategies for your work on campus.

Each chapter follows the same format, the same way you should provide consistency for your students to learn in your course design, and includes these elements:

- *Points to Ponder* is an overture to prepare your mind for the thinking and acts as a hook for the content.
- Vignettes provide real faculty and student experiences that set the tone for how the chapter content plays out in teaching and learning.
- Content is what you should know and how it can be applied in your teaching to provide significant learning. Boxes titled *Bright Ideas* provide stories that detail the experiences faculty have had in course design that worked well in our courses and that you can add to your courses. We also include *Jot Your Thoughts* boxes where you can write your notes so you don't lose your own good ideas while reading.
- *Reflect on This Chapter* contains questions for reflection as you develop a plan for using the content in your teaching practice.
- *Action Checklists* for each chapter are intended to help you apply the content to your course design.

## Chapter Overviews

### *Part One: Starting*

Chapter 1, "Preparing for Your Course Design," is the overture to planning for course design. As with any journey, some preparation is needed to set up the success of the endeavor. A discussion of significant learning leads to the examination of taxonomy frameworks. The identification of your course's situational factors leads to a deeper look at the expectations others have about your course, the characteristics of the learners, and your own characteristics as their teacher. Finally, your analysis of the situational factors will help you with the pedagogical challenges you need to address in your design.

### *Part Two: Designing*

In chapter 2, "Integrating Your Course Design," you will learn that designing your course properly allows you to teach interactively and provides students with significant learning experiences. You will have the opportunity to engage in Fink's (2013) integrated course design to develop and align learning outcomes, assessments, and activities in your face-to-face, blended, and online courses. An example of a completed three-column table (Table 2.5) demonstrates course integration that you can use as a model for your own course design.

Chapter 3, "Communicating in Your Course," focuses on planning integrated, multiple approaches to communicate to develop a welcoming and engaging environment for learning. A variety of communication tools and strategies are discussed to better engage students before, during, and at the end of the course to develop a more student-centered experience. Examples are provided so you can analyze the effectiveness of current strategies on the path to designing a communication plan that can be integrated into the course design.

Chapter 4, "Creating a Learning Framework," describes and summarizes research-based learning models and current thinking about learning processes as they relate to teaching and learning in various formats. This chapter provides the foundation for chapter 5 because it reinforces the course design model.

To practice the theory presented in chapter 4, chapter 5, "Developing Learning Activities and Techniques," describes learning activities as well as provides templates and sample activities and techniques appropriate to bridge the course outcomes to the assessments and to promote active learning and stronger student engagement.

As accessibility for all learners is critical for student success, in chapter 6, "Making Your Course Accessible," you will discover how to make your course and content materials meet requirements of the Americans with Disabilities Act (1990). A discussion of providing accommodations for student learning provides insights to broaden pedagogical practice, which benefits all students, not just those who need accommodations. These skills are also important to teach students so they can develop their own accessible materials in the course and the workplace.

Chapter 7, "Integrating Learning Technologies," illustrates that technology can serve as a great way to increase engagement and enhance the quality of learning experiences. Identifying a need and choosing appropriate tools and strategies to embed in the course can support learning activities, help students meet course outcomes, and prepare them for work after graduation. We include a discussion about choosing tools that will help faculty with course management so they can spend more time working with students.

### *Part Three: Assessing*

As understanding types of assessments and strategies to use multiple measurements to assess the whole student will make assessing student learning more fruitful, chapter 8, "Assessing Student Learning," includes developing backward- and forward-looking authentic portfolio assessments. We include an examination of the components of rubric development. A crosswalk comparison (Table 8.2) demonstrates how to link learning activities with assessment techniques. This is a valuable addition to assisting your course design as it provides ways to design using a blend of assessments and activities that are informal and formal or formative and summative, and offers a variety of learning types and possible technology requirements. Finally, a discussion of how faculty can use assessment results is included.

In chapter 9, "Assessing Course Quality," using the best practices of designing face-to-face, blended, and online courses provides opportunities to assess the quality of a course. Gathering student feedback in reflection activities and course evaluation surveys are ways to measure what is working and what can be improved to build a stronger course through continuous improvement.

Because faculty are expected to provide academic leadership in program and institutional assessment, chapter 10, "Assessing Your Program and Institution," discusses the need to integrate micro to macro levels of assessment from the student to the course to the program or department or to the institution by providing continuity for quality. Since some programs and departments and all institutions are required to measure their outcomes for accreditation, knowing how your course relates to the curriculum of the program or department and how these align with the institution's mission completes the overall assessment picture.

### *Part Four: Reflecting*

Reflecting on your teaching is key to continuous growth, improvement, and sustainability. Additionally, there are a variety of steps required for promotion and tenure. Chapter 11, "Reflecting on Your Teaching," focuses on what you can do to archive your work to monitor your performance and demonstrate your accomplishments as evidence of your quality work.

As with our students, we need to assess where we are in our practices and envision the pathway we want to take to achieve our goals. Reflection is the first step in thinking about your teaching and identifying where you are on your career pathway.

Chapter 12, "Learning How to Learn: Advancing Your Professional Development," is a discussion of how to use professional organizations and campus resources to help you create your professional development plan for career advancement.

The chapters in this book provide more than 70 Bright Ideas on teaching and learning with spaces for you to take notes so you can add your ideas to create an action plan for changes you want to implement in your courses, teaching, and professional development. That is the first step to making the changes you think will enhance your teaching and significant learning for your students. Each chapter has an Action Checklist based on the chapter content to help you organize your next steps.

Two additional chapters, which are available on our website (https://encoreprodev.com/book), discuss the needs of new faculty. The first chapter, "Making a Strong Start on Your Campus," focuses on key questions faculty have when starting in a new position or on a new campus. Ranging from logistics to garnering support from colleagues, this chapter will help them navigate the important challenges they need to address first to lead to success.

Because building a relationship with your supervisor is something that will benefit your work, the second chapter on our website, "Working Effectively With Your Dean and Department Chair," will help you understand the role your dean or chair plays in the administration and help you navigate your career. This person also plays a significant role in your life and can help guide your direction, provide wisdom during academic challenges, and assist you in growing professionally.

Our philosophy is that reflection on the teaching practice is one of the most important tools in learning and professional development, so we provide the space to write your thoughts throughout the book under Jot Your Thoughts. Make this book your own. We intend for you to be an author too, so write your reflections about what you are learning. Our goal is for you to use this book as a guide to refer to so often that the pages will be well worn as your progress in your teaching career.

In the back of the book, an area that is sometimes skipped over by the reader, we provided appendixes with additional material for use in your design. A glossary contains terms that may be new to you, and outcomes for each chapter have been provided to assist your learning. We also include an Additional Readings and Resources section for further reading and study.

Our team of educators took great pleasure in writing this book, and we are pleased that L. Dee Fink has written the foreword. The ideas presented here are tried and true. All the team members have stood in front of their peers and shared their strategies to improve faculty teaching and student learning. In return, they have helped thousands of students achieve their dream of a successful life and career while providing them with the confidence to change themselves in an ever-changing world.

All educators go through these steps in learning to teach and in developing significant learning. You are not alone. Our goal for this book is to provide you with a wealth of ideas to help you design courses that provide significant learning to change the lives of your students and help you achieve your mission and the mission of your institution.

# ACKNOWLEDGMENTS

As we reflect on the pathway to publishing, we would like to individually acknowledge the people who helped develop our careers and made this book possible. Ours is a collaborative team, and we have been fortunate to have worked with one another in faculty development for many years. Our individual strengths have helped each of us to grow as we have taught and made presentations together. We have easily passed the baton of leadership and content expertise to one another, recognizing how teaming our strengths could benefit our students and institutions. Collectively, we would like to thank those who went before us to lead and to teach us what we needed to know to design effective teaching and significant learning experiences for our students. Many of us have benefited from the work of L. Dee Fink. A special thank-you goes to Cheryl Neudauer for her contributions to several chapters of this book.

## Zala Fashant

Thank you to my higher education colleagues with whom I have had the honor of working during my positions in teaching, faculty development, and administration. Forming a team to turn great ideas into practice created a community of learners that helped my own growth. I want to thank Gordon Mortrude, education professor and mentor who helped fuel my desire to be the best teacher I could, and my former principal C. Elaine Burgess, who encouraged me to be my best by creating memory makers for students in the classroom and who helped launch my career as a college administrator. Further thanks go to my elementary, high school, undergraduate, and graduate students, who helped me realize that all learners share the same desires and fears and that common threads exist in all levels of education. As a faculty developer, I think back to the first time I heard a presentation by L. Dee Fink at an international conference. Thanks, Dee, for inviting me to coach faculty at your national workshops. Finally, I appreciate the support of family and friends who understand my desire to share what I learned with others to help them on their own teaching journey.

## Stewart Ross

It is always a challenge to thank people when there are so many to thank. However, I was fortunate to become friends with L. Dee Fink 16 years ago when I was a participant in an early workshop he was conducting on integrated course design. Just a couple of years later I became the founding director for the Center for Excellence in Teaching and Learning at Minnesota State University, Mankato, where I worked with more than 600 full-time professors over a 10-year period. I learned much during that decade, and I was also presenting workshops nationally and internationally on course design for Dee Fink & Associates and on active learning and other subjects related to quality teaching and learning at the university level. After more than 160 workshops, I am indebted to those faculty who not only learned how to improve their courses and create high-quality new courses but also helped me better understand the needs of faculty in terms of improving student learning. And I am indebted to the hundreds and hundreds of students I worked with in my teaching career. It is my distinct honor to have contributed to this book on teaching and learning, and I am forever grateful to Zala Fashant, colleague and friend for so many years.

## Linda Russell

My first and most important thanks go to the hundreds of students who over the years have taught me how to be a better teacher and a better human being. Also, a thank-you goes to my husband, John Mirocha, and my children, Erin and Jordan, who are my number one supporters. It has been a bit of a role switch for them to be rooting for me from the sidelines. Cheryl Neudauer provided valuable contributions to this book and was so much fun to collaborate with. Finally, I thank my good friend Diana Hestwood for the many brainstorming and processing sessions while writing this book and for 29 years of wonderful friendship and professional collaborations.

## Karen LaPlant

This book was the brainchild of Zala Fashant and wouldn't have been possible without his project management and writing and keeping us on task or Linda Russell's writing and editing or Jake Jacobson's, Sheri Hutchinson's, and Stewart Ross's writing. It is a book filled with what we have learned over the past 30 years. It is all the information I wish I had available when I began teaching in higher education. As attributed to Ben Franklin and several others: "Tell me and I forget, teach me and I may remember, involve me and I learn."

## Jake Jacobson

Creativity, teaching, writing, research, and publishing are team sports, and I am proud to have been working with and been supported by some the best in education from around the world. Nevertheless, first and foremost, my thanks go to my students; it is their trust that drove me to become a better teacher and later a faculty developer to teach those lessons learned. This is why I am able to engage in and meld the careers I love. *Explicit—Expliceat! Ludere scriptor eat.* Loosely translated, this means: "It is finished—let it finish! Let the scribe go out to play."

## Sheri Hutchinson

This book was created from the combined knowledge and skills of dedicated professional educators who serve their students around the world. The lessons in this book are from hard-fought battles on the educational playing field that isn't level for our students, much less for the faculty and staff. We wish to express our sincere thanks to everyone who helped lift us up and also to those who set up roadblocks along the way. We always appreciate the gracious supervisors we work with and are grateful for the less gracious supervisors who taught us life lessons on what we should not repeat. Thanks to Zala Fashant for being one of the gracious supervisors and for pushing us into this project, often with many polite and kind nudges.

# PART ONE

# STARTING

# I

# PREPARING FOR YOUR COURSE DESIGN

## Points to Ponder

In thinking about designing the courses you teach, consider the following questions to examine your prior knowledge:

- What are your experiences in teaching your courses as a new or midcareer faculty and how does that affect your course design proficiency? What data do you receive about your course's success? What measures do you use to determine how well the course is working?
- How well are students succeeding? What changes in content or practices will help students be successful in their careers?
- In thinking about your courses, which would you most like to redesign?

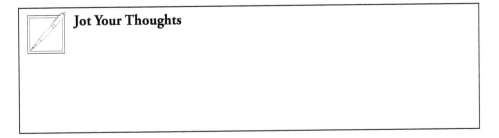

As the midsemester exams were graded, Catherine enjoyed a hot mocha at the local coffee shop. She reflected on her classes, students, teaching, and where she was in her career. In her seventh year of teaching full time, having been an adjunct for three years previously, so many things had changed. Catherine thought about what she knew now that she didn't know when she started.

She taught her first courses as mirror images of the way she was taught at her university. She hadn't struggled as a student so it was difficult to understand why her students didn't just get the content. As a student she was able to memorize well; apply the material; and ace the tests, even essay exams. As a graduate assistant, she got high ratings from her professor as she graded assignments and completed the work he passed on to her. She was glad that she provided a bit more feedback to her students now as it seemed to help them perform better.

Catherine was very confident in her current disciplinary knowledge. As a subject matter expert she had attended professional association conferences every other year to be sure she knew what changes were taking place in her discipline so she could modify her course content. Her students were performing fairly well. She referred them to the learning center as needed and worked with her department to offer study sessions. However, she noticed most of her students didn't take the opportunities for extra help. The course completion and pass rates were on par with her colleagues, matching the department average.

But something was nagging at Catherine. Could she make her courses and teaching any better? She had gone to some campus teaching and learning workshops, picking up some great tips here and there. She had learned about her students. Every time she had a student with a learning challenge she learned a bit more about making accommodations. She knew that some students weren't college ready. Perhaps they just needed to try harder, but she also wondered what she could do to help them succeed in her courses. She had inherited her courses and had made a few changes over the past five years. However, she still felt a bit trapped to teach like her peers. She had a mix of face-to-face and online courses. Students seemed to like the flexibility of online courses, but she felt a distance in communicating with them that she didn't feel when she met with her classroom courses. What could she do to bridge that gap?

Catherine knew how she learned but didn't understand how others learned. She gained some perspective by talking with the students who came in during office hours. What could she do to help students who were not great at the memorization and applying content like she was? She also began to wonder how her courses could be designed to make learning accessible to all her students from the start so she would need to make fewer changes to help them during the semester. Was there new technology that could help her communicate with her students and provide learning in a more significant way so students would benefit in their career long after they left her course?

Catherine gave tests and allowed students to choose projects in some of her courses. Was this enough? She knew students were passing tests but wondered if she was really assessing their mastery of the course outcomes. Hearing about some of her colleagues on campus who were assessing the quality of their courses, she wondered how her courses would compare to theirs. In a couple of years, Catherine's department is going to reapply for accreditation, and she wanted to be sure her courses would help the department in the evaluation. She was also asked by her dean to sit on a faculty committee to prepare for the institution's upcoming accreditation.

Catherine's reflection was giving her some insights. She knew she wanted her courses to significantly affect her students' learning, prepare them for their careers, and help guide them to successful lives. She opened up a book she got at her campus center for teaching and learning, *Designing Effective Teaching and Significant Learning*, and began reading.

## Planning for Course Design

Designing your courses to deliver effective teaching and significant learning is arguably one of the most effective ways to set students up for success. Our goal in writing this book is to assist you as you consider all the elements of course design and its overall impact on student learning, effective teaching, and institutional mission. Blending your prior knowledge and experiences with the content in this book will help you improve your current practice, making teaching even more enjoyable as you see your students more engaged in their learning. We have seen the impact of well-designed courses. We have worked with faculty worldwide to help them deliver the kinds of courses they have always wanted to teach. More important, in this book we share the stories of how faculty have transformed courses from theory to practice. As faculty developers and leaders in course design, we realize how course design models have expanded over the years. We start with Fink's (2013) foundation of integrating course design and provide additional design concepts to expand the course blueprint to implement plans for communication, accessibility, technology integration, and the assessment of course design as it fits into the assessment of programs and institutions and how you can use what you learn to meet your professional goals. Let's start this journey by discussing how you can prepare for designing your courses.

Fink (2013) explains the process of design that goes beyond creating an outline for delivering content. Using Fink's integrated course design approach, faculty develop an intentional course plan by considering the situational factors, reflecting on their big dream for what they want students to take from the course, developing outcomes and assessments first, and then adding the bridging learning activities. Fink (2005) provided the following steps in designing courses for significant learning: In the initial design phase (Steps 1–5), Designing Courses That Promote Significant Learning, if professors want to create courses in which students have significant learning experiences, they need to design that quality into their courses. How can they do that? By following these basic steps of the instructional design process:

- Step 1. Give careful consideration to a variety of situational factors. Use the backward design process.
- Step 2. Determine learning goals. What do you want students to learn by the end of the course that will still be with them several years later?
- Step 3. Create feedback and assessment procedures. What will the students have to do to demonstrate they have achieved the learning goals?
- Step 4. Develop teaching and learning activities. What would have to happen during the course for students to do well on the feedback and assessment activities?
- Step 5. Think of create ways to involve students that will support your more expansive learning goals.

Check to ensure that the key components (Steps 1–4) are all consistent and support each other in integrated course design (Fink, 2005). This abbreviated list of steps is a valuable resource for you in designing your course. See Appendix A for the complete document, where you will find descriptions for each of Fink's (2005) elements for course design. Chapter 2 will provide the opportunity to use this as you examine your own courses.

## Bloom's and Fink's Taxonomies

Many of you are familiar with the six levels of Bloom and colleagues' (1956) taxonomy: Remembering, understanding, applying, analyzing, evaluating, and creating. Many instructors incorporate a variety of these levels in their courses as they scaffold content and experiences to engage students in learning. It is best to use level-appropriate verbs to match where your course lies in the curriculum pathway. Anderson and Krathwohl's (2001) revised version of Bloom's taxonomy names six distinct levels of skills (as shown in Figure 1.1):

1. Remembering: recalling information; remembering facts, vocabulary terms, and basic concepts
2. Understanding: demonstrating the understanding of facts through comparison, organizing, providing descriptions or main ideas
3. Applying: using acquired knowledge to solve problems and navigate new situations
4. Analyzing: breaking down information into components, discovering the relationships between parts, cause and effect, identifying inferences and supporting evidence
5. Evaluating: judging the quality of information, ideas, or work based on criteria
6. Creating: putting together parts into a whole; developing models; synthesizing new processes, ideas, or products

If you were teaching the beginning course in a series of courses, you would tend to use more of the lower level outcomes to start and transition to using the higher level outcomes that are appropriate for the advanced skill levels you would like

**Figure 1.1** Bloom's taxonomy.

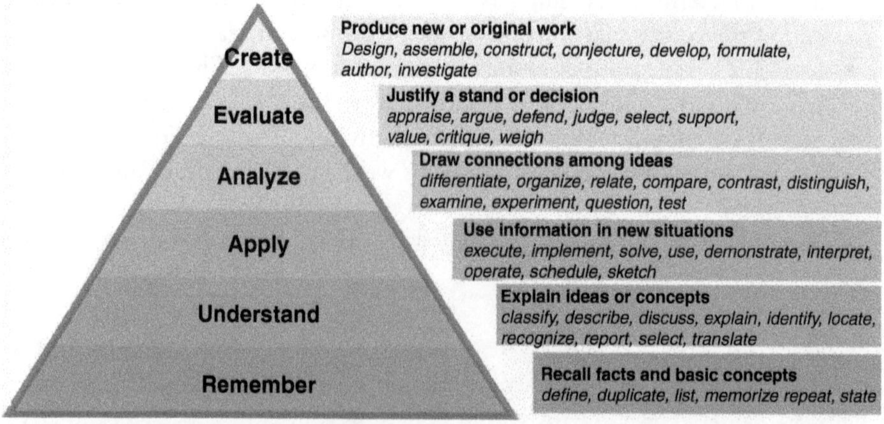

*Note.* Bloom's taxonomy includes the hierarchical domains of remember, understand, apply, analyze, evaluate, and create. From "A revision of Bloom's taxonomy: An overview," by D.R. Krathwohl, 2002, *Theory Into Practice*, 41, 212–218.

students to achieve as the course progresses. If your course is one of the final courses in curriculum, you would focus on the higher level skills knowing that students had mastered the lower level content in the foundation courses. Higher level course outcomes would be less about understanding at the knowledge or comprehension level and more about analysis, evaluation, or creation. It is possible to use all of the levels in the same course, but unless students will demonstrate new understanding in an advanced course, your outcomes will use verbs appropriate to the comprehensive and application levels and then move to the analysis and evaluation levels.

All levels of Bloom and colleagues' (1956) taxonomy are included in the first three domains of Fink's (2013) taxonomy. Fink wanted students to focus on how the course would transform them so that the results stayed with them after the course was completed. As shown in Figure 1.2, Fink emphasized that the course would add the domains or values of the human dimensions, caring, and learning how to learn, which would provide a lasting effect on learning through the course content as they moved on to other courses in the curriculum and, eventually, the workplace (Fink, 2013).

**Figure 1.2** Fink's taxonomy of significant learning.

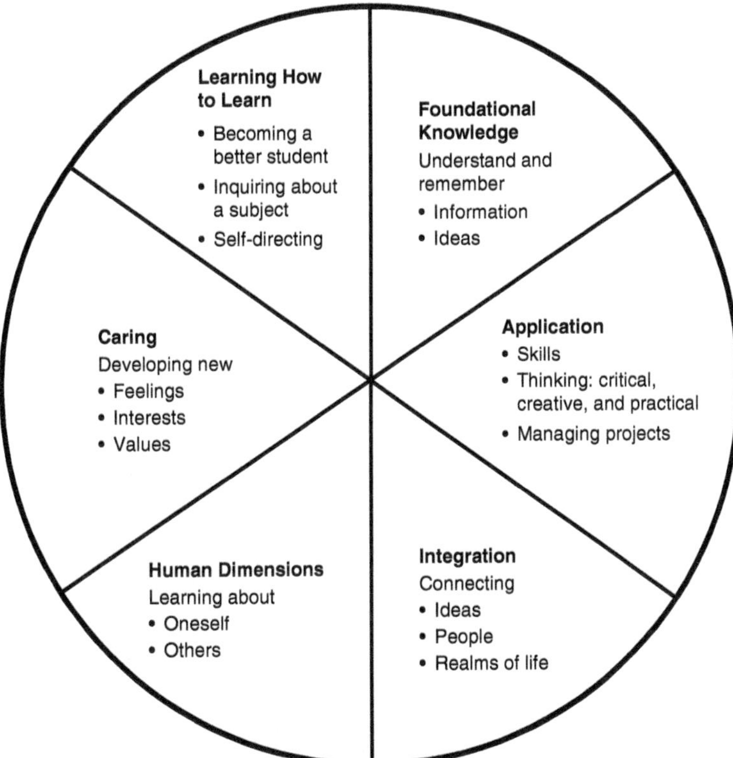


*Note.* Fink's taxonomy includes the domains of foundational knowledge, application, integration, human dimensions for self and others, caring, and learning how to learn. From *Creating Significant Learning Experiences*, p. 30, by L.D. Fink, 2003, San Francisco, CA: Jossey-Bass. Copyright 2003 by L.D. Fink. Used with permission.

In Fink's (2013) taxonomy of significant learning, course outcomes are created for all the areas. They are related to one another but aren't a hierarchy where you build on the lowest level to get to the highest level, which is why Fink's model isn't in the shape of a pyramid like Bloom and colleagues' (1956) but is instead in the shape of a circle (Figure 1.2) with the domains connected like pie pieces.

The following details the domains of the taxonomy of significant learning as seen in Figure 1.2.

- Foundational knowledge consists of new information, ideas, and content introduced in the course or from prior learning that students bring to the course from previous courses and experiences.
- Application is the demonstration of skills and critical, creative, and practical thinking through learning activities and measured in assessments.
- Integration of connections (through finding similarities and interactions) are made within the course, with other courses, and life-work experiences.
- Human dimensions include what students learn from the content as it applies to themselves and as they develop a deeper understanding by interacting with others.
- Caring is the adaptation to or changes learners make by valuing the ideas, feelings, and interests about what they are learning.
- Learning how to learn is what students discover about the way they learn in the course or discipline and being a self-directed, lifelong learner.

Fink's (2013) taxonomy provides a way to have a more outward-looking, beyond-the-course teaching philosophy for students by designing for the human dimensions, caring, and learning how to learn domains.

## Situational Factors

Each course has a set of situational factors (Fink, 2013), which are conditions that can affect the course delivery and its design. These factors can range from the size of the room and whether there are tables and chairs or desks to a reflection of what you, the instructor, bring to the learning experience. They help you identify the foundation for your course. The more in-depth the analysis of the situational factors is, the more valuable this step is in the course design process. Following are examples of situation factors:

- Specific context of the situation. These factors frame the course; for example, the time the course is scheduled, the way the course is delivered (online, face-to-face), the technology requirements, the physical classroom arrangement (lecture, lab), and where this course is offered in the curriculum.
- Expectations of others. Who are the stakeholders affected by this course? The answer here could be the students, other faculty, department, dean, advisory

board, and so on. What specific expectations will be in play for this course design? Is this a required course or elective course? How are students prepared for this course, and how does this course prepare them for what they take next and take away for use in their professional careers?

- Nature of the subject. What are the discipline-specific demands? Science, English, nursing, and business each require different ways of thinking, writing, explaining, and creating meaning. What does the discipline or field require of students on completion? Is the course centered on physical or mental skill sets? Are there safety considerations in labs or working areas?
- Characteristics of learners. Identifying the characteristics of the learners is key. Are your students ready for the level of the course—introductory or advanced? Do they have experience with online learning if your course is delivered online? Do you have students with learning challenges? What knowledge you acquire about the learners who tend to take this course will help you with its design.
- Characteristics of the teacher. This part is a self-analysis and a look at what you are bringing to the course. What is your level of teaching experience; are you a new or veteran faculty member? Is this the first time you are teaching this course, or are you teaching this course differently, perhaps online for the first time? Do you feel confident in teaching the course? Are you feeling any internal or external pressures in teaching this course? This is more personal even though it relates to the expectations of others previously discussed.

For each situational factor, reflect carefully on whether these conditions are in or beyond your control. In our workshops some faculty answer the question of control quickly before really thinking it through. Many times, with our guidance and deeper reflection, they realized there were things they could do to mitigate problems. If you can control the condition, then adjust accordingly. If the condition is beyond your control, you shouldn't waste valuable time trying to fix it or consider it greatly in the course design. Changing course catalog outcomes or requirements by accrediting agencies are examples of factors you may not be able to control. It is better to spend your time designing a course that embraces what you can't change and work with what you can adjust. Think about a current course you might like to redesign. How would each of these situational factors play into the construction of your new course? Table 1.1 will help you identify your course's situational factors.

Although all faculty understand the importance of reflecting on information that will affect teaching their courses, many take only a glance at the situation and context that frame their teaching. For instance, a new faculty member arriving on campus to teach four courses realizes the importance of answering some basic questions: How many students are in the course? What level in the curriculum is the course? What disciplines are represented? and What is the size and shape of the room? These are important concerns and need to be addressed; however, to design a quality course many more questions need to be examined. Consider the following:

**TABLE 1.1**
**Situational Factors**

| *Situational Factor* | *Your Course's Situational Description* |
|---|---|
| **Specific Context of Situation**<br>Class size<br>Course level: introductory, advanced, graduate<br>Meeting time and frequency<br>Delivery: classroom or lab, blended, online<br>Physical classroom conditions<br>Technology requirements | |
| **Expectations of Others**<br>Learning expectations placed on the course by:<br>• Curriculum<br>• Faculty colleagues<br>• Institution<br>• Profession<br>• Accreditation<br>• Society | |
| **Nature of the Subject**<br>Student perception<br>Theoretical, practical, or combination<br>Convergent or divergent<br>Important changes or controversies in the field | |
| **Characteristics of Learners**<br>Student attitudes to subject<br>College ready, advanced<br>Age or experience level<br>Prior learning foundation<br>Student life conditions: Full time, part time, family, working, professional goals | |
| **Characteristics of the Teacher**<br>Philosophy of teaching<br>Attitude about course or subject<br>Perception of students<br>Experience in teaching<br>Knowledge or familiarity of course content<br>Teaching strengths or challenges | |

*Note.* This planning form offers an opportunity to identify a course's situational factors. From *Creating Significant Learning Experiences*, by L.D. Fink, 2003, San Francisco, CA: Jossey-Bass. Copyright 2003 by L.D. Fink. Adapted with permission.

- Does this course lead into another course?
- Who are these students, and where do they come from?
- How do the skills and attitude of the teacher fit the needs of the students in this course?
- What accreditation issues need to be taken into account?

## Examining the Expectations of Others as External Audiences

We often analyze how to weave our courses into an established program or department curriculum. This is critical in delivering a comprehensive education that makes sense to our students so they can see the interrelatedness of the concepts they are learning. However, we also need to communicate the richness of the curriculum to external audiences including accreditation bodies, which we cover in depth in chapter 10, and the group of prime importance to our students, which is employers.

Isn't the major goal of higher education to position our students to be hired? Whether students are completing certificates, diplomas, or degrees, they need skills to compete in global markets. Many jobs today reach greater portions of the world than ever before. Teams work with colleagues who are in different time zones and continents and have a variety of cultural perspectives. Employers are looking for graduates who bring a greater depth of skills to the workplace. We have met with a variety of employers in more than 25 campus programs, departments, and general education advisory committees, and they unequivocally require the following skills from the graduates they are hiring:

- Problem-solving and analyzing data
- Critical thinking, decision-making, and exercising judgment
- Creative and innovative thinking
- Teamwork and managing people
- Written and oral communication
- Resiliency and persistence demonstrating cognitive flexibility
- Emotional intelligence, personal management, and professionalism
- Digital and social media literacy
- Self-motivation and a willingness to learn

Knowing what employers require has helped us shape the curriculum of well-designed courses to produce graduates who master these skills in course work and demonstrate them in the workplace. Not every course design needs to have outcomes for each of the skills listed here, but we need to be sure these skills are part of the curriculum. Educators need to ask, How does the design of our courses prepare students to obtain and succeed in the best jobs possible?

## A Deeper Look at the Characteristics of the Teacher

Anthony arrived on campus, hired just before classes started. His visit with the department chair was helpful in obtaining the proper forms, class schedules, and the key to his office. However, in terms of teaching, there was not much time to discuss challenges. He did mention to the chairperson that of the four courses, he felt comfortable with two of them, had some work to do for the third, and had never taught or even thought about what to do for the fourth course. The chair mentioned that he might contact some other faculty who have taught the courses previously or visit the office of the retired faculty member to gain a better understanding of the factors he would be facing in these courses. Anthony got the key to that person's office, where he found a possible textbook and a syllabus that had been used for years.

Anthony did not actually redesign the course. He rewrote the syllabus and chose readings for the course from the textbook, which was published several years prior and was not an area of the discipline in which Anthony had much experience. As with many faculty, he started with what artifacts he could find and taught the course as it had been taught in the past.

As he taught the course, he became uncomfortable with the text, so he researched new texts and ordered a new one for the spring semester. He knew he needed to redesign the course, so he took time during the course to keep notes about what he wanted to do differently. Anthony watched how engaged the students were in their learning and considered how he could develop better learning activities and assessments to demonstrate their mastery of the outcomes. He discovered that he needed to ask much better questions about this course and take a serious, in-depth look at the situational factors for solid clues on what the focus of the course should be and how he could create significant learning for his students.

As an educational leader, you design experiences for students to succeed. By applying the ideas offered here, you will provide significant learning. As the instructor, you have a limited amount of time and energy, so you have a choice to make: Be reactive or proactive. The reactive instructor responds to situations as they occur and works to correct them for each class every semester. The proactive instructor designs a course with the purpose of knowing that all the elements are in place and spends time interacting with students to guide their learning. The latter takes more time up front, but in the long run will save a lot of time and reduce stress as you don't have to make corrections during the busiest time of the semester—while you are grading, communicating with students and colleagues, and doing campus work.

## A Deeper Understanding of the Characteristics of the Learners

Knowing who your students are is the key ingredient in designing a student-centered course. Although this point is obvious, we are often busy with all the work we need to complete, so it is easy to forget our primary purpose. Integrated course design requires an examination of a course's situational factors. The analysis needed in identifying the characteristics of the learners helps you go beyond a one-course-fits-all or teach-to-the-middle design. As faculty, our mission is to develop learning outcomes and assess that students have mastered them. Knowing you will have many students from varying ages, cultures, experiential levels, prior learning knowledge, and skill abilities will help you design a course that will meet everyone's needs.

## Building Readiness for College Learning

Think about the students who may be taking your course. Your students might range from 16 years of age, taking advantage of concurrent enrollment in high school and a local college, to retired professionals returning as lifelong learners with varying educational backgrounds. They may be concurrently taking developmental course work or receiving academic support, or they may have entered your course after a rigorous college preparatory advanced placement or international baccalaureate program in high school.

Some students are the first in their families to attend a higher education institution. They may not have many role models, beyond their high school teachers, with any sort of postsecondary experience. Without brothers and sisters or parents who have paved the way and can offer guidance, they embark on a journey into the wilderness of attending a course like yours. They have few references to assist them. It was never expected that they would even consider going to college. They don't know what this experience has in store for them. It is easy for faculty to speak in the language of higher ed-ese, but at the same time students are trying to understand the meaning so they can succeed in your course. For more information see Appendix B.

The number of students entering college who are underprepared continues to increase. Kuh, Kinzie, Shuh, Whitt, and Associates (2005) reported that "a study conducted by the American College Testing program found that 49% of high school graduates do not have the reading skills required to succeed in college" (p. 1). Your students represent a variety of backgrounds and experiences. For example, they may

- come from cultural and linguistic backgrounds that are far removed from the academic culture;
- experience difficulties with aspects of mathematics literacy, reading, or writing;
- be diagnosed with mental illness or other conditions that make learning in college a challenge; or
- vary extensively in college readiness.

How can college faculty meet the needs of such a wide audience? This is the reality of considering the student side of the situational factors. In Appendix B we provide more information about working with academically underprepared students, usually those who scored below the acceptable pass rates on entrance exams and received developmental course work or support prior to or concurrently with college introductory course work.

Most new students will contend with some transition issues as they begin college. The reading and homework responsibilities outside class are greater, and the tests are significantly more difficult than most high school classes, so even very good students often have some challenges as they learn to navigate. However, if these students learn how to approach studying, taking notes, and talking with instructors, they usually will succeed. Many students haven't thought through how taking courses will affect them and their schedules. Balancing work and family responsibilities with the course's meeting time and workload is a change many don't fully understand until they are a few weeks into college life. Providing information on how students can prepare for this balance is helpful.

Many students are attracted to the convenience of online courses. Although this option may fit well into their schedules, some students don't understand the complexity of learning online, which requires greater independence and responsibility in learning content and meeting course requirements. One may also argue that teaching online is more difficult as well, because instructors need to build community in the course, which is more difficult to do in the online environment. The technology in the course learning management system (LMS) used to build this community is making this task easier; however, faculty and students need training to use the tools in an online course. A deeper discussion of this is found in chapter 3.

It is also helpful for faculty to facilitate a successful start to college by being explicit about the course performance expectations as well as designing the course in a way for students to have multiple opportunities to demonstrate their mastery of the content through applied practice in learning activities and assessment.

**Bright Idea**

What does it feel like to be a novice? You may have forgotten if you have not tried to learn something new in a long time. It's good for teachers to try something new: a new exercise or sport, a new hobby, or anything that puts you into the students' shoes. Try it. It will make you better. —**Linda Russell**

## Key Course Skills and Abilities

In thinking about the differences between the way experts and novices perform in your discipline, how do novices move toward becoming experts? Where are the trouble spots that seem to slow down many of your students? One way to better understand the student perspective is to ask your better students to explain how they read, study, talk, and write in your course. What is involved here is disciplinary literacy. According to Shanahan (2017),

> Disciplinary literacy is based upon the idea that literacy and text are specialized, and even unique, across the disciplines. Historians engage in very different approaches

> to reading than mathematicians do, for instance. Similarly, even those who know little about math or literature can easily distinguish a science text from a literary one.
>
> Fundamentally, because each field of study has its own purposes, its own kinds of evidence, and its own style of critique, each will produce different texts, and reading those different kinds of texts are going to require some different reading strategies. Scientists spend a lot of time comparing data presentation devices with each other and with prose, while literary types strive to make sense of theme, characterization, and style. (para. 6–7)

Thus, you must design the course in a way that will actively and explicitly teach and model the ways you read, talk, write, and think in your discipline. This design strategy will help all students, but it will make the difference for students who are less ready for college. In addition, you will have students who have learning challenges with sight and hearing and who will need additional design support. These challenges make the novice-to-expert pathway even more difficult. For most faculty, these kinds of challenges go well beyond what they experienced themselves as learners. This is an example of making your course accessible for all students. Chapter 6 expands on these ideas.

Identify the core concepts in your discipline that will be taught in your course. Seeing where your course is positioned in the curriculum is critical so you can introduce the appropriate concepts for student mastery. What are the foundational building blocks necessary to learn the concepts? What are the minimal performance expectations? These organizing principles of creating a quality curriculum are discussed throughout this book and specifically in chapter 9. They lay the groundwork for you to be able to identify levels of acceptable student work as you develop scoring rubrics that clearly describe your expectations. You can better diagnose a student's errors in thinking or conceptual understanding and provide them with the appropriate feedback if you have identified the steps in the learning process.

**Bright Idea**

Have your students who have successfully passed the course write a letter to a novice student on what helped them succeed in the course. Distribute the letters to students in small groups to discuss how this could help them this semester. For an online course, post several of the best letters in the course shell discussions and have your students write a reflection on what they learned by reading them. **—Zala Fashant**

## Course Accessibility for All Learners

Have you ever thought what it would be like if you were a student with a learning challenge? Increasing numbers of students with disabilities are pursuing postsecondary education. Accessibility design needs to create opportunities for students who are challenged by blindness, low vision, hearing impairments, mobility impairments, learning disabilities, health impairments, and psychiatric health impairments. If you have never experienced these challenges, then designing a course for students who need additional assistance may be beyond your scope of understanding. Thinking about accessibility on the front end of design helps you work with students immediately rather than learning which accommodations you will need to consider once the student enrolls in your course and then having to make the appropriate changes (Coombs, 2010).

The key is remembering that accessibility is not just about disability. Accessibility increases learning for all students. It is the cornerstone for inclusion, equity, and ultimately student success. It isn't just a positive design element; it is the law. Designing for accessibility doesn't take large investments of time. A few simple guidelines can help you evaluate your courses to ensure that all your students have the opportunity to perform at their best. Small changes to existing courses can eliminate barriers and provide all students with more equitable opportunities to learn and to demonstrate their learning.

Designing using a learning platform recognized for excellence in meeting these requirements will help you provide successful learning for all. Your campus resource person can tell you how the course learning platform supports accessibility. By converting your course materials, your students are able to view them or use their screen readers to view them. Doing so allows your students access to them and levels the playing field.

As previously discussed, students come from a wide variety of ethnic and cultural backgrounds. For some, English is not their first language. In most classes, students have a variety of learning preferences, skills, and experiences, all of which affect their approach to learning. The strategies to make course materials accessible using multiple methods helps these students learn as well. Chapter 6 covers specific strategies to be sure your course is accessible for all students.

## Helping Struggling Students Succeed

What do you do when students are not meeting academic expectations? Some of your students may be conditional admits who were admitted but have not met the entrance requirements, others may be on academic probation, and still others are graduates of developmental programming. All these students are at risk as they enter the college-level curriculum.

Even with special programming, advising, and academic support, these students have not magically been fixed and will continue to be the least familiar with college demands. Ideally, the college provides continued support in the form of supplemental instruction, tutoring, cocurricular options, and so on. They need a lot of practice to improve their study skills, testing skills, and appropriate college communication skills. There is no shame in not knowing what typical students know; instructors need to be explicit in instructions and make fewer assumptions. Being clear is not condescending. Developing checklists and rubrics for written work on assignments or assessments is important for all learners. Sometimes additional practice opportunities are necessary to allow more time on task to learn concepts, procedures, and skills. Allowing rewrites on some work or providing selected nongraded quiz questions to the entire class can be a confidence booster for some but a lifesaver for others. Additional practice is also great for students who have demonstrated deeper interest in the course, so it works for students who need extra help and those who have a greater interest.

A key aspect in teaching is to have a clear understanding of what it is like to be a novice learner in a discipline. This can pose a dilemma for some faculty on two counts: first, you are an expert who has studied and worked many years to gain deep learning in your field, so remembering what it is like to be a beginner may have faded away. Second, you may never have actually struggled in your discipline. You may have chosen your discipline because you had a passion for the subject, natural abilities, a drive to succeed in the area, or a deep curiosity about it, and you may not have had too many roadblocks thrown your way. Many of you may also have had a variety of role models guiding you, so you felt supported in your decision to go on to postsecondary work.

Most of us don't earn degrees in fields we dislike, fail at, or have fears about. Our students at the undergraduate level are not so lucky. They must take a wide range of courses in general education, even ones that strike fear into their hearts and keep them up all hours trying to understand the material. Did you take any courses in your general education requirements that made you wonder if you really needed them and you felt you were unprepared to take? Think about fine arts majors taking traditional science courses. If the design of the course doesn't allow them to bring their fine arts interests into the course as a way of applying the science content, then these students could dread the entire experience unless they happen to love science. For example, an interdisciplinary link could encourage music students to consider how temperature plays a part in tuning of instrument or in voice performance, or art students to describe how their medium reacts with other materials or the reaction that can take place in mixing types of paint, or the action on a clay sculpture being fired in a kiln.

Realizing that you are very different from most of your students in the lower division courses is a first step to teaching in an accessible manner. In our workshops, we discuss how some faculty may be perceptually challenged because they are experts, and the learning in this discipline may have come easily for them because of their interest in it. Master musicians attempting to give lessons to children beginning an instrument can suffer from this as they have forgotten the technical skills of beginning to learn how to play an instrument. This perceptual challenge is even worse if the teacher was a natural and learned to play the instrument quickly.

This difference is what often leads faculty to either not know how to advise a struggling student or to tell them to do something that is utterly unhelpful, such as "Just read the chapter again." You may be even further from the experiences that most of our developmental students have faced, not having gone through school failing classes or being told you just needed to work harder or being shamed in front of other students. Did you ever have the pressure of being required to go up to the chalkboard to show how you solved a math problem or stand in front of the class to spell a word you didn't know in a spelling bee? Many emotional aftereffects linger even years later for our most at-risk students.

Your understanding of the characteristics of all learners, those like you and, more important, those most different from you will make you the teacher who achieves significant learning. Learners will benefit from a compassionate instructor who realizes students need specific, helpful activities and support to find their way to successfully master the outcomes in your course. Moreover, it will transform their lives, so the success in your course provides lasting effects on their career and life. Appendix B provides additional suggestions to try with your students. You will find they help all students, but they really can mean a breakthrough for developmental students.

Some faculty don't take much time to reflect on the critical step of identifying the situational factors as they jump into the task of building a course. This is the cornerstone in the foundation of course design. Identifying the situational factors is a key first step. We have found that many faculty who use this research and reflection in their planning continue to find additional situational factors as they design their courses, adding to their own significant learning.

## Pedagogical Challenges

As you identify the course's situational factors, one particular factor often rises to the top; we call it the pedagogical challenge. Pedagogical challenges need to be addressed during the first class meeting for face-to-face or blended courses or during the first week of an online course. Developing the solid foundation and environment where students can feel safe and have the opportunity to be successful provides a gateway for students who say they dislike the topic of your required course. You can develop the motivation to learn and build the foundation for students to succeed in a course.

> A Midwest university has three distinct groups of students. One group comes from a metropolitan area where traffic is heavy, high schools have numerous advanced placement courses, and most students are prepared for attending college through advising and

other programs. Another group consists of students from very small rural communities with populations of a couple of thousand or so. These students find the university to be a huge, scary place full of people different from themselves. Another group is made up of international students. They vary greatly in their response to the university based on the country and size of the city they come from.

When these three groups are in a course, the faculty member needs to take some time to understand the different cultures and how to best design a course to embrace and value this diversity instead of allowing it to become a problem. In a classroom such as this it seems necessary to have some group work, if for no other reason than to help students benefit from the rich mix of ideas from those in the class.

Understanding the cultural richness and the level of learners' expertise will help you design a course that will provide pathways for student success (Gabriel, 2018). Identifying the situational factors that affect your course, and knowing which factors are in your control and which are not, is critical to designing significant learning. In speech courses, we often talk about knowing one's audience. Situational factors involve knowing your audience on a grander scale. The macro factors involve an external audience of employers, professional organization competencies, and accrediting organizations. Micro factors involve yourself and your students. What biases and perspectives do students come to this class with when they first enroll? What have they heard and what don't they know that you can address from the very beginning? Identifying your own biases will help you improve your teaching so that all students can be successful in your courses.

Completing thinking about your course's situational factors and pedagogical challenges is the first step in preparing for course design. As Fink (2013) has asserted, many faculty are perceptually challenged in their teaching as faculty are often talented in their discipline, and too often don't understand why some students have problems and don't learn easily or quickly. This seems to be one of the most pervasive pedagogical challenges faculty must understand and overcome in their teaching. In chapter 2 we discuss the additional steps needed for integrating course design.

## Reflect on This Chapter

Now that you have completed reading this chapter and thinking about the content as it applies to your work, please reflect on the following questions.

- How can Fink's (2013) taxonomy help you deliver the concept of significant and lifelong learning for your students?
- What courses do you currently have that need redesigning to provide significant learning for students?
- How does identifying situational factors and the pedagogical challenges help you prepare for course design?

**Jot Your Thoughts**

## Action Checklist

Use Checklist 1.1 to apply the chapter content to your practice and help you identify the steps for implementing these ideas in your teaching.

**CHECKLIST 1.1** Preparing for Your Course Design Action Checklist

| ✓ | **Course Design Planning** |
|---|---|
| ❑ | Downloaded *A Guide to Creating Significant Learning Experiences* (Fink, 2003) from www.deefinkandassociates.com/GuidetoCourseDesignAug05.pdf |
| ❑ | Identified the situational factors. |
| ❑ | Considered which factors are within my control and which are not. |
| ❑ | Identified which situational factor is my greatest pedagogical challenge. |
| ❑ | Read Appendix B: Knowing Your Students. |

# PART TWO

# DESIGNING

# 2

# INTEGRATING YOUR COURSE DESIGN

## Points to Ponder

In thinking about integrating the elements of your course design, consider the following questions to examine your prior knowledge:

- What do you really want your students to accomplish and take with them after they leave your course?
- How will your course prepare your students for their career and their personal lives?
- In thinking about one of your courses, how well are your learning outcomes, assessments, and activities aligned as they are integrated into your course design?
- Do you currently use a variety of assessments to demonstrate mastery of the course outcomes and a variety of learning activities to provide practice for students to prepare for successful assessments?

**Jot Your Thoughts**

Sitting at a roundtable as coaches at one of L. Dee Fink's conferences for designing courses for significant learning, we listened to faculty describe the courses they were currently teaching. As faculty learned about methods for course design, they identified the situational factors they needed to consider in designing their course. After discussing the factors, faculty were asked to dream about why they want to teach this course and what they want their students to take with them after completing this course.

So when we asked faculty to share their big dream for their course, many of them started with ideas like getting students to read the textbook, come to class prepared, complete assignments on time, and just show up for class. We wouldn't argue that each of these are important for student success, but these are not big dreams. Instead, many faculty know what they want students to be able to demonstrate when they leave the class, and it usually goes beyond skill sets. Faculty often want to develop their courses to help students become successful citizens as they achieve their professional and personal goals, which can be accomplished through an engaging course design. We asked them to rethink and go bigger. How will this course change learners' lives?

We urged the faculty to dig deeper into the big dream by understanding how to separate their hopes for completing work from what they wanted as big dreams for their students to achieve. The next round of responses was much more visionary. Many faculty gave a huge sigh of relief knowing that it was okay to design a course that would be more for students. They were excited to design a course that not only provided the right conditions for learners to achieve the course and department outcomes but also could take them beyond the end of the course and improve their professional and personal lives. One university faculty member said that this way of designing courses makes no course insignificant, and a technical college instructor told us that this style of design is a perfect match for the way he teaches as it aligns with technical education and meets employers' expectations.

## Why Faculty Teach

For most faculty, teaching students in courses designed using their big dream is really what they originally wanted to do. They wanted to be a teacher and mentor and develop learning that students remembered long beyond the end of the semester. They wanted to make a difference in the lives of their students much like someone had done for them. Designing courses this way delivered that opportunity.

Course integration is one of the most powerful strategies you can use in your teaching. Aligning learning outcomes, assessments, and activities is vital to the quality of the course, which needs to be in place to deliver significant learning for your students. As course design coaches we have seen hundreds of faculty transform their teaching and student learning. From what they tell us, faculty enjoy their teaching more after implementing their course redesign. They are proud to say that their students enjoy their learning more as well. Knowing that you have created a life-changing experience for your students is deeply gratifying and provides a way for you to have an impact on not only the students enrolled in your course but also each of the people they work with in the future and the ways they interact with their family and community.

## Course Design That Delivers Significant Learning

The word *curriculum* (n.d.) is from the Latin *currare*, meaning running or course, as in a racecourse—in other words, a pathway. For our purposes, it could be used in terms of a pathway that provides a well-practiced structure to guide vehicles or a rigid path that doesn't allow flexibility or movement because of the ruts created by others.

Integrated course design using the taxonomy of significant learning guides your students through learning activities and assesses their mastery of the outcomes. A well-designed course provides student-faculty engagement so the students aren't stuck in a rut with their learning. Students take your courses to learn from you as you are the expert in your discipline. They expect your course will show them a pathway to learning. The design of your course needs to be intentional for students to see why your content is relevant and how it will help them develop the skills they need to succeed professionally and personally. Knowing the course is designed well gives you the confidence of delivering the content in a manner that will allow you to spend your time teaching and working with students individually.

Most faculty want to share everything they know about the discipline with their students, but how much content can students absorb during the length of the course? Think of the last time you were at a buffet. Even if you arrived hungry, you couldn't begin to eat everything. You would have to choose carefully as you filled your plate being careful not to overeat and also saving have room for dessert. Your students are the same. They can only handle a certain amount as they find places to organize, store, and apply all the learning.

The design of a course and its integration into the curriculum are vital to student success. Content is layered from foundational to advanced. Early courses in a program build a strong foundation so that deeper learning can occur in later courses. A well-designed curriculum is cyclical as concepts link prior learning to new information at a higher level. Setting a strong foundation is important to support more advanced learning. Communicating your design is key for students to understand this learning pathway.

Overall course design is basically the same for online, blended, and face-to-face courses. Great design applies to all forms of delivery because the major elements for a course are the same. In this chapter, we examine the design elements that course designers use to improve their course design skills. Fink refers to this as designing courses leading to significant learning (Fink, 2003). To help you better understand the course design process discussed here, it may help if you focus on one of the courses you teach. It helps to think about a course that isn't going as well as you would like and that you think could be designed better. The redesign of this course isn't about tweaking it here and there. Instead it's about looking at the design through a new perspective, so you need to start from the beginning. The course outcomes may be predetermined and need to remain in your redesign. You may be able to repurpose some of the learning activities used previously if they are appropriate in your redesign, but don't center the redesign on your activities. They are not the starting point. Focusing on keeping the things you had will not allow you to succeed in redesigning because you will spend a lot of your energy trying to make things fit, blending the old with the new. Getting away from your current mind-set and thinking about what is possible in a new way by using your imagination and innovation for the new course will help you succeed in the redesign.

**Jot Your Thoughts**

## Your Big Dream

Although it is important to identify the situational factors discussed previously, they can sometimes involve conditions you may not be able to change. It is important to remember that these factors have an effect on the course and are a starting point to the design. To balance what may be limiting factors in the design, it is important for you to focus on your big dream for your students. Consider the following:

- How will taking your course influence students for the rest of their lives?
- In what ways will taking your course make a difference in the way students will be successful?
- How will your course provide insights that will enhance students' professional and personal lives?

By thinking about your big dream for this course you can communicate what you want the students to learn and how this learning will affect their lives beyond the classroom. As course design coaches, we have guided faculty in the redesign of their current courses, getting them to consider the full potential of what their course could offer learners.

For faculty whose big dream focuses only on basic foundational knowledge content, writing the outcomes for significant learning will be challenging. Big dreams go beyond using information to perform well on exams and receiving a passing grade for the course. A dream that only emphasizes memorization and passing exams is difficult to link to outcomes that extend beyond foundational knowledge. The richer the dream, the easier it will be to link it to learning outcomes based on Fink's (2013) taxonomy of significant learning. Rich dreams often refer to students' gaining confidence, understanding others better, seeing the connections of ideas in courses to the world around them, and so on. We discuss ways to write a broader set of outcomes by using all the taxonomy of significant learning domains (see Figure 2.1).

The following is an example of a rich big dream.

> This course will explore the "Materials Culture" by encouraging students to analyze issues related to consumption patterns of themselves, their communities, the larger society, and differing societies around the world. Students will realize the interconnected nature of their everyday activities, which may seem disconnected at first. What they watch and see can (does) affect what they buy. What they buy affects

> people and places around the world as well as the processes and systems of how "stuff" is sold and distributed. They will investigate their consumer power, impact, and limitations. Knowing the story behind the things that are bought, used, and tossed can help students to consume in ways that improve their lives and the lives of others. The intent of this course is not to discourage students from buying "stuff" but rather to equip them with knowledge and skills to help them be informed and empowered consumers. (Baines, personal communication, May 17, 2011)

For faculty who develop rich big dreams, full of meaningful ideas, moving from the dream to writing course outcomes is not a challenge. In the preceding dream, you may have started to see how thoughts could easily be translated into learning outcomes. By sharing your big dream with your students you communicate the purpose for the course, which answers the question that students often pose: "What am I going to get out of the course?"

Another example of a big dream comes from what many math faculty have told us in workshops. When asked to dream about what is really important to them for student learning beyond graduation they state simply that they want students in their

**Figure 2.1** Fink's taxonomy of significant learning.

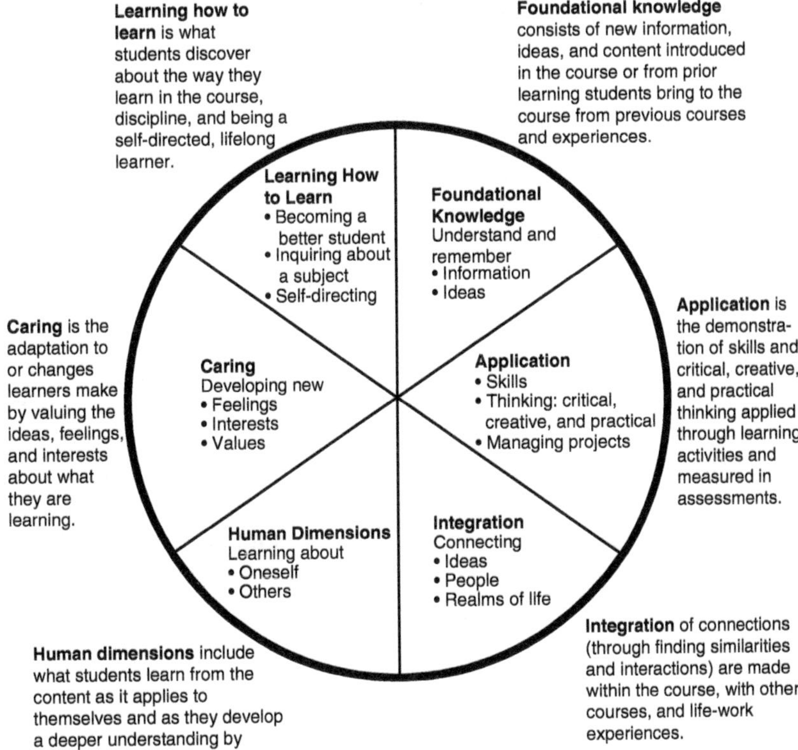


*Note.* Fink's taxonomy includes the domains of foundational knowledge, application, integration, human dimensions for self and others, caring, and learning how to learn. From *Creating Significant Learning Experiences*, by L.D. Fink, 2003, San Francisco, CA: Jossey-Bass.

courses to see the value of numbers in their life. This big dream statement applies to most disciplines. Replace the phrase "value of numbers" in math, with "value of _____" for your own discipline.

Math professors deal with students who have trouble understanding math day in and day out. Yet when asked to dream about the overarching goal for student learning, they said it was for students to care about the importance of numbers throughout their lives and to see how knowing about numbers could assist them in not only passing tests but also obtaining a higher quality of life. Foundational knowledge is crucial to math courses, and instructors were able to see the real-life value of the course once students left the institution. It is heartening to know many other instructors are realizing the importance of significant learning for students and the need for showing the connections of the course material to their life. This math instructor also saw the value of the human dimension of developing confidence in these math students if any learning was going to take place in his course.

Using the ideas of integrated course design, a history of dance instructor thought about what was really important for his students to learn and came up with the following life value for his course.

> This course is designed to engage the student with the importance of the human-body-moving-through-space that has informed the human experience from pre-literate times to today. It places our "embodied way of knowing" within a social, artistic, religious, political and cultural context. The student should experience an appreciation for the dynamic, varied and complex role that dance has played in human societies over time. In addition, the course is structured so that the students can learn how history is constructed by the questions that we ask, by the methods we employ, by the curiosity we bring to this subject. Many of these students have taken choreography class and it draws comparisons to how we creatively choreograph a dance to how we creatively engage with and construct our understanding of history. (Miller, personal communication, May 17, 2011)

As you can see, Miller developed a dream to help students benefit beyond the completion of the course, beyond checking the boxes for choreography content; it gets students to apply this learning to other areas in life. This allows students to link learned content to new thinking by showing relevance to experiences, a skill we wish all of our students had.

Now think about one of your courses. What do you want students to take away as they complete this course and move on to other courses or as they move on to their careers? Remember to go big. What is your big dream for your course? Write down your answer in the Jot Your Thoughts box.

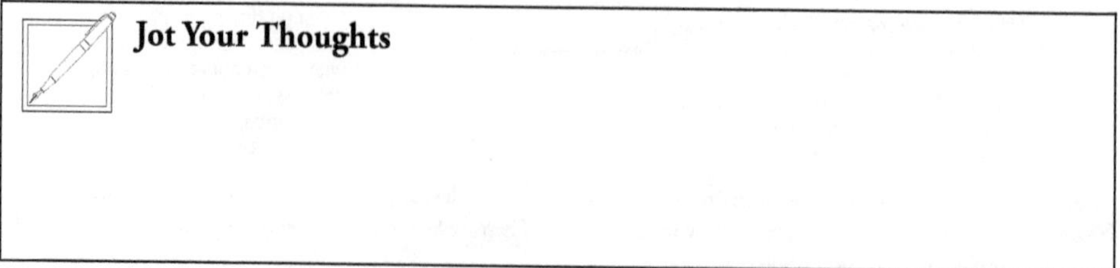

## Integrated Course Design

Now that you have identified the course's situational factors and your big dream, it is time to develop the main structure for the course. Aligning the learning outcomes (goals), activities, and assessments is perhaps the most important part of the design. You would be surprised how many faculty do not have these three elements aligned or haven't started by writing down their significant outcomes. Integrated course design starts with the situational factors (Figure 2.2) that are considered while designing and aligning outcomes, activities, and feedback and assessment.

Many faculty will design a course following a traditional, linear order. They think of a course idea, write down outcomes, think of the student activities, and add some assessments. The process of design is lengthy and very complicated and usually takes many shorter writing sessions over a period of weeks. One of the mistakes many faculty make is that they get excited about the learning activities, and by the time they get to the assessment they may be worn down by the lengthiness of the process or may not remember to connect the assessment with the outcomes. Thus, the assessment structure is rushed or incomplete, and the assessments don't always align with or measure the outcomes developed at the beginning of the design process.

Rather than using a linear beginning-to-end design model, integrated course design aligns the outcomes and assessments by using the backward design process

**Figure 2.2** Fink's integrated course design.

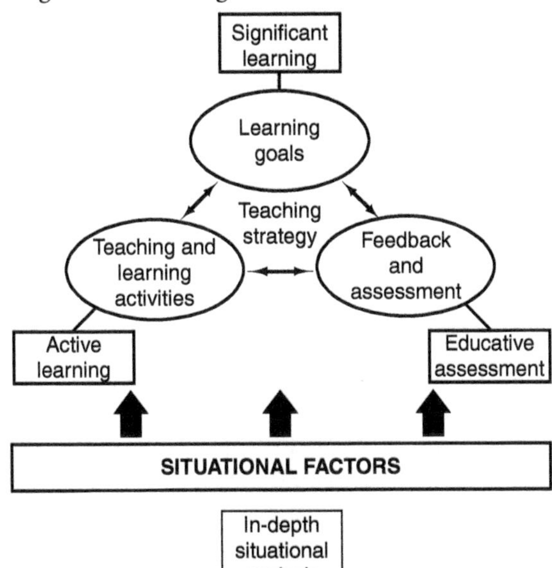


*Note.* This model illustrates the steps of Fink's integrated course design beginning with the analysis of situational factors to aligning learning goals (outcomes), assessment and activities to provide significant learning. From *Creating Significant Learning Experiences*, p. 127, by L.D. Fink, 2003, San Francisco, CA: Jossey-Bass. Copyright 2013 by L.D. Fink. Used with permission.

(Fink, 2003; Wiggins & McTighe, 2005). Begin by creating the outcomes, what you want students to learn in the course, and developing the formative and summative assessments to measure the mastery of the outcomes. Then you should decide on the appropriate types of learning activities to provide practice for students to apply the learning and determine how much time each activity will take.

Faculty seldom write course outcomes without some sort of discussion in their department or program. It is also critical to consider your institutional and program accreditation requirements. You may need to start with these outcomes as you redesign your course as they have been already approved and are part of the course catalog. You often have discretion in developing course unit objectives in your design that align with the outcomes and in developing the learning activities and assessments to measure how well your students are achieving the outcomes. You may need to start with the current course outcomes, but you can develop additional outcomes or unit objectives to fulfill the missing domains in the taxonomy of significant learning (Fink, 2013).

## Creating Learning Outcomes and Objectives

Writing significant learning outcomes and objectives shows students what they will be doing to improve learning during the course and demonstrates why the content is relevant to their learning and future career success. Consider your big dream in designing more targeted outcomes. Because the terms *goals*, *outcomes*, and *objectives* are often used interchangeably by institutions, we clarify our meanings for our discussion here.

*Goals* are grand overarching ideas. We do not use this term; instead, we will use *learning outcomes*, which are established for the course level. We use it in our syllabi, and it is used in the course catalog. *Learning outcomes* are the specific outcomes to be assessed to determine if a student has met the requirements for the course. *Learning objectives* can be thought of as suboutcomes to support the course outcomes. Objectives are used in units or weeks to break down outcomes into smaller and more specific items for assessment. *Outcomes and objectives* are measurable and written in a similar manner.

After attending one of Fink's campus workshops, a journalism teacher was making a serious effort to use this approach to design her general education course on the major news media in society. She was struggling with writing learning outcomes. We reviewed the big concepts she wanted students to learn by the end of the course, and after a period of silence, she blurted out, "Well, I want them to know everything in chapter 1, everything in chapter 2, and so forth." As you can imagine, we then discussed how to find a more specific and measurable set of learning outcomes.

She went back to work and ended up with a more significant set of outcomes. She decided that she wanted students as consumers of news media to be able to make a comparative analysis of the pros and cons of newspapers, journals, the radio, and TV as sources of news information. That is, when a major news event happened, these students would know the advantages and limitations likely to be associated with obtaining the news through each of these four media. She discovered that her outcomes for student learning were more than just knowing information, which would lead to significant learning experiences.

Some faculty make the following comment about their experience as a result of working on writing significant learning outcomes: The biggest challenge was limiting the number of course outcomes. Using Fink's (2013) taxonomy as a guide is a good exercise as it forces you to really focus on what you want the students to remember as they complete the course. Many faculty have never thought about the human dimension, caring, and learning how to learn domains (Figure 2.1) in the taxonomy related to course design. This is ironic as faculty want their students to think about caring for humans as clients, customers, or patients; value what they learn; and hope that students will continue to learn on their own. Once faculty wrote these significant learning outcomes, the course assessments and activities flowed more easily. Creating outcomes does require some deeper analysis as it is a new task for most. However, with some practice, faculty are able to identify these outcomes and bring them to the forefront of what they want for their students.

We have seen the following five major challenges in our work with faculty as they develop good learning outcomes for their courses. The first challenge from faculty is their course outcomes not linked to the dream. One of the most important parts of integrated course design is creating a dream of what the course might be. For most faculty this is a true aha moment where they realize the full potential of developing the whole student instead of focusing on foundational knowledge. Some faculty who develop quality dreams find it difficult to translate the dream into actual course outcomes because they have had little experience in writing outcomes or in reflecting on what they really want to accomplish in the courses they teach. Developing the skill to write quality outcomes that are related to big dreams takes practice. The key is asking, What do students need to know to make the dream come true? Once faculty develop the ability to link a richly textured dream to outcomes, the creation of an integrated course begins to move forward quickly.

The second challenge is they are writing content rather than developing outcomes. Faculty are accustomed to building courses around content rather than on learning. They often initially write learning outcomes based on specific content rather than writing outcomes that use the content to achieve the learning.

Wiggins and McTighe (2005) offer a framework for designing learning experiences very similar to that of integrated course design. Instructors know what they want or need to teach rather than understanding what and how students need to learn. Wiggins helps people understand this distinction in his workshops with the following exercise, as described by an attendee:

> Try to write some learning outcomes by asking yourself, "What do you want students to understand?" So complete the following sentence: "I want students to understand . . ." Then, after allowing some time to complete this, he [Wiggins] asks for some examples and receives comments such as: "I want students to understand

> the periodic table . . . to understand plate tectonics . . . to understand the styles of different musical periods." Then he points out: "These are not learning outcomes; these are examples of content preceded by a verb." (S. Ross, personal communication, January 20, 2019)

Faculty need to see the distinction between (a) wanting students to learn some content, that is, understanding concepts and memorizing information, and (b) seeing the possibility of multiple kinds of learning but only one of which is learning some content, or the foundational knowledge type of learning in the taxonomy of significant learning (Fink, 2013).

In a workshop, Ross asked faculty to expand their thinking about developing outcomes through the following exercise:

> Ask yourself the following question: By the end of the course, what is the one thing I want students to have learned? In answering this, allow yourself to use one verb. For example, a drama teacher thought about this, and for her course she answered: "To act." Ross pointed out that this was an application learning outcome (Fink, 2013).
>
> She then reflected on a follow-up question: For students to learn how to act, what else would they need to learn? She said she would want them to learn
>
> - some specific acting techniques for the application domain;
> - for the integration domain, the means to determine how the style and content of the play affects the way the actor interprets a particular role, showing the interaction between the play and the acting in it;
> - some information about different periods in drama history and the variation in acting called for by plays of those periods, for the foundational knowledge domain;
> - the ability to interact with other actors and the director for the human dimension–others domain;
> - for the human dimension-self domain, a recognition of an aspect of oneself or some personal experiences that allow them to make their character more vivid;
> - a commitment to doing the best possible job of acting every time they act, for the caring domain; and
> - to pay attention to what they learn about acting and themselves as an actor to improve as an actor every time they have an opportunity to act, for the learning how to learn.
>
> By starting with the central kind of learning for the whole course, she started linking to other kinds of learning and ultimately build a quality set of outcomes for significant learning.

The third challenge is faculty tend to write learning activities rather than learning outcomes, confusing activities with outcomes. This happens partly because they tend to spend much time on strategies for learning without taking the necessary time to reflect on what students should actually be learning. Writing an outcome like "students working in teams to answer questions about a case study" is not an outcome but rather an activity or means to achieve an outcome. "Students learning about how others think differently through teams" would be an outcome (human dimension–others).

The fourth challenge is getting faculty to choose appropriate verbs for learning outcomes. A learning outcome is a statement of what you want students to learn or be able to do as a result of the learning and feedback activities in the course. The statement needs to link to your dream for the course, be measurable, and be written in a way for students to understand. It is essentially a sentence-completion process. For example, the leading part of the statement is, "My hope is that by the end of the course, all students will be able to—," and the next word in the statement should be a carefully chosen action verb that is measurable. A listing of measureable verbs for each domain is discussed in the learning outcomes section later in this chapter.

The fifth challenge is getting faculty to create outcomes appropriate for each kind of significant learning. We provide a deeper examination of what you should consider in developing your learning outcomes with examples of outcomes in Table 2.1 later in this chapter. Note that the first three areas of Fink's (2013) taxonomy—foundational knowledge, application, and integration on the right side of Figure 2.1—work with the cognitive domain, whereas the last three areas—human dimensions, caring, and learning how to learn on the left side of Figure 2.1—work with the affective domain.

### *Foundational Knowledge Outcomes*

Most faculty are familiar with foundational knowledge because it refers to students learning the content of the course, and it has been the traditional driver of what many faculty teach. The outcomes form the basis or foundation for all other areas of the taxonomy (Fink, 2013).

How specific should foundational knowledge outcomes be? When designing the course and working up a statement describing the kinds of learning you want students to achieve, you do not need to specify every topic and concept of the course. In the syllabus and course shell, include a detailed list of the topics and knowledge expectations as unit objectives. When creating a learning outcome statement regarding foundational knowledge, you only need to identify the general categories of topics, concepts, or kinds of information you believe students need to understand and remember.

What verbs could you use for this category of outcomes? It is possible, but not advisable, to use *know* or *understand.* These are legitimate verbs, but they mean different things to different people because they are open to interpretation. They are also difficult to measure. We recommend using a verb that describes what students would be able to do. Some examples include the following:

My hope is that, by the end of the course, all students will be able to

- list the five steps involved in the scientific process,
- describe the meaning of plate tectonics,
- identify the four main factors in the course textbook as tools to use when analyzing a novel, or
- describe the elements that need to be considered in computer applications.

Using verbs like *describe* and *identify* has several advantages. They make it clearer to you what you want students to be able to do, they make it clearer to students what you want them to be able to do, and you are poised to develop your assessment activities to align with these outcomes. These outcomes are measureable.

Some common verbs used in foundational knowledge outcomes include *define*, *describe*, *explain*, *find*, *identify*, *label*, *list*, *match*, *name*, *outline*, *recite*, *select*, and *state*. All these verbs stress gaining information. A common mistake of some instructors, even after taking our workshops, is using verbs such as *apply* and *critique*, which don't fit in this domain. At the level of foundational knowledge, those skills are not developed yet; they are used in application outcomes.

### *Application Learning Outcomes*

Most faculty understand the importance of not only remembering or identifying ideas in a course but also taking this information to the next step and applying the ideas in real-world situations. This is where we suggest faculty create outcomes about critical, creative, and practical thinking. Being able to use information and ideas is imperative for careers and the general enjoyment of life. At the application level, students will be asked to do much more than memorize content for tests and exams. They will be asked to demonstrate the ability to use information to solve problems and make decisions.

An example of an application outcome could be, "My hope is that by the end of the course, all students will be able to design (develop, test, document) custom Windows computer applications."

You will note that in this application outcome students use the information learned in the class by designing computer applications. They are doing something to show they have a deeper understanding of the information because they able to design and develop, which gives students confidence that they really do understand this material and can do something important with it. Some common verbs used in application outcomes include *analyze*, *assess*, *critique*, *demonstrate*, *design*, *develop*, *modify*, *organize*, and *solve*. All these verbs stress using information.

### *Integration Learning Outcomes*

Some courses are not designed for students to integrate the ideas of the course they are taking into other courses and their careers. Typically learners focus only on ideas related to the particular content with few tie-ins to previous or future learning. Little time is spent demonstrating to students how the ideas being learned are interconnected to other courses they are taking; after all, there is not enough time for all the ideas to be covered in the course itself. However, we do a major disservice to our students if we don't help them see how ideas connect and how information from a course might be helpful with situations in their own life.

An example of an integration outcome for the previously mentioned computer course is, "My hope is that by the end of the course, all students will able to align computer programming solutions with business and personal interests."

The important part of this outcome is requiring students to make connections in their programming work with their business and personal interests. The instructor is now attempting to have students see how the course has valuable ideas while simultaneously encouraging them to connect those ideas to the business world where they will be working. The common verbs used in integration outcomes include *align*, *balance*, *compare*, *contrast*, *identify*, *integrate*, *organize*, *relate*, and *support*. All these verbs stress blending information.

### Human Dimensions Learning Outcomes

This type of affective learning is clearly different from cognitive learning, and some instructors struggle with figuring out what this might mean for their courses. However, with a little effort and imagination, most faculty are able to identify a learning outcome in this category that makes sense and sometimes even becomes central to the course as it applies to the dream they have for their students. In cases where course outcomes are already set by the institution, faculty are able to add this outcome to the list or integrate the idea into a preexisting outcome by adding it to unit objectives supporting the outcome. Once faculty realize this dimension is important to attaining their big dream for their course, they are eager to explore this area and add a human dimension goal for their course.

In one of our workshops, the participants were writing learning outcomes. A statistics faculty member raised her hand to express her dilemma. It felt like she was facing a stone wall that she could not get past. "In statistics, we solve problems. I can't see where human dimension learning is applicable to us," she said. There were about 30 people in the workshop, so we opened it up to the group, asking, "How many of you had to take a course in statistics when you were in graduate school?" A large number raised their hand. We then asked, "Of this group, how many of you had questions or some level of anxiety about whether you would be able to pass this course?" Most of the hands stayed up. Then we said, "And for those of you who did have some anxiety, would you have valued a professor who taught the course in a way that was designed to give you the confidence so you could do statistics?" There was a lot of nodding. The statistics professor also nodded and said, "I get it."

#### *Human Dimension–Self*

The first part of the human dimension domain of outcomes involves identifying learning outcomes related to students learning something about themselves, which includes a number of possibilities:

My hope is that by the end of the course, all students will be able to

- gain confidence that they can do something well;
- gain a new self-ideal, such as viewing themselves as a professional in their field; or
- express a sense of personal responsibility for doing excellent work in their field.

Sometimes people worry they do not see the difference between some kinds of human dimension–self learning and learning in the caring domain. An overlap is possible. For example, the outcome of students wanting to be professional engineers—a self-idea—can be viewed either as a human dimension or self outcome or a caring outcome. It can be legitimately viewed in either domain. What is important is to be able to imagine some outcomes in both categories. Often outcomes can overlap in areas, which is not a problem. The important thing is that you have included this dream-related outcome for your students. Caring is focused on students developing new attitudes and interests and valuing what they are learning. Human dimension is a broader introspection of oneself and one's relationship with others. It also guides students to become ethical decision makers. Writing an outcome about valuing could be used in both categories depending on the context.

*Human Dimension–Other*

This domain includes learning outcomes that involve students learning how to interact with others in a positive and effective way. This might involve goals like the following:

My hope is that by the end of the course, all students will be able to

- work with team members effectively, or
- interact well with people who have different ideas and who are different in age, race, religion, nationality, language, sexual orientation, gender, and so on.

We have seen two challenges when people try to write learning goals for this category. First, they write outcomes that refer to what they want students to do during the course, almost a description of a learning activity, which is a means to an outcome and not what they want students to be able to do by the end of the course and beyond. Faculty have written, "I want students to work together in class to solve problems." This would be better if expanded to "I want students to learn how to work effectively as part of a problem-solving group." This statement would open the course to a variety of activities that would help students develop skills to use in situations after the course is over.

A second challenge for faculty in writing these outcomes is that they have difficulty understanding how the human dimension–other could be relevant for courses in subjects such as natural sciences, humanities, or engineering. For these faculty, it is helpful to remember that their graduates will or at least can interact with other people regarding the subject matter being studied, and often the people whom students will later interact with will be different in one or more important ways from the students themselves. These interactions (discussions, collaborations, work relationships) lead to conflicts, disagreements, or misunderstandings in the class or the workplace. Some possible and potentially valuable learning outcomes for such courses might be the following:

My hope is that by the end of the course, all students will be able to

- discuss topics and questions about their field with family members or in social situations, or

- participate effectively on solving problems with others who are different from themselves or have different areas of expertise such as work teams or interdisciplinary projects.

Some common verbs used in human dimension outcomes include *act*, *argue*, *control*, *convince*, *debate*, *discern*, *discuss*, *display*, *express*, *follow*, *interact*, *manage*, *participate*, *organize*, *share*, and *volunteer*. All these verbs stress observing and applying course information to themselves and others.

### *Caring Learning Outcomes*

With the tremendous emphasis faculty and institutions put on foundational knowledge, caring outcomes can get lost in the pile of information. And yet students are seeking the value in what they are learning as it applies to their life. In workshops we often ask faculty to raise their hands if they would like students to care more about the subject they care so deeply about. It is rare not to have a room full of faculty with their hands raised with laughter echoing through the room. So why don't faculty include an outcome such as caring in their courses? One reason we have heard is that it is not measurable. However, attitudes have been measured in higher education and other places for many years. What could be more important than a group of students in an introductory course getting excited about the subject and looking into changing their major in that discipline based on this one course? At least we would want them to appreciate the content of your course and see how it can be valuable in the lives of other students and people beyond the classroom.

A history instructor used a verb we might expect in this domain's outcome: "Students will *value* the cultures and contributions of other immigrant groups as vital to their own human experience (i.e., their own personal, social, and national experience)." When students begin to value the course ideas, it leads directly to caring about the course. Although faculty tend to question writing caring outcomes, in many cases this becomes one of their most treasured outcomes in the course because it is the reason they teach in this discipline. Often faculty ask if they should list this outcome in the syllabus. This is an interesting question that seems to come from two concerns: One, the outcome can't be assessed, and two, the outcome will seem odd to other faculty or to the students who don't come to class to change their attitudes but rather to learn what they need to know to pass the course.

Many faculty who have developed a caring outcome for their courses report that students seem more engaged. Because the teacher values the importance of students caring about the course ideas, it leads to finding more exciting learning activities and assessments. Although caring may seem like a warm and fuzzy outcome, in the long run it can be crucial to students' engagement in a course and their development of the curiosity necessary to want to learn more even after the course is completed. Some see the importance this provides in getting students motivated to reach the final domain in the taxonomy: learning how to learn (Fink, 2013).

Let's review an example of a caring outcome. A faculty member created this outcome for a humanities, religion, arts, and society course: "Students will develop an interest in engaging with art and value its role in communicating abstract concepts about religion in society." In some ways, writing the outcome is the easiest part of the task. Next we need to find assessments and activities for students to master the outcome. The instructor developed a number of activities including having students read and react to testimonials on why this class is valuable written by two returning students who asked to be teaching assistants to experience the course again and guide others. Students debated or role-played various viewpoints in religious art controversies. Finally, students read primary and secondary sources on how lives are affected by art positively and negatively. The assessment of this outcome included students writing reflections about their own reactions to the abstract concepts and the news and stories about the examples that were provided. These reflections also included how this information could be useful in their future work. This provided an opportunity for them to share their values and how they grew in their caring for the content and experience of the course. This type of feedback from students provides an excellent tool to assess their progress and ways to measure the quality of the course design itself.

Caring outcomes may seem confusing at first, but it is easy to see from this example the power of this outcome in this course. Although foundational knowledge is important to students, this outcome forces the instructor to think creatively about how students might learn to care more about the subject itself. As this outcome is achieved, students will then become more engaged in the course and no doubt become more curious in the ideas being presented. Thinking back to the idea of situational factors and pedagogical challenges faculty face, bringing back recent graduates of the course to explain to the class its relevance in person or by video is an example of dealing with any lack of interest students may bring to a course, which can fester throughout the course.

Some common verbs used in caring outcomes include *act, comply, discern, display, express, manage, share, value,* and *volunteer.* All these verbs stress expressing values discovered during course learning.

### *Learning How to Learn Outcomes*

This is often an overlooked learning outcome for many courses. Preparing students to continue learning independently about a subject beyond the course should be one of the core outcomes of any course. If we can help students understand the conceptual structure of a subject of study (i.e., how it is organized and how to direct their own learning in relation to the subject) they will have the necessary tools for developing their skills and becoming more knowledgeable for the rest of their lives. In fact, this is critical in developing disciplinary literacy (the way experts in a discipline read, write, talk, and think), which is discussed in chapter 4. This requires caring about the subject, which is why these domains are linked. If we can succeed in promoting caring and learning how to learn, students can continue to be self-directed lifelong learners.

To illustrate the difference this might make for your students, imagine you are teaching a Spanish language course. If you asked students who had finished their required courses, "If you wanted to learn a new language, how would you do that?" a large percentage would answer, "Take a course in the new language." That kind of answer is couched in terms of the ways commonly used for learning a new language and is not a description of the process of learning a language, for which there are multiple mechanisms. If language instructors spent time teaching a conceptual framework for learning any language, students would have a process they could apply to learning any language with the help of learning materials like language CDs, apps, or even traveling to another country.

When instructors first see this as a possible outcome, they respond with a draft that is legitimate but small in scope for this kind of learning. We often hear something like, "Identify additional books to read on this subject" or "Continue to read professional journals on this subject." These are valid, but they lack a deeper look at and commitment to extending future learning. Developing a bibliography for future reading doesn't provide active learning in the current course. The outcome stating students will continue to read about the subject is difficult to assess. How would you know they will do it? This is always the issue.

However, you can use the bibliography activity with a larger set of materials and experiences by having students create a future learning plan to continue to grow professionally in the workplace or personally if the topic is more of an interest than a work position. You could assess this by developing a format and rubric.

Some common verbs used in learning how to learn outcomes include *create*, *decide*, *define*, *develop*, *formulate*, and *select*. All these verbs stress planning for future learning.

## Writing and Reviewing Your Learning Outcomes

A good resource to consult when writing learning outcomes is the syllabus rubric developed by Palmer, Bach, and Streifer (2014). Appendix A of this document contains an extensive list of verbs to use for each of the areas of the taxonomy of significant learning (Fink, 2013).

Now that we have examined how to write different types of outcomes using the taxonomy of significant learning (Fink, 2013), Table 2.1 demonstrates how a biology faculty member could design course outcomes.

Consider the following ideas from Fink (2013) as you prepare your course outcomes and unit objectives:

- Check with your dean or chair or campus curriculum committee for the number of outcomes you should have per course.
- Support your course outcomes with unit objectives, which is a great way for you to embed some of Fink's (2013) taxonomy into your course if course outcomes have already been established and you cannot add to them.

- Use verbs that are clear when writing outcomes. Some verbs such as *understand* may be vague and could be what some would consider passive learning. Action verbs lead to active learning. Describe what you want to see students being able to do in your course.
- Write the outcomes in language that students will understand. As you display them in your syllabus and throughout your course students will be able to better refer to them and see how they are related to their learning. If they aren't written in student-friendly language, add annotations to explain them.
- Use measurable outcomes and verbs for assessments.
- Write outcomes and supporting objectives at a level appropriate for the course. More advanced courses should have more advanced outcomes. Foundational courses don't need to have only foundational knowledge outcomes. Each set of outcomes plays a role in scaffolding the learning through the entire curriculum.

**TABLE 2.1**
**Fink's Three-Column Table: Learning Outcomes**

| *Taxonomy* | *Learning Outcomes* |
|---|---|
| **Foundational Knowledge**<br>Learners will understand and remember key concepts, terms, relationships, facts, and so on.<br><br>Describes what learners will be able to do with information. | Students will have a clear understanding of the well-defined concepts of cellular and molecular biology.<br><br>Students will be able to define pathological conditions in neurological as well as cardiological areas. |
| **Application**<br>Learners will perform or do important tasks.<br><br>Describes the kinds of activities and tasks learners will be able to perform based on the information they have acquired. | Students will be able to focus on a particular area of research that best suits their interests.<br><br>Students will be able to think systematically to solve a particular research question.<br><br>Students will be able to apply theoretical principles to lab practices, which would aid them in designing new protocols.<br><br>Students will be able to troubleshoot protocols. |

(*Continues*)

**Table 2.1** (*Continued*)

| *Taxonomy* | *Learning Outcomes* |
|---|---|
| **Integration**<br>Learners will identify, consider, describe the relationship between *X* and *Y*.<br><br>Describes the kinds of activities and tasks learners will be able to perform when they synthesize, link to, or relate specific information to other information. | Students will be able to relate pathological situations to the molecular basis. |
| **Human Dimension–Self**<br>Learners will better understand themselves.<br><br>Describes the kinds of activities learners will be able to perform when they apply the information to themselves and to their interactions with others. | Students will be able to confidently express their own hypothesis to others in a logical and concise manner. |
| **Human Dimension–Others**<br>Learners will be able to interact positively and productively with others.<br><br>Describes the kinds of activities learners will be able to perform when they apply the information to themselves and to their interactions with others. | Students will effectively communicate with others using evidence and discussion, as in journal clubs, which will also aid them in refining their own hypotheses.<br><br>Students will cooperate with others as they work together as a team. |
| **Caring**<br>Students will care more deeply about this subject or issues related to this subject.<br><br>Describes the kinds of activities students will be able to perform when they connect the information to themselves and their personal lives in a meaningful way. | Students will show they value the experience of contributing to their chosen field. |
| **Learning How to Learn**<br>Students will develop the ability to learn better (more efficiently and effectively) in this course and in life in general.<br><br>Describes the kinds of activities students will be able to perform to continue to learn more about this topic in the future. | Students will share information with others about topics learned.<br><br>Students will demonstrate ways they will continue to learn about their field. |

*Note.* This table provides examples of learning outcomes for each domain of Fink's taxonomy. From *Three-Column Table*, by L.D. Fink, http://www.designlearning.org/wp-content/uploads/2010/04/3-column-table-blank-2-pp.doc. Copyright 2010 by L.D. Fink. Adapted with permission.

Careful consideration should be given to writing course outcomes that align not only with the course learning activities and assessments but also with program, department, and institutional outcomes.

**Bright Idea**

In a classroom setting, provide the outcomes on the board that will be covered in the class session. Check each one off as you go through the list. Students may ask questions if they aren't sure they have mastered each outcome before you check it off. This also helps students who arrive late to class because they get oriented faster knowing what the class has already talked about. In an online course design you can include the outcomes in your learning units. Post the outcomes that are being taught and measured in assignments, discussions, and assessments. —**Zala Fashant**

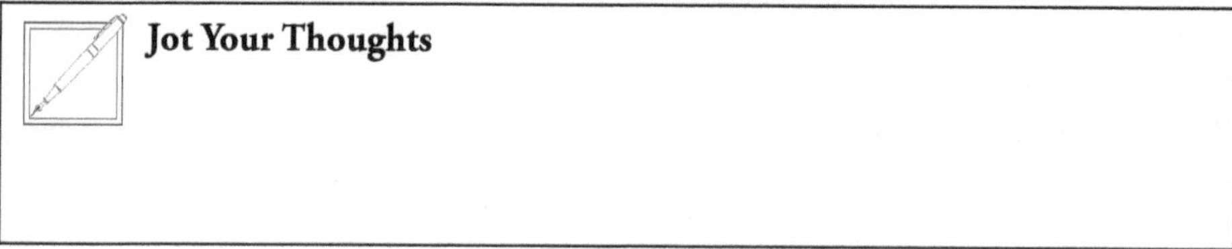


## Developing Assessments

Quality course design integrates a variety of assessments that are aligned and customized to measure learning outcomes. We discourage using only one or two types of assessment in a course as this practice doesn't measure a breadth of student progress. Let's examine the ways to use assessments effectively to engage students in their learning and measure student mastery.

As you approach the assessment, think about all the assessment choices that will best measure your outcomes based on the practice you will provide through your learning activities. Which of the following in Table 2.2 do you currently use?

We don't recommend using all these in a single course. For consistency throughout your course you should consider using four or five assessments to measure your learners' achievements, which provides a broader view in assessing ability. Students perform differently, some better by writing, some better by speaking, and some better through a demonstration. This doesn't mean that for each learning activity you need to give them a choice of writing an essay or creating a video presentation or an interpretive dance. You certainly can provide choices; however, you need to consider the workload of evaluating different forms of assessment with your schedule and the schedules of your students. If a student struggles on tests, and all you provide is tests, you aren't necessarily measuring how much they know about your course outcomes. You may be assessing only their ability to take tests.

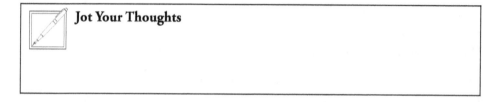

**TABLE 2.2**
**Assessment Types**

| *Forms of Assessment* | *Examples* |
|---|---|
| Writing assessments | Tests, quizzes, research papers, reflection papers, online discussions, reading reactions, essays, peer evaluation, project based, classroom assessment techniques case studies, learning assessment techniques |
| Oral assessments | Live speeches, oral and video presentations, classroom discussions, interviews, peer evaluation, debates |
| Hands-on assessments | Physical demonstrations, skill observations, portfolios, construction, performance tasks, model based, project based, competency based, graphic organizers, simulations, role play |

*Note.* This table provides forms of assessment and several examples of each.

It is critical to not only choose assessments that work well in your course and institution but also use authentic assessments that are used in professional workplaces. Self-check quizzes are a great way to provide feedback to you and your students on their progress; however, developing high-stakes tests that best measure foundational knowledge isn't the best practice in measuring all student learning. So if we are preparing students for their future work, assessing them the way they would be assessed in their career is part of the real-world experience we should provide.

## Types of Assessment

### *Formative and Summative Assessment*

Formative assessments occur along the learning pathway of the course. These lower stakes assessments form or guide the direction of learning, offer feedback to faculty about how students are progressing, and provide benchmarks for students to measure their learning progress. Examples of this type include unit or concept assessments delivered in tests, quizzes, online discussions, and assignments that measure unit objectives on the way to measuring a specific course outcome. They often carry less weight because they provide students with the opportunity to practice being assessed toward a larger assessment. In formative assessments students learn what they know and don't know well enough. By designing these assessments with a lower weight, students can progress by learning what they need to improve to demonstrate mastery of outcomes or competencies in the formative assessment without damaging their grade. In addition, careful consideration needs to be paid to the weight each formative assessment will carry in the final grade.

Summative assessments are the final higher stakes assessments that measure the degree to which a student has mastered the course outcomes. These assessments can be designed to measure more than one outcome. Summative assessments include capstone projects, student portfolios, and a comprehensive project or paper. These assessments use one assignment to measure all the learning that meets all the course outcomes. These assessments will carry more weight when determining the final grade. A balance of formative and summative assessments in your course design is ideal, and for students to be successful, planning for the weights of assessments is critical in your course assessment design plan.

### *Backward-Looking and Forward-Looking Assessment*

It is important to balance backward-looking and forward-looking assessments in your course design. Backward-looking assessments have been traditionally used in higher education, and many will recognize the following examples of questions found in this type of assessment:

- What is the definition of *race relations*?
- Who invented the Xerox copying machine?
- What were the dates of the Civil War?

Each of the answers to these questions require memorization. Examples of backward-looking assessments include tests that use multiple choice, true or false, and matching sets of questions. They are best for measuring foundational knowledge; they don't measure the other areas of the taxonomy well. Many learning platforms can automatically grade these kinds of tests and provide immediate feedback to students. The balance between backward- and forward-looking assessments may not be equal since backward-looking assessment best measures only one of the six domains of the taxonomy of significant learning (Fink, 2013), while forward-looking assessment measures the remaining domains. Backward-looking assessments can help students develop the foundation for extended learning.

**Bright Idea**

Pop quizzes don't effectively measure student achievement. Wanting to make sure students are reading material or studying throughout the week is a valid desire, but this can be accomplished more effectively with an engaging course design. Use the flipped classroom strategy to get students to read before class and assign a reflection on reading assignments about what the content meant to them and how they could apply the information in the workplace. Requiring this to be due in the course shell before a classroom meeting is effective and forces them to read. Assessments should be learning experiences, not gotcha assessments, which are more punitive than constructive. Think back to your own working experience. How many pop quizzes have you had? Your course should be designed to prepare students for their careers. **—Zala Fashant**

Your course should include forward-looking assessments, which provide a richer experience for students as it develops higher-level thinking. If you think back to the big dream for the course, you want to assess the body of content in your course (backward-looking for foundational knowledge) and assess applying the content in their future (forward-looking for the rest of the taxonomy). Forward-looking assessment questions could include the following:

- Discuss how you can use what you read this week in your current or future job.
- What will be the greatest reward for you as you assume the position for which you are preparing?
- How would you respond to a customer or colleague who has a concern about the service they received?
- What do you want to accomplish in this course?

Examples of forward-looking assessments include case studies, role playing, student research, inquiry, debate, and problem- and team-based learning. Take a moment to think about your course assignments and assessments. What kind of backward- and forward-looking balance do you currently have?

It is time to think about how you would align the assessments to the outcomes in your course. In Table 2.3, we can see how the biology instructor aligned the learning outcomes with the assessments in the taxonomy of significant learning (Fink, 2013).

Developing course quality assessment is discussed in more detail and examples of multiple forms of assessments are provided in chapter 8. See other examples of how faculty aligned their course outcomes and assessments in each of the domains of the taxonomy of significant learning in Fink (2013) and Barkley and Major (2016a).

**Bright Idea**

Tell your students what criteria you will use to determine their grade for your course. This tells them that you aren't determining the grade, they are. Students can grade themselves with the rubric and turn in the assessment and self-graded rubric, which provides a great opportunity to communicate expectations by discussing the differences between your evaluation and theirs. You can offer specific feedback as you explain why you may have given them the points you did. This way the assessment becomes an additional learning activity. You may find that more students achieve the highest standards because they understood the expectations. —**Zala Fashant**

**TABLE 2.3**
**Fink's Three-Column Table: Learning Outcomes and Assessments**

| *Taxonomy* | *Learning Outcomes* | *Learning Assessments* |
|---|---|---|
| **Foundational Knowledge**<br>Learners will understand and remember key concepts, terms, relationships, facts, and so on. Describes what learners will be able to do with information. | Students will have a clear understanding of the well-defined concepts of cellular and molecular biology.<br>Students will be able to define pathological conditions in neurological as well as cardiological areas. | Classroom assessment Techniques<br>Quizzes<br>Multiple-choice questions and descriptive tests |
| **Application**<br>Learners will perform or do important tasks. Describes the kinds of activities and tasks learners will be able to perform based on the information they have acquired. | The students will be able to focus on a particular area of research that best suits their interests.<br>Students will be able to think systematically to solve a particular research question.<br>Students will be able to apply theoretical principles into lab practices which would aid them in designing new protocols.<br>Students will be able to troubleshoot protocols as well. | Report assessment<br>Case studies (forward-looking assessment)<br>Reflections |
| **Integration**<br>Learners will identify and consider and describe the relationship between *X* and *Y*. Describes the kinds of activities and tasks learners will be able to perform when they synthesize, link to, or relate specific information to other information. | Students will be able to relate pathological situations to the molecular basis. | Oral presentations<br>Reflective writing<br>These formats would be subject to self-assessment and peer assessment |
| **Human Dimension–Self**<br>Learners will better understand themselves. | Students will be able to confidently express their own hypothesis to others in a logical and concise manner. | Survey or pre- and post-instruction questionnaire |

(*Continues*)

**Table 2.3** (*Continued*)

| *Taxonomy* | *Learning Outcomes* | *Learning Assessments* |
|---|---|---|
| Describes the kinds of activities learners will be able to perform when they apply the information to themselves and to their interactions with others. | | |
| **Human Dimension–Others**<br>Learners will be able to interact positively and productively with others.<br>Describes the kinds of activities learners will be able to perform when they apply the information to themselves and to their interactions with others. | Students will effectively communicate to others, discuss using evidence as in journal clubs, which would aid them in refining their own hypothesis.<br>Students will cooperate with others as they work together as a team. | Group discussions |
| **Caring**<br>Students will care more deeply about this subject or issues related to this subject. Describes the kinds of activities students will be able to perform when they connect the information to themselves and their personal lives in a meaningful way. | Students will show they value the experience of contributing to their chosen field. | Reflective writing-journal entries |
| **Learning How to Learn**<br>Students will develop the ability to learn better (more efficiently and effectively), in this course and in life in general. Describes the kinds of activities students will be able to perform to continue to learn more about this topic in the future. | Students will share information with others about topics learned.<br>Students will demonstrate ways they will continue to learn about their field. | Future learning plan<br>Self-assessment |

*Note*. This table provides examples of the alignment of learning outcomes and assessments for each domain of Fink's Taxonomy. From *Three-Column Table*, by D.L. Fink, http://www.designlearning.org/wp-content/uploads/2010/04/3-column-table-blank-2-pp.doc. Copyright 2010 by L.D. Fink. Adapted with permission.

**Jot Your Thoughts**

## Designing Learning Activities

The purpose of learning activities is to link the outcomes and assessments by providing students with the opportunity to practice what they have read in the content and learned in previous experiences and to create links to new information so they can demonstrate what they know and what they can do in assessments. When we think about learning, the learning activities will build thinking folders in the brain for a person to file the information in a systematic way so it is retrievable as needed.

Learning activities are "active"; that is why they aren't called learning "passivities" (Z. Fashant, personal communication, July 31, 2018). As you design your course, it is key for you to think about learning activities that will provide your students with the experiences necessary for them to fully understand and demonstrate outcomes that are measurable through assessment and that they are based on the kind of work they will encounter in their discipline in the workplace.

We use active learning for the following reasons:

- Students are given the opportunity to interact with the subject matter of a course.
- Students generate rather than receive knowledge; give students the opportunity to discover learning (Felder, Bullard, & Raubenheimer, 2008).
- Using active learning helps to eliminate distractions in the physical classroom such as personal cell phone use. Instead, make cell phones part of the an active learning lesson by polling students for answers anonymously and by researching additional information through Google Assistant and Siri in group work.
- The instructor facilitates rather than dictates students' learning. Instructors don't need the practice of delivering information, but students do need the experience of constructing their own learning.
- This is the type of learning that students will need to do in their future, so the more experience they have in the classroom the more prepared they will be to do it themselves in the workplace (Silberman, 1996).

Keep in mind that the learning activities are the most visible parts of the course for students, the tip of the iceberg that they see daily in your course's design. However, instructors know that much of the design is really the portion of the iceberg below the surface. Students will often ask, "What do I need to do in this course to pass?" The question that needs answering in designing learning activities is, What delivers significant learning experiences for students? Chapter 4 provides an in-depth examination of the learning process.

## Learning Activity Design

Reflect on the following list of practices regarding the challenges of developing significant learning activities. Some faculty use what they experienced as a student; however, we advise you to keep learning activities current. Duplicating former learning activities isn't a good idea unless they meet the following criteria. The activities in your course redesign should

- align with current course outcomes and assessments,
- provide the best ways for students to practice the outcomes to prepare them for the information and work experiences today, and
- lead intentionally to mastering outcomes and assessments.

Don't include activities because they are the latest or coolest things to do. You only have so many hours with your students, so you need to deliver only the best, most effective learning activities.

As you design learning activities, you need to predict the amount of practice a student needs to master outcomes. Consider the following in your analysis:

- Determine the level of your outcome. Lower level foundational knowledge outcomes usually need fewer activities, whereas higher level outcomes (application, integration, analysis) may need two or more.
- Identify the complexity and purpose of the activity. Will this activity meet one outcome or serve as practice for several? Is the activity part of a set of learning practices that support higher level outcomes?
- Analyze the time and equipment needed to complete the activity. Will students have full access to what they need to complete the activity effectively? Is the time or equipment limited? Should the activity be broken into chunks?
- Assess the effectiveness of the activities by having former students go through them and provide feedback.

Develop a learning activity to practice for multiple outcomes. It is perfectly acceptable to develop more complex learning activities that meet a couple of the outcomes at the same time. As learning activities take a major portion of a student's time, design one activity that will prepare students for more than one outcome. You may use portions of the course materials for several learning activities. Assignment rubrics will help students understand the outcomes they are practicing.

Keep learning active. Short lectures of up to 15 minutes to provide content with opportunities for students to learn by applying or analyzing the content are effective (Guo, Kim, & Robin, 2014). Significant learning takes place when students interact with content frequently. Providing activities for students to reflect, question, discuss, and process the information makes the lecture more interactive. Design your course so there are more voices or more hands moving at the same time. Greater engagement is a key ingredient of significant learning.

**Bright Idea**

Learning activities need clearly written instructions and expectations, effective time lines, communicated outcome alignments, and rubric criteria to meet high standards. You need to get in the head of a student when designing activities. They may be perfectly clear to you, but are they clear to your students? Find some trusted students and run the activities past them before you use it in a class, or ask another faculty member from another department for feedback.
**—Zala Fashant**

## Course Discussions as Learning Activities

The goal of integrated course design is to keep students engaged in the content and to use it to prompt higher-level critical thinking. Whether in the classroom or an online course shell, having students talk with one another is a strategy for creating significant learning experiences. One of the challenges for student engagement is students who think faster or are more confident answering more of the questions in a face-to-face class setting. Some students need more reflection time to organize their thoughts and present their ideas or answer questions.

The purposes of discussion are to (a) help participants reach a more crucially informed understanding about the topic or topics under consideration, (b) enhance participants' self-awareness and their capacity for self-critique, (c) foster an appreciation among participants for the diversity of opinion that invariably emerges when viewpoints are exchanged openly and honestly, and (d) act as a catalyst for helping people take informed action in the world (Brookfield & Preskill, 2005).

**Bright Idea**

A powerful tool to engage students in answering questions is to allow them to meet in groups. Asking students questions individually in a classroom setting can be intimidating. Some don't have the confidence or perhaps the knowledge to answer. However, questioning in a group setting builds that confidence. Some students need time to think about or research their answers. Even providing six seconds of wait time before responding isn't always enough time for all students to fully conceive their best answer. Some students benefit by listening to others' discussions. Asking questions of the group also gives faculty a chance to walk around the class and listen to multiple responses, praising students or guiding them to better answers. Questions requiring deeper thinking may be put in the online course shell for students to formulate answers after they have thought more about them. —**Stewart Ross**

Your course design can present discussions in a variety of ways, the first of which is thinking about the timing and purpose of the information to be discussed:

- Does the discussion and introduction to the material use students' prior learning to assess where they are in their knowledge the beginning of a unit? Do you want them to discuss what they know and propose ideas before you present new information in your course?
- Is the discussion a reflection on or reaction to material presented when you want to assess what students learned by having them interact with the content? Do you want them to analyze an author's view, synthesize solutions, or evaluate a situation in their responses?
- Discussions can allow students a chance to use backward- and forward-looking experiences.

As a learning activity or formative assessment, discussions are a great way to collect the students' evidence of thinking and understanding. When we develop discussion questions in a course, we try to get each student to use authentic answers, which are usually tied to their own experiences or to future experiences where they will use the content.

How will you present these discussions to gain the maximum learning opportunity for each student? A brief review of the strengths and weaknesses of the three delivery modes is presented in Table 2.4.

Using discussions in your course provides valuable experiences for learners. The opportunity to form your thoughts, whether orally or in written form, is a powerful way for students to organize their thoughts that model skills used in the workplace.

TABLE 2.4
**Course Discussion Analysis**

| *Delivery Mode* | *Strengths* | *Challenges* |
|---|---|---|
| Face-to-face classroom oral discussion led by instructor (question and answer) | Students and faculty can receive information and interact quickly. Greater student engagement can occur if this technique is used after a small group discussion, such as think-pair-share. | There is a possibility that only a few students talk (usually only one at a time); it is difficult to tell how many students really understand the material, as many sit quietly; quick-thinking and outgoing students will get the most attention. This method uses valuable face-to-face class time. |
| Face-to-face classroom oral discussion in groups | More students are speaking at one time, one per group. This method builds consensus as more ideas are being shared and analysis takes place. The instructor can visit groups, monitor discussions, and observe student participation. Students practice talking about the material and the instructor can check for understanding. This method is used in team-based learning (see chapter 5). | It is also difficult to tell how many students really understand the material. Quick-thinking and outgoing students talk the most, so there is a chance that some students will be passive in a group. This method uses valuable face-to-face class time but is useful since more students are participating. |
| Written discussion in a course shell | The instructor and the class receive information from all students. This method does not take face-to-face classroom time. A maximum number of thoughts are generated, which maximizes interaction. Students can prepare for more in-depth questions and reflect on their answers, which provides an opportunity for deeper learning. This method creates a documented source for assessment. Students construct their own learning and demonstrate written communication skills. | This method takes longer to complete, as you may need several days to get responses. It isn't as spontaneous. There is no assurance that all students are reading all responses. |

*Note.* This table analyzes the delivery modes for designing course discussions by listing strengths and challenges.

Table 2.5 shows how a biology instructor aligned the learning outcomes with the assessments and now the learning activities in the taxonomy of significant learning (Fink, 2013). Peggy Maki discusses the importance of integrating the learning activity assignments in a variety of ways to best master the outcomes:

> Assignments that align not only with specified outcomes and scoring rubrics or other metrics but also with course or education experience sequencing contribute to students' awareness of their progress toward achieving course-level expectations. Sequenced assignments, together with feedback to students and opportunities for them to reflect on their learning, help students learn about their patterns of strength and weakness as they prepare for a culminating assignment. On a larger scale, well-sequenced assignments across the general education program and major programs of study broaden and deepen students' understanding of the relevance and application of outcomes in diverse contexts other than the ones in the which they initially learned them. (Maki, 2017, p. 69)

See chapters 3 and 5 for more ideas about using discussions. For additional course design integration ideas for STEAM faculty see references in the Additional Readings and Resources section at the end of the book. You may also visit https://encoreprodev.com/book to read "Using STEAM to Power Your Course Design."

**Bright Idea**

Creating a rubric requires you to practice using it before you actually employ it for real grading. You will find that your students often turn in work that falls into gray areas, and your rubric language must zero in on distinguishing them. Try jotting down the errors or problems you find in the students' work, which then can be tallied (use the most frequent ones) and rewritten into language that can be used in a rubric. —**Linda Russell**

**Jot Your Thoughts**

**TABLE 2.5**
**Fink's Three-Column Table: Learning Outcomes, Assessments, and Activities**

| *Taxonomy* | *Learning Outcomes* | *Learning Assessments* | *Learning Activities* |
|---|---|---|---|
| **Foundational Knowledge**<br>Learners will understand and remember key concepts, terms, relationships, facts, and so on.<br>Describes what learners will be able to do with information. | Students will have a clear understanding of the well-defined concepts of cellular and molecular biology.<br>Students will be able to define pathological conditions in neurological as well as cardiological areas. | Classroom assessment techniques<br>Quizzes<br>Multiple-choice questions and descriptive tests | Provide lecture on information and ideas.<br>At the end of the lecture students are asked to write a concise summary of all concepts.<br>Assign any readings that fit here. |
| **Application**<br>Learners will perform or do important tasks.<br>Describes the kinds of activities and tasks learners will be able to perform based on the information they have acquired. | The students will be able to focus on a particular area of research that best suits their interests.<br>Students will be able to think systematically to solve a particular research question.<br>Students will be able to apply theoretical principles to lab practices, which would aid them in designing new protocols.<br>Students will be able to troubleshoot protocols. | Report assessment<br>Case studies (forward-looking assessment)<br>Writing reflections | Students prepare assignments on lab protocols based on concepts taught in the classroom.<br>Information could be gathered from books, online tools, direct lab experience (if any).<br>Reflective learning:<br>1. Introduce a case before a concept is taught.<br>2. Allow students to reflect on the situation.<br>3. After the lecture, return to the case.<br>4. Ask students to solve the situation based on information provided. |

| | | | |
|---|---|---|---|
| **Integration**<br>Learners will identify, consider, or describe the relationship between *X* and *Y*.<br>Describes the kinds of activities and tasks learners will be able to perform when they synthesize, link to, or relate specific information to other information. | Students will be able to relate pathological situations to the molecular basis. | Oral presentation<br>Reflective writing<br>(These formats are subject to self-assessment and peer assessment.) | Experience: Students choose a specific neurological or cardiological disease and make a presentation on the current knowledge of its causes. (Students select the mode of presentation: oral presentation, diagrammatic representation, or written format.) |
| **Human Dimension–Self**<br>Learners will better understand themselves.<br>Describes the kinds of activities learners will be able to perform when they apply the information to themselves and to their interactions with others. | Students will be able to confidently express their own hypothesis to others in a logical and concise manner. | Survey or pre- and post-instruction questionnaire | Experience: Students present their hypothesis for a proposed study aimed to advance current understanding of the chosen pathological condition. |
| **Human Dimension–Others**<br>Learners will be able to interact positively and productively with others.<br>Describes the kinds of activities learners will be able to perform when they apply the information to themselves and to their interactions with others. | Students will effectively communicate to others, discuss using evidence as in journal clubs, which would aid them in refining their own hypothesis.<br>Students will cooperate with others as they work together as a team. | Group discussions in course shell<br>Assess with a discussion rubric | Experience: Students develop a set of discussion topics, with writing prompts, on their research interest areas for the entire class. |

(*Continues*)

**Table 2.5** (*Continued*)

| *Taxonomy* | *Learning Outcomes* | *Learning Assessments* | *Learning Activities* |
| --- | --- | --- | --- |
| **Caring**<br>Students will care more deeply about this subject or issues related to this subject.<br>Describes the kinds of activities students will be able to perform when they connect the information to themselves and their personal lives in a meaningful way. | Students will show they value the experience of contributing to their chosen field. | Reflective writing-journal entries | Students share research findings about the topic that interests them. Research can include interviewing experts and others working in the field including graduates, discussing current trends and information, or forming panel discussions. |
| **Learning How to Learn**<br>Students will develop the ability to learn better (more efficiently and effectively) in this course and in life in general.<br>Describes the kinds of activities students will be able to perform to continue to learn more about this topic in the future. | Students will share information with others about topics learned.<br>Students will demonstrate ways they will continue to learn about their field. | Future learning plan<br>Self-assessment | Students enhance their existing knowledge by developing a reading list on topics of interest. Students will participate in an online forum to discuss the creation and analysis of experimental protocols. |

*Note*. This table provides examples of the alignment of learning outcomes, assessments, and activities for each domain of Fink's taxonomy. From *Three-Column Table*, by D.L. Fink, http://www.designlearning.org/wp-content/uploads/2010/04/3-column-table-blank-2-pp.doc. Copyright 2010 by L.D. Fink. Adapted with permission.

## Beyond Integrated Course Design

In addition to discussing the importance of integrating course learning outcomes, assessments, and activities in this chapter, we realize broader considerations are needed in course design beyond this framework. Student success initiatives on campuses involve much more to meet the challenges of student learners and a team of staff working collaboratively with faculty. The chapters in this book contain strategies to be embedded in the integrated course design framework, a sort of Integrated Course Design 2.0. Communicating in your course, course accessibility, integrating learning technologies, assessing course quality, and blending your course into assessments of your program and institution are critical design considerations to make your course relevant for all learners and at all levels. We discuss these further in the following chapters and provide strategies to develop quality courses and to help your students learn.

## Reflect on This Chapter

Now that you have completed reading this chapter and thinking about the content as it applies to your work, please reflect on the following questions.

- How have you developed the course outcomes and weekly or unit objectives for your courses? What resources do you use to choose action verbs to design course outcomes?
- How many types of learning activities and assessments do you use in a course? What assessments do you use to provide a polycentric measurement of your students' abilities?
- How do you currently measure your courses' quality?
- What is the big dream for each of your courses? Why do you think communicating this dream will help students perform better in your course?

**Jot Your Thoughts**

## Action Checklist

Use Checklist 2.1 to apply the chapter content to your practice and help you identify the steps for implementing these ideas in your teaching.

**CHECKLIST 2.1** Integrating Your Course Design Action Checklist

| ✓ | **Big Dream** |
|---|---|
| ❑ | Developed my course's big dream. |
| ❑ | Shared the big dream with students in the course shell and syllabus. |

| ✓ | **Course Outcomes** |
|---|---|
| ❑ | Created course outcomes or unit objectives linked to my big dream. |
| ❑ | Created one or more outcomes for each of the six categories of the taxonomy of significant learning. |
| ❑ | Developed outcomes that are measurable. |
| ❑ | Checked to make sure that course outcome verbs are active. |
| ❑ | Created outcomes that are appropriate for the curriculum level of the course. |
| ❑ | Developed outcomes and objectives that are written so students understand them. |
| ❑ | Aligned unit or weekly objectives to support course outcomes. |

| ✓ | **Assessments** |
|---|---|
| ❑ | Designed a variety of assessment types to measure outcomes. |
| ❑ | Created a blend of formative and summative assessments. |
| ❑ | Developed both backward- and forward-looking assessments. |
| ❑ | Considered the balance of teaching with assessing. |
| ❑ | Provided valuable and frequent feedback opportunities in the assessments. |
| ❑ | Developed evaluative rubrics for assignments and assessments. |
| ❑ | Designed opportunities for students to monitor their progress through frequent assessment feedback. |

| ✓ | **Learning Activities** |
|---|---|
| ❑ | Provided opportunities for students to share prior knowledge. |
| ❑ | Created learning activities to bridge outcomes to assessments. |
| ❑ | Developed activities that scaffold to prepare for the summative assessments. |
| ❑ | Chose active learning activities to promote student engagement. |
| ❑ | Eliminated learning passivities. |

(*Continues*)

**CHECKLIST 2.1** (*Continued*)

| | |
|---|---|
| ❑ | Designed course using a variety of activities to engage students appropriately. |
| ❑ | Created course discussions to promote deeper thinking and greater participation. |
| ❑ | Provided opportunities for faculty-to-student and student-to-faculty feedback. |
| ❑ | Provided opportunities for peer-to-peer feedback. |
| ❑ | Developed activities that reflect real-world working experiences. |
| ❑ | Planned the time needed and pacing to complete activities and provide feedback. |
| ❑ | Designed one or more learning activities for each outcome. |
| ❑ | Created activities with clearly written instructions, time lines, outcome alignments, and grading rubrics. |
| ❑ | Aligned course outcomes, activities, and assessments with the three-column table (Table 2.5). |

| ✓ | **Course Discussions as Learning Assessments and Activities** |
|---|---|
| ❑ | Created discussions including student and faculty introductions to build community. |
| ❑ | Developed discussions are based on students using critical thinking skills. |
| ❑ | Designed discussions in which students may use learning and work experiences. |
| ❑ | Aligned learning activity and assessment discussions to meet specific outcomes. |
| ❑ | Provided discussion grading rubrics. |

# 3

# COMMUNICATING IN YOUR COURSE

## Points to Ponder

Chapter 3 will focus on how communicating with students about your course design is critical to their successful navigation, mastery of outcomes, and course completion. In thinking about designing the courses you teach, consider the following questions to examine your prior knowledge:

- How do you currently communicate with your students in online, blended, and face-to-face courses?
- When do you currently communicate with your students?
- How confident are you that you are effectively communicating with your students?

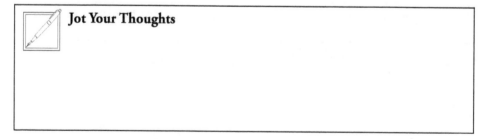

Samantha rushed into the dean's office and opened with "I didn't know I had to do this assignment by last Friday. It wasn't in the syllabus and I can't find it anywhere in the course information. This isn't fair!"

As dean, he always stressed the importance of communicating with students in all courses whether they are taught face-to-face, blended, or online. His role allowed him to assist faculty and students to talk with one another when the communication broke down. His first question to the student was, "Did you talk with your instructor?" She told him she had.

Samantha told him about how busy she is as a single mother, trying to work, taking courses full time, and tutoring her child with homework. Realizing all the stress she was feeling, the dean listened and told her that he would talk with the instructor, knowing that the reality of the situation needed the perspectives of both the student and the instructor. He picked up the phone and left a message for the instructor, Diane, letting her know he would send an e-mail with some details and would appreciate her help in solving this situation.

Diane was very responsive. She let her dean know that she and student had talked before Samantha made an appointment to see him. Diane was a little surprised that he had been contacted because she thought the problem had been resolved. He knew that students will often try other ways to get their full set of points.

Diane e-mailed a full set of course records including Samantha's grades, course progress, attendance, and correspondence regarding this situation. He appreciated the e-mail sent by Diane to Samantha after they first met that outlined the conversation and the final decision. This is what he needed to continue the conversation with Samantha, and he called her back the next day. Diane didn't need to make an accommodation for late work, but she asked Samantha to come back to talk with her about a way they could solve the problem. The two of them met and shared the resolution with their dean.

As a result of this interaction, Diane reflected about displaying due dates in the course shell with all the instructions for her assignments as well as on a page she could create for students of course assignment due dates. She hadn't used the course calendar in the learning management system but had put the due dates in the syllabus. Diane had communicated the information on the assignment calendar, but she recognized that having it in more than one place could help prevent this from occurring in the future with other students. Meeting with the person who coordinated the learning management system, she learned about a tool that could send out automated reminders to students about upcoming assignments.

Diane had the right to deny the student the opportunity to turn in the assignment late as stated in her syllabus, but instead of digging in her heels in she considered options. Having Samantha help with the solution—she chose to take a late assignment deduction—to find a way to make up some additional points with an additional assignment satisfied them both. Diane's course communication, which had been good, got even better. She continued to build a strong relationship with the student, modeling what could happen in the workplace.

## Course Communication Pathways

One of the most difficult tasks for instructors is developing an effective communication pathway for their students. Today's students have many forms of media vying for their attention and yours. Some of you may remember playing the game of dodge ball, which involves a lot of running around to avoid getting hit by balls and trying catch the ball to throw at your opponents. The balls in your courses are e-mail, texting, course-based learning management system (LMS) automated reminders, syllabi, checklists, calendars, announcements, discussions, faculty-created video messages, instant messaging, word of mouth, group work, file-sharing programs like Google Docs or Drive, and so on. With all these forms of communication, it is critical for you to design a clear and effective communication plan for your course using a variety of strategies. In this chapter we examine strategies you can use to communicate with your students, no matter which delivery method you use for your course, focusing on the elements of a course communication pathway, which include

- the reasons or purposes for the communication,
- the senders and receivers of the message,
- the schedule for communication, and
- the tools you can use to communicate.

We analyze these elements, and at the end of the chapter, you will be able to design your course communication plan. In the Points to Ponder, we ask you to think about how you communicate in your courses; reflecting on your current practice will get you ready for this discussion.

## Reasons for Communication

The terms *communicate* and *community* have the same root word. Through communication, a course community can be developed to retain students through increased engagement. While providing a more successful environment for students to achieve their goals through constructive feedback, you will help them monitor their progress and apply the learned skills they will use after graduation in the workplace.

Faculty know it is important but don't often focus on the value of modeling excellent communication. We may think our communication with students is about pushing out course information, but our strategies need to go beyond that. The most important connection a student makes related to success in the course is with you. Your design needs to provide intentional communication pathways that flow from faculty to students, students to faculty, and students to students. Students will always find ways to communicate, with or without you. The ways they communicate with you will provide the strongest learning experiences. Modeling communication is a way for younger students to experience well-designed written and oral communication as their main modes may focus on texts and tweets. Furthermore, you are demonstrating the skills they will need to master as they are practicing for communicating in the workplace.

Often we think students come to school knowing how to communicate. Most institutional learner outcomes include developing written and oral communication skills in students. We may fall short in preparing students if we think they accomplish those skills only in writing and communication courses. We promote a fallacy if we think quality writing is only important in the English department. This doesn't mean that instructors in every course need to assign a research paper. We need to consider the purpose for the communication and design the appropriate courses to teach the specific writing in their careers.

In our faculty development work with Fink's (2013) design principles, many faculty identify the need for their students to better communicate as an essential element in the situational factors and big dream. They recognize that building this skill with their students affects significant learning during their course and beyond.

How did most of us learn to communicate? From birth to pre-K we learned by watching how others communicated. We came to elementary school knowing to get messaging clues by listening to tone, watching facial expressions and body language, and by interpreting words. Some of us had a unit in our language arts book on how to answer and speak on the telephone. In high school or college we learned there were senders and receivers in a communication course and had to deliver speeches. For some, that was a terrifying experience. Some of us took speech or theater and learned how to be a character in front of a live audience, whereas others may have taught a course as a graduate assistant. We learned to speak as mentors and leaders who would need to teach communication skills to others.

Most of our communication pathways were developed through trial and error rather than structured learning, as most people assume that everyone knows how to communicate. Many of us learned to e-mail, text, leave a voice message, and video conference with little or no instruction. It isn't that instruction wasn't necessary, there just wasn't much available as technologies were quickly emerging and changing. The need to send a text message was often greater than the need to learn how to send a message effectively.

Teaching your students how to communicate through your course content needs to be part of your course design. As stated earlier, your institution may expect you provide experiences that support this learner outcome. Employers expect students to graduate from your discipline's program or department ready to communicate in the workplace, and your program's or department's reputation is measured in part by the quality of your graduates and their ability to perform. Part of the performance is communication.

In creating a course communication plan, you will develop better speakers and writers through modeling. You have the ability to challenge your students to think critically, listen actively, and work collaboratively, which are among the skills that employers require. Employers need graduates who are adept at using current communication strategies with robust written and video technologies. Today's students may be skilled at adapting to the latest communication apps without much formalized learning, opting instead for learning from others or by trial and error. This goes back to the concept of whatever is fastest, not the most effective. Many workplaces rely on employees who can effectively share information and work collaboratively using software that goes beyond social media apps. Students will need to build relationships electronically with colleagues in various locations throughout their careers, so providing them with opportunities to practice in the structure of your course benefits them.

There are other purposes for two-way communication besides building community. Using effective and timely communication methods in your course can also reduce confusion for students and allow them to get an answer to a question so that they can complete assignments. We recommend setting clear expectations for how students should contact you, as well as a reasonable turnaround time for your response. To facilitate the two-way communication, the instructor needs to explain how timely feedback will be delivered, taking into consideration the ways your weekend, holiday, and other nonschool days affect your ability to respond.

Another purpose for developing communication lines between you and your students is to allow students to stay in touch with you if they are unable to attend class for some period. Is there a way for them to check in with you, turn in assignments, access course materials, and so forth while they are away? This is helpful in the event of an extended illness, hospital stays, or family emergencies. Many of you can do so effectively by using the course's LMS.

To summarize, we have measured the results of intentional communication with learners as we developed courses using institutional, department or program accreditation, and employer-required frameworks. We encourage you to plan effective communication experiences to improve your students' ability to

- participate in the course community,
- meet your expectations,
- deliver their best work,
- achieve the course and institutional learner outcomes,
- complete the course in a timely manner,
- navigate the course successfully,
- build on your program's or department's reputation,
- meet employer expectations, and
- succeed in future learning and workplace opportunities.

In designing a course communication plan, you need to consider the purpose of the communication, what needs to be communicated, who the participants are, when the communication takes place, and how best to communicate. Before developing a communication plan, analyze the possible ways to communicate in the course, each of which is useful in face-to-face, blended, and online courses. You have students from all over the world with a wide range of background experiences in communication. Your audiences may extend beyond your students, and the most important may be your dean or chair who may be able to assist you when necessary.

## Ways to Communicate

Face-to-face communication is sometimes the most overlooked and yet the most used course communication tool in a typical classroom. Many students shy away from presenting information in the class, either because of timidity, a lack of experience or confidence, and differences in culture. Your course outcomes may not directly address oral communication, and yet it is one of the skills that you promote in your course. This skill is often listed in the institution's learner outcomes. Even in virtual online classrooms you can provide opportunities for students to prepare short video responses or longer presentations as ways to communicate orally. You can also use video conferencing in an online course if you schedule a designated common meeting time. Building confidence in your students is key for them to achieve their goals for employment. Few occupations don't require some personal face-to-face communication, and with ever-expanding global collaborations, the use of video conferencing has increased.

E-mail provides a means to send messages of any length with the flexibility to add graphics, documents, and short video attachments. It is easy to add links in an e-mail to direct readers to additional information, and automated emergency alerts can be sent from the institution to students. E-mail is a standard tool used in the workplace with the function of allowing archiving and searching by author and content. Most e-mail systems are robust in what they offer the users. Your institution may have identified e-mail as the official means to communicate messages to students, so it helps for you to support this tool for students to receive critical information.

Texting and instant messaging are ways to send short, timely messages to multiple devices. However, teaching your students to forward e-mail messages to their smartphones is an effective way of communicating course information as many students use their phones as their main communication device. We recommend this option because archiving text messages for an extended time may be a problem for phone storage and data plans. Texting may be an issue because it uses your phone number, which you may not care to give to your students. Our recommendation is to use the instant messaging, paging, or chat tool in your LMS, if available.

Course shell and LMS tools usually include an e-mail connection, instant messaging, and automated messaging reminders. Sending e-mails to students through the LMS is a convenient way for you to communicate one-on-one or with the entire class. Student e-mail addresses are usually automatically loaded into your course shell at registration. Your LMS may also have a way to send instant messages to students as they log into the course. Some LMSs allow you to send faculty-designed automated messages as reminders to your students, for example, sending an e-mail to students who haven't logged into the course after a few days and reminders of assignment due dates or upcoming assessments. Each of these can be programmed to be sent automatically, requiring little monitoring on your part during the course. We provide examples later in this chapter.

In the LMS course shell, you can usually create checklists, calendars, and announcements that can be stored permanently. The LMS allows you to set the times they are sent during the course. These weekly announcements can be displayed temporarily, avoiding long lists of information that is no longer needed in the course or permanently, depending on the content. This helps students find vital information posted in archived announcements.

The LMS usually has a number of communication tools that may benefit your ability to teach and your students' ability to learn in any delivery method. Some faculty in face-to-face courses use the course shell to post only the syllabus and grades. We ask you to consider using the LMS's communication tools and other features the course shell can provide in all course delivery methods. Some institutions require full use of the course shell, and others leave the amount of use to be determined by each faculty member. Our recommendation is to use the full set of tools in a course shell, which better serves students. From a faculty perspective, the array of tools provides you with many automated ways to communicate and free yourself up for more one-on-one teaching. By offering your students greater communication of their progress through the electronic grade book and assignment feedback tools, students can be more responsible for their own learning. From a student perspective, being able to communicate in many ways in one class using the full course shell and being limited in another class can be confusing and inconsistent. We recommend meeting with your LMS site administrator for training in how to use the tools, which can help your students learn and save you time.

Frequently asked questions (FAQs) in your LMS may reduce the number of times you have to answer the same question. Collect or keep notes about the questions you receive about assignments or other class activities, and then create an organized FAQs board, which can be organized by topics, projects, or assignments, so students can check first before contacting you. Creating a learning lounge or cyber café in the menu of your course shell is a great place to store FAQs and provides a place for students to post questions about their work. The community of learners can help answer these questions from one another in addition to the instructor's response to clarify information. This is a good model for the workplace; students need to learn to check available documentation or instructions before needlessly asking coworkers or supervisors for assistance.

Collaborative tools in your LMS or as stand-alone software applications are great ways for your students to work and communicate with one another. Your LMS may have the tools to divide students into groups for collaborative teamwork. Students can usually communicate through a group bulletin board and archive documents used in developing a final product. Applications like Google Docs and wikis allow students access to all work on the same document by adding information to the documents at the same time. This provides great flexibility for groups to meet and work collaboratively. If your LMS doesn't have the ability to create collaborative groups, Web applications like Basecamp will help students organize their work in groups by archiving shared documents. This can streamline communication about the workflow because the application provides change alerts as each group member completes portions of the assignments.

Group discussions take place in the classroom or the LMS environment. Faculty can establish clearly communicated writing prompts that guide students to post responses. Discussions are extremely effective ways to provide students with a place to reflect and interact on topics by sharing their perspectives as they learn from one another. Much like an in-class discussion, the instructor should interact with the students online in the course shell to guide the discussion into deeper thinking. Ways to engage students in discussions are also discussed later in this chapter.

Feedback from assignments and assessments is a valuable strategy to communicate expectations, explain areas of growth opportunity, and reinforce student-demonstrated achievement. By providing rubrics, you can communicate the standards to guide and identify students' performance levels. Your comments offer a valuable learning experience for students and give them targeted one-on-one time with you. Feedback can come in the form of verbal and written comments in all course delivery models. You may provide feedback in person during some in-class conferencing time or office hours. Your LMS or other software apps may provide ways to type and speak comments through the grade book or assignment drop boxes. The advantage is that students can replay the feedback throughout the course as they need it. For instructors, the ability to record the comments may mean they can provide deeper feedback because speaking is faster than writing. See chapter 8 for more information about how feedback affects educative assessment.

Course syllabi are your plans for delivering an outline and your expectations for the learning content. It is the student's guide to what they will learn and may need to change as the semester progresses to accommodate unforeseen circumstances. Learning activities or assessments might change. For this reason, many faculty consider it to be a living, or flexible, document. By providing the structure of the learning, the syllabus describes how your course operates. It also communicates with your dean or department chair what your expectations are in the course in case of students' misunderstanding. More about what you should consider to include in your course syllabus is included later in the Standard Syllabus Design section.

**Bright Idea**

Students often use their smartphones more often than other devices. It can be cumbersome to navigate through your LMS on a phone unless its design includes a phone app. When you plan methods to communicate, imagine students using a computer, tablet, or phone to access your course to see how they work as a response interface. Share this information with your students in the syllabus. —**Karen LaPlant**

## Communication Considerations

Communication is complicated, and as previously stated, the competition for attention is fierce. With so many sources sending us messages by mail, media, print, and handheld devices it is critical to consider how communication in your course is delivered and received. As a result of our extensive work with students and faculty, we ask you to reflect on the following as you prepare to deliver oral and written communication.

- Keep your purpose in mind. Stick to your message and deliver it as simply as possible. Some people may write like they talk with a lot of extemporaneous information, which becomes noise. Sometimes bulleted lists keep your communication clean and can act as a checklist. Remember that students may not be as skilled at separating the wheat from the chaff in written form.

- Listen first, act second. Often, students just need to talk. They may not even want your advice. In a world of telling, there is a limited amount of listening. When they do want to get your ideas, it may take them some time to formulate what they really want as they may be struggling with concepts and vocabulary. Be patient and guide them to form the correct question. By listening to others, you have time to think about the response you want to give them. This helps you to be your best. Less-experienced faculty may think they need to answer students to show them how much they know. There is plenty of time to do so, once the student has spoken. Ask students additional questions to help them discover possible solutions to their own challenges. One phrase to get students to expound on their ideas is, "Say more about that."
- It is okay to say you don't know. It is better to give a good answer than an uninformed answer. If you aren't sure how to answer, let them know you will contact them in a day or two with an answer. In that time you can get the correct information, speak with others who may have similar experiences, or provide them with resources. Students will appreciate your intention to find out the best answer, and be sure to follow up with them as quickly as you can so they know you are serious. You may want to put a reminder in your phone calendar to get back to the student.
- Sarcasm can be very dangerous. Many of us can remember a time when we got a sarcastic answer from someone we respected. It can change a positive relationship into a negative one very quickly, and it takes a long time to regain the trust lost.
- On a similar note, watch your use of humor. What is funny to some, is not funny to others. Humor is more about the ways people receive it than the way it is intended. Be enthusiastic and energizing. Students respect that. As with sarcasm, a misplaced joke can ruin respect and relationships. Additionally, in culturally diverse situations, humor does not necessarily translate and may only exacerbate confusion and feelings of intimidation.

**Jot Your Thoughts**

## Netiquette

One of the areas to address in your course communication plan and syllabus is establishing expectations for respectful communication, or *netiquette*. Students may be used to social media, but the communication in the course goes far beyond texting a friend. If you search the term *netiquette* online, you will find many recommendations to include in your course's netiquette discussion. Explain to your students that course communication is professional and matches the style they will need to demonstrate in the workplace. Your expectations may include the following:

- Using the subject line in an e-mail to identify which course they are in, such as CHEM 1020-04.
- Introducing themselves, for example, Hi, Mr. Jones, I'm Linda Russell from your CHEM 1020-04 class
- Writing in complete sentences and using correct grammar and punctuation
- Using emojis and abbreviations (e.g., IDK for I don't know) minimally or not at all
- Writing in a letter format (i.e., using paragraphs)
- Being courteous (i.e., no swearing, using all caps, etc.)
- Adding your perspective positively without criticizing others' viewpoints and pointing out the differences without judgment or accusations
- Keeping information about yourself and people you know private, for example, don't share sensitive personal information, use a phrase like "A person I know" instead of "My friend Collette Smith had cancer."
- Being patient with others who aren't as experienced as you may be because everyone is in a different place with technology, and everyone hasn't had the same learning opportunities as you (Mintu-Wimsatt, Kernek, & Lozada, 2010; Shea, 2004)

Netiquette rules can also apply to classroom discussions as well. Remind students they are practicing skills that are professional expectations adhered to by employees in the workplace.

## Engaging Course Discussions

In developing a communication plan for your course, it is important to analyze several aspects of course communication more deeply. We provide specific examples for your consideration as you reflect on how you are currently communicating with your students and how these practices could improve course communication.

### *Developing Effective Course Shell Discussions*

Think about a time when you were a student in a discussion in a class. Your instructor asked a question, and perhaps hands were raised and someone was called on to answer the question. Was that it, or was there more? How much time passed prior to the student being called on to answer? When the correct answer was given by the student, what were you thinking? If you knew the answer, you may have felt good about knowing it or felt disappointed because you weren't the person called on. If you didn't know the answer, you may have felt relieved because you didn't get called on.

Regardless, once the answer is provided, some students don't think any more about it because they are off the hook.

Remember being quizzed by a classmate with a stack of math flashcards? It may have been either a fantastic or a horrible experience for you depending on how well you knew your multiplication tables. Sometimes this activity was played as a game with you competing against a classmate. When you answered correctly you collected the flashcard in a pile in front you. If you won the game with a bigger stack of cards, the activity only reinforced what you already knew. However, if you lost, the faster student didn't give you much time to think about the right answer, and the activity didn't help you learn. The student with the bigger stack felt pretty good, and the one with a shorter stack felt bad. The same could be said about spelling bees in the classroom. The good spellers continued, and the poor spellers had to go sit in their seats. Do you think they were thinking about how to spell words any more once they were seated? In this case, all but one student lost, and there was little learning taking place for the rest.

Your course discussions shouldn't be a showcase for a talented few but a learning activity for all. Designing discussion questions is an important element in significant learning. In a face-to-face classroom, faculty can guide the discussion based on a set of questions and work with the answers students provide. We challenge you to consider the number of active participants in the classroom. Students are missing a rich learning experience if there is only one voice at a time participating in the classroom. Most discussions are set up like a tennis match. Instructor serves the ball, student returns, and the volley continues. Meanwhile, many students are inactive participants because there is only one ball.

Another way to promote greater engagement is to break the class into groups, which allows many students to serve and return the balls on multiple tennis courts. Using a think-pair-share strategy (King, 1993; Lyman, 1981), where students write down their thoughts individually and discuss them with a partner and then in a group or the entire class, works well to engage more students. Asking students questions and having them work in small groups to discuss answers increases participation and minimizes places for students to hide. This allows you to assess learning by walking around the classroom, listening to the student-run discussions. You have communicated your expectation that they need to participate.

In our teaching experience, the importance and effectiveness of course discussions has been discussed by many authors, specifically by those in the following:

> Although many useful strategies, techniques, and incentive systems are available to promote discussion, I have come to believe that the interpersonal foundation provides the crucial basis for lively classroom conversations. Some of the most cited works in higher education (e.g., Chickering and Gamson, 1987; Lowman, 1995) have asserted that a fundamental principle of effective teaching is increasing teacher-student contact and connection. Yet our classrooms can do more to meet students' needs for affiliation and promote engaging discussion. (Herman & Nilson, 2018)

Engaging, substantive discussions that deliver significant learning through intentional design are necessary in the face-to-face classroom and are even more important in the online classroom. Providing these types of discussions through learning activities and assessments build opportunities for measuring outcomes in the human dimension, caring, and learning how to learn domains of Fink's (2013) taxonomy. This is all part of teaching students to build community through discussing with others ideas on course content and the development of personal and professional relationships. The key is to teach students how to envision themselves in a broader sense, moving from a single-perspective view to a polycentric view of themselves in a more global structure or stage.

By using the discussions tool in your course shell in the face-to-face and online environments, you provide valuable ways to get all your students to think deeper as they increase participation. Using it in your face-to-face course is a great way to set up the thinking prior to having a classroom discussion and extend the discussion into deeper thinking outside the class session after the discussion.

Effective course discussions are intentional. They are a learning activity and serve as a way to provide formative and summative assessment (Herman & Nilson, 2018). For students, discussion assessments measure student mastery well as being authentic, observable, and measurable (Vella, 2002). Developing writing prompts that set a framework for the discussion need a proper balance. First, describe how the discussion prompt is linked to the course content. Second, write something to act as a hook that starts students thinking, leaving room for them to expand their thoughts with ties to the content, prior learning, and experiences. Finally, avoid prompts that are written in a way that only result in limited responses. The prompt need to allow students to build on one another's responses.

Don't include questions that require only a yes or no or short phrase answer. No instructor wants to read the same response 25 times. These kinds of prompts actually discourage discussions and do not promote deeper thinking as students are more likely to just check the box to finish the assignment.

Do include questions that provide room for analysis, interpretation, application to experiences, evaluations, and reasoning. Require additional resources to be included in the responses to bring in new and related information to inspire additional thought and participation by other students. Add a couple of questions to the prompt or an example that will spark thinking. These kinds of prompts encourage discussions and promote deeper and perhaps original thinking and provide a reason to engage.

Imagine you were taking a course on using discussion questions in the course shell or in small groups, and the instructor provided the following writing prompt for your analysis:

> How would you have students participate in discussions in one of your courses? Provide two examples of your best questions and describe how your students should respond. How do these help you bridge your outcomes to your assessments? Do you use these to check learning or as an outcome assessment in addition to a learning activity?

While students are answering the previous questions, you could provide follow-up questions for students during the unit to get them to think deeper such as,

- How would you improve the previous writing prompt to make it fit your needs?
- What advice would you provide other faculty in developing discussion writing prompts based on your experience?

These examples provide some latitude when thinking and providing responses. They also give you an opportunity to learn from your classmates' responses as you analyze them and learn more by comparing their answers to yours. We recommend you keep an archived bank of these additional questions to use in getting students to think deeper. Keeping these for use in future semesters is a time saver and can improve the quality of your ongoing discussion.

**Bright Idea**

An effective way to engage all students is to ask them to respond to the post previous to theirs and the one immediately following. Encourage them to post to others they find interesting. This helps make sure that more than a few posts get all the attention. —**Karen LaPlant**

### *Course Introduction Discussions*

To build community and teams, students should be asked to introduce themselves during the first week (Bain, 2004; Herman & Nilson, 2018). In thinking about designing the courses you teach, consider the following questions to examine your prior knowledge.

The students could be asked to provide an in-class or post an online introduction in a welcome discussion prompt. Learners could be asked to include some or all of the following in their introduction or by interviewing one another in a face-to-face classroom:

- What name do you prefer?
- What pronouns do you use (e.g., he, she, they)?
- What is your major?
- Why are you taking this course?
- How long have you been at this institution?
- What are your goals when you graduate? What type of job do you hope to get?
- What information about hobbies, interests, pets, and so on would you care to share?
- What questions do you have about the course?
- When you get a new electronic device, how do you like to learn how to use it (e.g., watch a video, read the instructions, play around with it, ask someone)?

This activity provides students with an opportunity to feel connected and network with classmates and the instructor. It can also provide a low-risk public speaking opportunity in a face-to-face classroom by having students talk about the topics with which they are most familiar. In using this introductory activity online, we recommend for you to require students to read each other's introduction and reply to one another in the course shell discussion. For greater participation, we suggest including in the directions or the syllabus that this is required and worth points. Assigning points to these introductions shows that you think knowing each other and building community is important. As a low-stakes activity, this allows students to practice submitting responses to discussion questions and prepares learners to participate in future course discussions in the format you expect as communicated through your discussions rubric.

The instructor should create an introduction as well. You can answer the same questions provided to the students. Many students enjoy this as it puts you on par with them so you seem both professional and approachable (Bain, 2004). A great place to build this welcoming connection is in the course shell by using a short video or a document that you can also send with the syllabus in an opening e-mail to your students prior to the course start. You could include some of the following topics:

- State your name so students learn how to pronounce it, which helps students whose first language isn't English.
- Identify your preferred gender pronoun (e.g. she and her, he and him, they and their)
- Explain your role as the instructor and say how students should address you (Ms., Mr., Dr., first name?)
- Tell students how they can benefit by making an appointment during office hours for help or stopping in, even just to say hello.
- Share your philosophy of teaching and learning and your big dream with them so they know how this course will help them in the future beyond the end of the semester (Harrington & Thomas, 2018).

**Bright Idea**

Keep in mind that communication styles are culturally influenced. For example, there are differences in eye contact, handshakes (and in some cultures, women and men should not touch, including shaking hands), body language, and so on. Some students are taught not to question or disagree with their teachers and to address instructors using only formal titles. Some cultures do not use last names, so some might prefer to call an instructor Dr. First Name. Is it all right for students to call you professor or by your first name? Tell students what you prefer in your syllabus. —**Linda Russell**

### *Creating Discussions as Learning Activities*

As stated earlier, using discussions as a learning activity provides an opportunity to elicit deeper thinking. When beginning these discussions, ask students questions in which their responses will demonstrate evidence of their thinking. We recommend your questions

- be open ended,
- link to previous learning,
- offer opportunities to include personal and work experiences,
- require some research and data mining,
- allow authentic or original responses tied into previous learning and knowledge,
- provide enough detail so student can't answer with short responses,
- inspire further discussion by posing questions to other students and the instructor,
- provide multiple ways to answer using varying perspectives and evidence, and
- allow the opportunity to develop a theory or model.

Your interaction in course shell discussions enhances student learning. Some faculty believe that threaded discussions are a place for students to interact, and at the end of the week will be read and assessed. This isn't what you would do in the typical classroom. You wouldn't start a discussion with a prompt and then leave the classroom. In a course shell, the learning goes deeper if you are interacting with students' posts. You can ask additional deeper questions that guide the discussion and gives other students more information for responding by using a read and react strategy. We recommend monitoring responses, and rather than responding to only one student who has a question, use the responses of several students to pose a new question that all students could respond to. Sometimes if you only ask one student a question who is responding to the post, others may think you don't want to hear from them.

In addition, to make blended course discussions significant, introduce discussions in the classroom and continue them in the course shell. This can be a great motivator for students to dive into the discussion once they have had time to reflect and get their thoughts flowing.

**Bright Idea**

You can provide an opportunity for additional points for online discussions if students pose new questions or respond further to the new questions you posed. These could be bonus points or a requirement for students to respond to two of their classmates and respond with an additional post to your additional post or question during the week. —**Zala Fashant**

**Bright Idea**

Be sure to include your rubric for discussions in the writing prompt for discussions. Providing a set of responses as a discussion post during the first week of the course could provide students with examples of posts that receive a variety of scores to help them understand what their posts should reflect to receive maximum points. —**Zala Fashant**

### *Reflective Assessment Discussions*

Faculty can benefit greatly by asking students to reflect on their learning throughout the course. It not only helps your students learn but also provides you with feedback about your teaching and course design. Student responses will confirm what is going well in the course and provide insights on how you could improve instruction. Include a question for each unit that asks students for feedback on what they found most valuable in the course materials, discussions, and concepts. Reflective thinking is often underused. Offering this opportunity in course shell discussions takes little class time. For students, it personalizes learning and can be used to assess human dimension, caring, and learning how to learn course outcomes. Discussion prompts help students analyze how they learn. Ask them to tell you how they can apply what was learned to the type of work they will be doing in their future. This is an example of Fink's (2013) forward-thinking and meaning-making assessment that we discuss more in chapter 8.

**Bright Idea**

Monitor your discussion responses. It is important for you respond to all students in your course. Some students provide more detailed and perhaps higher quality posts, and it is easy to engage more often with these students. To ensure fairness to all students by making them feel a part of the course, monitor the number of times you respond to each student. This is an important best practice if your goal is to create an environment where all students can grow. Keeping a spreadsheet of who you respond to is a quick way to make sure you aren't engaging with some students more than others. Most students are proud when the instructor gives their contribution to the discussion a positive response and makes them feel like a valuable member of the class. —**Zala Fashant**

## Communicating Through Course Syllabi

Your course syllabus is the backbone document that provides the structure for the students and you to follow. This document should guide the navigation of the course from beginning to end, so it needs to be clear and comprehensive (Palmer, Bach, & Streifer, 2014). Besides providing value for the course, your syllabus serves to answer questions about policies and procedures at your institution.

The syllabus is the overture to your course because it introduces all the themes and policies you use throughout the semester, and

> reconceptualized as a motivational tool, the syllabus can be an extremely useful resource for students and an opportunity for faculty to think critically about the course as a whole. Faculty can use the syllabus to map out the learning path for students and as a mechanism to start building a learning community within the course. When faculty create a new syllabus, or revise an existing syllabus, it is the perfect opportunity to step back and reflect on the purpose of the syllabus and how to make the most of this important resource. In essence, the syllabus can be used as a motivational course design tool, communicating to students the goals of the course and the path students can take to meet with success. When faculty view the syllabus as a potential tool to enhance the learning experience in terms of motivation, communication, accountability, and curriculum mapping, the end product will best serve students and faculty. In other words, the syllabus needs to be thought of not as a set of rules and expectations but rather as the foundational document that sets the stage for student success and acts as the planning tool for faculty. (Harrington & Thomas, 2018, p. 3)

The syllabus can also answer questions even if the course is transferred to another institution. Developing a template for your syllabi using a style template that meets Americans with Disabilities Act (1990) requirements will assist in resolving disputes with students. A well-designed syllabus demonstrates the content, procedures, and policies of the course if any challenges are escalate to the level of your dean or administration.

Finally, course syllabi are often written in an academic style that may include terminology and formatting unfamiliar to students, especially novices in the discipline (Nilson, 2007). If you want students to use the syllabus, it needs to be student centered or it will be brushed aside. If your institution requires a template format, you could use annotations to help students understand the language.

## Standard Syllabus Design

Your institution may have a syllabus template for you. Other institutions have requirements for what must be included in a syllabus or a suggested checklist of minimal requirements. Check with your colleagues, department chair, or dean for the expectations at your institution. If you are designing your own syllabus, our recommendations were collaboratively developed by faculty and administration at one of our institutions. Items in our template are based on best practice recommendations by faculty in their work with Quality Matters (QM; 2018a) and by requirements for federal compliance by your institution's accreditation body.

As you construct your course syllabus, we suggest including the following. The content headers were created through a faculty-administration collaboration we participated in to standardize syllabi at one of our institutions. Many of our faculty were participating in formal peer reviews, so we integrated the QM (2018a) standards into all course syllabi. (See chapter 9 for a discussion of QM standards.)

- Opening: program name; course prefix, number, and name; course schedule identifier and section; credit hours; semester or dates if partial semester; course delivery format (e.g., face-to-face, blended, online)
- Faculty: contact information
- Course information: description, learning outcomes, course requirements, grading policies (QM standard), reference to institution's learner outcomes and values, course instruction schedule
- Course materials: texts and references including ISBNs (QM standard), tools and supplies including software (QM standard)
- Campus emergency notification: alert information process
- Last day to withdraw from a course: links to the drop and add policies on the institution's website
- Required technology skills (QM standard)
- Required technical access (QM standard)
- About the course: a place to share your teaching philosophy and big dream (Fink, 2003)
- Student handbook and calendar: Provide website links for students to access the student handbook and calendar
- Academic integrity policy
- Attendance policy
- Netiquette (QM standard)
- E-mail communication process
- Support services (QM standard)
- Academic difficulty (QM standard)
- Weekly course schedule

The detailed version of our recommendations for syllabus design, including descriptions for the subsections, can be found in Appendix C. In addition to this institutionally created syllabus model outline, others have similar and different ideas on what to include in your course syllabus (Bain, 2004; Davis, 2009; Harrington & Thomas, 2018; Nilson, 2007; O'Brien, Millis, & Cohen, 2008).

Knowing that your syllabus is an effective tool to communicate the structure of your course, you may want to assess its quality. Chapter 9 provides well-designed rubric examples to help measure the quality of your syllabus components.

**Bright Idea**

Students don't get overly excited about covering the outcomes during the review of the syllabus in your course. They tend to scan through them on the way down to find out what they need to do for the course. Display the list of learning outcomes during the first class session or during the first week of online discussions to have students identify which outcomes were most important to them. You can project them on a whiteboard and ask students to come up and put a star next to their top three choices with a marker. In an online course, the students can write about their top three in a discussion post. This provides a sense of prior learning in the students and gives you a chance to see the areas where you may need to provide more instruction. It was your first opportunity to assess your students. This also helps them identify what they will learn and start the buying in process to see the relevance this class will have on their future. —**Zala Fashant**

## Visual Syllabus Design

According to Canada (2013), "For many, the syllabus is the academic equivalent of an appliance manual. Everyone expects one, but reading it is another matter" (p. 37). When we asked our students, they told us they do not and likely will not read a syllabus. Most faculty create a syllabus that is teacher centered with information the instructor thinks is important. You might consider what a student really wants to know at the start of the class and make your syllabus more learner centered. Ask your students who have taken the course what major questions they had about the course. Some of the information on the syllabus is needed one time, and some of it is needed to be referred to many times throughout the semester. Thinking about the order and format of the syllabus can make it more engaging and useful for students. Syllabi often have very similar text-intensive structures. Including some visuals to help students identify text content, such as concept maps or compare-contrast tables to communicate syllabus information can help to show students the link between your course outcomes, assessments, and activities (Nilson, 2007).

Students today are connected to media devices, most of which are now handheld. Learning has moved from text based to media based. Frankly, a syllabus filled with text doesn't interest students, it feels laborious. What are faculty doing to make their syllabi more engaging so students will refer to the document often to guide their progress in the course?

Let's examine the positive aspects of the graphic syllabus (Nilson, 2007) and the interactive syllabus (Richards, 2001):

> Graphics work so economically because of what Larkin and Simon (1987) call "perceptual enhancement," which means they communicate information on two levels at once: through their individual elements and through the spatial arrangement of

> those elements. At the same time, all the relevant concepts and relationships, all the important information, are displayed simultaneously as a whole, giving the view a "computational advantage" (Larkin & Simon, 1987). The various elements are easy to locate, facilitating the extraction of information, and the interrelationships among the elements are evident in the spatial arrangements, shapes of enclosures, and colors, without the mind having to interpret or infer them. (Nilson, 2007)

For some students, graphics can help them retain information or make it easier for them to find the place in the document to find the information.

The interactive syllabus (Richards, 2001) is a means to help students visualize the syllabus to set a foundation for them to begin to construct their own learning. Often this syllabus is presented on a Web-based platform, which provides active links to learning opportunities and visual models, graphs, and other learning objects can exist.

Although many versions of the interactive syllabus have been created by faculty, Richards (2001) helps define the structure in the following:

> The "look and feel" of the Interactive Syllabus remains discretionary with every instructor. In working with faculty from a variety of disciplines in the development of their interactive syllabi, it has become clear that a table used as a conceptual map with three or four columns (images, topics, readings/viewings/listening, and resources) and as many rows as is required (weeks of the semester, topics to be studied, etc.) works well. (p. 2)

This style of a syllabus provides

- a constructionist manner of learning where students are able to explore and build on the resources provided,
- a visual layout of course content that can be either structured or more free flowing allowing students to innovate depending on purpose of the course and the discipline,
- an opportunity to weave a mind map concept into LMSs,
- a menu for course content that is easy for students to explore and revisit as needed throughout the course making all content available all the time as they build on their learning, and
- a visual layout of course materials that isn't text intense and can be found at a glance versus scrolling through pages of text content.

There are special considerations in using this syllabus. Numbers and alphabetical order are discouraged as they are displayed on the syllabus in a hierarchical manner. Greater explanation is usually required because this type of organization may be unfamiliar to them. Technical requirements for access to audio or video files will need to be communicated along with URLs for plug-ins. The ability to play course materials on a variety of devices and options for low and high bandwidth are required so that all learners have access. The open-range type of learning where students need to direct their learning may not provide enough structure for some students. However, faculty can design the amount of openness they want in the course design (Richards, 2003).

Today, much of a graphic or interactive syllabus can be loaded into a course using your institution's LMS. Students click on the links that take them to a page in your course that plays the video or audio file, displays a diagram or illustration, or takes them to a website that offers a virtual tour or simulation.

When using visuals in your syllabus and course, you need to think about accessibility. Visuals in electronic documents need to be described using alt (alternative) tags, text or audio descriptions, or captions. Alt tags are additional descriptive text that appear when a cursor hovers over an image, an object, or a hyperlink. Screen readers will voice this text for learners with sight impairment. The graphics in visual syllabi may use colors to designate context meaning. For example, color-blind students can find this detrimental as they may not be able to distinguish the appropriate color designation. If you create a visual syllabus, you might also maintain a text-based syllabus and provide both for students as part of accessibility. Syllabi could also be broken into sections, which could be posted in the course shell menu individually, for example, where to get help, grading, course policies, and institutional policies. See chapter 6 for a further discussion of the Americans with Disabilities Act (1990) requirements, and use of style headings to help students find information.

Students recognize the importance of course content based on the amount of space and time items are given. This is true about the course syllabus. Students will glance through the syllabus because they may not realize its utility and then proceed to ask you questions about the material you provided. You have the opportunity to show them that your syllabus is used not only for the beginning of the semester but also throughout the semester by drawing students' attention to it in your course.

Students will understand the importance of the syllabus based on the time you spend explaining it to them during the course orientation; your philosophy will be passed on to your students (Fornaciari & Dean, 2014). In face-to-face courses, faculty spend on average 26.6 minutes discussing the syllabus (Thompson, 2007). In online courses, getting students to use the syllabus at all is a greater challenge as many of them will focus on the sections about what they need to complete as deliverables. In other words, they want to know, "What do I need to do to get an A?"

In workshops on syllabus design, faculty have asked if they should have a complete, detailed syllabus or a one- or two-page version. Communication of the elements of the syllabus has been made easier as it can be designed into the course shell of the LMS. Students need the details. Remember that this document is the course guide. It needs to lay out all the course and instructor expectations. However, expecting students to digest the details of a document of more than 10 pages in a single activity is unrealistic. Tell your students that all the information is there for them to refer to as necessary, and you can use the technology in your LMS to communicate the elements throughout the semester. Think about grouping the material into the following sections (you may consider designing your syllabus chronologically based on what students need to know):

- Before the course begins
- On the first day or week of the course
- During the first few weeks of the semester
- Around the middle of the semester
- Toward the end of the semester
- After the semester is over

In thinking about syllabus content in this manner, you can set up news announcements and automated e-mails in the LMS to review the key points while students refer to the syllabus throughout the semester.

**Jot Your Thoughts**

## Communicating Through Learning Management Tools

Blended or online courses can have advantages because they serve students who can work independently and need a flexible course schedule. You will need to provide greater attention to communication to ensure that students don't feel disconnected in the virtual classroom environment. You can increase student engagement and build community by using your LMS tools such as announcements, chat and instant messaging, discussions, e-mails, and automated messaging.

- Make announcements viewable for students as they log into the course pertaining to each new unit with corresponding outcomes and upcoming assignments and assessments.
- The chat feature in your LMS can be used to answer questions and clarify information.
- You can design a discussion area for students to ask questions and for clarification with threaded or guided discussion opportunities, as discussed previously.
- Examine the effective use of automated messaging tools.

Automated messaging tools in LMSs like D2L Brightspace's intelligent agents or Blackboard's notifications can be an effective way to deliver reminders to students automatically, taking less of your teaching time to monitor progress. We provide an example here. (More specific examples to help you design intelligent agents can be found in Appendix D.)

## Welcome to the Course

To: [This automated message is sent to each student.]

> Hello [Student Name],
>
> I see that you have accessed the [Name of Course] online course. I hope you are as excited as I am for this learning opportunity. My name is [Instructor Name], and I am your instructor for this course.
>
> To achieve the course outcomes, it is important that you keep up with the schedule of the course activities. Please read the course syllabus and schedule in [LMS Name] carefully.
>
> If you have questions or concerns, please contact me through my e-mail at [instructor e-mail address]. Remote office hours are available online via webinar by scheduling an appointment.

Setting up automated messages in in your LMS can help you provide every student with timely feedback throughout the course. This tool saves time as you don't have to painstakingly go through the grade book, discussions, and course management tools to get the data needed to send e-mails individually to each student. Keep in mind the adage "Set it, and forget it" to help you reach students effectively by spending less time managing and more time teaching.

## When to Communicate

Many faculty begin course communications on the first day of class. However, communicating with your students prior to the beginning of the course may help them better prepare for their individual needs and answer their questions about the following:

- Computer compatibility or software requirement: Sending an e-mail to students with these requirements and inviting them to log into the course may ease their concerns by knowing they will be ready to go on the first day. Let students know when the course shell will open. When possible, we recommend opening the course shell a few days prior to the start date of the course so that students can explore your course to get comfortable with how it is designed. This helps them prepare to begin learning activities.

- Textbook acquisition: Whether students are picking up their textbook at the campus bookstore or ordering them online, they may need a week to receive their text. Notifying them early will help them with assignments during the first week of class to avoid having to catch up after the course has begun.
- Time management: Ask students to plan their schedule accordingly so they can participate in the course and maintain their personal and professional responsibilities.
- Technical skills: Informing students about special skills they need for the course will help them plan to be ready. Refer them to online videos or written resources to help them learn about these skills.
- Student e-mail account: Using their e-mail before class begins helps students make sure everything is working for them. Sending them the preceding information and the course syllabus and inviting them to ask questions ahead of time help students feel more comfortable on Day 1.

Some students struggle trying to grapple with all of this on the first day of class, so helping them prepare the week before the course begins better enables them to start on time. The following is a specific example of the information you can send to your students via e-mail prior to the beginning of the course.

> CCIS 1005 Computer Security Awareness—Online Spring
>
> This is a fully online course using [Name of LMS]. This is not a self-paced course so you need to be aware of due dates. To be successful you need basic computer skills, Internet access, the required textbook, and a student e-mail account to download and install Office 2016 software.
>
> There will be a course orientation webinar online from 5:00 p.m. to 5:45 p.m. CST on Tuesday, January 9. Watch for the link in your student e-mail later this week and in [the LMS] announcements or news when the course opens online at 5:00 p.m. For other questions, please contact [Instructor at e-mail address].

Frequent communication equals connection. Connecting with students in a timely manner during the course helps retention and success, as illustrated by the following:

- Students who have frequent contact with faculty members in and out of class during their college years are more satisfied with their educational experiences, are less likely to drop out, and perceive themselves to have learned more than students who have less faculty contact (Cross, 1998).
- The more intensely students are engaged and involved in their own education, the more likely they are to do well, be satisfied with their educational experience, and stay in school (Pascarella & Terenzini, 1991).
- Students who interact with their teachers develop a support network and are more likely to persist in classes (Tinto, Russo, & Stephanie, 1994).

Some of your students will use weekly communication as a lifeline, which guides them to complete course work. This is especially true with students who are new to the institution and higher education or are in the early courses of your program. You are developing their ability to see themselves as successful college students in this new environment. As much as we would like them to come prepared for the experience, it is better to provide more information than needed. We found the following strategies to be effective in communicating with our students weekly:

- Send course announcements with reminders about upcoming work or events and other course-related information.
- Participate in course discussions. Students enjoy seeing your comments in the course discussion. It builds the course community so there is a feeling of everyone working together rather than learners completing assignments on their own.
- Provide feedback to assignments and assessments to the entire class and individually. Compliment students as a group when some start to turn things in early and when the group has done outstanding work. Frequent feedback to individuals keeps students motivated and connected to the course content and to their instructor.
- Use automated LMS tools as reminders. Setting up automated messages provides communication with students about course progress, freeing up your time to provide unique, individual feedback to improve student performance.
- Send encouraging e-mails about progress and assistance. Automated messaging can encourage participation and assistance and allows you to communicate with students who need some additional or more extensive help.

The final time to communicate with your students is at the conclusion of the course. This is an opportunity to remind students to provide feedback using the course survey evaluation or one last course reflection in an e-mail or in a discussion question. Additionally, it is a good time for you to remind them to register for next semester and give them information about what they need to do next in their program or major.

## Course Communication Plan

Hume said, "The art of communication is the language of leadership" (as cited in Paymar, 2012, p. xx). Implementation of a course communication plan is critical to promote significant learning and deliver student success. As you think about a broader blueprint to course design, we expand on the alignment of course elements to include communication. The takeaway from this chapter is to integrate course communication into your course design. Now that we have discussed the purposes, tools, and schedule for communication, examine the graphic organizer

**TABLE 3.1**
**Communication Plan**

| *What (Purpose)* | *Who (Sender)* | *To Whom (Receiver)* | *When (Schedule)* | *How (Tool)* |
|---|---|---|---|---|
| Course welcome and syllabus | Instructor | Students | Week prior to start of course | E-mail and course announcement |
| Announcements to inform the progression of the course | Instructor | Students | Weekly or more often as necessary | Announcement tool in the LMS |
| Unit discussions: interaction with course materials | Instructor and students | Other students and returned to instructor | Weekly | Course discussion tool in the LMS |
| Group course assignments | Instructor and students | Other students and returned to instructor | By units throughout the course | Course discussion or grouping tool in the LMS |
| Absent | Instructor | Students | Weekly or more often as necessary | E-mail or intelligent agent in the LMS |
| Missing work | Instructor | Students | Weekly or more often as necessary | E-mail or intelligent agent in the LMS |
| Completed work | Instructor | Students | Weekly or more often as necessary | E-mail or intelligent agent in the LMS |
| Grade concern | Instructor | Students | Weekly or more often as necessary | E-mail and intelligent agent in the LMS |
| Impending instructor withdrawal due to lack of attendance | Instructor | Students | Near the date of withdrawal | Announcement tool, e-mail, or intelligent agent in the LMS |

*Note.* This table provides an example of a course communication plan.

in Table 3.1 as you begin the development of your plan for intentional course communication.

According to Whyte (1950), "The single biggest problem in communication is the illusion that it has taken place" (p. 174). A tip for your communication plan is to keep track of the various items students have asked you about. Decide in your plan the most efficient and easiest method to facilitate future communications to save time and improve the flow of information for you and your students.

Developing a purposeful communication plan ensures critical course information sharing and promotes enhanced learning. This open communication builds a community of collaborative learners. Some of the most meaningful learning comes through student-to-student interaction. Students mentoring and teaching one another by sharing their learning is some of the best learning, and recognizing this, helps you design a better learning environment that promotes the leadership students will need to achieve in the workplace.

## Reflect on This Chapter

Now that you have completed reading this chapter and thinking about the content as it applies to your work, please reflect on the following questions:

- Based on the strategies presented, how might you improve your course communication plan?
- Which communication strategies would you add to your online, blended, and face-to-face courses?
- Based on what you learned in this chapter, how can you increase student engagement through the communication strategies?

**Jot Your Thoughts**

## Action Checklist

Use Checklist 3.1 to apply the chapter content to your practice and help you identify the steps for implementing these ideas in your teaching.

**CHECKLIST 3.1** Communicating in Your Course Action Checklist

| ✓ | **Course Communication Opportunities—Which do you currently use?** |
|---|---|
| ❑ | In-person communication—face-to-face and blended courses |
| ❑ | Web conferencing—online courses |
| ❑ | E-mail |
| ❑ | Texting, instant messaging |
| ❑ | Course LMS tools: messaging, automated messaging |
| ❑ | Frequently asked questions (FAQs) |

(*Continues*)

**CHECKLIST 3.1** (*Continued*)

| ❑ | Collaborative tools (LMS groups, Google Docs) |
|---|---|
| ❑ | Classroom discussions—in-person speaking |
| ❑ | Classroom discussions—course shell written responses |
| ❑ | Written or spoken feedback—instructor-to-student or student-to-student |
| ❑ | Course syllabi |

| ✓ | **Effective Course Discussions** |
|---|---|
| ❑ | Developed a variety of deeper thinking spoken questions. |
| ❑ | Created writing prompts for discussions requiring analysis, interpretation, application, evaluation, and reasoning. |
| ❑ | Provided opportunities to add new resources and information. |
| ❑ | Designed Socratic follow-up questions for students that dig deeper. |
| ❑ | Provided an opportunity for student introductions. |
| ❑ | Posted an instructor introduction in the course. |
| ❑ | Provided feedback and interaction to student responses during each unit. |
| ❑ | Developed reflective and forward-thinking opportunities for authentic responses. |
| ❑ | Discussed the ways students can model netiquette during the course. |

| ✓ | **Course Syllabi** |
|---|---|
| ❑ | Reviewed course syllabus for missing standard content. |
| ❑ | Considered using a visual syllabus. |

| ✓ | **LMS Tools** |
|---|---|
| ❑ | Designed communications for the announcement and news features. |
| ❑ | Considered uses for chat, instant messaging tool. |
| ❑ | Analyzed the robustness of the discussions tool. |
| ❑ | Designed opportunities for students to discuss or work collaboratively in groups. |
| ❑ | Planned for use of the e-mail tool. |
| ❑ | Checked for an automated messaging tool and learned ways it could assist in communication. |

| ✓ | **Frequency of Communication** |
|---|---|
| ❑ | Developed messaging before the course begins. |

(*Continues*)

**CHECKLIST 3.1** (*Continued*)

| | |
|---|---|
| ❑ | Reviewed ways to message during the units of study, weekly or more. |
| ❑ | Created summary messaging at the end of the course. |

| ✓ | **Course Communication Plan** |
|---|---|
| ❑ | Identified the purpose for each message. |
| ❑ | Listed who is sending each type of message. |
| ❑ | Listed who are the receivers of messaging. |
| ❑ | Scheduled when messages are sent. |
| ❑ | Analyzed the best tools for each type of message. |

# 4

# CREATING A LEARNING FRAMEWORK

## Points to Ponder

Chapter 4 examines how students learn and will help you develop your understanding of why this is an essential element in course design. In thinking about integrating the elements of your course design, consider the following questions to examine your prior knowledge:

- What is your role in teaching? What do you understand is the difference between delivering content and facilitating learning activities?
- What did you learn (maybe more than once) that you have never used?
- How did you learn to learn in your discipline?

As the student in the following vignette discovered, using active study methods encourages more than just memorizing results in better test scores.

> Stacey, a business student, was referred to the learning center because she had failed the first two exams in two business classes. When asked how she studies for the tests, she replied, "Well, you know, I look over my notes. Then I try to read all the chapters." We introduced her to a method of making study cards, which required her to ask several questions about each term or concept. There aren't always answers to each question, but it requires more complex thinking than just terms and definitions. It works best if the student does this after reading, from memory, or for retrieval practice. Her immediate response was, "You have got to be kidding! I don't have time for that!" We persisted. She went home to study for the upcoming test.

When she left the office, it didn't seem likely that she had taken in any of the explanation of how this could help her nor how it was better than looking over her notes and chapters. What a surprise then, when we discovered Stacey had earned a 94 on the test. She had spent the entire evening making a study card for every bold-faced term in the chapters, using the set of questions from our meeting. She said at first it felt very mechanical; she was just checking to see if there was an answer to each question, and then moving on. But—and this is the important part—at some point she realized that she would recall connections between ideas and add them to her cards. She began to see the relationships between and among the concepts. She reported that she actually was chuckling during the test because, as she said, "It was like I already knew what the questions were going to be!"

## Why Don't Students Know How to Study and Learn?

When students seek help and are asked about their study methods, they often say they are reading and rereading, highlighting, searching for and watching videos, reviewing lecture notes and slides, and summarizing with extensive notes. These methods can help with remembering and understanding, but research shows that if teaching and learning are focused on these levels, students do not retain their learning and are not able to transfer it and use it (Bransford, Brown, & Cocking, 1999). Many students think these methods have worked for them in the past, and they may be reluctant to change or may not know how to change. To help them develop higher level learning skills, we need to include low-stakes and scaffolded class activities and assessments that provide frequent, supportive feedback to show them that these produce better and longer lasting learning.

When you get a new electronic device, how do you like to learn about it? Do you

- play around with it until it works,
- ask someone who already owns it for help,
- read the owner's manual,
- watch a demonstration video and then try it out, or
- watch a lecture or review slides?

How is learning about a new electronic device similar or different from how you learn when you are taking a class?

You could use the previous questions with your students to get them to think about their learning, but these questions also show that how we learn about many things in our life is not necessarily how we learn in formal educational settings. In the history of humans, learning by lecture is a relatively new technique, and it was important when an elite few were the holders of knowledge. The word *lecture* (n.d.) is from the Latin meaning to read. As we can now access information from almost anywhere, students can read on their own, and we can shift our teaching methods to help students develop effective habits of mind and cognitive capacities.

**Bright Idea**

A great use of backward-looking assessment is reflection on how learners mastered the content. A great use of forward-looking assessment is developing a plan to learn new material in the future. Using this plan as an assessment provides a way to measure learning-how-to-learn outcomes. —**Zala Fashant**

Although many colleges and universities offer stand-alone how-to-study courses or workshops, the students who are encouraged to enroll in them are often relegated to the course because of failure, academic probation, or conditional admission status. Most college students may never be exposed to a systematic study of how people learn, best practices for learning (high-level, long-lasting learning), or practical methods for creating their own toolbox for learning. Also, students are often not aware of their own learning or do not have an understanding of concepts or processes they are supposed to learn. They don't monitor their comprehension, nor are they checking it periodically. Metacognition is our "awareness, understanding, and control of our own thinking" (Ormrod, 2017, p. 116). Learners who have strong metacognitive abilities can reflect on their learning and also direct their learning to make progress. Metacognition is one aspect of critical thinking and can be guided and coached by effective instruction.

College faculty have long complained about their students' lack of intellectual prowess, preparedness for college work, and effort. An oft-quoted report that Harvard and Yale needed to hire Greek and Latin tutors for its underprepared students in the 1600s and 1700s reminds us that this is not a new problem (Cowie, 1936; Pearson, n.d.).

The reality is that many students have not developed effective learning skills. They might have found school easy and were not challenged by their curriculum until they arrived at college or until they progressed through college where concepts are more difficult or courses run at a faster pace. Students may have had breaks in their education because of relocating with family or a job change. They may have had stressful life situations that drew attention away from school. They may have grown up in a school system that focused on teaching to the test and with decreased academic challenges.

Many students who arrive in our classes have developed skills for listening to lectures, watching videos, reviewing slides, reading and rereading and highlighting textbooks because their assessments were mostly multiple-choice questions that tested their ability to remember and understand, and they may have performed very well. However, if students use these methods, they do not retain much of their learning and cannot use it in new courses and situations. Therefore, we need to design our classes to help students learn how to learn. Research on how we learn shows that many of our traditional teaching methods and students' study methods do not actually support human learning (Boser, 2017; Brown, Roediger, & McDaniel, 2014; Dunlosky, Rawson, Marsh, Nathan, & Willingham, 2013; Kamenetz, 2015).

## Facilitating Quality Learning

For faculty who attended school in a formal educational system, much of their learning was through lectures, where other effective teaching methods were not modeled. If they make it to graduate school, they likely have learned to learn despite how they were taught.

Faculty are usually hired because of their credentials from graduate school and beyond. Their learning in the discipline often does not include the important aspects of their role as an instructor: how to design courses, materials, and learning activities that promote learning and help students develop these essential skills. The course design discussions in previous chapters should help you think about how you design your course, but how to plan activities to facilitate learning is the goal of this chapter.

## Identifying Learning Bottlenecks

One approach to teaching emphasizes the role that faculty play in observing where and when students run into what they term *bottlenecks* in the course (Middendorf & Shopkow, 2018). Each discipline is unique, and the experts who deeply understand the frameworks, key methods of thinking, and underlying concepts shape thinking (often referred to as disciplinary literacy). Accordingly, the experts have the best chance to take note of the places in a course or curriculum where students tend to get stuck and to think about the way they would handle it and model that mental action, providing practice and feedback for students. This is referred to as "decoding the discipline" (Middendorf & Shopkow, 2018, pp. 5–6). Middendorf and Shopkow (2018) also note that novice learners cannot be expected to internalize all the intricacies of learning in a discipline without some setbacks. The expert's role is to mitigate those setbacks, or bottlenecks, in a structured manner.

## What Is Learning?

Ormrod (2017) defines *learning* as "a long term change in mental representations or associations as a result of experience" (p. 6). Ambrose, Bridges, DiPietro, Lovett, and Norman (2010) said learning is a process, involving "*change* in knowledge, beliefs, behaviors, or attitudes, and is the *result of experiences*" (p. 3; emphasis added). Notice that learning is not cataloging a set of facts and information but involves experiences that change our mental models for the long haul. It is not memorizing facts and regurgitating them during exams. Key to this definition is that we must have the experiences ourselves; thus for learning to occur in our formal education systems, we must create opportunities for students to have the kinds of experiences that lead to long-term changes in their mental models.

## How Does the Brain Learn?

Numerous sources tell us how the brain works in learning. Cognitive psychology, brain science, and physiology describe neurons' growth and synaptic connections, showing that as we learn, our brains literally grow new connections, providing us with neural networks of related knowledge and skills (Bresciani Ludvik, 2016; Doyle & Zakrajsek, 2019; Hockenbury & Hockenbury, 2013; Smilkstein, 2011; Wolfe, 2001).

Students (and faculty) often have a fixed mind-set that intelligence and the ability to learn is predetermined (Dweck, 2006). Students will often say things like they are not good at math or they cannot learn languages; however, it is more likely they have not developed the skills or learning strategies for these disciplines. People with a fixed mind-set often see feedback as criticism or as a signal of failure. People with a growth mind-set think that with practice they can learn and improve. They often see feedback as an opportunity to improve. Research has shown that certain areas of the brain do grow when learning new tasks (Maguire, Woollett, & Spiers, 2006; Woollett & Maguire, 2011). Helping students develop study strategies to learn in your discipline and providing supportive feedback along the way can help them shift from a fixed to a growth mind-set.

An important note here is that learning isn't one size fits all. What works in English composition may not work in a physics lab. Learning in a design course is different from learning music theory. Each discipline requires at least some unique learning strategies, and the instructor needs to communicate how students can best learn and succeed in the discipline. Sharing these strategies with students right from the beginning of the course helps students learn without depending on much trial and error. Having students reflect on how they best learn, based on your shared strategies, helps them identify how their brains store and use the content. This intentional teaching of the disciplinary literacy skills of your field is essential for students to succeed. McGuire (2015) offers 33 strategies for teaching students how to learn better, including the following:

- Give a learning strategies presentation to students immediately after returning the first quiz or exam.
- "Clearly articulate assignment expectations to students and provide rubrics and exemplars if possible" (p. 172).
- "Provide guidelines for working effectively in teams" (p. 172).
- Introduce "switch days" (p. 172), during which students will be called on to teach some of the concepts.

Research shows we can take in small bits of information at a time, about seven numbers or four verbal phrases, into working memory (Ormrod, 2017). To get something into long-term memory, learners need to make connections to things that are already in long-term memory. For example, connecting new information to previous learning or experiences facilitates this transfer. We also need to strengthen connections by returning to the material at a later time, spacing our practice, and performing retrieval (Brown et al., 2014).

Chunking up material also helps reduce the overload as students plow through dense chapters loaded with new concepts and new vocabulary (Miller, 1956; Oakley, 2014). The concept of *cognitive load*, introduced by Sweller (1988), is the amount of information we are processing in our working memory at one time. It is limited, as mentioned earlier, so when students must multitask in their learning, they experience the feeling of overload. Faculty can mitigate this by pointing out the things that are most important so students can attend to those first. Also, being specific about the outcomes you expect at the end of the task will help students focus. You can chunk the material by providing stopping points with a few questions that students should be able to answer at that point. Just like a piano teacher teaches hands separately then hands together, you can allow students to gradually put parts together into a smoother, conceptual whole by modeling your thinking aloud, clearly showing them the mental pathways to arrive at conclusions, or weaving related parts that combine to create a more complex idea (Ormrod, 2017).

When learners are novices, certain aspects of learning become critical. According to Ambrose and colleagues (2010), it is difficult to know what to pay attention to; everything seems equally important. This is why students resort to memorizing disconnected terms or facts. The content seems like an endless list of factoids rather than clusters of related information, some of it large concepts and some of it details that help explain the large points. Experts have more than one organizational structure for new information, such as a musician who does not just see the musical notes as individual notes but as chords and motifs. Novices need examples and practice to be able to recognize these structures. Some examples of practice are using advanced organizers (e.g., an outline or map that summarizes a class or unit) and activities where students complete tables, maps, pathways, time lines, categorization, or other tasks that require them to practice thinking about relationships and processes.

## Effective Study Methods

Your overall course design can enhance students' own study methods by its alignment of learning outcomes, learning activities, and assessment methods. These connected aspects of your course serve as a road map for your students. When students are clear about what is expected and get plenty of practice (with feedback), they will be most ready for the learning assessments. However, they still need to review; practice more; and solidify concepts, skills, and processes to be fully prepared. Students tend to use study methods they are familiar with, even if they don't get the results they hope for. In Dunlosky and colleagues' (2013) metastudy, the following study methods were found to be the most effective:

- Self-testing, such as practice tests
- Distributed practice, the opposite of cramming
- Elaborative interrogation, asking a lot of why or how questions
- Self-explanation, as if one were teaching
- Interleaved practice, mixing up practice by doing different types of learning in study sessions
- Making connections among concepts, that is, seeing relationships among ideas

Students' most popular study methods are often ineffective. Dunlosky and colleagues (2013) also found that highlighting, rereading, summarizing, and keyword mnemonics were all ineffective study tools.

Faculty can facilitate effective study methods in the design of the course by

- including many opportunities for students to practice retrieving their learning such as providing sample test questions, implementing frequent low-stakes testing, and adding cumulative questions to all tests;
- suggesting that students break down their studying into chunks over a longer period of time or supplying a sample schedule;
- modeling why and how questions in class;
- having students explain concepts to a peer in class and having the peer ask questions; and
- mixing up practice opportunities, much like a math textbook provides a mixed review, which is similar to what is expected on an exam (Brown et al., 2014; Schwartz, Tsang, & Blair, 2016).

By intentionally including these elements in the course, these essential skills become mainstream in student learning for success.

**Jot Your Thoughts**

## Why We Lecture Less

The most common method of teaching for many college faculty is the lecture. It is what faculty know and how they were taught as students. Lecture is a great way to cover a large amount of material in a fairly short time. It is orderly and teacher centered, and covering material in this manner gives the illusion of learning (Brown et al., 2014).

Unfortunately, lectures are not very compatible with the way the brain learns. As mentioned earlier, short-term memory can only hold four verbal items, and we need to make connections to previous learning to get information into long-term memory and reinforce these connections by returning to information later and by practicing retrieval. Therefore, lecture results in minimal learning, and it is also superficial. Most of the learning from lectures takes place when students review their lectures outside class, and too much of that learning is focused on memorizing and understanding what was covered. With technological advancements in slide show programs and online platforms, students often request instructors to post lecture slides and may assume there is no need to attend class. When choosing class or online activities, think about what students can do when they have the opportunity to interact with you and their classmates. When designing courses, shift their intake of information, for example, from readings to class preparation, so that students can practice higher level skills when they have your support and the support of their classmates. Many faculty use the flipped classroom concept to achieve this (Bergmann & Sams, 2012).

The average adult attention span is quite short—some say 6 to 10 minutes (Guo et al., 2014), and most of us are likely distracted even during that time. Although researchers dispute the exact number of minutes we can be attentive, it is generally agreed that it is easier to extend our attention when we know more about the subject (Smilkstein, 2011). But that does not apply to our students. Their attention drifts partly because of the cognitive demands of listening to someone talk about a subject they are largely unfamiliar with and lack a sufficient foundation in. Students need some change to occur to pull them back to an attentive state, and they need time to make connections. We are constantly taking in sensory information, some of which we need to ignore so we can focus on the learning activities and put the information into our working memory.

But remember that our working memory can only hold about 4 verbal items, and we need to get them into long-term memory by making connections to what is already there. Many lectures are 50 to 60 minutes long, so if students' attention is lost after only 10 minutes, then much valuable class time is spent talking without much learning. It is often recommended for lectures to be interspersed with small changes to keep the students engaged. A short question-and-answer session or a minute of asking them to try this or solve that can make a lecture more effective.

**Bright Idea**

Even a small change can refocus students' attention or provide a break for discussion. If you're using PowerPoint slides for your presentation, press *W* to make a blank white screen. Pressing *B* will make it a black screen. —**Linda Russell**

However, during any lecture, the person who is most engaged, doing the most thinking, and likely deepening their understanding of the content is going to be the lecturer. If you think of the course as a tandem bike, the lecturer is riding in the front, doing the majority of the pedaling, steering, and braking. The lecturer points out things to see along the ride. The students are sitting on the second seat. Some may be pedaling, and some may have their legs stretched out, not pedaling at all. They don't have the full view in front of them; they are mostly looking at the back of the instructor. The students aren't steering, so they have little control over the direction of the bike ride.

Therefore, we should flip our thinking about our interactions with students in a classroom or online. Rather than providing a lecture broken up with some activities, we should break up our activities with targeted explanations, ideally based on what students are struggling with or not understanding during the activities. We can even put the students in charge of the course activities; have them sit on the front seat of the bike, set the direction by steering, and point out the important things to see.

## Uncover the Content Versus Cover the Content

To learn, students must practice the exact skills you will be assessing. A common way to think about a curriculum is for instructors to cover the topics or content. In contrast, Karl Smith refers to "uncovering the content" (K. Smith, personal communication, May 6, 2005). However, if we cover a lot of content, students will focus on remembering and understanding a lot of content, identified as foundational knowledge in Fink's (2013) taxonomy of significant learning. They will then not retain it or be able to apply it in the future. Instead, think about the skills you use as a professional in your field. What do you want students to be able to do with their learning? This ties into the human dimension, caring, and learn how to learn areas in Fink's taxonomy of significant learning. By including activities that get beyond foundational knowledge, you will be addressing more areas of significant learning.

What is an acceptable load for learning? When designing a course for language learners, for example, it is recommended for students to learn 5 to 10 words per week (Heller, 2018). Think about how many new terms students are expected to learn in a unit in your class. Additionally, there are context- or discipline-specific words that our students might not know (e.g., economics, advocacy, variable). If our students have not yet developed a large vocabulary, they might also have to think about or look up general terms we use (e.g., *deleterious, mimic, benevolent*). All of this increases the cognitive load, or their brain bandwidth, needed to read or listen and focuses their attention on defining words versus making conceptual connections.

## Facilitating Deep Learning

As noted earlier, students have learned to focus on study methods for remembering and understanding. Textbooks indirectly encourage this by carefully listing all the new vocabulary at the end of each chapter and including dense content. Students try to commit to memory maybe 40 or more new words. Students think the focus is to remember the terms and their definitions and understand what they read. They have developed and used these methods in the past, which are relatively easy and have worked for them.

Bloom and colleagues (1956) described the cognitive domain in terms of levels of complexity in thinking and learning, which was later revised by Krathwohl (2002), who reordered the last two levels so that *evaluating* precedes *creating*, as shown here:

- Remembering: some information in each field needs to be memorized for each recall
- Understanding: being able to put information in one's own words
- Applying: using the information to do something new, such as make a prediction, perform a calculation, carry out a task
- Analyzing: seeing how parts are connected, classified, and make up the concept or whole
- Evaluating: making judgments about the value of ideas (What is the best course of action? What is the first thing you should do?)
- Creating: making something new, compiling, designing—writing a paper, creating a video, designing an experiment

Bloom and colleagues' (1956) taxonomy is thought of as a hierarchy, where lower levels of learning are needed before higher levels can be attained. For instance, we need to understand something before we can apply it. At the lowest level, students remember something they have memorized. If you can look at the textbook or class materials and find the answer without understanding it, such as a term and its definition, it is the lowest level of thinking or learning—remembering. If a student can listen to a lecture, read a book, or watch a video and nod along because it makes sense, or if they can summarize it in their own words, they are at the next lowest level of learning—understanding.

Many students never get beyond these levels, so they don't really learn in the way that most faculty are hoping they will. They won't be able to use this information because in all likelihood, they don't actually retain it, especially if it is not meaningful and connected to other learning. As previously mentioned, the taxonomy of significant learning (Fink, 2013) lists this same level of remembering and understanding as foundational knowledge, essential to understanding concepts for deeper learning.

Students need practice at all levels of these taxonomies if they are to become proficient in skills or gain mastery of outcomes. As faculty, we should create ways that students can practice memorizing, explaining, using, taking apart, verifying or judging, and putting together the concepts and skills that we teach. Our assessments also should include tasks for students at the cognitive levels we expect of them. Our classroom activities should provide low-stakes opportunities for students to get supportive feedback and identify gaps in their learning, develop study strategies, and build the skills they will need for our assessments. In other words, our class activities should be aligned with our assessments, and both should be driven by our higher-level learning outcomes. We want to avoid the scenario that was reflected in one student's comment, "Mickey Mouse lectures; Einstein tests!" She was frustrated that the in-class experience only addressed foundational topics and skills, but the exams were assessing higher level skills, such as application and analysis.

Sweet, Blythe, and Carpenter (2017) describe the "4 R's" (p. 12) they believe will get students thinking at the higher levels of Bloom's taxonomy: receive, retrieve, rate, and reflect. After receiving information, students can demonstrate retrieval through practice during learning activities or quizzing. They should be expected to use critical thinking to rate the value of arguments, and last, they need to reflect on their learning, using metacognition.

## Short Active Learning Techniques

Learning is most effective when students are actively engaged in activities that address various levels of learning, whether they are in class or studying on their own (Felder et al., 2008). We want our courses to be places of energetic thinking, questioning, and responding. Some practices promote passivity, which decreases learning. When students are passive learners, they put the responsibility for learning on the instructor instead of accepting responsibility for themselves. Learning occurs as a result of much practice; it is not something we hand out to our students. How can we offer more active learning and, thus, practice, in our classes? We recommend the following to bring students on board with a more active approach:

- Start active learning strategies from the first day of class. Use icebreakers so students can meet their classmates, activities such as a team quiz to discover important policies in the syllabus and activities to connect prior learning to the first unit in your class.
- Explain why you are using active learning methods. Link them to your teaching philosophy and research data on learning.
- Change your practice slowly. If you are currently using lecture-based instruction, implement one or two active techniques at a time to build your confidence.
- Develop a new lesson or unit that starts with an activity, such as a discussion, instead of a lecture.
- Choose low-risk activities, such as polling or practice quiz questions. Further examples are discussed later in this chapter.

Ideally, your classes will be designed so students will be doing most of the remembering and understanding work before they come to class. To motivate them to do this, students will need to see a benefit. If your class sessions or online materials repeat what is in the textbook, students will stop reading them. You could also add low-stakes online or in-class quizzes so students can earn some points for doing the reading. If students shift doing their remembering and understanding work to before class sessions or online presentations, then class time can be used to move to higher levels of learning when they have the support of you and their classmates.

**Jot Your Thoughts**

## Reality Check

Have you been taught content you've never used, like memorizing names of capital cities, historical dates, or steps in chemical reactions, but then never used them as a professional in your field? Are students learning things they will never use in their career? It seems we often teach things in our fields because we always have without asking ourselves why. As knowledge expands, selecting course content becomes increasingly difficult. One way to reduce content and to free up more time for deeper and active learning is to remove the parts students will not need.

The truth is, no one will run up to your students in the workplace and demand, "Define *osmosis*!" or "Explain hydraulics!" In contrast, they might need to select and use intravenous solutions based on the principles of osmosis, so you could provide students with patient scenarios and ask them to select the correct intravenous solution. They might need to fix a hydraulic system, so you could provide them with problems to troubleshoot and ask them which steps to take to diagnose and fix the problem. Thinking about the skills they will need in future courses and in the workplace will help you select activities to include in your course.

How we access information has changed. In the past, students depended on instructors to provide the information in their courses and fields, but now, with new technologies, they have access to information from many sources. Today more than ever we need to teach students how to most efficiently and effectively access information and use critical thinking to select credible sources and evaluate content. Information itself is rapidly changing, so rather than requiring students to memorize facts that may change, we should focus on teaching them the skills to continue to learn new information, as Fink (2003) describes in the taxonomy as learning how to learn.

Textbooks can affect the way you think about designing your course as well. When selecting a textbook, it is important to consider how it structures the content. What is the organizational structure—chronological? by system? political versus topography? This may determine the way you will have to approach the content.

And if your textbook has a different organizational structure from what you use when you teach, you will have to design your activities so that students can learn how to organize their knowledge and make connections. For example, if your book presents the human body by body system (bones, brain, sensory structures), and you want your students to understand the body's head, you will need to help them make these connections.

Textbooks are published partly on the basis of what has been published before, what other publishers are including, and what a majority of instructors might purchase. It is easy to be lulled into thinking that if a topic is in a particular textbook, then it should be taught in the course. Although most publishers offer custom textbooks, you can usually just choose which chapters you'd like to use, but most publishers do not allow you to select content in chapters. Open educational resources (OER) are educational materials that are in the public domain or introduced with an open license. They are free, and they may be adapted as needed by the user. for delivering course content are becoming more popular for this reason (see chapter 7).

## Developing Low-Stakes Activities

Frequent low-stakes activities in the classroom or online provide students with opportunities to practice, retrieve, and develop skills. Low-stakes activities help students identify gaps in their learning, decrease the illusion of learning, and provide support and opportunities for targeted feedback that can lead to improvement. These are low stakes because they might be for practice without points, points awarded based on completion, or a few points earned based on a score, ideally with more than one opportunity to earn the points. Low-stakes activities will help decrease anxiety, which is helpful as anxiety can decrease learning (Wolfe, 2001). In addition, when students feel less pressure, they are less likely to cheat.

We recommend the following low-stakes techniques:

- Include frequent think-pair-share activities in which students think about a prompt, pair up with another student to discuss it, and share their thoughts with the whole class (Angelo & Cross, 1993). There are many variations, such as write-pair-share or think-pair-square (first forming a team of two then a team of four). This is one of the easiest activities to include in a class as it gives all students a chance to participate, even if they are only comfortable doing it with one other student. Often students are more likely to share with their own team if they see that someone else has the same concern or if they are asked to share what their classmate has said.
- Instruct students to do a quick write or one-minute paper (Angelo & Cross, 1993). There are many prompts you could use including, "Write one thing you know for sure, one question you have at that moment, one key concept, one question that might appear on the exam." Collect and read the papers to see where students have misconceptions or need more help.

- Ask students to illustrate the concept you are explaining. You might ask students to draw a map, stick figure, diagram, flow chart, provide an analogy, or build a model. You could bring a box of supplies to encourage this (e.g., colored paper, markers, glue, Play-Doh, scissors, etc.)
- Use an online polling tool, such as Socrative or Poll Everywhere, and students' own devices to ask sample quiz questions or get feedback. This is a great way for students to see how a test question will be constructed and how you expect them to be thinking. For a low-tech version, you could give students different colored index cards or cards marked A, B, C, D, E they hold up to vote so you can get a quick idea of their learning. If there is a lot of disagreement on an answer, ask students to talk to someone with a different answer to convince them they are correct and then vote again. You could also provide short team quizzes and have students write exam-type questions. Research shows that in-class quizzing and getting something incorrect then getting feedback improve learning (Brown et al., 2014). This is referred to as *effortful retrieval.* Learning also increases if students are tested before studying the material (Brown et al., 2014). Brown and colleagues' (2014) research shows that that if students try working a math problem before they are taught the method, even if they cannot solve it, they perform better after they are taught the method. The effort of thinking the problem through and then later being taught the necessary explanations seems to create stronger connections and results in better learning.
- Include content samples, not just students' reactions to their learning. If students are writing or drawing the concepts of the course, collect their papers to get feedback about gaps in learning or misconceptions. Students can do this either anonymously or with their names. This is also a way to take attendance and to award a few low-stakes points for attending and completing tasks. If you do this frequently, hand out half sheets of paper so they are all the same size and easier to handle. If you teach many sections, ask your copy center to cut papers in various colors then use a different color for each section. Using scratch paper can reduce costs, and it model recycling.

**Bright Idea**

None of these activities create much work for you. You can read through the papers very quickly and decide ahead of time if any points or attendance or participation credit will be assigned. Handle them once: read, score, and record.
**—Linda Russell**

What if you have large classes that seem less conducive to teamwork and active learning? Pairs activities can be used in any size class. Pairs work may also be viewed more positively by students than working in larger groups, and it is more easily structured so there is less social loafing. It is also easier for students to hear one another in larger classes. You may need a signal, such as flicking the lights or ringing a bell or using an Internet timer on screen to corral them back to attention, but they'll get used to it. Online polls, as mentioned earlier, can easily be used in large classes as well as cards you provide that are marked A, B, C, D, E or True and False that students hold up to reflect answers to multiple-choice or true-or-false questions projected on a screen.

Silberman (1996) suggests the following activities for pairs:

- Brainstorm what students already know about an upcoming topic or the key points in the last class or the class preparation materials and readings.
- Discuss a reading using a prompt or question.
- Interview each other about a concept or position.
- Question or quiz each other.
- Recap the information that was just presented.
- Develop questions to ask the instructor about the day's content.
- Take turns explaining how to work a problem with one student acting as the accuracy checker, then switch roles for the next problem.
- Compare notes from classroom preparation, such as reading notes, or a lecture.
- Respond to an instructor-posed question.
- Take a practice quiz and explain how they eliminated options to reinforce the kind of thinking involved with a multiple-choice test.
- Create a table to compare and contrast two or more concepts.

**Bright Idea**

Research shows that hand-written notes are more effective than those written on a computer, and having a device or a computer in class has been shown to decrease learning unless the device is being used for the class (Mueller & Oppenheimer, 2014; Ward, Duke, Gneezy, & Bos, 2018). Encourage students to write their notes. —**Linda Russell**

Low-stakes activities can also be scaffolded so that students can develop higher-level skills. Scaffolding involves using previously taught skills to teach new, more complex skills (Brown et al., 2014). Gradually, the students need less of the earlier structures and can work without the building blocks. For instance, if you want students to learn how to study by making concept maps, you could first provide a complete concept map, have them complete one that is partially filled in, have them reconstruct one you made, give them the main points and have them arrange them, and then finally have them complete one from a reading (Crowe, Dirks, & Wenderoth, 2008). If you want them to write a research paper, have them brainstorm topics and search terms, draft a thesis statement, turn in a reference list, turn in the first page or section, then turn in a draft.

Scaffolding also helps to space practice, interleaving different skills, and interrupt the task to allow percolation, all of which have been shown to increase learning

(Brown et al., 2014; Ormrod, 2017). Scaffolding also helps target the level of learning to help students build confidence while they develop skills for more complex tasks. Because students often underestimate how long it takes to complete something (e.g., study for a test, write a paper) and have competing demands on their time, scaffolding can help them break up a larger task. This will produce higher quality work that will be more pleasant and easier to grade for the instructor, and students will increase learning and feel more success.

Interleaving is usually described as practicing different activities in one period, such as studying history and math in the same evening. But with one subject, interleaving could be achieved by combining types of activities, such as reading, taking a short quiz, making a set of flashcards, writing a short summary of key points, or predicting an outcome.

Low-stakes and scaffolded activities also provide opportunities for frequent feedback. If students are doing activities in class, such as learning to build a concept map, they get immediate feedback from their classmates and from you. If they are working on parts of a paper, they could get feedback from other students in class or online or you could give them feedback on the steps of the activity.

Feedback can help students identify gaps in their knowledge and skills and help them target their improvement with more practice. Providing rubrics and checklists can help students see expectations and can help you and peers provide feedback (see chapter 8). Adding opportunities for feedback without a grade, such as practice quizzes or points for completion but not for correctness, can decrease emotion and increase their use of feedback (Dweck, 2006). The tone of the feedback affects students' response to it, so try to keep a supportive tone. Students will feel like they belong in your class if your feedback shows that you are noticing their successes, clearly pointing them in a better direction that is doable for them, and indicating that you believe they can get there. Using language such as "You haven't quite got it yet" provides students with a different way to look at short-term failure; they may not have it yet, but they will get it eventually if they keep working on it. This is a good counter to the frequent attitude that students have when they make errors or experience failure: They give up too soon and approach it with a fixed mind-set, assuming they are not capable of ever getting it.

Low-stakes and scaffolded activities with frequent feedback also allow you to assess where students need more help, resources, or instruction. If students turn in a one-minute paper about the main idea in class, and they misidentify it, you could address this in the next class and improve on this for the next semester. If students have trouble identifying key terms for a concept map, you could repeat this practice in a future unit and provide some help with picking out key terms.

## Longer Term Activities

After you've successfully used some of the lower risk activities to build a foundation, you can move to longer term activities that can be repeated or developed over weeks.

Longer types of active learning gives students time to get used to your style, goals, and expectations. Some examples of longer term activities ask students to

- critique or peer review each other's work, such as an essay question, or a short paper using a rubric or a set of criteria (see Appendix E for sample rubrics);
- analyze a case problem, an exercise, or an experiment;
- create a poster about a particular concept;
- research and present a short explanation of a process, concept, or argument; or
- create a portfolio of their best work to be showcased at the end of the unit or term.

The goal of active-learning strategies is to promote higher level, more complex learning and to develop independent learning strategies and move from more guided practice to learner independence. Your students will not focus on memorizing if you ask them to do other kinds of thinking, such as analyzing, using or carrying out actions, judging, and creating new ways to express concepts. The goal is to decrease the time they listen, watch, read, and summarize and increase the time they spend applying, predicting, connecting, comparing and contrasting, reorganizing, evaluating, and creating, all of which are skills employers tell us they are looking for in the workplace.

## What Role Does Forgetting Play in Learning?

Brown and colleagues (2014) describe the value of forgetting. It isn't the forgetting part that is so essential to learning, it is *effortful retrieval*, which is a way to recall information to apply it to further learning. This happens best when we use spaced practice methods. We forget part of what we learned in the space (days or hours) between practice sessions. We focus hard to recall what we've forgotten, and in doing so, we begin to notice the salient points and begin creating the mental models that help us see the concepts as whole units rather than individual facts. It is as if our brain created a sort of macro program to understand the concept. For example, when we learn to drive a car, eventually with plenty of spaced practice, we form mental models for shifting gears (on a manual transmission) or parallel parking or merging into traffic (Brown et al., 2014). Faculty can provide tasks that promote effortful retrieval by inserting cumulative questions in their quizzes or other activities that require students to recall what they learned earlier. Some textbooks offer cumulative reviews or quizzes for students to practice this important type of retrieval practice.

## Pacing the Learning

When you design your courses, you make decisions about how to pace your content over the semester or term. Some concepts take more time to learn through practice or have more detail; others are perhaps more familiar to students and won't take as much time.

But pacing affects you and your students in other ways. It is difficult for everyone to keep learning energy high over the span of many weeks. For the best learning, students need to get feedback from you quickly after each assignment or test. The way you schedule student work affects your time to grade and provide helpful feedback. The following are some suggestions for organizing and pacing assignments and exams:

- Stagger your assignment and assessment due dates for each class you teach so you don't get inundated at one time. Make one course's assignment due one week and another course's the next week (although this may not work if you teach four sections of the same course). Develop an assignment and assessment schedule for all your courses to see how all the work for the semester will be turned in. You don't want major projects for all courses turned in during the same week of the semester.
- Make the first day of the week the day the class begins as all classes don't begin on Monday. You don't have to make all assignments due on Sunday by 11:59 p.m. You probably won't be checking the assignment submittal drop box at midnight, ready to begin grading. Consider making your due dates correspond more closely with your weekly class times.
- Create a drop box for late papers in your course shell. Students can submit them when they are done, and you don't have keep rechecking past drop boxes. Communicate your late-work policy clearly. We always want students to complete the work, so consider deducting points for late assignments rather than giving them a zero. That way they have to at least complete the assignment, and the tardiness still negatively affects their grade. If assignments involve authentic practice, you want students to complete them. In the real world, depending on the field, we may not be severely penalized if we turn in work beyond a deadline; however, this varies with the type of work, the setting, and perhaps the discipline.
- Don't make the major learning assignments and projects due on the last day of the semester. Your feedback from their work is a tremendous learning opportunity. If these are due in the final week, you won't be able to provide valuable feedback, nor will students have time to read and reflect on it. Consider having due dates within a week or two of the end of the semester so you can grade assignments and provide feedback. Students can write a reflection assignment about how and what they learned from the last assignment or project while you are grading, or if there is a final exam, hold class review sessions. However, as final exams usually follow a campus schedule, you won't have control over their timing.

You may want to get ideas from your colleagues about how they handle their workload. Designing an assignment work plan will help avoid having too many assignments to grade in a limited time so the amount of work doesn't pile up. You want to be able to give timely feedback, and your students need to use that feedback to improve for the next assignment.

## Matching Your Teaching to Learning Outcomes

Your teaching and learning activities are tied to your learning outcomes for the course or unit. If you have written the outcomes carefully and determined the assessments for each, it will become clear which activities students need to practice to prepare well for the assessments, even capstone assessments. This is where backward design will really be helpful. As you design learning activities, predict the amount of practice a student needs to master the outcomes. Consider the following in your analysis:

- Determine the level of your outcome. Lower level foundational knowledge outcomes usually need fewer activities. Higher level application, integration, and analysis may need two or more.
- Identify the complexity and purpose of the activity. Will this activity meet one outcome or serve as practice for several outcomes? Is the activity part of a set of learning activities that scaffolds to higher-level outcomes?
- Plan for the time and equipment needed to complete the activity. Will students have access to what they need to complete the activity effectively, or is the time or equipment limited and the activity may need to be broken into chunks or completed one part at a time?

## Reflect on This Chapter

At this point you may be feeling overwhelmed with the notion of completely rethinking how you teach your students. Many faculty cannot fathom reworking every day of class using this new paradigm of facilitating learning experiences rather than lecturing. We suggest you start small, trying one new activity such as think-pair-share. Get feedback from your students using quick writes or anonymous surveys, and then tweak as needed. It can be somewhat scary to cede control of the classroom, but in taking small steps it can be very liberating. In a way you are experiencing exactly what students experience when they enroll in a course as a complete novice: some fear, some excitement, and mixed emotions. Now that you have completed reading this chapter and thinking about the content as it applies to your work, please reflect on the following questions.

- What is the best use of course time?
- For blended and face-to-face courses, what do you need to be together to accomplish?
- How can you get students to uncover the content instead of you covering it?
- What will students be able to do as a result of taking your class, and how can you give them practice doing it?

**Jot Your Thoughts**

## Action Checklist

Use Checklist 4.1 to apply the chapter content to your practice and help you identify the steps for implementing these ideas in your teaching.

**CHECKLIST 4.1** Creating a Learning Framework Action Checklist

| ✓ | **Understanding the Learning Process** |
|---|---|
| ❑ | Reduced lecture time and develop more engaging learning activities. |
| ❑ | Organized materials and presentations into shorter, roughly 10-minute chunks to support learning. |
| ❑ | Analyzed the difference between delivering content and facilitating learning activities. |
| ❑ | Planned the time needed and pacing to complete activities and provide feedback. |

| ✓ | **Understanding Research-Based Study Strategies** |
|---|---|
| ❑ | Developed a plan to model assumptions, logic, and other disciplinary literacy skills and overtly teach them to students. |
| ❑ | Created ways to suggest and provide practice for research-based study strategies. |

| ✓ | **Choosing Materials and Content** |
|---|---|
| ❑ | Selected materials and content to support a diversity of student backgrounds. |
| ❑ | Aligned my content directly to my learning outcomes and course assessments. |

| ✓ | **Plan Low-Stakes Activities** |
|---|---|
| ❑ | Aligned learning activities directly to my learning outcomes. |
| ❑ | Developed early, lower point activities to provide practice for higher stake activities and assessments. |
| ❑ | Designed activities to begin immediately in the course so students get comfortable with them. |

# 5

# DEVELOPING LEARNING ACTIVITIES AND TECHNIQUES

## Points to Ponder

Chapter 5 provides tools to create active learning opportunities for significant learning in your course design. In thinking about integrating the elements of your course design, consider the following questions to examine your prior knowledge:

- Activities take too much class time, don't they?
- Students don't prepare for class. If I don't lecture, how will they learn?
- What if my students resist activities and tell me they'd rather I lecture?
- It gets too noisy and chaotic when I do activities. How do I restore control of the class?
- Should I assign points to activities? That sounds like too much grading.

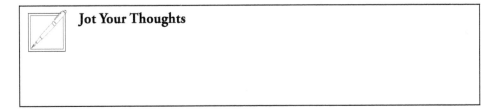


Rhonda, a new faculty member in the philosophy department, stopped in to see the center for teaching and learning leader for some advice. She was concerned about her three-hour class offered once a week. She taught like she was taught—she lectured. She used the textbook as an outline for the class and guide what content to include. Partway through one class, she thought, "There are people here who are teaching experts. I need to connect with them." She sought faculty development opportunities to learn other research-based strategies, and she tried to understand the research on how students learn. Rhonda learned that most of us can only hold about four pieces of information in our working memory before we do something with it, which suggests that students should be doing activities interrupted with short explanations. Students retain and transfer their learning more if they use active learning and focus-level skills, but all students need help developing their strategies to do this. Rhonda was very worried that students taking her three-hour class weren't really getting to apply their learning by listening to lectures without breaks.

She looked at the course's outcomes, assessments, and activities. It was time for her to redesign, keeping in mind that she wanted to use active learning activities to prepare students for the assessments of the outcomes. She considered using more of the course shell tools to improve instruction as she got to work. Her goal was to use more activities and fewer lectures in her class.

She made changes in each of her course's units to provide more active learning practice opportunities. She checked to make sure that the assessments were aligned with her outcomes and that the learning activities were designed to help students demonstrate mastery in the assessments. She met with a trusted colleague who supported her desire to redesign her course to show her how she changed the course. Once implemented, Rhonda was surprised how she gained valuable information during the activities about what the students were and were not learning. She was able to use this to help students immediately and to improve future classes. She realized she was able to monitor and help her students learn more on their own through designed experiences. She better understood what the idea of uncovering or discovering the content was.

Rhonda was able to change from a lecture-only approach to a class plan that gets students to read the content before coming to class. Class time was only for activities plus short impromptu lectures when students struggle with a concept. Students wanted to listen to these explanations because it was just-in-time information that applied directly to what they needed. Class attendance increased, students wanted to come to class as participants, their engagement increased, they mentioned how they enjoyed the class, and assessment results improved. She now sees evidence that more of her students are learning deeply as well as learning how to learn in her discipline.

## Getting Started With Effective, Significant Learning Activities

Significant learning consists of integrated course design that provides a framework for engaging students with content, and the students are actively participating in and even designing their own learning experiences. On day one of the course, you have the best opportunity to communicate this triad: faculty to students, students to faculty, and students to students. When the course design embraces this philosophy, the maximum amount of learning can be achieved as it enhances the experience for students and faculty.

Active learning equals high engagement. *Active learning* is defined as any instructional method that engages students in the learning process. In short, *active* learning requires students to participate in meaningful learning activities and think about what they are doing (Brame, 2016). In contrast, lectures tend to allow students to be passive. Although some lecturing is appropriate and can be helpful, if you reduce lecture time and substitute high-quality learning activities as described in this chapter, your students will be more engaged and will learn more deeply.

We encourage you to start your active learning the very first day. If you begin your semester with expectations of full participation in class activities, your students will adjust more easily, and you will receive less resistance. Also, activities foster a climate of community, which leads to students getting to know each other better, supporting each other, and helping each other. We teach in diverse, multifaceted spaces, and it is good for us to model and encourage positive interaction, collaboration, and mutual respect. Activities can appeal to a diverse audience as well. Discussing ideas honors oral traditions; a combination of listening, writing, drawing, and discussing is inclusive of many types of learners with multiple preferences for taking in and working with information. As we know that one size does not fit all, it is incumbent on us to provide a variety of learning experiences for our students.

As you introduce your course on the first day of class, we encourage you to use an activity, perhaps a think-pair-share about your syllabus. Although collaborative, this activity does not require students to divulge personal information to complete strangers and is not threatening. It will get them accustomed to doing rather than sitting in your class.

Think-pair-share is an example of a classroom assessment technique, and there are many, after Angelo and Cross (1993) introduced them years ago. These methods provide an activity for students and give you information about their progress or proficiency about a topic. Most are short, easily assessed, and add to the documentation you gather about your students' learning. Barkley and Major (2016b) have built on Angelo and Cross's work and are also an excellent resource for developing active learning assessments.

Activities can be used before, during, and after learning takes place. You might ask your students to think, write, talk, or draw about a topic you haven't introduced yet to get a sense of their perceptions and background knowledge. Also, we know that learning occurs when we can tie or connect new learning to previous learning. Using the activities as learning reinforcers and checks is also valuable.

### *Think-Pair-Share*

In think-pair-share, students are presented with a question and given time to think about it individually for a few minutes before pairing up with a classmate to discuss it. The pairs either report to the class or discuss the questions with another pair. This is a good way for students to begin talking with each other and building community in the class. It can also be more content related. For instance, if you want your students to familiarize themselves with the library, you could give them questions that require a visit (or online visit) to locate resources or to conduct a sample search.

Some faculty enjoy a scavenger hunt by posing questions from the syllabus. For example:

- When is our first quiz?
- What is the late homework policy?
- Office hours are on what days?

Variations of this activity include write-pair-share or think-pair-square (forming first a group of two then a group of four). The following prompts (which do not require students to divulge private information) can be used as a get-to-know-you activity that also serves as practice for pair-share activities:

- What are you looking forward to learning in this class?
- What was the last book you read?
- What is the best class you've ever taken and why?
- What sport would you like to be good at?
- What is one thing we would not know by looking at you?
- If you could learn another language, which one would you choose?

These activities can be done in the classroom and are easily reproduced in the course shell for the online or blended experiences. The scavenger hunt and introductory icebreaker activities can be offered through a discussion prompt or quiz tool. This may help students who need some reflection time to prepare a response, including introverts, culturally diverse students, learners whose first language isn't English, and so on.

Later, your prompts could be higher level why and how questions on topics from your course. They serve very well as methods for getting high-quality discussions going. For example:

- Why do you think this activity will help you in your future work?
- How will knowing this help you in future courses in your program?

### *Background Knowledge Probe*

According to Barkley and Major (2016b), using a questionnaire that allows you to find out how well your students are prepared for the course, unit, or topic will help you anticipate trouble spots and pacing as you teach. You can adjust the questions to solicit information about how confident students feel about the topics and what they might like to learn.

### *Quick Write: One-Minute Paper*

Writing is a good tool to get students started on their thinking. In the previous activity, we mentioned that write-pair-share is one technique. Another writing activity that may not involve sharing is sometimes referred to as a one-minute paper, but the amount of time can vary. Originally developed by Charles Schwartz and documented by Wilson (1986), this paper can be used as a classroom assessment technique to find out what your students might still need more instruction on. For example, you might have students respond to the following:

- What is one thing from today's class you are confused about?
- Describe one thing you learned today that you feel you completely understand.
- Write one question you have about today's class.

You can also use this method for students to practice retrieval using open-ended questions, like the following:

- What are the components of classical conditioning?
- What are ways operant conditioning is different from classical conditioning?
- Why do we need oxygen?
- Why does __________cause_________to___________?
- What is the difference between ____________ and _________________?

You can skim through the papers to get a feel for how your students are learning the content and use that information to decide what to review more, explain differently, or rework. You can give everyone who turns one in a little credit in the grade book, or they can be anonymous. Angelo and Cross's (1993) book offers more ideas on how to follow up with in-class writing activities. This quick assessment can provide you with valuable results on the effectiveness of your activities including your directions, instructions, structure of activities, timing, and so on. Using this feedback helps you make the experience better for other activities in the course and when you repeat it. If it is confusing for students, you may decide to replace this activity in the future.

### *Student Feedback Through Discussion*

Discussions may be used for reinforcement or deepening learning and also assessment of learning. Facilitating discussion is an important tool to engage students in the content, disciplinary methods of inquiry, and a diagnostic tool for you. As Brookfield (1986) and Brookfield and Preskill (2005, 2016) have emphasized, collaboration in learning is a critical factor in teaching adults. Unfortunately, discussions can often deteriorate into a stilted question-and-answer session with few students participating and without faculty input. Providing encouraging feedback on student responses and posing new questions can help students dig deeper. This is the classic Socratic method, which also works well in the course shell where students and faculty have the time to reflect on the discussion, and all students can participate.

In the face-to-face classroom, providing time for reflection before discussion can allow more students to feel ready to contribute. As in the think-pair-share activity, the think time sends the message to students that reflection and thought are expected and valued, not just blurting out answers. Using groups involves more students than the one who is asking the questions (the teacher) and a few responding students.

Discussions can be initiated using a variety of strategies. The first is thinking about the order of the information presented. Other questions to consider before planning to use a discussion in your course include the following:

- Is the discussion used as a way to assess students' prior knowledge of a new topic? Do you want them to discuss what they know and propose ideas before presenting information?

- Is the discussion a reflection on or reaction to course materials in which you want to assess what students learned by interacting with the content? Do you want them to analyze an author's view, synthesize solutions, or evaluate a situation in their responses?
- Is the discussion an avenue to allow students a chance to use both backward- and forward-looking experiences?

As a learning activity or formative assessment (occurring along the learning pathway of the course as opposed to the end of the course), discussions are a great way to collect the students' evidence of thinking and understanding. When we develop discussion questions in a course, we try to get each student to use authentic answers that are usually tied to their own experiences or to future experiences in which they will use the content. Faculty are not the only ones who can pose discussion questions. Allowing students to pose questions in a discussion thread is a very engaging way for them to demonstrate higher level thinking. In more advanced courses in your curriculum, having student groups facilitate their own discussion or writing prompts adds another level of activities and assessment of learning and provides a workplace-related experience to your course.

**Bright Idea**

You will learn a lot about your course design by listening to or reading the student responses to questions in discussions. They will tell you which of the resources you provided were the most valuable, which will help you as you update the course in the future, or what to keep and what to change. **—Zala Fashant**

Designing discussions needs intentionality by faculty (Herman & Nilson, 2018). Knowing how to use discussions to gain the maximum learning opportunity for students is critical. The comparison of discussion delivery modes in Table 5.1 can help you plan the best use of them in your course design.

Asking questions that align with your learning outcomes is key to a good discussion. This demonstrates that the discussions, whether used for assignments or assessments, are intentional. Discussions are best used for higher level thinking: analysis, evaluation, creation (Bloom et al., 1956). Words and phrases such as *why, how, compare, contrast, break down, make a judgment, set a priority, suggest a solution to a problem,* and so on will elicit more complex thinking from students. These types of questions generate more authentic versus rote responses, demonstrating evidence of student thinking. See chapter 2 and chapter 3 for more on facilitating discussions.

**TABLE 5.1**
**Course Discussion Analysis**

| *Delivery Mode* | *Strengths* | *Challenges* |
|---|---|---|
| Face-to-face classroom oral discussion led by instructor (question and answer) | Students and faculty can receive information and interact quickly. Greater student engagement can occur if this technique is used after a small group discussion, such as think-pair-share. | There is a possibility that only a few students talk (usually only one at a time); it is difficult to tell how many students really understand the material, since many sit quietly; and quick-thinking and outgoing students will get the most attention. This method uses valuable face-to-face class time. |
| Face-to-face classroom oral discussion in groups | More students are speaking at one time, one per group. This method builds consensus as more ideas are being shared and analysis takes place. The instructor can visit groups, monitor discussions, and observe student participation. Students practice talking about the material and the instructor can check for understanding. This method is used in team-based learning. | It is also difficult to tell how many students really understand the material. Quick-thinking and outgoing students talk the most, so there is a chance that some students will be passive in a group. This method uses valuable face-to-face class time but is useful since more students are participating. |
| Written discussion in a course shell | The instructor and the class receive information from all students. This method does not take face-to-face classroom time. A maximum number of thoughts are generated, which maximizes interaction. Students can prepare for more in-depth questions and reflect on their answers, which provides an opportunity for deeper learning. This method creates a documented source for assessment. Students construct their own learning and demonstrate written communication skills. | This method takes more time to complete, as you may need several days to get responses. It isn't as spontaneous. There is no assurance that all students are reading all responses. |

*Note.* This table analyzes the delivery modes for designing course discussions by listing strengths and challenges.

**Jot Your Thoughts**

## High-Engagement Activities

There are many approaches that engage students, use teams or groups, and allow longer, more in-depth projects. The following are some of the most common methods, and our resource section at the end of the book provides sources on the ones that would be most useful for you:

- Inquiry-based learning begins by posing questions, problems, or scenarios so that students may identify and research issues and questions to develop their knowledge or solutions (Lee, 2004).
- Process-oriented guided inquiry learning is student-centered group learning in which self-managed teams use carefully constructed materials that guide them through the data, much like following the scientific method (De Gale & Boisselle, 2015; Lewis & Lewis, 2005; Şen, Yilmaz, & Geban, 2015).
- Problem-based learning is any learning environment in which the problem drives the learning; it is an important part of team-based learning (Duch, Groh, & Allen, 2001b).
- Team-based learning goes a step further than cooperative learning because students stay in the same group for an entire semester, transforming groups into teams (Duch et al., 2001a).
- Case studies are real-life stories or problems that prompt students to integrate their classroom knowledge with their understanding of real-world situations, actions, and consequences (Yin, 2018).
- Service-learning is an educational method that entwines experiential learning and community service (Heffernan, 2001; Jacoby, 2014; Strait & Lima, 2009). It meets educational objectives through real-world experiences while tapping students as resources to benefit their college and communities.

### *Quizzing to Deepen Learning*

As a metastudy of learning methods by Dunlosky and colleagues (2013) found, one very effective method for deep learning is testing, which requires effortful retrieval. This can be self-testing or teacher-created low-stakes quizzing. Short quizzes can be used in several ways to check students' learning at various points in a unit. These are not pop quizzes but planned, short quiz formats that are low risk for students. Some faculty like to conduct individual quizzes, followed immediately by group quizzes. The same quiz or similar quiz is used in both cases and allows students to test their knowledge and understanding and then get feedback from their classmates as they work together on it a second time. Average the points between the individual and group efforts, or devise a different way to award points. There are also scratch-off answer sheets available that give students instant feedback about their answers to quiz questions (Epstein, n.d.).

The purposes of short quizzing are to

- get a snapshot of how your students are learning;
- give them the opportunity to practice an effective learning technique, effortful retrieval (Brown et al., 2014);
- reward your students for keeping current with the course; and
- learn from each other immediately after taking the short quiz in groups or in a group reflection on the quizzes.

These quizzes might consist of only five questions, but they should focus on the most important concepts from the previous class period or lesson, thus reinforcing those concepts.

Short quizzes also promote a second effective learning method: distributed learning (Dunlosky et al., 2013). There is a time gap between what students learned in the previous class session and the quiz. The quiz serves as a second look at the content. If you include one cumulative question from earlier sessions, you've made the quiz even more useful for learning by making sure that students continue to remember earlier concepts, processes, or information as they move ahead in your course. These shorter quizzes are not the same as big tests. They require students to keep up with the course, but they will not count as heavily toward a course grade as tests might. They serve more as an activity than an exam. They can be a diagnostic tool for you as well; you will see immediately where students are confused or need additional practice, so you can make adjustments as needed. These quizzes can be offered by using the course shell quiz tool, so you can use them in all types of course deliveries, and they can be completed outside class.

### *Online Polling, Card, or Finger Polling*

Project a test question (multiple-choice or true-false format) on the overhead screen or use a Web tool such as Socrative or Poll Everywhere and have students answer. There are different ways to view the results, but you and the class get immediate feedback. Some students may not have a device, such as a smartphone or a tablet, so make it easy for everyone to answer. A low-tech method is to use cards marked A, B, C, and so on that the students make or you provide. Then they just hold up the card with the letter that corresponds to the multiple-choice answer. Using cards of different colors makes it quick and easy to see how many got the correct answer, and what the common errors are. Students can also hold up fingers for the choices instead, but it's a bit harder to see the patterns.

Some students might be reluctant to participate for fear of being incorrect. You could tell the class that this activity is not to judge students but to collect feedback about your teaching and whether they understand the content before moving on. You could also have students hold cards directly in front of them in case they are uncomfortable with the students around them seeing their responses. If you notice that many students do not have the correct answer, you can instruct them to find a student who has a different answer, convince him or her that the first student is right, then have them answer again.

### *Draw a Picture*

Some concepts can be illustrated or diagrammed. Learning to sketch concepts can become an excellent review tool for students. For example, ask them to

- draw two rectangles and show how to find the perimeter for one and the area for the other;
- sketch a cross-section of the layers of skin, labeling each;
- make a simple drawing of one characteristic of Gothic architecture; or
- draw an example of a pinnate leaf and another of a lobed leaf.

You could also use this activity to assess what students think or know about a concept before it is addressed or as a start to a discussion. For example, students could be asked to draw energy to find out what they know or to draw a scientist to start a conversation about our perceptions of the people who pursue science as a discipline.

### *Advance Organizers*

Advance organizers to enhance learning, which have been advised for decades (Ausubel, 1960), are visual displays of concepts or information that show the framework or structure of the ideas. Often they are charts or tables but can also be diagrams, drawings, or other figures. In this chapter we provide several examples or templates you can adapt as needed for your discipline. You can model how each is created by filling in part of the information for students and having them complete it. By showing students the salient points, how to compare and contrast them, and how to categorize, you are scaffolding instruction about your discipline; that is, you are teaching disciplinary literacy skills. Your students will learn how to make these organizers themselves after a time, and you won't need to continue to provide them unless further topics are very complex and you offer them as a navigational tool.

### *Categorizing*

One aspect of many disciplines is learning the ways concepts are categorized, which is another facet of the disciplinary literacy of the field. You can help students learn the constructs that are used in your discipline by conducting activities that ask students to group, separate, contrast, and combine ideas, theories, concepts, and other information. For example, asking them to name five things that contributed to the Great Depression provides students with sorting or categorizing and retrieval practice. This activity is also referred to as a knowledge grid and requires students to demonstrate analytical skills and the categories related to the topic or discipline (Barkley & Major, 2016b). The table and sorting activities in Tables 5.2, 5.3, and 5.4 are other

TABLE 5.2
**Comparison Table Example**

| *Salient Points to Compare* | *Classical Conditioning* | *Operant Conditioning* |
|---|---|---|
| **Basic idea** | *Student explains* | *Student explains* |
| **Response** | | |
| **Acquisition** | | |
| **Extinction** | | |
| **Spontaneous recovery** | | |
| **Generalization** | | |
| **Discrimination** | | |

*Note*. This graphic organizer provides the structure to compare classical conditioning to operant conditioning.

TABLE 5.3
**Periods in Architecture History**

List the following architectural styles under their appropriate historical period:

| | | |
|---|---|---|
| Materialism | Neoclassiciam | Inventionism |
| Confucianism | Gothic Scholasticism | Indism |
| Rococo | Skycraperism | Totalitarianism |
| Ecoism | Regionalism | Absolutism |
| Rationalism | Victorianism | Anti-Urbanism |

| **Ancient and Pre-Renaissance** | **Renaissance** | **Early Modern** | **Modernism** | **Beyond Modernism** |
|---|---|---|---|---|
| | | | | |
| | | | | |
| | | | | |
| | | | | |
| | | | | |

*Note*. This architecture history graphic organizer requires students to fill in the substyles under each historical period by choosing from the list provided.

TABLE 5.4
**Finish the Time Line**

| *Date* | *Summary of Major Events*[a] | *Details*[a] |
|---|---|---|
| 1938 | Hitler announces Anschluss (union) with Austria. | Hitler annexed Austria and demanded liberation of German people from a region of Czechoslovakia; Chamberlain tried to attempt a settlement. |
| September 30, 1938 | Treaty of Munich | |
| March 1939 | Invasion of Czechoslovakia | |
| March–April 1939 | Britain rearms, assures Poland | |
| Late August 1939–May 1940 | Britain and France declare war. | Why is it called the Phony War? |
| April–May 1940 | Hitler invades Denmark and Norway. | |
| May 10, 1940 | | |
| June 4, 1940 | | |
| August–October, 1940 | | |

*Note.* This organizer allows students to fill in important events in World War II. It can be expanded as needed. From *Timeline of World War II*, by K. Burns and L. Novick, 2007, www.pbs.org/thewar/at_war_timeline_1939.htm. Copyright 2007 by WETA, Washington, DC, and American Lives II Film Project.

[a]Student fills in blank cells.

ways to practice sorting. SoftChalk (https://softchalk.com) is an online tool to use with your learning management system (LMS) to develop interactive tables modeled after Tables 5.2, 5.3, and 5.4. Students can manipulate the information and you can create a key to show them how well they did.

In Table 5.2, students are asked to compare two psychological concepts: classical conditioning and operant conditioning. They fill in the appropriate information using the prompts in the left column. This is an excellent study tool.

Table 5.3 requires students to choose from architecture styles to fill in the blank areas under each period in history. This type of organizing can be used in many ways, such as using photos of buildings instead of the names of the styles. Students can be asked to go beyond matching styles to categories and describe features that explain why they belong in a category.

In Table 5.4, students fill in the blank cells, describing important events in the time line of World War II.

In Figure 5.1, students fill in the steps for computations with fractions, which serves as a good study tool.

**Figure 5.1** Fractions mind map.

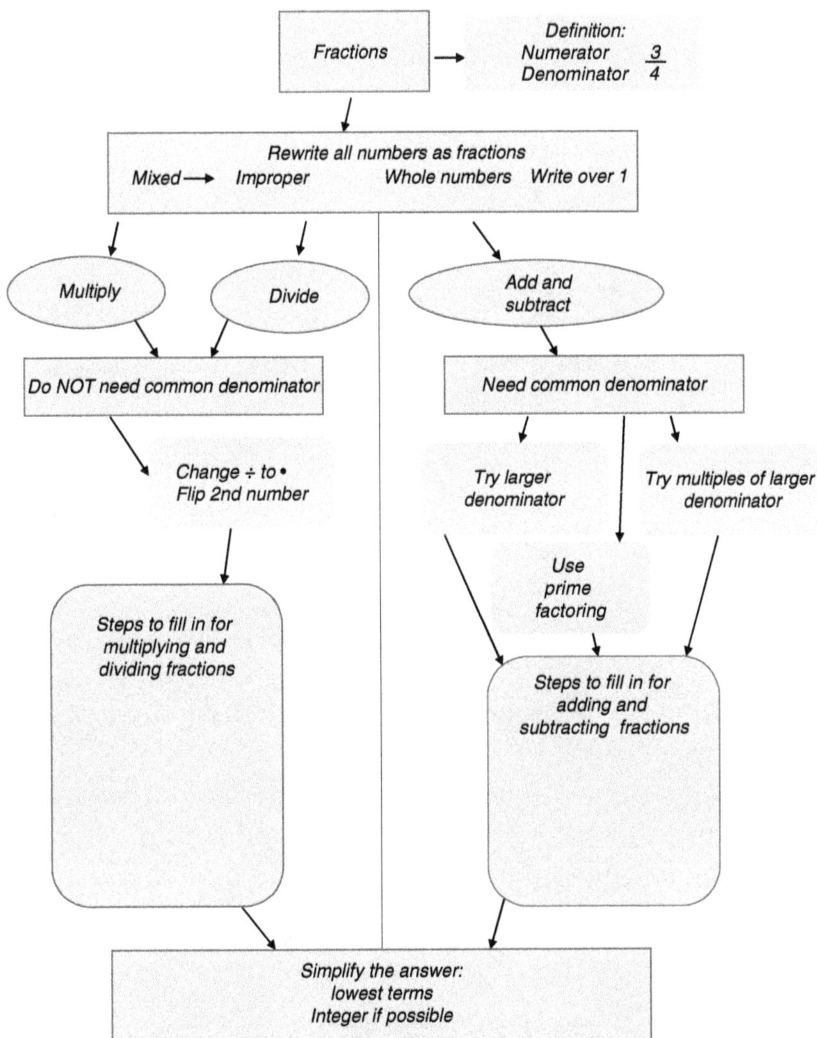


*Note.* This organizer lists the steps to follow to multiply, divide, add, and subtract fractions.

## *Fill in the Pathway*

Barkley and Major (2016a) refer to the type of activity in Figure 5.2 as a sequence chain. Others use the term *pathway*, which is often used in biology and health-related fields. For example, a physiology pathway model is a way for students to see the big picture in human physiology. When the class is learning what happens when a person has a reflex response to a stimulus, students can use the model pathway to identify exactly what occurs in the reflex response and where it occurs. Figure 5.2 is the model, based on Silverthorn (2015). Figure 5.3 is an example of students' work.

**Figure 5.2** Pathway model in physiology.

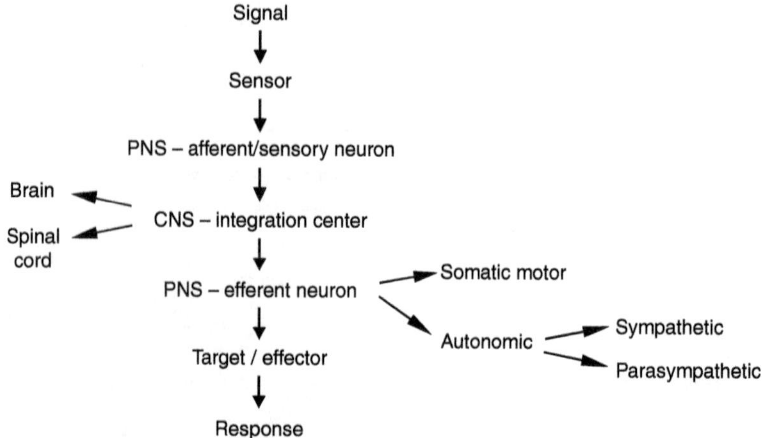


*Note.* PNS = peripheral nervous system; CNS = central nervous system.

**Figure 5.3** Student's example of a pathway.

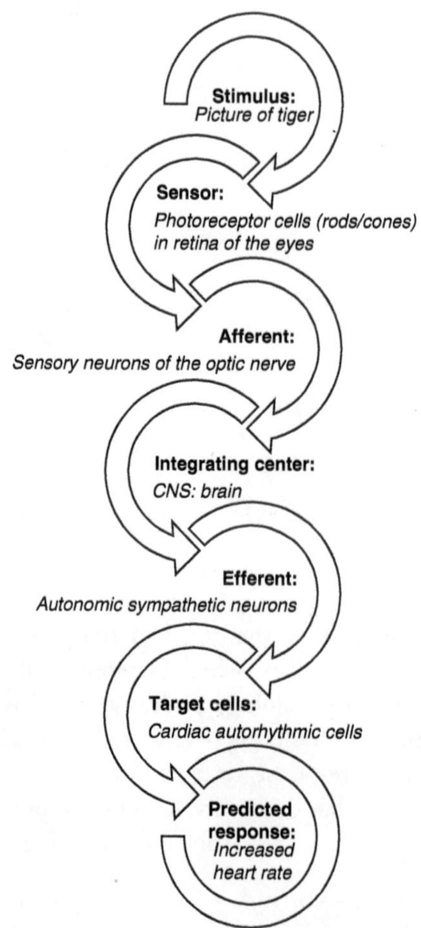

### *Gallery Walks*

In this activity, students work collaboratively on solving a problem, making a chart, or sketching a concept on sheets of paper from a flip chart and then display each group's work on the walls. Students then move around the room, looking at each group's work posted on the walls. They might use a rubric to rate the quality or thoroughness of each, or they might just take a few notes of things their group didn't think of or would like to try next time. This kind of activity allows group work to be shared with the entire class without asking individuals to stand up and give a report, which is sometimes hard to hear in a large class.

**Bright Idea**

If you have concerns about using tape on the walls of a classroom, use painters' tape. It can be removed without damaging the wall's surface. Gallery walks and Four Corners require students to move around the room. These activities may need to be accommodated for students with mobility and sight challenges.—**Linda Russell**

### *Four Corners*

Four corners, or stand where you stand (Barkley & Major, 2016a), is another type of polling, this time with movement. If there are four choices to answer a question, students can go to the predesignated corner that represents the answer they think is correct. This works very well for issue discussions in which there might be two or more points of view on a particular issue, and students can move to the corner of the room to show which one they agree with. This might be the basis for further discussions, debates, writing assignments, and future four-corner voting activities after the students learn more about an issue.

### *Jigsaws*

Jigsaws are collaborative learning activities in which each person in a group has one job, like one question to answer or one part to learn. If you have five groups of four in your class, each person is designated A, B, C, or D in each group. Separate all the As, Bs, Cs, and Ds into four groups, each of which is assigned a task, and tell them to work together to try to become experts on their assigned question or part. Then they return to their mixed groups and share information so that the group is able to answer all four questions or provide all four parts. The activity can be extended to group presentations or poster boards. According to Herman and Nilson (2018), "The jigsaw method helps students acquire and understand new information, debates, and task-based discussions add experience, and thought-focused discussion encourages reflective dialogue" (p. 25).

### *Student-Generated Study Materials*

College students must learn to create their own study and learning tools. By using some of the previous methods in class, you are modeling for students what works in your discipline. They can learn to create their own versions of such models as they prepare for exams or work on projects. It is best if study materials allow students to practice the most effective learning methods. Research has shown that the following promote longer lasting and deeper learning:

- Self-testing
- Distributed practice (the opposite of cramming)
- Elaborative interrogation, asking a lot of why or how questions
- Self-explanation, as if teaching it
- Interleaved practice, mixing up practice by doing different types of learning in one study session
- Making connections between old learning and new and with experiences and applications to abstractions

### *Making Study Cards*

This technique has been used for many types of learning and for many levels of education. Study cards, or flashcards, can get students beyond memorizing terms and definitions if creating the card requires thinking about several aspects of the concept, not just the definition. One way students can practice effortful retrieval is to try to make the card without referring to their notes or materials. Students might create the cards as a study or review tool or as an in-class activity. They may not be able to answer all the question prompts, but entertaining the questions helps students think more like experts. Table 5.5 shows what questions to ask for three types of study cards.

On the front of the study card, the student writes the term, principle, or concept spelled correctly, indicating pronunciation if necessary, and noting the source (chapter or page number, website, and so on). On the back of the study card, the students ask each question listed in Table 5.5 to determine if there is an answer. Figures 5.4, 5.5, and 5.6 are specific examples of study cards that make use of the questions listed in Table 5.5. Figure 5.4 is an example of a study card for the term *constructivism*, Figure 5.5 is an example of a study card for the term *metacognition*, and Figure 5.6 is an example of a study card for the process of blood typing.

Now that you've seen three different study cards, you can see that every card doesn't need to answer exactly the same questions about a concept. But when students start to pose the questions, they are going to learn more about the concept than just its definition, which enhances learning.

**TABLE 5.5**

**How to Make Study Cards**

| *Generic Study Card Questions* | *Customized Physiology Study Card Questions* | *Customized Theories Study Card Questions* | *Your Customized Questions* |
|---|---|---|---|
| The definition in your own words | The definition in your own words | What phenomenon does this theory explain? | |
| An example from the book, lecture, or your own | An example from the class materials or another source | What exactly is the theory; describe all aspects of how it works. Include all relevant terms that are part of this theory. | |
| How it works (if it is a process) | How it works | If possible, provide a clear example of this theory at work. | |
| What it does, if it does something | If something causes it to increase, what effect will it have? | Who developed this theory? | |
| What effect it has on other things (terms, concepts) | If something causes it to decrease, what effect will it have? | When did he or she develop it? | |
| What it is a part of | What it is a part of (in which larger structure or category can it be found)? | How does this theory fit into some general movement or way of thinking in the discipline? | |

(*Continues*)

**Table 5.5** (*Continued*)

| *Generic Study Card Questions* | *Customized Physiology Study Card Questions* | *Customized Theories Study Card Questions* | *Your Customized Questions* |
|---|---|---|---|
| What is part of it? | What is part of it (which smaller structures or concepts are found in it)? | How is it similar or different from other theories about the same phenomenon? | |
| What it is related to (any other terms from the chapter)? | What it is similar to? | Is this theory generally accepted, or is there some controversy about the theories that explain this phenomenon? | |
| What it is distinguished from (what it isn't)? | What it is different from (what it isn't)? | | |
| A drawing, chart, mnemonic device, or other method you will use to help you remember it | A drawing, chart, mnemonic device, analogy, connection to something in your life, or other method you will use to help you remember it | | |

*Note.* This table shows different types of questions that students can ask (and answer) when they make study cards.

**Figure 5.4** Example of a study card: Constructivism.

***FRONT OF CARD***

Constructivism
Ch. 7, p. 423

***BACK OF CARD***

**EXPLAINS WHAT?**
How people learn.
**DEF:** Humans construct knowledge and meaning from experiences.
**EX:** We assimilate new info, then accommodate it by reframing our existing mental constructs; failure leads to learning
**WHO/WHEN:**
Piaget and others
**RELATED TO:**
Philosophies of education and learning
**IMPLICATIONS:**
Responsibility for learning resides with learner; instructor facilitates, provides guidelines, creates environment

**Figure 5.5** Example of a study card: Metacognition.

***FRONT OF CARD***

Metacognition
Ch. 5, p. 185

***BACK OF CARD***

**DEF:** Awareness/understanding of own thought process
**EX:** Planning, monitoring comprehension, assess performance
**WHAT IT DOES:**
Helps us perform cognitive tasks
**EFFECT ON LEARNING:**
Improvement, better self-awareness
**PART OF:**
Learning theory, memory, self-regulation
**ITS PARTS:**
Knowledge/awareness, regulation, experiences; involves planning, monitoring, and evaluating
**TYPES:**
Content knowledge, task knowledge, strategic knowledge

**Figure 5.6** Example of a study card: Blood typing.

***FRONT OF CARD***

Blood typing
Ch. 24, pp. 797–799

***BACK OF CARD***

**DEF:** Procedure used to determine which antigens are on red blood cells from donated blood, to prevent rejection of the blood.

**EX:** A+ blood will agglutinate when anti-A or Anti-Rh antibodies added. So patients with Anti-A or Anti-Rh cannot receive A+ blood.

**HOW IT WORKS:**
Presence of antigens determined by splitting donated blood samples into 3 test samples. Each is combined with one of the 3 antibodies specific for red blood cell antigens: Anti-A, Anti-B, Anti-Rh.
Positive agglutination means the antigen is present.

**INCREASES, WHAT IS EFFECT?**
More antigen on the surface of red blood cells, more agglutination

**DECREASES, WHAT IS EFFECT?**
Less agglutination

**PART OF:**
Clinical screening to determine compatibility of donated blood to recipient.
Also used in prenatal care to determine potential of an Rh mother (leads to lysis of Rh+ of fetus)

**ITS PARTS:**
Antibodies specific for red blood cell antigens and red blood cells with unknown antigens.

**SIMILAR TO:**
Tests used to determine presence of antibodies in blood; often used to determine if a patient is infected with known viruses. Also related to MHC typing (HLA) in organ transplants.

**DIFFERENT FROM:**
Not a method for determine antibodies present in a patient.
Only for red blood cells.

**Bright Idea**

You can ask students to turn in a few of their study cards as extra credit when they take their exam as an incentive for them to create cards as a study tool. Scan or photograph (with their permission) the best ones to show future students. **—Linda Russell**

## Reflection Activity

To encourage application of the concepts learned and personal reflection on learning, a written assignment called an insights-resources-application can be useful (Barkley & Major, 2016a). It has three parts: Students write about new insights they have gained, discuss resources they feel have been particularly helpful in the learning experience, and provide an example from their own life that is related to the readings or other materials. Often students are not expected to think about their learning, and yet reflection is an important part of deepening a learning experience and making it more meaningful. It also enhances the development of metacognitive strategies.

## Management of Activities in Class

Whether organizing students into groups or having them move to other parts of the room, activities require more classroom management than sitting and listening. Some faculty fear that activities take more time, and when faced with the other logistical aspects, they give up altogether. It is a matter of planning on your part to get students accustomed to your activities and ready to move in and out of them without much ado.

Hand out playing cards to put students into groups (e.g., all number threes in one group), or form base groups that are assigned for the semester. Put your instructions on different colored sheets of paper and group students according to the color of their instruction sheet. In large classes, it is sometimes easier for students to stay put and work with the students behind or in front of them.

Activities can also become noisier than many college faculty are ready for. The room may feel chaotic and messy. We strongly suggest using a signal to get students to turn their attention back to the large group or the instructor. Let them know before starting the activity that you are going to ring a bell, sound a tone, play a song using your phone, clap your hands or raise your hand, use an online timer projected on the screen, or something else. Caveat: Do not attempt to use your voice to bring your students back to order. You can harm your voice, and students long ago learned to ignore teachers who yell.

### *Time Management of Activities*

It is difficult to predict how long some activities will take. When you try an activity, write down how long it took, or any other suggestions to yourself about pacing, so you can improve the next time. Some faculty like to have a few longer activities and then a couple of shorter ones to fill in if there is time. Others keep a list of favorite activities along with the timing for each one.

Once you know the general amount of time that most of your students take to finish an activity, it is perfectly acceptable to set a time limit. If the activity is too open ended, students may not manage the task well. They can get bogged down on one question or just waste time. However, a challenge is that students work at different paces, so try to have an extra something that students can do if they finish before others. For example, if they are working on a practice quiz, suggest they try to write some of their own questions. If it is a discussion, try to add some extra questions to discuss if they finish early, such as, How does this connect to other learning in the class?

### *Resisters to Activities*

Sometimes students will react negatively to participating in learning activities. We suggest starting on day one with an activity to firmly demonstrate that this is how your class works. We believe telling students why you make various decisions about how class is conducted helps allay students' concerns about participating. Discussing some of the research on learning, sharing your own experiences or struggles with learning, and urging students to keep an open mind so they can learn more, and maybe in less time, are all ways to communicate your reasons for using activities.

You can also use classroom assessments to get feedback. For example, try one and one: one thing to keep and one thing to improve. Compile the findings and report back to your class. You can use this to show that different strategies work for different students, for example, "Five of you want to keep the skits and 12 of you want to remove them." You might also use assessments to increase some activities and decrease or improve others. Practice quizzes are a popular activity that students find very helpful.

## Grading or Assigning Points to Activities

We suggest awarding points for learning activities, but there are many ways to do this that will not increase your grading load very much at all. Most faculty use methods to award small point values on a 0 to 1 approach (e.g., 0 = absent or non-participating, 1 = acceptable). Even just a check mark that counts a certain amount will do. These points are essentially participation points, not actual assessments of the quality of the learning, but they impress on students the value of attending class.

College faculty show what we value when we attach points or a grade to an activity or a task. Students will be quick to call out an assignment as busy work if they see nothing in return. Although we wish all students would do our assignments and activities for the sheer joy of learning, we must acknowledge that many students don't. What we hope is that by getting students' buy-in for the activities because of the points, they will also discover they are learning more effectively, doing better on assessments, and perhaps even enjoying the active nature of the class.

For longer or more complex activities that are turned in, you can use rubrics, which are scoring guides that provide clear criteria for acceptable and exceptional work or clarify the line between unacceptable and acceptable work. Developing them takes time, but it usually speeds up the grading process. In addition, when students ask why they received a certain grade, it is easy to show them where they did well and where they still need improvements, because it is all right in the rubric. See chapter 8 for more on rubric design and samples of rubrics in Appendix E.

## Reflect on This Chapter

We provide ideas for many activities in this chapter, but you don't need to do them all. Choose a few, try them, and see how they go. For another collection of helpful tips, see McKeachie (2014), now in its 14th edition. As you consider your classes and methods of teaching, what changes in delivery do you plan to try first? What activities appeal to you right now? You will find that some of the classroom assessment techniques and learning assessment techniques are very easy and quick to try, and other activities require more planning and preparation on your part. Now that you have completed reading this chapter and thinking about the content as it applies to your work, please reflect on the following questions:

- What is a good day-one activity for your classes?
- Which advance organizers would work in your discipline or course?
- What kind of writing and talking would you like your students to do?

**Jot Your Thoughts**

## Action Checklist

Use Checklist 5.1 to apply the chapter content to your practice and help you identify the steps for implementing these ideas in your teaching.

**CHECKLIST 5.1** Developing Learning Activities and Techniques Action Checklist

| ✓ | **Activities** |
|---|---|
| ❑ | Selected a course opening icebreaker. |
| ❑ | Planned for advance organizers work in courses. |
| ❑ | Chose at least two active learning methods to try this semester. |
| ❑ | Selected a few classroom assessment techniques to integrate in courses. |
| ❑ | Identified high-engagement activities to integrate. |
| ❑ | Planned to use or expand discussions either face-to-face or online this semester. |
| ❑ | Aligned course activities with outcomes and assessments using the three-column table (Table 2.5). |

(*Continues*)

CHECKLIST 5.1 (*Continued*)

| ✓ | **Grading** |
| --- | --- |
| ❑ | Analyzed the point distribution for low- and high-stakes activities in my course. |

| ✓ | **Reducing Lecture Time** |
| --- | --- |
| ❑ | Reduced lecture time significantly by offering content in a more engaging way for student learning. |
| ❑ | Identified active learning opportunities for students to replace lecturing. |

| ✓ | **Managing Activities—Face-to-Face Classrooms** |
| --- | --- |
| ❑ | Selected a method of keeping time for activities. |
| ❑ | Communicated the signal for learners to complete small group discussions to return to a whole class summarization and move to the next activity or topic. |

# 6

# MAKING YOUR COURSE ACCESSIBLE

## Points to Ponder

Chapter 6 emphasizes the importance of, and strategies for, designing courses that are accessible for all learners. In thinking about designing the courses you teach, consider the following questions to examine your prior knowledge:

- What do you currently do to make your course accessible for your students who have learning challenges?
- What tips, resources, and information do you need to make courses more accessible?
- What campus resources do you know of that can assist you in understanding and implementing accessibility improvements?

Sara received an e-mail from the Accessibility Resource Center that states a student in her class needs to have tests read to her as an accommodation. Additionally, the e-mail states the student should receive 1.5 times the normal testing time. Also, on the previous night, one of Sara's students stayed after class and told her about his memory loss after a traumatic brain injury, so he asked if it was okay for him to record her class lectures. Sara could relate to the memory loss because she had an aunt with something similar, but having tests read aloud and longer test time? Is that fair and for real? To add to her confusion, just last week, her campus sent out a notice that all content posted online has to be accessible and 508 compliant. What is this accessibility and 508 compliance that campus staff keeps talking about?

After feeling ill equipped to understand the requests from the Accessibility Resource Center, Sara sought assistance and read books about diverse student populations and accessibility and spoke with colleagues about students with learning challenges. She visited the Accessibility Resource Center to learn more about the campus processes regarding accommodations. Her campus offered accessibility and learning challenge seminars so she could learn how to become better at identifying and working with these students in her classes. She also learned how to make her course materials accessible, which was much easier than she had expected. Sara found that working with all students, even the ones who challenge her, provided a rewarding opportunity. She learned more about them and something about herself too. Sara felt she became a better teacher by understanding the legal and ethical reasons campuses embrace all students.

## Creating an Inclusive Environment

We are all familiar with the kinds of accessibility features now common in building design, streets and sidewalks, home building, and the like. Referred to as universal design, its features include automatic door openers, lowered drinking fountains, curb ramps on sidewalks, and shower handles and paddle doors instead of round doorknobs, which are all examples of modifications to objects that allow physically disabled people to be more independent, full participants in society. We may be less familiar with the kinds of accessibility that we provide in educational institutions. According to the Center for Applied Special Technology (n.d.), universal design

> is a set of principles for curriculum development that give all individuals equal opportunities to learn. Universal Design for Learning (UDL) provides a blueprint for creating instructional goals, methods, materials, and assessments that work for everyone—not a single, one-size-fits-all solution but rather flexible approaches that can be customized and adjusted for individual needs.
>
> The UDL principles are based on the three-network model of learning that take into account the variability of all learners—including learners who were formerly relegated to "the margins" of our educational systems but now are recognized as part of the predictable spectrum of variation. These principles guide design of learning environments with a deep understanding and appreciation for individual variability. (paras. 2–3)

Universal design principles go beyond assisting students with accessibility challenges. They take into account the ability of course content to reach all students by broadening the perspectives to include diverse student populations with respect to ability, disability, age, reading level, learning style, native language, race, and ethnicity. In other words, universal design is really about creating an inclusive educational environment (Burgstahler, 2015; Tobin & Behling, 2018).

We generally think of meeting the needs of disabled students when we discuss accessibility. The Rehabilitation Act (1973) was the first government action for the civil rights of the disabled, and was the forerunner of the Americans with Disabilities Act (ADA; 1990). The Rehabilitation Act was the first attempt in the United States to formally create a level playing field with penalties for noncompliance.

Section 504 (1973) of the Rehabilitation Act provides educational accessibility for the K–12 and higher educational systems of the physical components of the institution and the classrooms (e.g., doors must have automatic openers and be wide enough for wheelchairs or other assistive equipment to pass through. Section 508 (1998) is an amendment to the Rehabilitation Act to address advances in technology. It states,

> Section 508 of the Rehabilitation Act of 1973 . . . as amended, mandates that Federal agencies "develop, procure, maintain, or use" information and communication technology in a manner that ensures Federal employees with disabilities have comparable access to, and use of, such information and data relative to other Federal employees, unless doing so would impose an undue burden. (Section 508, I.A.1, par. 1)

Even though this statute refers to federal employees with disabilities, it covers all institutions that receive any form of federal funding. This amendment then directs us to make software, hardware, websites, videos, and other information technology accessible. We can make our educational system accessible to disabled people by

- removing physical barriers;
- providing alternative methods for students to demonstrate their proficiency, such as having a test read to them or allowing extra time on tests;
- providing alternative communications, such as interpreters for hearing-impaired students;
- providing accessible materials, websites, or course shells so disabled students can use tools such as screen readers; and
- rethinking our curricular priorities to make sure our policies and requirements are actually pertinent to the learning outcomes of the course.

We cannot cover all aspects of accessibility in education in this chapter, so we focus on the role that faculty play in supporting disabled students by providing courses and content materials that are accessible and by providing appropriate accommodations for their learning.

## Understanding the Legal Terms

The U.S. Department of Education (2013) uses the following definition of *accessibility* in many of its resolution agreements with educational institutions:

> Accessible means a person with a disability is afforded the opportunity to acquire the same information, engage in the same interactions, and enjoy the same services as a person without a disability in an equally effective and equally integrated manner, with substantially equivalent ease of use. The person with a disability must be able

to obtain the information as fully, equally and independently as a person without a disability. (para. 3)

The ADA (1990) and the term *reasonable accommodation* provides the legal foundation for providing accessible learning environments, materials, and tools. The definition of *accessibility* is quite broad. The term *accommodation* in the educational context is the method used to make accomplishing educational tasks possible for a particular student. For example, to make your exams accessible, certain disabled students are allowed to take more time than your nondisabled students. Accommodations, "do not compromise the essential elements of a course or curriculum; nor do they weaken the academic standards or integrity of a course. Accommodations simply provide an alternative way to accomplish the course requirements by eliminating or reducing disability-related barriers" (American Psychological Association, 2019, para. 2).

## Knowing Your College's Services

Your institution should have an accessibility services office (often called *disability services*, but we prefer the less pejorative term *accessibility*). Find out how this office communicates with faculty about the needs of students and ask the staff the following:

- Will the office inform you about necessary accommodations for individual students?
- Will the student be the one who communicates the accommodations information?
- What kind of documentation is used or required by students to receive accommodations?

Students frequently inform us they need extra time on tests, a note taker, or extended deadlines without having an official document from the accessibility services office to verify the request. It is important to follow up on such requests to ensure you're offering accommodations to students who are recognized by the office.

## Understanding Student Needs

Having a deaf student in class will likely make you realize how often you turn away from students while you talk, such as talking while writing on the board. Until you have a sight impaired student, you may not be aware of the amount of visually important materials, videos, or websites, you use as learning materials. And until you have a student with a learning challenge, you may never understand why some students seem to understand everything clearly in class yet do poorly on written assignments and exams. Faculty certainly cannot be expected to know about every kind of learning challenge, but as you gain experience with a broad range of students, you will learn about the many kinds of barriers that affect people's lives. Many teaching techniques that you use, as well as materials you provide, can be made more accessible to all of your students but will be especially important for some of them.

Knowing how to work with students who are challenged by any of these conditions is difficult until you learn how to best reach them personally and academically. Also, keep in mind that having had a student with a certain condition doesn't mean you are prepared to work with another student who has the same condition. Taking into consideration all students' abilities to learn in the design of your course is a challenge as you develop the course and its content delivery. As you choose your learning activities and assessments, consider alternative ways to provide the same learning with an alternate plan. It is easier to work this into your design prior to the start of the course than it is to redesign your course once it has begun.

## Considerations for Teaching Accessible Courses

You are responsible for complying with the Rehabilitation Act (1973), Section 504 (1973), and Section 508 (1998), which pertains to course materials, presentation, websites, videos, course shells, and other learning methods and materials. That means you are required to make your Word documents, PowerPoint presentations, webpages, videos, spreadsheets, and PDFs accessible for students.

The good news for instructors is that creating accessible content requires minimal effort because of advancements in technology, which provide you with the opportunity to design instruction that maximizes ease of learning for all of your students. Many students, with and without learning challenges, benefit from accessible content. For example, deaf students aren't the only students who benefit from the use of closed captioning for videos. Students who are in places where they don't have the ability to use speakers or headphones use closed captioning while watching a video, along with students who may not understand the accent of the video presenter and may prefer to read the captioning. Some students may prefer to read content that is in the video. They may choose to read the material first so they better understand the content as they watch the video. Learners whose first language isn't English may also benefit by seeing and hearing the content of a video to verify their comprehension. By making the content accessible, you remove barriers for students and improve their course success and retention.

### *Print Materials*

Most faculty use Microsoft Word, Excel, PowerPoint, and PDFs to create course learning materials. Since 2010 Microsoft's Office Suite has had a built-in accessibility checker and information to help you make your documents more accessible. This checker will analyze your text, tables, and images and provide instructions on how to make changes to improve the content accessibility. Contact your information technology (IT) help desk or accessibility services office to assist you.

Creating structure for your document's content provides important information about how the content is organized and allows all users to efficiently navigate the document and fully use the content. You can establish the formatting style when creating a new document so that your application automatically uses that structure throughout the document. This is especially important for students who use a text-to-speech reader to help them access and learn from print material. The following areas can all be formatted correctly by using the accessibility checker:

- Styles
  - Styles are used for titles, headings, and subheadings and to add boldface or emphasize important text. When you use the styles tool instead of just selecting bold, someone using a screen reader can access your document because screen reader technology will interpret your title or heading for the reader who cannot see that it is bold.
  - Autoformatted bulleted and numerical list items are accessible.
  - A table of contents is automatically built from the styles you applied.
- Tables
  - Table headings and data cells are organized logically.
  - Tables have the header row assigned and checked for readability using an accessibility checker, such as is provided in the tools in Microsoft Word.
  - Alternative text (alt text or alt tag) is a descriptive phrase that explains the nature or contents of a table for those using a screen reader.
- Hyperlinks
  - Hyperlink names are meaningful and subject oriented. For example, instead of a "click here" link, name the page, such as "click for the Learning Center page."
  - Hyperlink URL addresses begin with http:// or https://.
- Images
  - All images need an alt tag that describes the image for those using a screen reader or are unable to view the image.

Using these practices while creating content makes the content visually attractive to learners and will help your visually impaired students who use a screen reader to understand documents, tables, and images.

We recommend starting with your syllabus in a Word document. Apply the suggestions from the accessibility checker to improve the formatting. If many items have to be corrected, it may be easier to recreate this document in a stylized format rather than using your current syllabus.

Structuring your documents to make the text, tables, and images accessible is your first step. The State of Minnesota's Information Technology Services Office of Accessibility offers a website to check your documents with the accessibility checker and add alt tags to your images and tables so when you save the document as a PDF, you will then also have an accessible PDF (Minnesota Information Technology Accessibility, n.d.). You can share the document electronically, online, or in any learning management system (LMS) so your students can interact with the documents that are accessible using a screen reader, for example. The site also has instructions and a tutorial so you can learn more about creating accessible materials. Many other websites, such as WebAIM (n.d.), also provide this training information.

### *Course Shells and Websites*

Many LMSs are designed with accessibility in mind; however, it is up to you to make certain the course content is also accessible. If you provide links to websites, you can check if they are accessible by using the free accessibility checker from WebAIM (n.d.). A number of resources are available to assist you in thinking through the design of an online course from an accessibility perspective (Coombs, 2010; Nilson & Goodson, 2017; Seale, 2014).

### *Videos*

Videos to welcome students or complement course content need to be captioned for compliance with Section 508 (1973) and Section 508 (1998) so all your students can interact with and learn from your videos. Simply attaching a written transcript of the video text does not fully comply with the legal requirements. Software applications today provide an easier way to create closed captioning for videos.

> **Bright Idea**
>
> One way to create captions is to write a script for your videos and then add it to your video captions. —**Karen LaPlant**

Captioned videos provide access to content for students with auditory processing challenges and help students whose first language isn't English and benefit from hearing and seeing the content. Learners accessing information in public spaces who can't play the audio are able to read the video content. Adding captions to the video ensures that all your students can readily access the course content. For example, an Internet search of captioning service providers will give you available resources for integrating captions into your course materials. We recommend several captioning services in the Additional Reading and Resources section (p. 315, this volume).

Adding video captioning is possible using YouTube, which includes instructions in the Video Manager tool. We suggest checking to see if your campus or department has its own YouTube channel, or create one of your own. Listing your videos as private means they are not searchable by outside audiences, and you can also disable the function to receive comments.

Accuracy in such things as language, grammar, and spelling is very important in captioning. A rule of thumb many experts use is 99% accuracy, which leaves very little room for error.

According to the Federal Communications Commission (2018), captions should meet the following criteria:

- Accurate: Captions must match the spoken words in the dialogue and convey background noises and other sounds to the fullest extent possible.
- Synchronous: Captions must coincide with their corresponding spoken words and sounds to the greatest extent possible and must be displayed on the screen at a speed that can be read by viewers.
- Complete: Captions must run from the beginning to the end of the program to the fullest extent possible.
- Properly placed: Captions should not block other important visual content on the screen, overlap one another or run off the edge of the video screen. (para. 2)

Automatic caption creators on various video streaming sites generally do not meet the high accuracy rate for captioning. The actual language is often inaccurate with little to no attention to proper spelling, grammar, music, or noise notifications; hence, you will most likely need to edit the captioning. Editing the captions can take as much or more time than creating accurate captions yourself. This is why we recommend writing a script for your video to use to record your presentation and for captioning.

**Bright Idea**

You may want students to watch a video or lecture before they arrive in class so they have prerequisite knowledge for a planned lab or activity. The flipped classroom approach allows students to pause and rewind pieces of the lecture or video they might have missed the first time and puts less pressure on students who need more time to process the information than a class session typically allows. —**Zala Fashant**

## Teaching Students to Make Documents Accessible

As faculty, it is our responsibility to remove learning barriers from course content and documents, and our students need to know how to do this as well. You may have students creating spreadsheets, working in groups, sharing documents to gather feedback, and presenting final projects for classmates to critique. All these documents need to be accessible to all their peers. Knowing how to do so is a marketable skill your students will take with them into the workplace. Consider including tip sheets in your course resources and make checking for accessibility part of your assignment rubric.

**Jot Your Thoughts**

## Policies and Pedagogical Considerations

One aspect of curricular accessibility is examining your course policies and your teaching philosophy. We often have assumptions about what normal college expectations are, and these assumptions are based on our own learning experiences in higher education. We have become comfortable with the 50-item and 50-minute multiple-choice exam, the notion that students must take their own lecture notes, and the idea of firm deadlines on student work. How are all these practices actually related to or support learning in our courses? Is it absolutely necessary to be able to take a test in 50 minutes? Does it really matter who takes lecture notes? Semesters end, so deadlines eventually play a role, but do we need to be rigid in how we think about acceptable time frames for students to complete projects, homework, or exams?

Timed tests or other in-class work is especially challenging for many students for many reasons. Think about the role of time. What message does it send about learning and thinking to have a rigid, short time frame for exams? In online testing, short time limits have been part of the solution for Internet cheating, but is there some other way to limit searching the Internet for test answers? In face-to-face classes, the notion of one minute per question is quite arbitrary. You can shorten tests or give them more frequently, create take-home tests, or offer online tests as an alternative to in-class tests, all of which can be helpful for all students, not just disabled ones.

Recording class presentations and lectures is another way to make your class accessible to the person who is absent that day, the student with learning challenges who takes notes very slowly, or the hearing-impaired student who reads your script of the recording. Posting lecture notes online also assists students who are struggling with the content so they can verify their notes are accurate, and it helps those who need more time on the material and those who have difficulty taking notes.

Having some kind of deadline for submitted work is a fact of life, although in education we are often far stricter about it than in most workplaces. How often are you penalized for finishing a project late? Deadlines can be flexible in almost any situation. There are excellent reasons to have firm deadlines, such as students showing their incremental progress and having time to practice their skills over time as opposed to doing everything at once. There are good reasons for faculty too; you want to pace yourself with grading, you don't want to hand back quizzes if several students have not taken them yet, and you certainly don't want to run into a time crunch at the end of the semester when you have a grades-due deadline looming. On the other hand, you might provide a window of time for work to be submitted. Students might wait until the last second, but they would still have the advantage of flexibility if the task reasonably could be finished by the beginning of that window, and the students who need more time would have it.

Offering choices for some of the student work is another way to provide accessibility. If an oral presentation to the class or just to you would fulfill the learning outcomes of a writing assignment, could it be an alternative for interested students? Criteria would need to be the same for all demonstrations of learning. However, if the class is a writing class, then writing is essential to the outcomes of the course, so an oral presentation would not be appropriate.

Ask yourself the following questions:

- Do my policies and practices actually relate to my learning outcomes?
- Is time a significant pedagogical factor?
- What are the student behaviors, time lines, and work that are essential to the course?

When we have clear pedagogical reasons for our policies and practices, it becomes much easier to determine how to modify a task for accommodations, as well as how to rethink aspects of the task to make it more accessible for everyone. For example, giving students some element of choice can promote an inclusive, respectful learning environment for all. We recommend discussing how the organizations who hire your students work with these challenges. Matching your expectations to their expectations would help students make the transition from school to work.

## Accessibility Technologies

A variety of technologies helps students interact with your content. It is important for you to be aware of the most common technologies students will use, and perhaps you would enjoy using some of these technologies to speed up writing and reading time by transferring speech to text or text to speech. Your campus may have site licenses for some of these technologies.

Text-to-speech technology for your printed material, speech-to-text capabilities, and screen readers provide accessible interaction with content and meet the needs of each student. Table 6.1 provides a comparison of options for interacting with your content and offer accessibility and a more personalized learning experience.

## Interacting With Students With Disabilities

At the beginning of the chapter we discussed the inexperience most of us have in working with students who may have a variety of learning, psychological, or physical

**TABLE 6.1**
**Text-to-Speech Technologies**

| *Software Application* | *Purpose* |
|---|---|
| Dragon Naturally Speaking (Nuance.com) | Speech to text, also is used by mobility-restricted individuals to navigate websites |
| ReadSpeaker (Readspeaker.com) | Online and offline text-to-speech solutions for websites, mobile apps, e-books, e-learning, and so on |
| Jaws (Job Access With Speech; Freedom Scientific.com) | Screen reader for computer users whose vision loss prevents them from seeing screen content or who need to use control keys versus the mouse to use a computer |
| Read & Write Gold or Texthelp (Texthelp.com) | For students who prefer to listen to their documents, Web pages, or PDFs instead of *reading* or anyone who needs a little help with *reading* and *writing* |

*Note.* This table describes four text-to-speech technologies that are available to enable students to have material (online and offline) read aloud.

challenges. We also need to consider the biases we have regarding people who have challenges we don't understand. It is critical to separate the challenge from the person as we gain a deeper understanding of how we can best work with individual students. Opening our minds and becoming aware of our biases and reactions is a first step.

You may be curious about the nature of a student's disability when approached with an accommodation request. Be aware that it is up to the student to disclose or not disclose the details of a disability. The accommodation request will not identify it; it will simply state the accommodation, such as extended test time. The most appropriate and respectful question you can ask a student is, How do you think your disability will affect your learning in this class? The student might know the answer and have good suggestions based on successful strategies that other faculty have provided or may not if your course is in an unfamiliar area. In that event, you and the student might check in with each other periodically to see how things are going.

## Your Course's Accessibility

Throughout this chapter we discuss a variety of ways to meet the needs of all your students. Accessibility isn't about just making accommodations for one or two students who may have learning challenges. Everyone has at least occasional learning challenges, and although these practices may help some specific students, they are generally helpful for a majority of students. Implementing these practices in your course design and adding them to existing courses can help you retain students and provide an environment that offers a greater opportunity for success.

## Reflect on This Chapter

Now that you have completed reading this chapter and thinking about the content as it applies to your work, please reflect on the following questions:

- How do you currently handle requests for accommodations, and who is the campus person to contact for more information?
- How can you select your curriculum content and instructional strategies to maximize learning for all students?
- Which accessibility strategies will you integrate into your course design?
- What steps do you need to take to make your course more accessible?

**Jot Your Thoughts**

## Action Checklist

Use Checklist 6.1 to apply the chapter content to your practice and help you identify the steps for implementing these ideas in your teaching.

**CHECKLIST 6.1** Making Your Course Accessible Action Checklist

| ✓ | **Legal Understanding and Defining Terms** |
|---|---|
| ❑ | Downloaded or bookmarked the ADA compliance information. |
| ❑ | Developed an understanding of what *accessibility* means. |
| ❑ | Realized the need to make accommodations for learners. |
| ❑ | Contacted the accessibility services staff on campus to learn how they can help with students who need accommodations. |
| ❑ | Identified campus staff who can assist in making course materials accessible. |
| ❑ | Identified campus staff who can help with universal design and facility accommodations for learning and access. |

| ✓ | **Providing Accommodations** |
|---|---|
| ❑ | Designed classroom to help students who need physical accommodations: adjustable seating, work spaces, ramps, lighting, and so on. |
| ❑ | Analyzed changes to provide pedagogical accessibility. |

(*Continues*)

**CHECKLIST 6.1** (*Continued*)

| | |
|---|---|
| ❑ | Eliminated course timed tests unless required by industry standards. |
| ❑ | Provided a process for students to submit late assignments. |
| ❑ | Developed instructions to teach students to make documents accessible. |
| ❑ | Recorded course content (audio or video) with captioning. |
| ❑ | Identified the tools in the LMS to provide accessible content. |

| ✓ | **Making Printed Materials Accessible** |
|---|---|
| ❑ | Found the Check Accessibility tool in Microsoft Office applications. |
| ❑ | Checked course documents for the proper use of styles. |
| ❑ | Checked document table headings and data cells are organized logically and header rows are assigned. |
| ❑ | Ensured hyperlink names are meaningful (subject oriented). |
| ❑ | Eliminated the use of "click here" that won't identify the address for a screen reader and used URL instead. |
| ❑ | Started all URL addresses with http:// or https://. |
| ❑ | Labeled images with subject-oriented alt tag (e.g., 2018 Ford F-150) or labeled *decorative* if appropriate. |

| ✓ | **Making Video Materials Accessible** |
|---|---|
| ❑ | Created and posted written scripts for videos to assist learners, realizing this is not fully compliant for some students. |
| ❑ | Identified campus resources to help make closed-captioned videos. |
| ❑ | Verified all course videos are closed captioned including self-created, YouTube, and vendor videos. |
| ❑ | Researched text-to-speech and speech-to-text software opportunities and identified campus staff to offer recommendations or information on access to this software. |

# 7

# INTEGRATING LEARNING TECHNOLOGIES

## Points to Ponder

Chapter 7 examines the planning and pedagogical considerations needed to integrate learning technologies in course design. In thinking about designing the courses you teach, consider the following questions to examine your prior knowledge:

- What technology do you currently use in delivering your course?
- What experiences have you had with integrating technologies? Do you consider yourself a novice, an intermediate user, or an expert? What are your biases about using technology?
- How could course technology provide opportunities to enhance interactions, engagement, and encourage collaboration?

**Jot Your Thoughts**

At a workshop conducted by a local publishing company, Rashida ended up leaving with so many ideas of new things to try in her course that she was a bit overwhelmed. When she returned to campus, she spoke to a colleague who offered some sage advice: "Just think of one item that is troubling you the most in your courses, and instead of trying to use all the ideas at once, focus on the one area that would make the biggest difference first. Then perhaps consider some of the others."

Rashida chose an issue she was facing in the computer lab: getting students to pay attention when she needed to show them something. Too often she struggled to gain control of 25 to 30 students in a classroom with computers as they were checking their e-mails and social media sites. At the workshop, she was introduced to software that could solve this challenge.

With the software downloaded on the computers in the lab, Rashida could freeze the students' computer screens and display the information she wanted them to see as their only option. She could also select an individual student's screen and share information with just that student. It seemed like a great way to get a student's attention and individualize instruction. Rashida tested the application in the computer lab before class and confirmed that it did what she wanted it to do. When the students entered the class, they noticed the difference the computer screen immediately. Instead of checking e-mail and surfing the Internet, their only option was viewing Rashida's presentation. She finally had the students' attention as she started class. She was happy that she had seen this classroom management software because it gave her control over what students could see during hands-on learning activities. Rashida could now monitor and interact with students individually in a controlled setting. Her students were now more engaged as they focused on the content.

## Assessing the Need for Technology in Your Course

Technological toys are so tempting. Many of us have hopes and dreams of what new technologies would do to improve our lives. Today students have access to information like never before. Faculty have greater opportunities to connect students with this information and harness the power of such a large network of communication at their fingertips. Familiarizing yourself with your campus and the technologies you and your students have access to is crucial when learning about technology for your classroom. No matter the delivery mode, classroom, blended, or online, you can integrate the resources necessary to develop more interactive lessons into your teaching practice and formulate your technology learning plan for each of your courses. We say each of your courses, because technology plans aren't one size fits all. What works for one may not meet your needs in your other courses or those of your colleagues. Often, course technology is scaffolded much like content and skill development. Classroom management software tends to work more broadly across courses.

At educational and technology conferences we see all kinds of exciting, great technologies to use. Thinking you have to use all the latest whiz-bang techniques, you end up going back to campus overwhelmed, not knowing where to start.

Much like course design, your technology integration needs to start with (a) outcomes, what you want your students to do; (b) assessment, how you know they are doing what you want them to do and that the technology is working the way you want it to; and (c) analyzing the software applications that will make the learning activities engaging. The questions you should ask yourself as you assess your course's technology needs include the following:

- What student learning needs will technology meet?
- What can't I do now that technology will allow me to do?
- How can technology help me better relay information to my students?
- Will the technology improve the quality of my course?
- What technology will my students use in the workplace?

Without examining the answers to these questions it is easy to think that you should use technology to solve problems that don't exist or fill students' time with activities that don't improve the learning experience. Since each learning activity uses valuable course time, choosing the proper technology is critical. Using technology just to have technology in your course isn't necessary. Integrating technology by weaving it into the course work intentionally leads to significant learning. Also with the cost of implementing technology into a course, not to mention the potential cost to students, you need to be sure that the return in meeting outcomes is a worthwhile investment.

Most of our institutions have already invested in a course learning management system (LMS) that may come with a robust set of technological tools that can help your students be successful in the course. How familiar are you with all the LMS tools you currently have? Be careful not to invest in new applications that duplicate what you can already do. Also, are you currently using these tools to manage your course? See chapter 3 for more about using specific LMS tools.

## Good Reasons to Implement Technology

It is important to not get caught up in the notion of absolutely having to use this technology in your course. As the instructor you must analyze the reason behind implementing technology. The first part of your analysis should be examining the course outcomes. If adding technology to your course will help students meet the learning outcomes better, then you have a case for implementation. The following are good reasons to integrate technology into your course:

- The technology will give students better practice, methods, or access to information or experiences that will help them master the learning outcomes better than they do now.
- Students need to work with the technology found in the workplace that you are preparing them to enter.
- Students should learn, or remain current with, widely used technological innovations.
- Active learning and student retention and engagement are priorities, and certain technology stands to improve them.

Technology shouldn't be the tail wagging the dog. If you must change your course content to fit the technology, then you need to reexamine why you are using the technology. In addition, the technology needs to blend into what you want students to demonstrate. New technology often needs to be taught to students. You can't assume they will just adapt to an unfamiliar technology; some will and some will not. Unless demonstrating the use of the technology itself is a course outcome, students need to be comfortable using the technology to better master the content outcomes. Otherwise, you will not be sure if your assessment is measuring a lack of content mastery or identifying difficulty in using the learning technology.

## Identifying Your Classroom's Current Technology Tools

Some faculty arrive in the classroom 10 to 15 minutes before the start of class, turn on the computer, activate the projector, plug in adapters, open a PowerPoint presentation, and begin to discuss a topic. But what if the classroom is set up differently from what you are accustomed or is new to you? What do you need to be aware of to have a more successful teaching and learning experience? Do you know whom to contact if you need assistance? If you can get to your classroom several days or weeks prior to teaching, you can begin to explore what you have on your computer and the student computers.

In reality, getting the technology you need for the classroom begins long before you step into the classroom to begin working with students. If you can't get to the classroom before you teach, contact a person in information technology (IT) who can let you know what software and hardware you will have access to at the teaching station. If you plan on the students using computers, find out what your options are for scheduling classroom labs or a set of laptops. Keep in mind that IT departments may need a few weeks to process your request for software installation. Campus room schedulers may need the same amount of time to change your class's meeting place to a computer lab.

## Communicating Your Course's Technology Requirements

As you are designing your course, developing your syllabus, and reviewing your textbook, make a list of the technologies you will need so you can communicate the requirements to your students using the course shell and syllabus. Explain how the technology will deliver the best learning activities to meet your course outcomes or how students will use the technology in the workplace. Industry-standard technology may be expensive, but your students must become proficient in it to find employment. You may be able to convince some of your business and industry partners to donate software for use in your program.

Your textbook selection may also have technology, such as downloaded programs or cloud-hosted software. If you need software installed on your computer, on the teacher station in classrooms, or on student lab computers, contact your IT department well in advance. Some campuses send out notices each year to determine what software programs need to be on campus computers. Other campuses only add programs when you request it and sometimes it involves a cost, so your dean or supervisor needs to budget for this technology.

Consider the following questions to identify the requirements your course will need as you develop your technology plan:

- How many types of devices will this technology work on, such as a computer, phone, or tablet?
- Do all your students have access to devices to use the technology?

- How will your students access the software off campus? For online-only students, is there assistance in downloading and installing? How will they access the software, and what is the cost to students? Failing to make sure students can access software can frustrate students. Ask your IT department if the campus help desk will be able to support your students.
- Will you have a computer lab available to introduce students to the software? Is the Wi-Fi capability fast enough in your classroom or students homes if they are not in a lab? Is there a website portal for students to use instead of downloading materials?
- What are the requirements for personal computers that your students will need to complete assignments outside class?

Technology expectations and specifications should be listed in the course description if possible, so your students will see what is needed when they register, and they should definitely be in your syllabus. Although the general consensus is that today's students are all computer or device savvy, just because they are using apps on their phones doesn't mean they know much more about computers than the apps they are using. Many have very limited knowledge when it comes to educational technology use. Your technology plan should

- clearly communicate hardware requirements;
- ensure the software will work on a personal computer, Mac, tablet, cell phone, or all these devices;
- name the operating system and version they need to have on their computers;
- display a system test provided by the software company or your campus IT department, if possible, so students can check that their system is up to date; and
- include a resource guide for students to access help if they have questions or problems.

**Bright Idea**

Remember that usually you are not permitted to download software onto classroom computers, so planning ahead is essential. If you discover a new technology you wish to use with your students, you will need to request to have it installed; your campus may not even allow midsemester software changes. IT departments have a work schedule, and your installation will need to be in the queue. —**Karen LaPlant**

## Technology Template

We developed a technology planning table you can use to begin to identify and understand exactly what technology will be needed for your classes. Include the hardware, computer specifications, and software you require. List the classes that will need these items and any other special requirements. Do this even if the only technology is Office 365 so that you remain aware of the needs. Always include this in your syllabus and other materials so that students know what they will need. Table 7.1 provides an example to begin your technology list for all your classes.

Ask your IT department staff the following:

- What are the specifications of the classroom computers?
- Can faculty save content on the computer itself to use again in a future class session?
- Can faculty have a network or cloud drive to save content that is accessible off campus?
- When is the computer hard drive reimaged? (A school may wipe out all the saved information on a computer to reformat it; typically once per semester.)
- Does IT send a warning before it reimages the classroom computers? (This is important if you have saved PowerPoint presentations or other materials. If the computer is reimaged and you don't have a backup, you must spend additional time downloading the materials again.)
- How do you request software or hardware for the classroom? What is the time frame for acquiring and what is the cost of adding software?

**Jot Your Thoughts**

## Fighting the Technology Monsters

You and your students may be from different generations and have very different approaches to technology. In general, younger students are assumed to be *digital natives* (Prensky, 2001). They have been exposed to sophisticated hardware, software, and apps for most of their lives. They are native speakers of the technical lingo and know all the varied uses of cell phones or other types of technology. You may find that these students

- like stimulation and have a game-based mentality,
- prefer to be active and may have a short attention span,
- want immediate gratification and feedback,
- feel entitled to rewards such as participation trophies or an easy A, and
- focus on their practical and immediate needs versus long-term learning.

TABLE 7.1
**Course Technology Plan**

| *Needs* | *Installation* | *Courses* | *Other* |
|---|---|---|---|
| **Hardware Needed**<br>❑ PC<br>❑ Mac<br>❑ Either PC or Mac<br>❑ Printer access<br>❑ Printer name<br>❑ Printer location<br>❑ Permissions or code | ❑ IT staff<br>❑ Yourself<br>❑ Faculty<br>❑ Other | ❑ Needed for all courses<br>❑ Needed for individual courses:<br>❑<br>❑<br>❑<br>❑ | ❑ Cost and budget<br>❑ Approvals<br>❑ Communication<br>❑<br>❑ |
| **Computer Specifications**<br>❑ OS: Windows 10<br>❑ Mac iOS 11<br>❑ Other | ❑ IT staff<br>❑ Yourself<br>❑ Other | ❑ Needed for all courses<br>❑ Needed for individual courses:<br>❑<br>❑<br>❑ | ❑ Cost and budget<br>❑ Approvals<br>❑ Communication<br>❑<br>❑ |
| **Software Needed**<br>❑ MS Office 2013<br>❑ Office 365<br>❑ Adobe Professional<br>❑ Accounting<br>❑ Java<br>❑ Python<br>❑ Other | ❑ IT staff<br>❑ Yourself<br>❑ Faculty<br>❑ Other | ❑ Needed for all courses<br>❑ Needed for individual courses:<br>❑<br>❑<br>❑<br>❑ | ❑ Cost and budget<br>❑ Approvals<br>❑ Communication<br>❑<br>❑ |

*Note.* IT = information technology; MS = Microsoft. This table provides a sample of course technology considerations.

You may feel you are competing with technology for the engagement of your students. Some students may race ahead and ask questions before you are ready to address them. Other students may be using the technology differently from how you had hoped, or they may not understand how you intend for them to use it. Faculty may feel pressured to be experts on every aspect of technology used in the course, but in reality, your students may be more familiar with some of the technologies than you are, so use their knowledge to your advantage. Ask students who are savvy to help students who need some mentoring; this is an excellent way to acknowledge prior knowledge and experience.

Students arrive in class with smartphones, tablets, or laptops that they are eager to use, but you will need to show them how to use these items in an educational context. Rather than banning cell phones from the classroom, you can find ways the students with smartphones can use the technology to learn. Get students involved with interactive tools that harness the power of their smartphone. Polling apps are ways for students to team up to discuss class content and select the answer they have agreed is correct. The results can be displayed anonymously on an overhead screen in the classroom, perhaps in the course shell, or on an app for online students. The results are great ways to promote further discussion and analyze a variety of perspectives. Many online courses use a polling tool in the LMS to provide the same experience (see Table 7.2 for specific third-party apps.).

Technology is great when it works, but it can fail us, or we can fail to use it correctly. When failure happens, you must handle the ups and downs by implementing

**TABLE 7.2**
**Collaborative, Organized, Online, Learning (COOL)**

| *Collaboration* | | |
|---|---|---|
| *App or Software* | *Location or URL* | *Use* |
| Facetime | www.apple.com | Video conferencing for meetings with iPhone, Mac, iPad |
| Facebook Groups | www.facebook.com/groups | Private classroom group and student study groups |
| Google Classroom | classroom.google.com/u/0/h | Collaborative workspace |
| Kahoot | kahoot.com | Games and polling |
| LinkedIn | www.linkedin.com | Professional networking |
| Office 365 | www.office.com | Creating documents and presentations |
| Office Lens for iPhone and iPad iPhone or iPad app | iPhone or iPad app | Using camera to document and capture screenshots and whiteboard material |
| OneDrive | www.office.com | Share documents and archive |
| Screencast-O-Matic | screencast-o-matic.com | Screen capture tool |
| Skype | https://education.microsoft.com/skype-in-the-classroom/overview | Web conferencing |
| Socrative | www.socrative.com | Quiz creation and collaboration |
| Trello | trello.com | Shared content and project management |
| Twitter | twitter.com | Short messaging |

| *Organized* | | |
|---|---|---|
| *App or Software* | *Location or URL* | *Use* |
| Basecamp | basecamp.com | Share documents and archive |
| One Drive | www.office.com | Share documents and archive |
| Trello | trello.com | Shared content and project management |

(*Continues*)

**Table 7.2** (*Continued*)

| *Online* | | |
|---|---|---|
| *App or Software* | *Location or URL* | *Use* |
| Adobe Connect | www.adobe.com/products/adobeconnect.html | Web conferencing for projects and online office hours |
| Apple Apps | www.apple.com/ios/app-store | Variety of apps for course integration |
| Google Chrome Extensions<br>• Grammarly<br>• SoapBox<br>• ReadSpeaker Translate | www.google.com/extensions | Grammar checks, text-to-speech, video recording, translation |
| Microsoft App Store | Launches from Microsoft Word, Excel | Variety of apps for course integration |
| Microsoft Education Center | www.microsoft.com/en-us/education | Training opportunities |
| Respondus Lock-down Browser | www.respondus.com/products/lockdown-browser | Locks down a student's browser during online testing |
| Zoom | www.zoom.us | Web conferencing and online office hours for advising |

| *Learning* | | |
|---|---|---|
| *App or Software* | *Location or URL* | *Use* |
| Dragon Dictation | www.nuance.com/dragon.html | Speech-to-text recognition, dictation, and transcription |
| GCF Learning | edu.gcfglobal.org/en | Student learning tutorials |
| Google Docs & Sheets | www.google.com/docs/about | Tutorials |
| Hoonuit | www.hoonuit.com/home | Study guides and tutorials, formerly Atomic Learning |
| Lynda.com | www.lynda.com | Student research and technical training<br>Check your campus or local library system for a free membership |
| Jing | www.techsmith.com/jing-tool.html | Screen capture |
| Kahn Academy | www.khanacademy.org | Student learning tutorials |
| Merlot | www.merlot.org | Curated open education resource materials and content creation tools |
| Office 365 Forms | forms.office.com | Education forms and surveys |

(*Continues*)

**Table 7.2** (*Continued*)

| *Learning* | | |
|---|---|---|
| *App or Software* | *Location or URL* | *Use* |
| Open Text Library | open.umn.edu/opentextbooks | Peer-reviewed, free, openly licensed textbooks |
| Respondus Test Bank Network | www.respondus.com/products/testbank/index.shtml | Generates tests within your LMS constructed from banks of possible questions |
| Saylor | www.saylor.org | Open-source textbooks and courses |
| Udemy | www.udemy.com | Accessibility standards and training, includes a website accessibility evaluation (WAVE) tool |

*Note.* This table provides suggested options for course technology integration.

a back-up plan. When technology isn't working the way you want it to, and you can use the savviness and problem-solving skills of those experienced students, do the following:

- Have students test several similar technologies for you. Let them know ahead of time that they are the testers and will be the experts; in this way, the students feel like their input matters and are more engaged. Former students may also enjoy critiquing technology you are considering. They know what you expect and can compare the new technology to the way they learned.
- Talk to your students and use a technological snag as a way to regroup and teach the critical thinking skills you have embedded in your course. Students want to know what and how content relates to their next course or their career, and this can lead to their love of learning. Take advantage of this by showing the importance of testing technology that is being used in the field, and use your failure as a teaching moment. Say things like, "This happens at work, and it could cost you, so we can fail here without costing the company anything."
- Show them you have planned for challenges and are teaching them resilience skills: admit-accept-revise-move on. Admit the issue, list resolutions, accept that things will be different, and move on, but talk about resiliency and the ability to adapt and change gracefully. Students should learn to be comfortable with mistakes and fix them rather than worrying or panicking. Use this situation as a teachable moment. Chapter 4 discusses encouraging students to develop a growth mind-set; this is a good time to model it. You are a learner too, and you can show them that mistakes lead to learning.
- Remind students that failure is a part of learning. Many past innovations succeeded only as a result of a myriad of failures or by accident. We don't learn

by success alone. We often learn more by analyzing failures, and this type of learning makes you more successful in the future.

## Reimagine the Use of Technology

Imagine teaching the same way every day as if there were only one way of learning. You may eventually get bored, and the same thing happens for students. Variety makes learning more interesting. Technology can make a repetitive teaching task easier, or it can shorten a time-consuming task. Consider how technology might work for you in teaching; for example, what tasks in teaching bog you down? Some faculty have said that following up with students about calendar reminders, due dates, and missing assignments fills up teaching time and takes away from providing feedback on student work, which produces significant learning. Tools in your LMS can help you automate the reminders and provide ways to offer rich individual feedback in an efficient manner (see chapter 3).

How can you help your students succeed by designing technology-supported learning activities in your course? Sometimes you will teach in less than optimally designed classrooms. Perhaps students have to follow your PowerPoint presentation from the back of a large classroom, a situation that is less conducive to engaged learning and accessible learning for all students. Request to teach in a computer lab to share your presentation on the students' computer screens so they can see it right in front of them. Some classroom management systems offer students the opportunity to watch your PowerPoint presentation or software demonstration on their own computer or on large overhead screens. Students may learn better with the material directly in front of them rather than looking up at the screen at the front of the room. You can also see what they are viewing at your teaching station, which helps you monitor their attention and progress. When you want to demonstrate something for the entire class, these classroom management software solutions allow you to freeze students' screens, remove access to Internet searching, and focus their eyes on what you are doing.

Another way to reimagine the classroom is to have students view media or read print materials before class, either to demonstrate an essential task or provide background information, often referred to as flipping the classroom (Bergmann & Sams, 2012). You can create videos or link to existing videos available on sites such as YouTube or on your textbook publisher's website. Posting videos or their links in the course shell is a great option for introducing material and reinforcing previously learned content; plus, the videos can be watched multiple times. This allows you to spend precious class time engaged in more hands-on practice activities, and students can always reinforce their learning by watching the video again.

You can search for videos on YouTube, get them from your textbook publisher, find an open source site, or create your own. Videos that are no more than 15 minutes provide targeted learning, and the chances of your students watching them will be greater. Providing an outline that contains the timestamp (the minutes and seconds) in a video where a concept is discussed helps students review the material. Some LMSs record the amount of time your students are logged into the video learning module, which can tell you which students watched it.

**Bright Idea**

Knowing how many of your students have watched a video gives you an opportunity to send an automated message or e-mail through your LMS to remind those students who have not logged into the video to watch it. —**Karen LaPlant**

## Integrating Video Content

It is easier than ever before to search for video content online. Sites like YouTube, TED Talks, and even publishing company websites have material available to use. When assigning a video as required or optional material, it is essential for instructors to watch the entire video prior to using it in the course to be sure the content is suitable for the students' skill levels. It also needs to comply with accessibility standards. Many times videos include content not discussed in class, which causes confusion and prompts questions from students.

There are a variety of tools available for you to make your own videos. Your IT department will know what licenses your institution has for creating and editing videos. If there are none, many apps and software programs are available, several of which are in Table 7.2. Web browsers such as Google Chrome provide extensions that allow screen and video recording. Creating your own videos helps you customize your content. After you create your video, you can upload it to YouTube and set it as unlisted so only your students can view it once you give them the link. Screen capture and video editing software, such as Camtasia (or for a free open source alternative, CamStudio), is widely available. Keep your video content to five- to seven-minute clips so that your students are able to access and watch on a variety of devices using varying Wi-Fi connections (Brame, 2015). Type transcripts of what you say in the video and provide the text for students in the course shell. Some apps provide automated captions and are accessibility compliant (see chapter 6).

## Integrating Apps and Social Media

Choosing effective apps and social media can increase student engagement and may improve learning experiences. In Table 7.2 we use the acronym COOL (collaborative, organized, online, learning) for a few suggestions for technologies and their purposes to improve the mastery of learning outcomes, which contains a list of apps for each technology type. To be included, a technology app must be engaging and fulfill a real need for the learning environment. The apps we have listed follow our guidelines of being easy to use, well established, commonly used, secure—with few or no privacy issues—and engaging.

A variety of software apps are available for Web-based platforms and devices such as iPads. Applying these learning technologies to course outcomes can be done using Carrington's (2015) padagogy wheel.

### *Collaboration, Sharing, and Publishing*

Connecting to social media is a way to link your course to broader content. Following content-oriented groups or individual experts on Facebook or Twitter is a relatively simple technique. For example, showing business students how to connect with companies or other social movements online helps students learn about their professional communities and keep up with the weekly challenges. Assigning discussions in your course shell is a best practice to get students talking about issues in their future profession.

Bringing experts into the classroom no longer requires a personal visit with easy-to-use Web conferencing software such as Skype, Adobe Connect, WebEx, Zoom, or other technologies like Facebook Live, Google Hangouts, or even FaceTime. Students can develop a set of questions collaboratively and have a live question-and-answer session with an expert. We also suggest recording these sessions, with the guest's permission, to post in your course for future use. Building a library of these experts allows students to individualize or enhance their learning by choosing a session from a field they are interested in or to learn from someone on topics they are not as familiar with.

Group work and project management is possible remotely with the use of collaboration software. Researching information and simultaneously taking notes using a shared technology can help groups work together in the classroom and online by Web conferencing. Students can also work on their own to complete a shared document during the week asynchronously. Options like OneNote, Trello, Google Docs, VoiceThread, and Sway engage students while allowing them to use technology that is also used in the workplace.

Other collaborative publishing and sharing ideas include the following:

- Facebook groups that provide an opportunity to participate in activities like service-learning and to connect with organizations or companies that may be related to your topic, such as local governing boards or specialists in your field of study. These groups or individuals often promote and deliver valuable new content through Facebook groups.
- LinkedIn is a key hiring and professional networking service that provides opportunities to connect with specialists in your field and market yourself or find employment. LinkedIn also allows posting and connecting to experts. The publishing option is great for classes requiring essays by allowing students to publish articles on the site.
- Blogs are important resources for updated and new content. For example, Stack Overflow is a blog for technology specialists to find possible solutions

to difficult coding problems. Find the important blogs in your field and use them as resources for your students or have your students post or reply, with your approval.

- Twitter is used for many topics, from political elections to a wide variety of social issues. Professionals in all fields recognize the value of the service for posting quick important updates. Students can comment using Twitter feeds created for your classroom, and experts can respond and or add ideas. Additionally, Twitter requires short posts, so students can learn the important skill of writing briefly and clearly.
- Podcasts are increasingly popular for a wide variety of topics. Gray (2017) offers ideas for using podcasts in education. Gray's topics include the technical aspects of developing and planning podcasts and tips for making quality podcasts.

### *Virtual Field Trips*

Budget cuts and online classes no longer need to preclude students from field trips to experience content beyond the classroom. Virtual field trip links can be embedded into your content so you can provide engaging learning activities for your students. In the early days of the Internet, faculty would use images of pictures and places and create their own tours, but now many historical landmarks and organizations have developed their own virtual exhibits and tours. YouTube 360 offers virtual reality videos or 360-degree views of locations and events. Rather than using valuable class time to go on a field trip, consider having students take a virtual tour of a location outside class using a Web browser and develop online or classroom activities to share their experience.

### *Using Technology for Quizzes and Tests*

Whether you give pretests, short quizzes, or longer exams, using technology can free up class time and provide immediate feedback to your students. In addition to your LMS's quiz tool, Quizlet (https://quizlet.com) is an application with an option for creating quizzes. Like polling tools, Quizlet allows you to create online quizzes, and it also allows students to create their own study cards or practice tests. Textbook publishers that also have technologies to create quizzes offer premade quizzes and tests to accompany textbooks. Some campuses may have a license to use quiz software, such as Respondus Test Bank Network, for creating quizzes that blend into your LMS.

**Bright Idea**

To further engage students, have them help develop quiz questions. Review their questions and post the best ones in the LMS quiz tool or use a third-party polling system. You can also have students post quiz questions on the course's discussion board. —**Sheri Hutchinson**

## *Simulations and Game-Based Learning*

Many publishers and open source resources now offer engaging technologies that motivate students to learn. Simulations, gamification, and other game-based active learning can provide practice for workplace applications. As we discussed previously, using simulations, virtual reality, and gamification allows students to construct or uncover their learning. It also provides a different way of looking at the learning taking place. For example, virtual reality

> grabs and holds the attention of students. This has been documented in the reports of a number of research studies. Students find it exciting and challenging to walk through an environment in three dimensions, interact with an environment, and create their own three dimensional (3D) worlds. (Pantelidis, 2017, p. 63)

Simulations are available through publisher textbooks and online resources and bring real-world experiences into the course when it is time to apply them. The real experience may be difficult for students to participate in because of cost, opportunity, distance, and so on. Simulations reproduce the experience so students can integrate course content into situations they may face in the workplace. Simulations can be used for science labs, health care procedures, welding and trades, and other disciplines where costs of materials, scheduling of space, access to experts, and other limiting factors are barriers to the experience.

Digital media simulations provide students with a host of advantages and benefits, including the following:

- They are personalized, providing an engaging student-centered approach to learning.
- They are multimodal. Learning this way enables students to employ multiple modes of learning, and learning by doing provides the most effective way to transfer short-term knowledge into long-term memory.
- They provide virtual internships that prepare students for what lies ahead when they must apply for jobs. Theory does not build a skilled workforce; application and long-term competency development do. Lifelong learning is a habit, not an event.
- They are plug and play, extremely easy to use learning tools.
- They are accessible on demand around the clock, around the globe. Students can access sessions on their schedule, practice at their own speed, and reuse and practice as much as they need.
- They allow failing forward because they take place in safe environments where the potential for teachable moments is high and the consequences for mistakes are low. (Beckem & Watkins, 2012)

Simulations using virtual reality are excellent ways to deliver learning experiences if they meet your course outcomes. Virtual reality could work well when

- a simulation could be used;
- teaching or training using the real thing is dangerous, impossible, inconvenient, or difficult;
- a model of an environment will teach or train as well as the real thing;
- interacting with a model is as motivating as or more motivating than interacting with the real thing;
- travel, cost, or logistics of gathering a class for training make an alternative attractive;
- shared experiences of a group in a shared environment are important;
- the experience of creating a simulated environment or model is important to the learning objective;
- information visualization is needed, manipulating and rearranging information using graphic symbols, so it can be more easily understood;
- a training situation needs to be made really real;
- it can make perceptible the imperceptible;
- developing participatory environments and activities that can only exist as computer-generated worlds;
- teaching tasks involving manual dexterity or physical movement;
- it is essential to make learning more interesting and fun;
- the disabled need the opportunity to do experiments and activities that they cannot do otherwise; and
- mistakes made by the learner or trainee using the real thing could be devastating or demoralizing to the learner, harmful to the environment, capable of causing unintended property damage, capable of causing damage to equipment, or costly. (Pantelidis, 2017, pp. 64–65)

Gamification is a motivational, reward-based method used in a number of online learning activities. Items such as coins, badges, points, or other rewards are earned by students while motivating them or helping make detailed content easier for them to understand. Games teach strategy and skills because they require close attention in an active, fun setting. If you played *The Oregon Trail* (Rawitsch, Heinemann, & Dillenberger, 1971) computer game back in elementary school, you needed to plan for the journey and to make good decisions to problems encountered along the way. If you did, you met success, and if you didn't, you never saw Oregon. You were able to succeed or fail in a safe environment. As in many games, your skills improved while you played. You learned what to do and what to steer away from, and you made mistakes and were able to practice enough times to move on to the next level successfully. The action made the activity motivating and for many students provided the means to persist and prevail.

Imagine teaching a course on urban planning and development or architecture. A game that leads you through the elements of design and possible problems could support course concepts well. Critical thinking, problem-solving, and collaboration skills can all be developed as students work to achieve the goal of the game. These applications of real-world experiences reinforce significant learning by making the material stick.

Finally, the simulation and gamification experiences as learning activities must be aligned with the course outcomes and assessments (Pantelidis, 2017). Using these just for fun or to be cool isn't a good use of the students' time during the semester. Ask yourself these questions: Does this activity meet the outcome, promote significant learning more effectively, and will it help students succeed on the outcome assessment?

## Open Source Materials

As you search for technologies, apps, and other online resources, consider open source peer-reviewed content. Open educational resources (OER) are teaching, learning, and research resources in any medium that reside in the public domain or have been released under an open license that permits free use and adaptation by others. OERs include full courses, course materials, modules, textbooks, videos, tests, software, and any other tools and materials used to support access to knowledge. A number of open source textbooks also include interactive lessons and embedded quizzing technology. You can supplement your learning with your own quizzing and interactions using software such as SoftChalk (https://softchalk.com), which is available for purchase. You may develop your own interactive lessons by using additional content authoring tools, such as Adobe Captivate.

Textbooks are becoming increasingly expensive for students, who paid between $1,250 and $1,420 for textbooks and course materials in 2018–2019 (College Board, 2019). A complicating factor is that students often don't have the funds to purchase textbooks immediately; in fact, 59% of students report they have had to wait for their financial aid money to purchase textbooks (Ernst, 2015).

OERs can help students save money, but you must evaluate the quality of the materials before you offer them to students. The following are some things to check:

- Make sure the organization or person is reputable. Look for other materials this organization or person has produced, and read any reviews.
- Check that the material provides up-to-date content. You may have to supplement with current Web links or other sources.
- Read all the permissions carefully to be sure you are able to use the material as you intend. A Creative Commons license is a clear indication that the material is available for open use and allows users access to "distribute, remix, tweak, and build upon [their] work, even commercially, as long as [users] credit . . . the original creation" (Creative Commons, n.d., para. 1).
- Certify that an OER is indeed an OER by confirming that there are no copyright, contract, or privacy issues with the contents.

In addition to these considerations, you should evaluate the materials from a readability and comprehensibility standpoint. Read samples of the content to find out if it is appropriate for the level of your students and course (Microsoft, 2019). Check several different samples from the beginning, middle, and end of the material for consistent readability.

Comprehensibility involves the general look of the material on the page or screen, as well as textbook-type features designed to help the reader navigate the material, which should have

- good margins so that the whole page doesn't look jammed with words;
- headings that separate the material into sensible sections;
- vocabulary that is clearly marked as important (boldface or italic) and definitions or explanations that are easy to find;
- guiding questions or end-of-chapter questions for discussion;
- graphic explanations, such as charts, tables, graphs, photos, or drawings that augment the text;
- a table of contents;
- an index; and
- no obvious typographical or other writing errors, which are more common in self-produced materials and can be very difficult for English language learners or students whose reading and vocabulary skills are lower.

OER Commons (2019) is a public digital library of OER where you can build content, resources, or lesson plans and then publish them for the benefit of educators and learners everywhere. You may also choose to use a resource that someone else developed, such as a textbook. Other sources for OERs include the following:

- Lumen Learning (OERs and courseware)
- MERLOT (simulations, games, courses, and more)
- University of Minnesota Open Textbook

Many large universities offer open source courses and textbooks with instructor materials. Using materials from these courses can supplement your course design. The scope of your course may be different from that of Harvard's or Yale's, and the intended audience may also not match yours. Again, you must determine that the materials are at the appropriate skill level for your course and students. As discussed in chapter 1, your situational factors, pedagogical challenges, big dream, and course outcomes are your unique factors to consider, so they may be different than many of the open source courses. We recommend that if you find some course materials elsewhere, it is critical for you to design your own course with content that meets the needs of your students: Course design isn't one size fits all.

**Jot Your Thoughts**

## What Is Cheating in the Internet Age?

Instantly retrieving information is the way of the modern world. However, we are doing students a disservice if we don't require them to search for additional information to foster problem-solving and innovative thinking. We have a great opportunity to teach our students how to research appropriate information and learn to select material from credible sources.

Having such access to information can also increase the opportunity for students to be dishonest (Luckin, 2018). Dehn (2003) suggests that academic dishonesty is widespread:

> Regardless of how we feel about our curriculum's contribution to academic dishonesty, the first step in improving our academic ethical environment is accepting the possibility that the potential for cheating is widespread. In fact, in light of data that suggests increasing student acceptance of cheating behavior and increased admission of cheating by students, it is likely that if we haven't recently detected any academic dishonesty it is because we haven't been looking. When one combines these changes in student ethics with how much easier committing plagiarism has become thanks to the PC and Internet, we can understand why cheating is on the rise. (p. 190)

Many students copy and paste digital content as they post on social media; they say it seems to be an accepted practice because everyone is doing it. You are working with students who see a meme and pass it along in text messages or develop their own memes by adding words to photos they have downloaded. The standard practice students are used to in social media is that everything is fair game.

Teaching students to use technology responsibly is part of the learning process. Many students tend to cheat or skip over the proper way when they don't know how to do something. Be sure you addressed your expectations in the academic integrity and netiquette portions of your syllabus and course shell. Reminders on assignments that point to these policies will demonstrate that you consider them important, and you can build a better understanding for students to help them balance their practices. Remember, they have spent thousands of hours on social media. Our experience as faculty is that we want to instill deeper integrity in our students. Learning to cite their sources is part of a professional code of conduct that needs to start in your course and continue as a life skill they demonstrate in the workplace.

Many faculty who use technology for testing are concerned about cheating. In this context, we define *cheating* as to looking up answers on the Internet while taking an exam. Setting a short time limit on the test discourages students from taking extra time to search for answers. However, a time limit puts extra pressure on students, contributes to anxiety, and sets up a perceived adversarial relationship between students and faculty. Another solution is to use software that keeps students from accessing the Internet on the campus computer they are using to take the test. They still might be able to use a smartphone; however, in a controlled situation you can place limits on smartphone availability. Finally, you can use your LMS to generate exams that produce randomized questions as well as randomized answers.

Keep in mind that using quizzes and exams applies to Fink's (2013) foundational knowledge and Bloom and colleagues' (1956) remembering and understanding levels of their taxonomies. Assessing higher level domains in the taxonomies require students to know this information and be able to do something with it. In a course designed for significant learning, you should choose authentic student performance and response assessments that require more than recollection and repeating facts to demonstrate deeper thinking and skill demonstration. See chapter 8 for more on creating authentic assessments.

## Mobile Learning

Faculty and students have the opportunity to create quality experiences for learning on the go using their mobile devices. From a course management standpoint, faculty can receive communications from students through smartphone notifications, which can improve their ability to quickly respond. Using handheld devices, faculty can also upload additional course content through LMS tools to offer greater just-in-time learning. Because more students own smartphones than ever before and because of the robust offerings of these mobile devices, faculty can design authentic assignments and assessments that bridge written content to applied real-world practice. We have to examine if students are ready for this now or will be soon. The Pew Research Center (2018) examined home technology use and found the following:

- The vast majority of Americans (95%) own a cell phone of some kind. The percentage of Americans who own smartphones is now 77%, up from just 35% in 2011. Ninety-four percent of adults ages 18 to 29 own smartphones; ownership by men is 80%, women is 75%, and is nearly evenly distributed among Whites, Blacks, and Hispanics. About 80% of adults with some college own a smartphone, and 91% of college graduates own one.
- Data on the use of other technologies by U.S. adults ranks ownership of computer and laptops at 73%, tablets at 53%, and e-readers at 22%.

- Home broadband usage is decreasing, with about 20% of U.S. adults who own smartphones dropping broadband; 28% of these are ages 18 to 29.
- Some 84% of American households have at least 1 smartphone, according to a survey conducted in fall 2016 (Pew Research Center, 2017). Desktop and laptop computers are nearly as common; 80% of households have at least 1 of these devices. Tablet computer ownership is somewhat less widespread with 68% of households with at least 1 tablet. Household incomes of less than $30,000 rely more heavily on smartphones.

Smartphone ownership has increased so much that for most students it is their first means of communicating and being connected. The devices are convenient because users can connect to the Web to access courses and research, take photos and videos, and record discussions and conferences. We are not dictating that your course design has to use this technology, but we encourage you to consider using a tool that is fairly accessible to your students and could increase their engagement.

The focus on redesigning learning spaces in a course needs to include a discussion of how mobile learning plays a role. We once considered these devices distracting in the classroom. Instructors told students to shut them down to avoid interrupting learning, but it is different when it comes to mobile learning. Physical spaces are being designed for greater active learning classrooms, instructional labs, makerspaces, team-based classrooms, and collaborative spaces (Educause, 2019). Makerspaces are labs designed to build on foundational learning through constructivist activities by providing available materials for inquiry and invention. Virtual classrooms need cloud space that provide an equal opportunity for access, even for students whose home computers may be limited in capacity. In physical and virtual classrooms, mobile learning can play a significant role when students perform tasks to demonstrate mastery of outcomes.

Mobile learning has increased in popularity because of improved capabilities of devices and users. Today smartphone and tablet owners can take photos of their experiences anywhere in the world and upload them instantly to social media platforms. We see our friends touring the Louvre, listening to the chiming of Big Ben, sailing the Greek isles, and being on safari in South Africa in real time. This ability is a great way for students to create content to demonstrate learning mastery and for faculty to assess outcomes. No longer does technology need to get in the way; no studios, special lighting, microphones and cameras, or electrical equipment is needed. Individual or team-based learning through technology can be easily integrated into course design to engage students and prepare them for the workplace. According to Educause (2019),

> The use of mobile devices has made content creation easier because smartphones and tablets include cameras to take photos and videos and a microphone to capture audio. This hardware, paired with powerful and intuitive mobile apps and increasingly available Internet access, has created a revolution of content creation and

> sharing. With capabilities including Bluetooth, GPS [global positioning system], and NFC [near-field communication], mobile devices can create new interactive and personal experiences. Even the most basic smartphone can be paired with an inexpensive Google Cardboard to create an immersive experience. Powerful apps allow students to quickly reference content or explore a concept in a new way. (p. 21)

The use of mobile learning in course design requires the following five considerations as situational factors: digital equity and accessibility, retooling or rethinking the teaching practice, digital literacy and fluency, campus resources, and planning for future technologies.

### *Digital Equity and Accessibility for All Learners*

*Digital equity* is defined by Educause (2019) as "comparable access to technology, particularly to broadband connectivity sufficient to access unbiased, uncensored content and to enable full participation on the World Wide Web" (p. 18). Some challenges to consider in choosing mobile learning technologies start with checking broadband connectivity and speed. These can vary from urban to rural areas, national regions, and other countries. Course technology access and navigation can vary depending on the device. Can your learning method be accessed by multiple devices? Finally, as discussed in chapter 6, accessibility challenges may be a barrier for some learners. You will need to plan for these situations and provide an alternative and equal learning opportunity.

### *Retooling the Teaching Practice for Full-Time and Adjunct Faculty*

According to Educause (2019), "The shifting nature of the instructor—from transmitter of knowledge to facilitator and curator—has accelerated the need for strategically planned faculty support and a reevaluation of the role of teaching and instruction" (p. 19). If the use of mobile learning is a change for your course, you will need to identify the role you will play in delivering learning. Pedagogically, what will you do differently from what you did in the past? What skill development will you need to use this new tool comfortably in the course? How will you become an expert so you can help your student novices? If the department or program is initiating changes in the curriculum to develop mobile learning integration, will all faculty, full time and part time, learn to use the technology? We recommend that they all should for consistency.

### *Digital Literacy and Fluency for Learners and Faculty*

Digital literacy is a bit like picturing runners at the starting line for a race. They need appropriate shoes, gear, knowledge of the course, and training. Learners need equipment, skills, and access. Good runners know the course as a part of their plan to perform their best. They know the elevation changes, where there is shade and wind, when to increase or decrease their pace, and when to hydrate at water stations.

Students need more than basic digital skills. They also need to recognize how to navigate the technology and apply this ability to their future work and career. According to Educause (2019),

> Digital fluency is the ability to leverage digital tools and platforms to communicate critically, design creatively, make informed decisions, and solve wicked problems while anticipating new ones. Merely maintaining the basic literacies by which students and instructors access and evaluate information is no longer sufficient to support the complex needs of a digitally mediated society. Learning solutions are designed and deployed using increasingly sophisticated technology, creating a need for learners to gain new skills to meaningfully engage with those tools. Digital fluency requires a rich understanding of the digital environment, enabling co-creation of content and the ability to adapt to new contexts. Institutions must not only support the uses of digital tools and resources by all members of the organization but also leverage their strategic technologies in ways that support critical thinking and complex problem solving. (p. 14)

### *Campus Resources to Support Mobile Learning*

Resources are needed to implement a shift to mobile learning. Faculty development is necessary for instructional design and technology integration. In the course design, faculty need to provide the user agreement information and instructions on how apps will be used to complete course work. According to Educause (2019),

> As devices have become more powerful, the affordances of mobile learning have grown dramatically in recent years, especially through AR [augmented reality] and VR [virtual reality] applications that allow learners to experience and experiment in a more authentic way than ever before. For instance, SkyMap allows people to connect astronomy concepts to the real world by holding their phone up to the sky. (p. 22)

## Future Technology

The one thing we do know is there will always be new technologies to use in teaching. Our experiences with smartphones and other devices using retinal scanning, facial recognition, and fingerprint activation tell us that our ability to know who learners are and authenticate their work will be improved. Virtual environments may assist us in delivering simulation experiences in the classroom and the homes of learners. The size of devices continues to make them portable and useful in new ways. Watches monitor our movement and vital signs, access e-mail, and connect to our phones. Phones that record visual data, provide access to research sites, and offer connectivity almost anywhere are prompting new applications that make learning instantaneous. We are able to talk with people worldwide in real time, and we can ask virtual assistants to provide us with data on a wealth of topics, which changes the learning landscape from what you need to know, to what you can access in seconds. According to Educause (2019),

> Virtual assistants are expected to be used for research, tutoring, writing, and editing. Similarly, virtual tutors and virtual facilitators will soon be able to generate customizable and conversational learning experiences currently found in a variety of adaptive learning platforms. (p. 32)

With computers using 3D printing and artificial intelligence, robots vacuuming our floors, great robot pets, and more, the tricorder scanners on *Star Trek* and the lifestyle of the Jetsons are closer to reality. Learning will follow suit. Imagine students going to the replicator to create 3D artifacts from archaeological digs or the parts of the anatomy for study. And as technology progresses, we will be able to use all our senses to enhance the learning experience. Embracing change and new ways of learning will provide you with opportunities to keep your course current and your students engaged. Start with what you need today to solve the high-priority learning challenges as you dream about what your course might look like in 10 years.

## Reflect on This Chapter

Now that you have completed reading this chapter and thinking about the content as it applies to your work, please reflect on the following questions:

- How can using technology make student learning more engaging and help students learn at their own pace?
- What ways can integrating technology help you with your teaching, and how would your role as the instructor change?
- Which technologies discussed in this chapter could improve learning in your courses?
- What technologies will your students need in their future careers?

**Jot Your Thoughts**

## Action Checklist

Use Checklist 7.1 to apply the chapter content to your practice and help you identify the steps for implementing these ideas in your teaching.

**CHECKLIST 7.1** Integrating Learning Technologies Action Checklist

| ✓ | **Analyzing Course Design for Technology Integration** |
|---|---|
| ❑ | Selected the learning outcomes that are conducive to using technology. |
| ❑ | Analyzed technology software, apps, hardware to understand course use and integration. |
| ❑ | Identified ways learning technologies will improve student learning, meet industry needs, and increase student engagement. |

| ✓ | **Resource Procurement** |
|---|---|
| ❑ | Discussed course technology needs with department, chair, dean, or supervisor. |
| ❑ | Worked with an advisory group to identify workplace technology needs and industry standards. |
| ❑ | Met with campus IT staff to learn the process to get technology installed. |
| ❑ | Learned the process to budget for new technologies for future budget cycles. |

| ✓ | **Evaluation** |
|---|---|
| ❑ | Planned for evaluating learning technologies use and effectiveness. |
| ❑ | Developed a student feedback process to assess new technologies. |
| ❑ | Established the means to gather feedback on technologies related to workforce needs from an advisory group. |

# PART THREE

# ASSESSING

# 8

# ASSESSING STUDENT LEARNING

## Points to Ponder

Chapter 8 analyzes multiple uses for effective student learning assessments to get the maximum impact with minimal time through course design. In thinking about designing the courses you teach, consider the following questions to examine your prior knowledge:

- What do you currently know about assessing student learning?
- How could you use testing as an assessment? Is all testing assessment?
- How could you blend multiple methods to assess student learning and improve your course?
- In what ways could course assessment be used beyond determining a student's final grade?

Lan had been teaching in the surgical technician program for 5 years, and she was getting frustrated that her students seemed to have so much trouble with 2 of the learning outcomes of the course on instrumentation: Students will be able to identify each of 35 common surgical instruments and specify each instrument's use in surgical procedures. Lan thought it should be very easy for students to master this, but every semester it took 5 to 6 weeks before all the students had passed the exam. The class spent so much time on this single unit that she ended up rushing for the rest of the semester to catch up.

The departmental assessment, which had not changed in many years, was an objective test consisting of matching photos with the names of the instruments and multiple-choice items on what each instrument is generally used for. Lan attended a seminar on active learning methods that gave her an idea for changing the way she taught the unit and prompted her to follow up with a meeting with her department chair to discuss alternative assessments.

The department chair and Lan decided that the exam should be more of a practical exam, rather than an objective test. What do medical surgery technicians actually do in the hospitals? They get the schedule of procedures and make sure the appropriate instruments are ready and organized for the surgical team. This became the basis for the new exam.

Instead of lecturing, Lan created small work teams and gave each team a complete set of 35 instruments. The task was to determine what each instrument was called, what it was used for, and in what typical instrument sets it would be included (for common procedures). The teams received several surgery scenarios and practiced setting up the lab according to each requirement. Her students were very engaged as they divided up the instruments and tasks for learning about them in the textbook, online, and in other class materials. The groups were expected to teach each other so that everyone had the same knowledge base. Practicing setting up the lab for a range of procedures ensured that all students experienced several scenarios and had the opportunity to sort the instruments, label them, and create the sets for surgery.

The assessment became more authentic. Each student was given 3 scenarios and required to select the necessary instruments, label them, and create the sets needed for the procedure at hand. The assessment had changed from an objective test focusing on memorizing to a practical clinical exam that emphasized the skills needed in the workplace. The pass rates for the 2 learning outcomes skyrocketed from 50% to 90%. After observing this turnaround, Lan approached her dean to discuss how to best report the changes she had made in a broader way. She prepared a report for her advisory committee, and she also included the information in her program's annual report.

## What Is Assessment?

The word *assess* (n.d.) comes from the Latin *assidēre*, which means to sit beside. Assessment isn't the same as judgment; both are often perceived differently by the receiver. For all of us, assessment in the form of judgment can feel hierarchical. When assessment feels like judgment to the student, it can stifle motivation. Perhaps most formative assessment should be called *feedback* instead. It feels more like the Latin definition of *to sit beside*. If faculty think about providing assessment by pulling up a chair and sitting next to a student, the feedback has a whole different feeling from a grade on a page or in an electronic grade book. It is a feeling of teaming between student and mentor.

Feedback is part of a constructivist learning philosophy in which students use course materials to think of content in the human dimension, caring, and learning how to learn domains (Fink, 2013). Rather than saying build it and faculty shall judge, the assessment should say build it with feedback, so you can build it by yourself in the future. Assessment, in our thinking, is a part of a person's life and not just the snapshot used to determine a grade in a course. The philosophy is completely different.

Many experts have devoted entire books to the topic of assessment (Banta & Associates, 2002; Maki, 2010; Silva, 2008, Walvoord & Anderson, 1998). One helpful resource is Astin and colleagues' (1993) principles of good practice, which helps to guide our thinking about assessment in the general sense.

## Principles of Good Practice for Assessing Student Learning

The following principles for assessing student learning can also be helpful when thinking about how to avoid plagiarism and cheating in online courses:

1. The assessment of student learning begins with educational values.
2. Assessment is most effective when it reflects an understanding of learning as multidimensional, integrated, and revealed in performance over time.
3. Assessment works best when the programs it seeks to improve have clear, explicitly stated purposes.
4. Assessment requires attention to outcomes but also and equally to the experiences that lead to those outcomes.
5. Assessment works best when it is ongoing not episodic.
6. Assessment fosters wider improvement when representatives from across the educational community are involved.
7. Assessment makes a difference when it begins with issues of use and illuminates questions that people really care about.
8. Assessment is most likely to lead to improvement when it is part of a larger set of conditions that promote change.
9. Through assessment, educators meet responsibilities to students and to the public. (Walvoord & Anderson, 1998, pp. 189–191)

These broad brush strokes of defining *assessments* can work well for assessing all levels of assessment—assessing student mastery of outcomes in courses, measuring the quality of course design by the ways students are able to progress, and using the data to report on the quality of program or department evaluations.

## Assessing the Student Versus Assessing Student Learning

Assessment in a course provides two opportunities to learn what is occurring. The first, which is the one we are most familiar with, is assessing the student. We equate this assessment to giving individual grades. The second assessment, which we may not be as familiar with, is assessing the larger picture of how learning occurs and how students are progressing in mastering the course concepts as a group. At times, these assessments are interrelated, meaning they can be administered at the same time. Let's examine this second assessment opportunity on our way to discovering ways to measure individual student learning.

Isn't all testing assessment? Many faculty assume that testing is the same as assessment. They believe that when giving quizzes and exams, they are assessing student learning, and in some cases they might be. It is more helpful to look at the purposes of tests versus assessment.

Testing students is usually conducted to assign individual grades that are recorded in the grade book to assign grades at the end of the course. Assessment activities measure mastery of outcomes or diagnose holes or gaps in student learning according to the learning outcomes of the assignment, unit, or course. There is an overlap. Many faculty use quizzes and tests to see overall how their students are doing in terms of mastering the learning outcomes for the course.

Assessment activities are used for the group of students and their success or mastery, not individual students. According to Walvoord and Banta (2010), "Assessment is the systematic collection of information about student learning, using the time, knowledge, expertise and resources available, in order to inform decisions that affect student learning" (p. 2). In addition, assessment has action as a goal: Something will be done with the information gathered, whether it is improving instruction, curriculum design, or institutional efforts (Walvoord & Banta, 2010). The purpose of assessment is to learn more about how students are progressing toward mastery and then to reflect on what can be improved in instruction and course design to better meet those outcomes.

## Internal Assessment of Student Learning

Assessment of student learning as a whole begins with course outcomes. As you write learning outcomes, you should also identify the evidence that demonstrates mastery to know what your students are achieving. Evidence can include behaviors, products, writing, problem-solving, action, and skills that show students' proficiency. For example, if the learning outcome is "Convert metric weight units to English weight units and vice versa," you may consider the following to be subparts of the outcome:

- Students should be able to convert all the weight units you have determined to be relevant; that is, milligrams, grams, kilograms, ounces, and pounds, but perhaps not hectograms, dekagrams, decigrams, or centigrams, which are used less commonly.
- Students should be able to accurately work with very large and very small numbers.
- Students should be able to convert problems that arrive at an even answer as well as those that result in decimal or fractional parts.

This careful consideration of including many ways students should be able to show mastery of the skill of conversion is thorough and multifaceted. It is not just one or two problems, it is many, which can be administered over multiple class sessions.

To design an assessment for the outcome "Convert metric weight units to Imperial weight units and vice versa," you would create a series of problems for students to solve and then aggregate the performance data as a class to see if students as a group are performing as expected. If your goal is for 80% of the students get at least 80% of the items correct, you can easily find out if the class is underperforming and what problems exist. The assessment need not be given all at once like a test; items can be embedded in homework, labs, or in-class work over time. Then you can decide if reteaching is needed before moving on to the next topic. Your aggregated data set is a snapshot of your students' performance of an outcome. It provides important information to you and to your department about overall student achievement. This type of assessment is unrelated to individual student grades.

For department assessment, some would select a set of common test items to put on an exam that is given to all sections. For example, perhaps a standard 5 or 10 items would be included on the Unit 3 test, even if each instructor wrote a different exam for Unit 3. Those standard items would be analyzed as an assessment of all the students in the multisection course. The same items would be assessed each semester. Why would this be helpful? Many department directors want to improve the matriculation of students through their courses, and gaining an understanding of how students perform on selected high-value skills can identify where course improvements can be made. Results could even help a department director figure out in which course certain skills or concepts are best taught to improve the flow of learning from course to course. This same strategy can be used across multiple disciplines to measure institutional-level learner outcomes such as critical thinking and oral and written communication, among others.

## External Assessment of Student Learning

External assessment instruments can also serve as tools for course improvement or teaching improvement. Licensure exams are one such tool. If the course outcomes are aligned with the licensure test's outcomes, the data from those exams may be used to determine needed improvements or accolades. In one such program, we observed an analysis of the federal air traffic controller exam that zeroed in on a few key areas of the program that needed additional time. It was very helpful for the faculty to understand that even though they taught those concepts, the students had not learned them as needed to score well on the test items. It caused some valuable internal reflection and redesign of course modules and how much time to spend on each.

Having a language class take a practice proficiency exam such as the Test of English as a Foreign Language (Educational Testing Service, 2019d), *Test de Connaissance du Français* (*Centre international d'études pédagogique*, 2018), or *Diplomas de Español como Lengua Extranjera* (Spanish Diplomas, 2019) can serve assessment purposes and give students a chance to practice taking an exam for which they might be preparing to meet international work requirements.

Nursing students have long practiced for their state board exams using sample tests, some with questions from previous years' exams. These practice exams don't just provide familiarity with the topics and the question styles, they also provide detailed rationales for why the incorrect choices are wrong and why the correct choices are either correct or better answers. Incorporating this type of exam review into each semester of nursing can help students become more familiar and comfortable with test items, the multiple-choice format, and the pressures of a high-stakes licensure exam.

For general education, examples of available instruments are the Collegiate Learning Assessment (Council for Aid to Education, 2019) or the Proficiency Profile (Educational Testing Service, 2019c). Assessment tools to measure specific skills range from the undergraduate-focused California Critical Thinking Skills Test (Insight Assessment, 2019) to the familiar graduate school and professional exams like the Graduate Record Examinations (Educational Testing Service, 2019a) and the Professional Assessment for Beginning Teachers (Educational Testing Service, 2019b). As Maki (2010) points out, standardized exams provide a history of validation and reliability studies to support their use as well as evidence of students' knowledge and skills that are measurable with test questions. They can be used to track student learning if used in a formative and summative manner. The standardized exam can also be used to meet external mandates for graduates and to evaluate programs of study. However, they do not provide evidence of the "strategies, processes, and ways of knowing, understanding, and behaving that students draw on or apply to represent learning" (Maki, 2010, p. 207). Nor can they accurately represent the complexities of learning. Because these tests are not tied to the institutions themselves, they are not helpful in gaining information about the pedagogy and practice of a particular institution.

## Assessing the Individual Student in Your Course

Returning to what assessment means to the students mentioned at the beginning of this chapter—to sit beside—let's listen to how their perception of assessment sounds. When students are focused on a grade versus learning, their experience and motivation are completely different. For example, here are some comments from grade-oriented students:

> "I think that without regularly scheduled exams I would not learn and remember very much."
> "I do not find studying at home to be interesting or pleasant."
> "I will withdraw from an interesting class rather than risk a poor grade."
> "I get irritated by students who ask questions that go beyond what we need to know for exams."(Walvoord & Anderson, 1998, p. 44)

The following are comments from learning-oriented students:

"I find the process of learning new material fun."
"I enjoy classes in which the instructor attempts to relate material to concerns beyond the classroom."
"I discuss interesting material that I've learned in class with my friends and family."
"I try to make time for outside reading despite the demands of my coursework." (Walvoord & Anderson, 1998, p. 44)

What comments do you think your students are making about assessment in your courses? Most faculty would enjoy hearing the comments from the learning-oriented students, and how you design your course's assessments can make that happen.

In our courses we have determined that student assessment should no longer be about grade stratification, where only a few students are able to get an A. Employers want all graduates to be proficient at the highest level in performance competencies. None of them were calling us to ask if we can give them the names of students who received Bs and Cs. They want the best employees who can walk into the workplace and apply their thinking and skills to the work. They want to hire the students who already demonstrate proficiency in learning so they can take on new work by learning new skills in the workplace.

## Educative Assessment

In working with faculty, the lines between creating learning activities and assessments are often blurred. Significant learning comes from meaningful feedback during course activities and feedback provided through formative and summative assessment. Assessment without providing meaningful feedback is a missed opportunity as it meets only the need of the faculty to provide a final grade for the course. That is why we do not recommend measuring the majority of a student's progress by quizzes and tests. Students learn little by examining the results of these assessments. They receive a score, a percentage, or a grade, whose meaning is minimal, and they learn little from these results to understand or identify ways to improve. Our experience tells us that students often have more questions about how they are doing in the course and begin to focus on how to make a number improve than to improve their knowledge and skills.

Fink's (2011) educative assessment consists of three components. Assessment is forward-looking, uses criteria and standards, and provides self-assessment and feedback opportunities (see Figure 8.1).

The most common and typical assessment of student learning has long been exams. The multiple-choice question exam has been as popular over the years for testing as the lecture has been in preparing students for the exams.

A typical exam is an example of backward-looking assessment. Students read a text and other materials, attend lectures, study for a period of time, and are then given an exam where they are expected to remember the information and select the correct answer from among three of four possible answers, which can involve a certain

**Figure 8.1** Audit-ive and educative assessment.

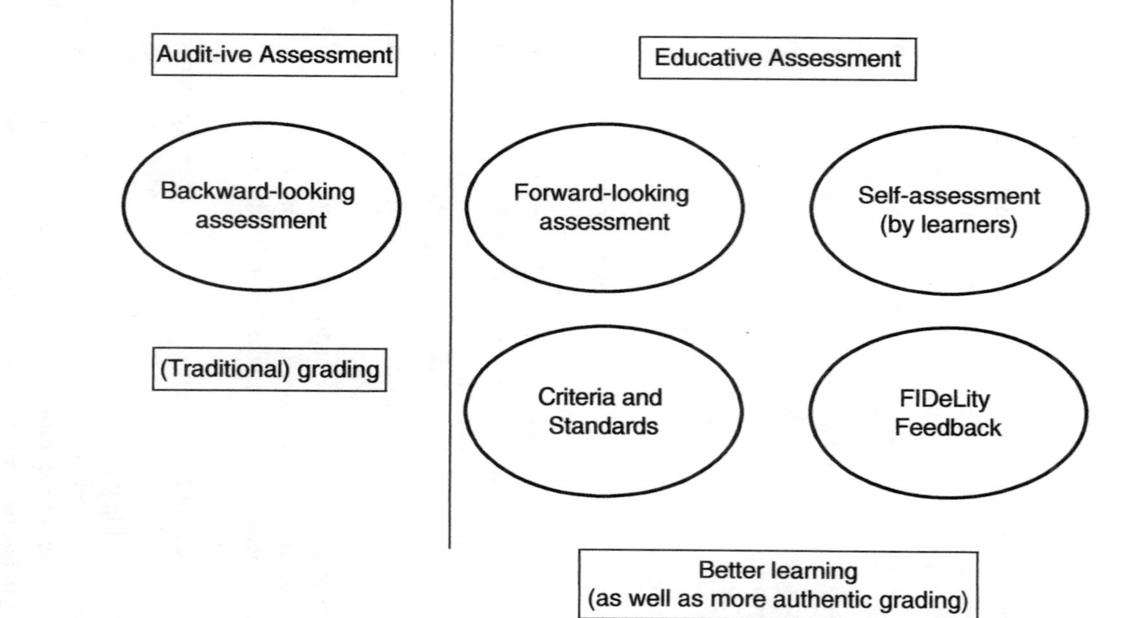


*Note*. This figure illustrates Fink's model for audit-ive and educative assessment. From *A Self-Directed Guide to Designing Courses for Significant Learning*, by L. D. Fink, (2011), http://www.bu.edu/sph/files/2011/06/selfdirected1.pdf, p. 14. Copyright 2011 by L.D. Fink, 2011. Adapted with permission.

amount of guessing. The reason this is called backward-looking assessment is because the exam requires students to look back on what they have learned in the course. In most cases the exam has little or no connection to real-world experiences but rather asks students to hold in their memory facts and figures that can be used to find the correct answer on the test.

Forward-looking assessment puts students into authentic situations where they are expected to actively use the foundational knowledge learned in the course. This type of assessment requires the students to look into the future through analysis and predictive exploration, visualizing problems and their place in creating solutions rather than reciting facts. In short, students are asked to demonstrate an integrated use of prior experience and skills developed in the course. Backward-looking assessment has its place in a course to assess foundational knowledge, and forward-looking assessment allows students to use information learned to make decisions and connections that will be valuable to them after the course is completed.

Criteria and standards are necessary so that students and instructors can measure the learning taking place in the course. An example of this is the use of rubrics to assess student work. Students must know what will be evaluated and how they will be assessed. Constructing criteria and standards provides the framework for students to meet your expectations. Providing these criteria for each assignment and samples of exemplary work are the means to get students to see the level they need to achieve. The more you do this early in the course and curriculum, the more it increases the quality of work students produce.

Self-assessment is crucial for students' learning so that in time they don't need to depend on the instructor or experts to know what high-quality work is. Ultimately, by the time the students complete the course and receive their degree, they must be able to identify high quality and know how to improve poorer quality work in the field. If students do not learn to assess their own learning, they will miss one of the most powerful aspects of the feedback process.

Another element of integrating educative assessment in your course is to provide FIDeLity feedback (Fink, 2013). FIDeLity feedback is frequent, immediate, discriminating based on criteria and standards, and delivered in a loving, respectful, and supportive manner (see Figure 8.1).

Students receiving frequent feedback remain connected with the course. As discussed in chapter 3, students are barraged with constant media feedback. Your course doesn't need to match this media marketing blitz, but keeping your feedback in the forefront of students' attention is key. Reacting to and applying the feedback is a way to further engage them to keep the learning from feedback relevant.

Similarly, feedback that is delivered after some time doesn't make it relevant to the learning experience. Immediate feedback doesn't mean within hours, but determining the timeliness of providing feedback makes it useful. Assignment feedback that is offered after a couple of weeks in a semester course won't have the same impact as feedback that is delivered soon after the due date. Consider your schedule for delivering feedback as you design the assessments.

As previously mentioned, assessment feedback that isn't discriminating doesn't help students learn. Base your comments on how students are meeting the course criteria or standards to personalize the feedback and provide a path for students to improve where needed.

Finally, feedback needs to be constructive and delivered in a loving way. Consider how the student will receive the feedback. Even difficult news can be helpful if you deliver it in a respectful, supportive, professional tone. Feedback shouldn't just be judgment. Help them with solutions, offer ideas. They may have submitted what they did because they didn't make connections to the rubric criteria or apply directions. If you just tell them they didn't meet the expectations of the assignment, they won't learn. We recommend for students to self-assess and use some peer-assessment strategies using the rubric before they submit it to you. This is valuable to them and gives you the chance to spend your time helping with the bigger picture feedback rather than things they can correct themselves. This deeper feedback is where you get to help shape learning and where you as the expert guide novices, starting where students are developmentally and moving them to where you want or need to them to be.

The key question to ask yourself when designing an assessment of a learning outcome is, How will I know a student is performing adequately? Although tempting, you can't rely on thinking you'll know it when you see it. What you will actually know is what the best and the worst performances are. But the critical point to understand is to develop a clear line between what is acceptable at this level, and what needs work. You will be thinking of what is acceptable student work for the level of your course, that is, first year, premajor, or capstone. Keep in mind that first-year students who may be novices or students who are nearly experts in capstone courses will need to be assessed differently.

In evaluating some basic concepts, the right answers may be clear. But for more complex concepts, assessing becomes multilayered. In mathematics, for example, partial credit may be given to a student who works a problem using correct methods but makes a small calculation error. Writing assignments, essay questions, projects, oral presentations, creating products (computer network or program, building furniture, creating art, making a website), and other student work are more complex to grade than simply marking them right or wrong.

To clearly define the line between acceptable and needs work, some kind of scoring guide is useful. Rubrics can help you isolate the critical aspects of the criteria you are using for scoring and can speed up the grading process as well. Rubrics also help students better understand how they were graded. When rubrics are used for everyday assignments, students should view a copy of one before they attempt to complete an assignment to use as a checklist to be sure they have addressed all the criteria. If the assessment spans several instructors' courses, creating a good rubric enhances interrater reliability (multiple assessors across a department) and as a result may increase the consistency of expectations as well.

It may seem like we just put the cart before the horse, discussing scoring guides before the design of the assessment, but we did not. The very first thing is to know clearly what behavior, writing, presentation, and product you are looking for (the outcome); isolate the criteria you will be using to assess; clarify the line between acceptable and needs work; and, finally, develop assessment and assignment tasks that will elicit the work you intend to evaluate. Doing so follows the backward design principles.

## Rubrics: Tools to Measure Learning and Provide Feedback

Rubrics should provide a clear description of the task, some kind of scale for grading, the dimensions or criteria you will be using to evaluate the work, and descriptions of each level on the scale (Stevens & Levi, 2012). The structure of designing rubrics can follow this form as shown in Table 8.1. We provide additional details to complete the rubric cells.

### *Description of the Task*

The rubric should clearly name the topic of the assignment or assessment, place brief directions for the assignment or assessment at the top of the rubric so students see them as well as the grading scheme.

### *Scale: Some Ideas for Language*

Scale refers to the titles or headers for each column of the rubric:

- The scale of points is displayed in columns left to right from low to high or high to low (see Table 8.1). Some argue that starting with the highest points or descriptor (e.g., exemplary) to the left next to the criteria encourages students to attempt to reach those.
- Numbers or points alone can work.
  - For simple or lower scoring rubrics, a single point value (4, 3, 2, 1) can be offered for each column.
  - For more complex or higher scoring rubrics, a range of points could be offered in each column (0–5, 6–10, 11–15, 16–20).
- Words alone could work if the activity is for formative assessment and designed for improvement only. For example:
  - Exemplary, proficient, marginal, unacceptable
  - Sophisticated, competent, partly competent, not yet competent
  - Advanced, intermediate high, intermediate, novice
  - Distinguished, proficient, intermediate, novice
  - Accomplished, average, developing, beginning
  - Excellent, acceptable, needs work
  - Excellent, proficient, developing, beginning
- A combination of words with points is often used.
- A scale of three, four, or five levels are all workable options and may be determined by the sophistication of the assignment or assessment.

**TABLE 8.1**
**Template for Rubric Design**

| ↓ Description of Task (Assignment or Assessment) | | | | | | |
|---|---|---|---|---|---|---|
| **Course Discussions: Post your responses to each set of weekly discussion prompts** | | | | | | |
| | Scale → | **Excellent** | **Proficient** | **Developing** | **Beginning** | ← Column Level Descriptors |
| ↓ Dimensions | Scale → | **4 Points** | **3 Points** | **2 Points** | **1 Points** | ← Points (or choose range below) |
| **Criteria** | **Score** | **20–16 Points** | **15–11 Points** | **10–6 Points** | **5–0 Points** | ← Range of Points |
| **Discussion Content** | | **Highest standard** | **Medium high standard** | **Medium low standard** | **Lowest standard** | ← Dimensions (criteria) descriptions |
| **Writing quality (spelling, grammar, sentence construction)** | | **0 errors** | **1 error** | **2 errors** | **3 or more errors** | ← Dimensions (criteria) descriptions |
| **Discussion support (experiences, additional sources)** | | **Highest standard** | **Medium high standard** | **Medium low standard** | **Lowest standard** | ← Dimensions (criteria) descriptions |

### *Dimensions (Criteria)*

In Table 8.1, the dimensions, or criteria, are listed vertically in the first column on the left.

- Break the task down into components, such as organization and usage.
- Dimensions are stated in neutral terms (not just something like "good organization").
- Think of these as all the aspects to assign points for or to consider when determining the final grade.

### *Description of Dimensions*

The descriptions you provide for each dimension are the key for students to recognize the level of their achievement or performance.

- Start by identifying what an excellent (or the highest level) of performance will look like.
- For the other levels, specifically describe what might be the problem, omissions, lack of quality, and so on.
- These descriptions really help students understand the difference between a B and a C, for example.
- When grading, the instructor can circle various parts of the description to visually see where the student's work falls.
- Keep written descriptions in the same format in the same order. Change the description for each column based on level of performance standards (high, high to medium, medium to low, or low) so a student can easily see the differences in performance levels.
- Quantifying descriptions provide specific expectations so it is helpful to use numbers whenever possible: 0 errors, 1 to 2 errors, 3 to 4 errors, 5 or more errors; or provide 1 example, 2 or more examples, 5 or more examples, and so on.

For more examples of rubrics see Appendix E. Several others presented in chapter 9 are ways to measure the quality of your course design.

Before you use a newly developed rubric, we advise getting some feedback from a colleague or trying it out with your students on a sample assignment. Faculty have told us that they know exactly what they want for the highest standard (exemplary) and they can identify what is the lowest standard (beginning). Many, however have difficulty distinguishing between the middle scale areas of performance such as proficient, intermediate, and developing. This is the toughest part of rubric writing; we all can see the As and the Fs. It is much harder to nail down the Cs and the Bs or the C minuses from the D pluses. Students can't tell the difference either, and for a rubric to really be helpful, it should clarify the grading for them as well. When they see what you have circled or marked on the rubric, they should understand better how they can improve. A well-constructed rubric will make grading easier and more consistent for you and communicate clear expectations to your students.

Rubrics measure student learning as they progress toward the mastery of the outcomes in a course. However, rubrics are rarely used as a way to improve your course. Recording the number of students who fall under the headings of outstanding, proficient, and developing at the top of the rubric can provide you with much feedback on how to redesign the learning experiences and ultimately improve the course so more students achieve the higher standards. If your students are achieving the desired levels of proficiency and development, ask yourself what you can do to provide a pathway for more of them to move to the outstanding level. This can also be a way to reflect on your own level of expectations to determine if you are assigning points fairly to the criteria you established. Faculty can be so used to the fact that only a few students can get an A that we sometimes think only a few can be outstanding. However, this is not to say that everyone gets a trophy for participation. Being an objective assessor is critical to this process.

**Bright Idea**

Creating a rubric requires you to practice using it before you actually employ it for real grading. You will find that your students often turn in work that falls into gray areas, and your rubric language must zero in on distinguishing them. Try jotting down the errors or problems you find in the students' work, which then can be tallied (use the most frequent ones) and rewritten into language that can be used in a rubric. —**Linda Russell**

## Designing Course Assessments

The types of assessments you choose will depend on two basic criteria: the skills or tasks your students need to practice to achieve mastery and the future tasks your students need to perform on the job or in their academic positions. The more aligned your assessments are with the outcomes and desired future behaviors and skills, the more consistent and authentic your course will seem to students and other stakeholders. There are many course assessment types; we provide the following selection that can be used in a variety of disciplines.

### *Classroom Assessment Techniques and Learning Assessment Techniques*

Classroom assessment techniques and learning assessment techniques are informal assessments, usually quick, and offer helpful information about your students' mastery of individual concepts. A mix of these informal assessments and more formal assessments is an excellent way to gain a deeper understanding of your students' progress.

**Bright Idea**

You will learn a lot about your course design in reading students' responses to your questions. If you ask them to reflect on the unit's reading and video materials they will tell which of the resources were the most valuable to them. You might use discussion questions to informally see how your students are mastering the course concepts. This will help you as you update the course in the future by indicating what to keep and what to change. —**Zala Fashant**

### *Portfolios as Assessments*

Portfolios have long been used in the arts. It is more recent that they have become assessment tools in other disciplines. They may be used for one course, a capstone course, or as a show portfolio in an entire program that showcases a collection of a student's work. Fink (2003) and others have written about learning portfolios, which may include a collection of artifacts and provide a narrative for a learning experience, whether from one course or from several (Cambridge, 2010; Eynon & Gambino, 2017; McDonald, 2012; Reynolds & Patton, 2014). Many faculty may not be comfortable with teaching their students how to construct an ePortfolio. Providing professional development for faculty in creating portfolios in general may be the first step in offering this assessment (Eynon & Gambino, 2017; Zubizarreta, 2009).

The narrative part of a portfolio requires students to reflect deeply about what they have learned and how it has affected them or will contribute to their chosen careers. This requires backward- and forward-looking analysis. The artifacts provide the evidence that learning and reflection have taken place. Self-reflection is an important part of closing the loop in the learning-teaching cycle. It causes students to think about learning goals; personal goals; setbacks; recovery from setbacks; their own efforts; ideas for improvement; future applications of the learning; and, of course, their big dream. Self-reflection contributes to metacognition as well as motivation and self-efficacy. We believe that when used with classroom assessment techniques (CATs), such as one-minute papers, reaction papers, or other reflective activities, the portfolio can be powerful for the student and the instructor alike.

If you plan to have students produce a portfolio, it begins on the first day of class. You provide the structure and the rules for the portfolios beginning with the outcomes of the course and the type of acceptable evidence of mastery that students may include. A scoring rubric should be developed and given to students at this time as well so they can refer to it as they are compiling their work and planning their approach. We recommend a reflection component to support the learning how to learn domain (Fink, 2013). Throughout the course, you will need to guide students, provide opportunities for them to select work that will go into the portfolio, and offer reflection time in the form of short responses to writing prompts or other chances to begin that part of the process. Herman, Aschbacher, and Winters (1992) offer the following caveat:

> There are two issues related to selecting the dimensions of scoring criteria for portfolio assessment: (1) What are the criteria for selecting the samples that go into the portfolio, and (2) What are the criteria for judging the quality of the samples? Prior to considering criteria for judging portfolios, you will need to determine whether the portfolio should be rated as a whole, or as individual samples. (p. 75)

## *Group and Individual Projects and Presentations*

One of the ways faculty can prepare students for careers in the workplace is to provide experiences in which students can present information they have learned. These individual and group opportunities will help students with public speaking, organizing of content, researching and editing content, and developing visuals to support content. Providing clear rubrics with criteria is necessary so all parts of the presentation are prepared, and the expectation of full participation by each member is clear in group situations. You can decide if you would like each group member to evaluate the participation of each of the other group members and themselves as a part of the grade. This can keep groups accountable to one another especially if most of the work is done outside the course. If you do this, we recommend that group members write a short description with a rubric to justify the points they assigned.

Presentations can be made using video or Web conferencing technology as used in the workplace. Employers are looking for employees who can work in teams and can deliver presentations successfully. Effective oral communication may also be an institutional learner outcome that can be measured to show how students meet this goal for school accreditation. By presenting this information, students can learn content from one another, and they can also receive feedback from experts in the field who watch the presentations online or in person.

## *Research Papers*

One of the most traditional ways of measuring student learning has been assessing a research paper. The strengths of this assessment are that they provide

- an individual demonstration of outcomes mastery,
- researching skill development in choosing quality discipline sources,
- writing skill development through a logical structure to communicate messages, and
- the opportunity for detailed individual feedback about discipline-specific writing to demonstrate organizational and analytical thinking.

Active learning takes place as students engage in the research and organize the information through writing. Further active learning can take place if the papers are available to other students in the course shell and by oral presentations to share the knowledge they have gained in their research.

Often these papers are turned in to the instructor for a grade without opportunities for discussing the process, sharing with classmates, and getting helpful peer feedback. It is often used as a summative activity turned in at the end of the course with no outlet for future use in the course or tie-in to future learning in other courses in the curriculum. Instructor feedback is often received after the course is completed. Students may look only at the final grade and read only a couple of the comments, so the value of the feedback and future implementation may be diminished.

Our suggestion would be to assign these papers earlier in the semester. By using other course activities to support writing the research paper, such as discussion posts and turning in sections of the final paper, you will help students rise to the challenge of providing quality work. Furthermore, presenting these papers in class before the end of the semester allows students to use the feedback in other course work, or by linking this assignment to the next course in the curriculum to use what they have gained, students can apply it to future work.

Using a rubric for research papers makes them fairly easy to grade. The rubric criteria support students in digging deeper to offer critical comparison and analysis and better meet what is expected of them in their careers. Consider developing a common program or department rubric to help students develop and expand the disciplinary literacy skills they will need. Using other course activities to give students practice in doing so will help them rise to the challenge.

### *Journals and Reflective Writing*

Having students reflect on their course learning experience is a very valuable way to get students to find inner connections with the content. Using journals and reflective writing is a chance for students to use backward-looking and forward-looking assessment. You can design the assessment to have students share their experiences, express their perspectives learned from the material, and discover ways they can use what they have learned in future learning and working experiences. Providing opportunities for students to reflect on and predict how to apply their learning is a way to assess the human dimension, caring, and learning how to learn areas of the taxonomy of significant learning (Fink, 2013).

### *Critique of Professional Performance, Art, Theater, and Music*

All of us have opinions about the quality of performing and visual arts. Many of these opinions are determined by a feeling, not a set of criteria. If we experienced comfort, we may have enjoyed it and labeled it good. If the experience made us uncomfortable, we may not have enjoyed it and wouldn't want to repeat listening, viewing, or watching it. Rubrics are especially useful to identify the key criteria to help evaluate the product. One of the criteria may include the aesthetic impression a performance or work delivers; however, using the elements of the arts to assess the product will outweigh the feeling it evokes.

As in other types of course work, feedback by the instructor and students during the creative process makes up a majority of the learning and assessment. Music and theater directors provide constant feedback during rehearsals, through the use of skill description and imagery, to move students closer to the vision of excellence in performance to achieve what the author or composer intended. Visual artists guide students through practice revisions that lead to the final product that is partially determined by student artists as they hone the skills needed to communicate the art form (e.g., sculpture, painting, photography, or film).

Another assessment commonly used in the fine arts disciplines is self-assessment. Students describing their impression of the work is a way of moving them from listening to expert external feedback to internalizing the assessment feedback so the students can value their own abilities and learn from their learning and carry it forward to future experiences. Activities can include conversations with faculty one-on-one and between peers during practice or through reflective writing or critique after practice. This step is critical to moving students from novices to experts, and as you may have realized, this isn't unique to the arts but applies to all disciplines (Haugnes, Holmgren, & Springborg, 2018).

As managers who supervise employees, we need skills in evaluating performance. Understanding the criteria of this type of assessment is a necessary skill for all employees. Perhaps more than any other area, this assessment carries over to an individual's personal life as well. Evaluating these areas by using a performance rubric helps to take the emotional perspective out of the assessment and ties it closer to a well-established set of criteria to guide our evaluative eye. In each of the criteria, it is important to move away from how it makes you feel to what you see and experience during the evaluation.

### *Student-Developed Plans for Learning How to Learn*

A valuable way for students to continue their learning is to have them develop their future professional learning plan. In doing so, students can see why what they learned in your course will help them continue learning in additional courses in the curriculum and beyond. This also prepares them to think about how they will continue to grow in the workplace by developing a professional development plan. Developing an assignment or assessment sets the tone of why this is important for students and professionals. Sharing some of your goals from your professional development plan is a great way to model how these types of plans help us achieve professional and personal outcomes.

## Developing the Pathway for Summative Assessment

Much like developing learning activities that provide practice to prepare for assessment, your course's plan for assessment needs to carefully take into account how students will have practice being assessed using the means you have chosen to measure mastery. Providing student practice for assessments uses a baby-steps philosophy. Smaller, lower stakes formative assessment provides practice as you lead students to summative, higher stakes assessment. This concept is logical, and yet we have observed and evaluated hundreds of courses where a faculty member has used only the final, high-point, high-stakes summative assessment. Developing an overall plan to focus on your course's assessments helps you see the flow of assessments over and above how they blend with the alignment of learning outcomes, assessments, and activities. The plan helps you see how this all comes together so you can answer the following questions: Will students have time to complete each level of work and be able to apply their learning to future course work? Will you have time as the instructor to assess and provide feedback to students in time for them to apply it their future work?

## Assessment Versus Learning Activities

In our work with faculty, many had difficulty in deciding if a learning element was an activity or an assessment. Let us work from the premise that the same type of exercise can be used for either. As a quick review, learning activities are used to practice concepts that are later assessed in formative or summative stages. The following are four types of learning activities from Fink (2013):

1. Active, which includes hands-on and discussion exercises
2. Passive, which includes reading and lectures
3. Connecting, which includes how to tie information together from past learning to present and future learning
4. Reflective, which allows students to consider their growth in learning, how they learned, and how they can best use what they have learned

Some learning activities can be a combination of these. One of the most common team learning activities involves active and connecting learning. Can you think of an activity you would use in a group situation in which students are interacting with one another and taking previously learned content and connecting it to new content? This is easily done in a lab where students build foundational knowledge on the use of equipment so they can conduct a more complex experiment. For example, in nursing you learn to draw blood before moving to preparing for a blood transfusion.

In Table 8.2, active learning may also be reflective or connecting depending on how you design it. In an authentic project students may be asked to demonstrate active learning and also reflect on what they learned and how they might use it. Alternatively, they may be asked to connect learning with the concept by predicting how they think they connect or how they could see the connection.

Along with these learning activities, it is easy to include formative assessments, informal and formal, to check student understanding. These assessments are similar to the activity, and in some cases, once students have practiced a skill, the final run-through of the activity can be used as the formative assessment. Informal formative assessments may or may not carry points. If offered formally, assigning points for the work might be a stronger consideration as it may save time by providing a measure of student performance and giving you the information to conduct a summative assessment.

Informal assessment indicates to students and faculty how the learning is progressing and provides them with a compass to direct future learning, measuring the direction and duration of additional learning. Informal assessments take the form of CATs and peer-evaluated drafts of work, for example. The feedback can be used on the path to more formal assessment. This assessment may not have points assigned or perhaps offers completion points only. Informal assessments are usually considered formative assessments.

As stated previously, formative assessment occurs along the course's learning pathway, whereas summative assessment usually takes places at the conclusion of instruction and learning for each course outcome. All summative assessment doesn't have to occur at the end of the course. In fact it is better to assess the outcomes as they are completed throughout the course to provide feedback to students. Moreover, students won't have to demonstrate an extensive list of outcomes during the final week of the course. Your assessment plan may also include projects that measure several outcomes through a single summative assessment using a megarubric, which takes into consideration the criteria measured with individual rubrics for formative assessments earlier in the course.

## Student Progress: Reaching Milestones

Imagine yourself running a race. You may be the elite runner who knows what you need to do to cross the finish line. Other novice runners need to concentrate on getting to the next water station as they see the finish line in terms of achieving several shorter segments. Your students may view your course and your program in the same way. Some of your students are self-motivated and able to complete the course by crossing the finish line. Others need to progress by achieving benchmarks or milestones throughout the semester. Which kind of learner were you when you were in college? When faced with a large project on your campus, like redesigning a course, do you look at the finish line, or do you like to celebrate short-term victories?

If you have designed your course with only the finish line in sight, you may lose students along the way who need to accomplish short-term victories on their way to crossing the finish line. Some LMSs let you award badges at each leg or unit completion of a course to show students they were successful in achieving a set of criteria for outcomes or competencies based on faculty-developed rubrics. In addition to a score in the grade book, this badge provides tangible proof of success. It also provides motivation for students to continue as they look forward to earning their next badge. For some students, these short-term wins or evidence of progress keeps them engaged in a course. Students are able to save their artifacts that receive badges in an ePortfolio, providing a way of monitoring students' outcomes or competencies in a program or department.

This is a powerful tool to motivate students to achieve more in your course. Setting the criteria for each badge is fairly easy and something you would do in the design of the course anyway; it communicates expectations to the students, and it delivers motivation through technology automatically that requires little of your time during the course itself.

## Final Considerations

### *How Does Testing Fit?*

Giving tests may be the most common method of assessment for many faculty and administrators, but as you see in Table 8.2, there are dozens of ways to assess student learning, informally and formally, and for formative and summative purposes. Some faculty have concluded that traditional testing is not as effective as more authentic activities, and other faculty like a combination. Furthermore, your department or institution may require formal summative exams, such as final exams.

The classic objective exam of multiple choice and true or false is best used to assess foundational knowledge. As we've discussed, foundational knowledge is important—indeed, all else is based on a solid foundation—but the other areas of the taxonomy (Fink, 2013) are equally important for deep, long-lasting learning. To assess the application area of the taxonomy, objective questions are less helpful. Exams that use essay questions and word problems, or case studies, or are based on clinical performance are better for assessing students' abilities to apply their learning to new situations. For assessing the integration area, essay exams that allow students to show they can pull together ideas from several parts of a course or unit work best. Oral exams can also accomplish this, but they require one-on-one contact, and most of us have too many students to do this.

Let's look at the foundational skills in the nursing outcome of drawing blood. It is easy to construct test items to verify that students can identify the steps and equipment involved in the procedure. But at some point, students' actual blood drawing skills must be examined in the clinical setting.

We don't recommend exams to assess Fink's (2013) caring, human dimension, or learning to learn domains. However, in Table 8.2, notice that test analysis is one of the activities or assessments in the learning how to learn area, which involves having students try to learn more about themselves by conducting a self-analysis of their testing including preparation as well as performance skills. Students often begin to see patterns in their own errors and learn how to avoid them in future exams. They may also realize they make errors because of anxiety during tests, which is something they can learn to improve.

**TABLE 8.2**

**Taxonomy Crosswalk for Assessment and Learning Activity Types**

| *Taxonomy Domain* | *Informal Versus Formal Assessment* | *Formative Versus Summative Assessment* | *Assessments and Learning Activities* | *Learning Types (Active, Passive, Connecting, Reflective)* | *Technology Options Learning Management System (LMS)* |
|---|---|---|---|---|---|
| **Foundational knowledge** | — | — | Readings | Passive | Text, Internet, LMS |
| | Informal | Formative | Think-pair-share | Active | Paper, whiteboards |
| | Informal | Formative | One-minute paper | Active, reflective | Paper, whiteboards |
| | Informal | Formative | Polling, quizzing | Active | Smartphones, clickers |
| | Informal | Formative | Advance organizers | Active, connecting | Paper, whiteboards |
| | Both | Formative | Concept maps | Active, reflective | Paper, whiteboards |
| | Informal | Formative | Draw a picture | Active, reflective | Paper, whiteboards |
| | Both | Both | Four corners | Active, reflective | Physical space |
| | Formal | Summative | Oral, video presentation | Active | Projector, LMS |
| | Both | Both | Discussions (live, written) | Active, reflective | Paper, LMS |
| | Informal | Both | Study cards | Active | Index cards |
| | Both | Both | Student self-assessment | Reflective | Paper, LMS |
| | Formal | Both | Written paper | Passive | Paper, LMS |
| | — | — | Lecture | Passive | Live, video, LMS |
| | Formal | Summative | Objective tests, exams | Passive | Paper, LMS |

| **Application** | — | — | Readings | Passive | Text, Internet, LMS |
|---|---|---|---|---|---|
| | Formal | Both | Case studies | Active, reflective | Paper, LMS |
| | Both | Both | Gallery walks | Active | Posters, whiteboards |
| | Both | Both | Four corners | Active | Physical space |
| | Both | Both | Jigsaws | Active | Posters, whiteboards |
| | Formal | Summative | Oral, video presentation | Active | Projector, LMS |
| | Both | Both | Discussions (live, written) | Active, reflective | Paper, LMS |
| | Both | Both | Student self-assessment | Reflective | Paper, LMS |
| | Formal | Both | Gaming, simulations | Active, connecting | Computer, projector |
| | Formal | Both | Role playing, dramatization | Active | Physical space |
| | Formal | Both | Portfolios | Active, reflective | Binder, ePortfolio |
| | Formal | Summative | Authentic projects | Active, reflective, or connecting | Paper, LMS |
| | Formal | Summative | Written paper | Active, passive | Paper, LMS |
| | Formal | Summative | Essay, application exams | Active, connecting | Paper, LMS |

(*Continues*)

**Table 8.2** (*Continued*)

| *Taxonomy Domain* | *Informal Versus Formal Assessment* | *Formative Versus Summative Assessment* | *Assessments and Learning Activities* | *Learning Types (Active, Passive, Connecting, Reflective)* | *Technology Options Learning Management System (LMS)* |
|---|---|---|---|---|---|
| **Integration** | — | — | Readings | Passive | Text, Internet, LMS |
| | Both | Both | Gallery walks | Active | Physical space |
| | Both | Both | Jigsaws | Active | Posters, whiteboards |
| | Both | Both | Advance organizers | Active, connecting | Paper, whiteboards |
| | Informal | Formative | Concept maps | Active, connecting | Paper, whiteboards |
| | Both | Both | Four corners | Active | Physical space |
| | Formal | Both | Case studies | Active, reflective | Paper, LMS |
| | Formal | Summative | Oral, video presentation | Active | Projector, LMS |
| | Both | Both | Discussions (live, written) | Active, reflective | Paper, LMS |
| | Formal | Both | Inquiry-based learning | Active, reflective, or connecting | Paper, LMS |
| | Formal | Both | Problem-based learning | Active, reflective, or connecting | Paper, LMS |
| | Formal | Both | Team-based learning | Active, reflective, or connecting | Paper, LMS |

| | | | | | |
|---|---|---|---|---|---|
| | Both | Both | Student self-assessment | Reflective | Paper, LMS |
| | Formal | Both | Gaming, simulations | Active, connecting | Computer, projector |
| | Formal | Both | Role playing, dramatization | Active | Physical space |
| | Formal | Both | Portfolios | Active, reflective | Binder, ePortfolio |
| | Formal | Summative | Authentic projects | Active, reflective, or connecting | Paper, LMS |
| | Formal | Summative | Field experience | Active, reflective, or connecting | Location |
| | Formal | Summative | Situational observation | Active, reflective, or connecting | Location |
| | Formal | Summative | Written paper | Active, passive | Paper, LMS |
| **Human Dimension Self, Others** | — | — | Readings | Passive | Text, Internet, LMS |
| | Formal | Both | Case studies | Active, reflective | Paper, LMS |
| | Formal | Summative | Oral, video presentation | Active | Projector, LMS |
| | Both | Both | Discussions (live, written) | Active, reflective | Paper, LMS |
| | Formal | Both | Inquiry-based learning | Active, reflective, or connecting | Paper, LMS |

(*Continues*)

**Table 8.2** (*Continued*)

| *Taxonomy Domain* | *Informal Versus Formal Assessment* | *Formative Versus Summative Assessment* | *Assessments and Learning Activities* | *Learning Types (Active, Passive, Connecting, Reflective)* | *Technology Options Learning Management System (LMS)* |
|---|---|---|---|---|---|
| | Formal | Both | Problem-based learning | Active, reflective, or connecting | Paper, LMS |
| | Formal | Both | Team-based learning | Active, reflective, or connecting | Paper, LMS |
| | Formal | Summative | Service-learning | Active, reflective, or connecting | Paper, LMS, location |
| | Both | Both | Student self-assessment | Reflective | Paper, LMS |
| | Formal | Both | Gaming, simulations | Active, connecting | Computer, projector |
| | Both | Both | Journaling | Reflective | Paper, LMS |
| | Formal | Both | Role playing, dramatization | Active | Physical space |
| | Formal | Summative | Portfolios | Active, reflective | Binder, ePortfolio |
| | Formal | Summative | Authentic projects | Active, reflective, or connecting | Paper, LMS |

| | | | | | |
|---|---|---|---|---|---|
| | Formal | Summative | Field experience | Active, reflective, or connecting | Location |
| | Formal | Summative | Situational observation | Active, reflective, or connecting | Location |
| | Formal | Summative | Written paper | Active, passive | Paper, LMS |
| **Caring (Valuing)** | — | — | Readings | Passive | Text, Internet, LMS |
| | Formal | Both | Case studies | Active, reflective | Paper, LMS |
| | Both | Summative | Oral, video presentation | Active | Projector, LMS |
| | Formal | Both | Discussions (live, written) | Active, reflective | Paper, LMS |
| | Formal | Both | Inquiry-based learning | Active, reflective, or connecting | Paper, LMS |
| | Formal | Both | Problem-based learning | Active, reflective, or connecting | Paper, LMS |
| | Formal | Both | Team-based learning | Active, reflective, or connecting | Paper, LMS |
| | Formal | Summative | Service-learning | Active, reflective, or connecting | Paper, LMS, location |
| | Both | Both | Student self-assessment | Reflective | Paper, LMS |

(*Continues*)

**Table 8.2** (*Continued*)

| *Taxonomy Domain* | *Informal Versus Formal Assessment* | *Informal Versus Formal Assessment* | *Assessments and Learning Activities* | *Learning Types (Active, Passive, Connecting, Reflective)* | *Technology Options Learning Management System (LMS)* |
|---|---|---|---|---|---|
| | Both | Both | Gaming, simulations | Active, connecting | Computer, projector |
| | Both | Both | Journaling | Reflective | Paper, LMS |
| | Formal | Both | Role playing, dramatization | Active | Physical space |
| | Formal | Summative | Portfolios | Active, reflective | Binder, ePorfolio |
| | Formal | Summative | Authentic projects | Active, reflective, or connecting | Paper, LMS |
| | Formal | Summative | Field experience | Active, reflective, or connecting | Location |
| | Formal | Summative | Situational observation | Active, reflective, or connecting | Location |
| | Formal | Summative | Written paper | Active, passive | Paper, LMS |

| **Learning How to Learn** | — | — | Readings | Passive | Text, Internet, LMS |
|---|---|---|---|---|---|
| | Formal | Both | Case studies | Active, reflective | Paper, LMS |
| | Both | Summative | Oral/Video Presentation | Active | Projector, LMS |
| | Formal | Both | Discussions (live/written) | Active, reflective | Paper, LMS |
| | Formal | Both | Inquiry-based learning | Active, reflective, or connecting | Paper, LMS |
| | Formal | Both | Problem-based learning | Active, reflective, or connecting | Paper, LMS |
| | Formal | Both | Team-based learning | Active, reflective, or connecting | Paper, LMS |
| | Formal | Summative | Student self-assessment | Reflective | Paper, LMS |
| | Formal | Summative | Journaling | Reflective | Paper, LMS |
| | Formal | Summative | Portfolios | Active, reflective | Binder, ePortfolio |
| | Formal | Summative | Future learning plan | Active, connecting | Paper, LMS |
| | Informal | Both | Test analysis | Active, reflective | Paper |

*Note*. This table offers a crosswalk comparison of possible assessments and learning activities for each domain of Fink's taxonomy.

## *What Should You Do With Your Results?*

Assessment results are for filling in the grade book, right? Although that is one important reason for collecting this valuable student mastery data, consider additional uses for the data once the final grades have been submitted. Results of assessments might be for you only, for your department's data collection, for your dean or other administrator, or for your college's assessment initiatives. For some disciplines, an outside agency may be interested in your assessments (Palomba & Banta, 2001). In fact, the top two uses for learning outcomes assessment are regional accreditation and program accreditation (National Institute for Learning Outcomes, 2018). However, according to Kuh and colleagues (2015), an important aspect of assessment is "to move the assessment of student learning from an act of compliance to the use of assessment results to guide changes that foster stronger student and institutional performance" (p. x). In fact, many faculty conduct periodic assessments just for their own information to compare from term to term how students have learned an outcome or to check on learning in a new course or topic. It's very helpful to see what kinds of problems students are having to determine how your teaching could improve next time you teach the content.

You should keep results of assessments even if you don't plan to share them. If you gather several over time, you may see patterns of improvement in learning that should be part of your teaching portfolio, you might use the results to lobby for curriculum development in your department, or you might see a need for some professional development for yourself or others.

Departments and programs may conduct assessments to verify that students are on track to matriculate to the next course in the sequence or are ready to take a licensure exam. Capstone assessments are designed to provide assurance that graduates are operating at acceptable levels in a range of skills that culminate in a graduation ready student who may go on to a career or further schooling. These results may be shared with stakeholders, such as program advisory boards, regents, boards of trustees, and others.

Colleges and universities often use assessment results as part of the reaccreditation process. Find out how your institution makes use of outcome assessments and offer to contribute to the pool of knowledge. Also, some campuses have common competencies all students are expected to reach by the time they graduate or transfer, and they may be periodically assessed. Critical thinking is one such competency. Every department or program should be able to assess for this competency, so think about how you might do that in one of your courses. The Association of American Colleges & Universities (2019) Value Rubrics are an excellent resource for rubrics on topics such as critical thinking, written communication, quantitative literacy, ethical reasoning, and 12 other competencies.

## *What If Your Students Perform Poorly?*

What if your students do not perform adequately on your assessment of an outcome? Let's return to the purpose of assessment. We said one of the uses of assessment is to improve teaching or the curriculum. It is a tool for informing you about your students' skills in a particular area and should not be used punitively.

If students perform poorly on assessment of an outcome across several sections, you can't ignore it as a one-off event. Something must be happening or not happening, and it deserves analysis. Ask yourself the following:

- Did the assessment match the outcome?
- Did the instruction match the outcome?
- Did students have multiple times to learn and improve on the outcome before being assessed?
- Did students have a foundation to perform at this level of learning?
- Was enough time provided to practice the content or skill to prepare for the assessment?

Alignment is key. If there is a disconnect between either the teaching of the learning activities and the outcome or the assessing and the outcome, students will likely not do well. Or if the assessment looks quite different from the practice assignments or activities that the students experienced, they may not be able to shift to a new method or recognize that it is the same. For example, if math students practice lots of computation problems on slope, but the assessment has many word problems about slope, students may not be able to set up a problem correctly to work it out. Setting up a problem and computing a problem are two different things; the tasks are not equivalent. Be sure your students practice the type of work any assessment will require. This is not teaching to the test as much as it is giving students a chance to practice what they will be expected to do.

Time on task is also a factor in learning and assessment. Learning takes time as well as repetition. Give students enough time to practice the tasks, so when they take the assessment, they are comfortable and ready.

**Bright Idea**

Keep a document somewhere in your computer files labeled Teach Better. When something goes wrong, make a note in this document with a clear explanation so you will remember it. Later, when you are getting this course ready for the next semester, review these items and find solutions for them. —**Linda Russell**

### *How Can Assessment Help Your Department or Program?*

Because assessments may be used to help an entire department examine the learning outcomes in a program or a group of sequenced courses, it can be extremely useful to carefully assess learning outcomes at several points in a curriculum. For example, if assessments show that students are still not mastering an important concept in the third course in the sequence, plans could be made to return to that concept more deliberately in the first and second courses.

Faculty at one campus discovered that beginning chemistry students did not understand dimensional analysis, which is used in balancing equations. The prerequisite math course instructors and the chemistry instructors all agreed that the math course could begin teaching this type of analysis, and the chemistry instructors would actively teach it again in the context of chemistry. Once both sets of faculty deliberately taught the concepts and gave students practice, the students overall did much better on the assessment of dimensional analysis in chemistry. This collaboration benefited student learning and gave faculty a chance to work together across disciplines.

This level of measurement for outcomes is a best practice regardless of whether your program or department is accredited or not. Your institution needs to demonstrate this level of assessing outcomes for its accreditation; the more you can do to demonstrate this mastery is important for that accreditation and to show employers what your students can do for employment (see chapter 10 for more about how student assessment is used for program, department, and institutional accreditation).

Throughout this chapter we examine the layers of the assessment of student learning. We offer a variety of ways to assess student mastery of outcomes in courses and how to blend a variety of assessments to provide a multidimensional perspective of how students are achieving. We also discuss how you can measure the quality of your course design often by analyzing the results of your students' success on your assessments. Finally, we look at what you can do with your results and how they can help you strengthen your program or department.

## Reflect on This Chapter

Now that you have completed reading this chapter and thinking about the content as it applies to your work, please reflect on the following questions:

- What should I do if my students aren't meeting the learning outcomes?
- Have I made sure my assessments measure the course's learning outcomes?
- In reflecting on the multiple means of course assessment presented, how could I enhance the types of assessment I use in my courses?
- How can the assessment I conduct in my courses help my department?
- How can assessment help my department?

**Jot Your Thoughts**

## Action Checklist

Use Checklist 8.1 to apply the chapter content to your practice and help you identify the steps for implementing these ideas in your teaching.

**CHECKLIST 8.1** Assessing Student Learning Action Checklist

| ✓ | **Assessing Through Learning Outcomes** |
|---|---|
| ❑ | Aligned my assessments to my course learning outcomes and activities. |
| ❑ | Developed an understanding that testing my students is for individual assessment and grading purposes. |
| ❑ | Considered ways that assessments can provide insights of aggregated student performance on selected learning outcomes for program or department improvement. |

| ✓ | **Using Rubrics** |
|---|---|
| ❑ | Learned the basic elements of a scoring rubric. |
| ❑ | Created rubrics that include descriptive language for each criterion at each scoring level. |
| ❑ | Practiced by test-driving rubrics before using them for actual scoring in the course. |
| ❑ | Received feedback on course rubrics from students or colleagues. |
| ❑ | Determined a method to apply rubrics in my grading system. |
| ❑ | Established a goal of developing rubrics for discussions, assignments, and assessments in all my courses. |

| ✓ | **Assessment Planning** |
|---|---|
| ❑ | Developed a course assessment plan with the help of Table 8.2. |
| ❑ | Have included informal and formal assessments. |
| ❑ | Designed formative and summative assessments to measure student mastery. |
| ❑ | Created backward-looking assessments for foundational knowledge outcomes and forward-looking assessments for the outcomes from the other domains. |
| ❑ | Analyzed how the same experiences can serve as a learning activity or assessment depending on where in the course they are placed. |
| ❑ | Used a variety of learning types (active, passive, connecting, reflective) appropriately for designing assessments. |
| ❑ | Considered the technology needed to deliver learning in a face-to-face, blended, or online environment. |

(*Continues*)

**CHECKLIST 8.1** (*Continued*)

| ✓ | **Purposes of Assessment** |
|---|---|
| ❑ | Used course assessment results to improve course design and teaching methods. |
| ❑ | Analyzed course assessment results to improve program or department student mastery, retention, and matriculation in courses to improve curriculum. |
| ❑ | Use assessments to gauge student mastery before they take a licensure or other standard exam. |
| ❑ | Considered how to use portfolio assessment as a learning tool, a capstone experience, or to showcase students' work. |
| ❑ | Analyzed course assessment results as a part of reflecting on the quality of teaching practice to develop a personal plan for improvement. |

# 9

# ASSESSING COURSE QUALITY

## Points to Ponder

Chapter 9 examines ways to assess the quality of your course's design. In thinking about designing the courses you teach, consider the following questions to examine your prior knowledge:

- How do you know that your course is good?
- What strategies do you use to measure your course's quality?
- What feedback opportunities do you use for students to tell you about their experience in the course?

Luis just got back from a meeting with his dean where he was discussing the previous semester's course evaluations completed by his students. Sitting at his desk, he stared at his computer knowing he had to do something about the design of his courses because he was feeling overwhelmed and disappointed with the results of the evaluations. His dean encouraged him to address the feedback he got from the students and change some aspects of the course. He needed to figure out where to start, decide what was good about his course, and what needed improvement.

For a few semesters now, the students had complained about the textbook and wondered if he cared about their progress in the course. He felt he was being reactive to issues, spending most of his time fixing problems rather than teaching and working with his students.

In talking with a colleague who had just returned from a workshop on assessing course quality, he decided he needed more specific feedback on what he needed to do to improve the design of his course. He reviewed the course evaluations and realized his students hadn't really been complaining as much as they were offering some good ideas. This was a good starting point.

Luis started to use the ideas to make some changes. He gathered a group of students he trusted and asked them to look through his redesigned course. He agreed that the text was getting old and a bit dry, so he replaced it. He also realized that he could ask students to bring some of the resources they had found to class. His colleague had been allowing more discussions in the course shell and had students reflect on what they thought was valuable in each of the units, so he used that idea for feedback. He added more frequent feedback on assignments in his new version of the course. Using an outline his colleague got at the workshop, he added some of its elements and asked her to look at his course redesign.

The students and his faculty colleague recognized the value in the changes so he was feeling better about this course now. Luis decided to use this redesigned course next semester. He also signed up for the next workshop that covered strategies that make courses more engaging so he could learn from other faculty what was working in their courses. If these changes worked, he could apply many of these ideas to his other courses.

## Striving for Quality

In our learning experiences we often wondered how we were doing in our courses. Not much has changed; the universal question from our students from elementary school to graduate school is, "Am I doing well?" As faculty, administrators, and course designers we need to be asking the same question. Measuring the effectiveness of your course is an essential component of course design, and no one designs a course perfectly before teaching it. Think of designing a course like buying a new vehicle; first you research it, look at the features, and then test-drive it before you purchase it. The first time you teach the course you designed is akin to taking it out on the road. Before you leave the lot you need to have the seat and mirrors in the correct position. Once on the road, you will notice other things that you will want to adjust. This isn't a failure, it is a normal part of the course design process. During the life of a course, you will continue to make changes to the design and assess the quality of the course and the experience your students are having in their learning. Course design follows a continuous improvement model.

The following are reasons for measuring your course's quality:

- Your course needs to remain current to provide significant learning experiences for students, and measuring quality ensures that it does. You will continue to find new or better teaching materials, integrate technology to improve learning, or update content based on new discipline standards and competencies.
- By knowing your course design is solid, you focus your time on teaching students directly, not working with the technical operation of the course. You improve your ability to teach by having the time to meet students' individual needs.
- Great design can actually make your course workload lighter and more enjoyable as you see your students grow.
- Measuring course quality builds your teaching confidence. You will identify what you need to change based on assessment, and once changes are in

place, you'll know that you are providing significant learning. You can also participate in teaching and learning conversations with other faculty and your administration. Your work on improving quality course design can be a goal in your professional development plan.

- You will have answered the question, "Am I doing well?"

In this chapter we examine several strategies for measuring the quality of your courses using the practice of continuous improvement. You can use many of these strategies on your own informally, which is the first step in the pathway to prepare for formal course quality evaluations. Diamond (2008) uses a systems approach, high faculty ownership, and gaining the support of the institution. Smith (2016) focuses on online delivery. Also, Dunn, McCarthy, Baker, and Halonen (2010) offer a set of guiding questions to consider as you begin thinking about course quality. Their benchmark approach considers identifiable thresholds of quality for a course, program, or discipline.

## Before You Teach: Test-Drive Your Course

Prior to teaching a course we recommend that you ask others to test-drive it. Using preteaching feedback from colleagues from inside and outside your department, or former students if you are redesigning a course, is a helpful way to identify challenges. Having other sets of eyes examining your course is important to ensure your design work is understandable by all. In the middle of the design process, you might get tunnel vision and miss some of the peripherals that make the student experience better. Student feedback helps keep your course learner centered. We recommend taking a small risk and opening yourself up for feedback from those you trust to be honest with you by doing the following:

- Ask a colleague to review your syllabus and your class schedule and critique the sequencing and pacing of your course delivery, as well as your planned assignments, activities, and assessments. Smith (2016) describes syllabus and schedule review methods to use for online courses. She also includes the way the course is organized, how students can get the repetitions they need, and how generally understandable the materials will be for students.
- Compare your course to one of a colleague who is teaching another section of the same, previous, or next course in the curriculum sequence to see how your course connects to the other and prepares students to be successful.
- Check pacing, workload, and assessment methods to consider how your course aligns with department expectations.
- Share assignments, project ideas, exam questions, and ideas with colleagues.

Designing a course as a collaborative process provides the opportunity to test it so you know you are offering a quality experience to your students. Failing to share your design is a missed opportunity to eliminate barriers to your teaching and student learning. Designing in isolation doesn't allow you to capitalize on ideas that collaboration provides. Your design goal should be to provide the greatest degree of significant learning the first time you teach the course.

## Assess Your Course Syllabus

The major document communicating your course design and its policies is your syllabus, which is a one-stop walk-through of course expectations to help students be successful and to communicate to internal and external audiences, like your dean or chair, curriculum committees, and transfer and accrediting agencies, what is covered and the degree to which content is covered. Your self-assessment of the document's effectiveness and completeness will help you prepare to publish it to audiences. As you design your syllabus, your institution may have a template it requires you to use. Ask if it is permissible to add additional information. Two quality resources we offer here will help you design your syllabus.

The first resource was developed by Palmer and colleagues (2014) and provides a syllabus rubric guide and scoring sheet focusing on the following areas:

- Learning goals and objectives
- Assessment activities
- Schedule
- Classroom environment

A supplemental rubric includes details on scoring learning activities. Appendix A in Palmer and colleagues (2014) provides an extensive list of verbs that best fit when writing outcomes for each domain of Fink's (2013) taxonomy of significant learning and when designing a variety of thinking and skill performance activities.

A second rubric resource from the University of Cincinnati (n.d.) provides assessment criteria for the following broader range of syllabus elements:

- Visual appeal
- Course overview
- Student learning outcomes
- Course resources
- Prerequisite, corequisite, breadth of knowledge areas
- Electronic communications policy
- Attendance policy
- Academic integrity policy
- Special needs and accommodation policy
- Pass or fail, audit, withdrawal policy
- Course calendar

We recommend using both of these rubrics as a checklist for some of the best practices in syllabus assessment.

Many authors who have published syllabi offered a means to assess the quality. Another checklist and rubric we found helpful and provided a slightly different criteria is from Harrington and Thomas (2018).

## Measuring Quality as You Teach

There are several ways for you to measure the quality of your course. We follow the principles of formative assessment and suggest you find ways to evaluate the quality of your course design, activities, and assessments. The purpose of formative assessment is to provide checks on progress toward mastering learning outcomes. Similarly, you can use the methods we describe next as mini assessments of how well your course is meeting your goals for students. Making the effort to glean feedback on your course during the term also sends a positive message to your students that you care about improvement and their learning experiences. When you are willing to make midcourse corrections, you gain credibility as a standard bearer of excellence, and you also end up with a better course the next time you teach it.

### *Formative Course Assessments*

A valuable way to measure the quality of your course is to use the information from students' course evaluations. Course evaluations can be provided informally by the instructor as a formative assessment during the course and as a summative assessment at the end of the course. These informal assessments are for your eyes only and should be used to continually improve your course. Your institution most likely has a formal course evaluation process to obtain student feedback. Be sure to find out what the process is and get a copy of the formal course evaluation so you know how you and your course will be evaluated. These formal assessments will probably be sent to your department chair or dean as well.

You can check to see how your students are progressing throughout the course to help you address any issues before students fill out the final course evaluation at the end of the course. It is vital to course correct throughout the semester. Some faculty think that it is best to ask students about their attitudes and reflections about the course at the end when students have gone through all the content and activities. This is a bit of a fallacy for a couple of reasons. Students make up their minds about a course in the first few weeks and will have determined if you are involving them in their learning, if you are providing feedback on their work that helps them progress in the course, and if the workload makes sense and matches the outcomes that will help them in their career.

Another reason that this is a fallacy is that your course design shouldn't have all the bells and whistles at the end of the course. For retention, students need engaging learning activities that hook them into wanting to learn more from start to finish. The course design shouldn't replicate a fireworks display with a flourish of several explosions at the beginning to pique interest, followed by one flash at a time to make the show last longer, and conclude with a big bang experience so everyone will walk away happy. Course design needs to provide a series of fulfilling experiences to motivate student learning.

A final reason is that assessing the course sooner during the semester conveys that you care about student learning and are are willing to make adjustments during the course. In a variety of course evaluations, we have usually seen an assessment item similar to this: "My instructor cares about my progress in this course." Knowing the perception of your caring about their progress helps you make corrections as needed.

Whether you teach face-to-face, blended, or online courses, the discussion tool of your learning platform's course shell is a great place to collect and archive information about your class. This serves as a place for you to assess student learning, and with the right questions you can collect some great feedback that will help you improve your course.

Ask students to reflect on their learning. If they indicate they are struggling with any of your content, you can improve it by building a stronger foundation or setting up the course differently so it makes greater sense to them. Offer them opportunities to critique course content such as the readings, handouts, and videos. Let them tell you what they found meaningful. From these critiques you can measure the effectiveness of what you have provided. Providing a board for them to post and discuss materials they find online can show you what is important to them, and perhaps they will find some great articles for the resource section of your course or to use as additional readings in future courses. This is also a way to help students dive deeper into the course content to meet their individual learning interests. A tip we gave earlier in the book is to have students identify the course outcomes they most relate to or want to learn more about. Allowing them to post additional resources they discovered in their learning is a way to help them fulfill their personal learning and meet the learning how to learn outcome.

What do you do with the informal feedback you get from students? Openly address the concerns students have in the class, and tell them why you designed the course the way you did. If you can make a few tweaks in the course to improve based on the feedback, you will really show your students you mean business when it comes to creating a significant learning environment. Even if you cannot change something midstream, you can explain why. Make sure that you provide this information in the course design so the next time you teach the course, you won't have to cover the same concerns. The feedback may provide you with ways to better present, or bridge, material for stronger learning connections.

### *Classroom Assessment Techniques and Learning Assessment Techniques*

As you can use formative assessments to provide students feedback on their course progress, you can gather feedback on your course design using classroom assessment techniques (CATs). Angelo and Cross's (1993) handbook includes 50 CATs. Many of these were developed prior to the explosion of online courses, but they can be easily adapted to this format. Barkley and Major's (2016b) learning assessment techniques (LATs) include excellent strategies for face-to-face and online courses. They are aligned with Fink's (2013) taxonomy of significant learning as well, and to make sure you have assessments for each of the categories, use their reference guide (Barkley & Major, 2016a). These formative assessments usually take minutes to complete and provide excellent information on how well your students are learning. It helps your students reflect on their learning and can help them learn how they best learn.

### *Benefits of Using CATs and LATs*

When used frequently by faculty, CATs or LATs

- deliver day-to-day feedback that can be applied immediately;
- provide useful information about what students have learned without the amount of time required for preparing tests, reading papers, and so on;
- allow you to address student misconceptions or lack of understanding in a timely way; and
- help to foster good working relationships with students and encourage them to understand that teaching and learning are ongoing processes that require full participation (Iowa State University Center for Excellence in Learning and Teaching, 2019).

Looking through the CATs and LATs provides you with a clearer picture of how students are learning prior to using a more structured formative or summative assessment. It will prevent you from being surprised that your students didn't understand the content when there are higher stakes results. When you see what students haven't learned, you can communicate additional information or restate content in a different manner using e-mail, class discussion at your next meeting, or in the course shell. Clarifying the unclear information and reviewing it by reteaching should be done quickly so students don't remain confused for very long.

For students, CATs and LATs can

- help develop self-assessment and learning management skills;
- reduce feelings of isolation, especially in large classes;
- increase understanding and ability to think critically about the course content;
- foster an attitude that values understanding and long-term retention; and
- show that you are interested and supportive of their success in your course (Iowa State University Center for Excellence in Learning and Teaching, 2019).

CATs and LATs reinforce much of Fink's (2013) course design principles of human dimension, caring and learning how to learn, as we discuss next. These can easily be used on discussion boards in the course shell, which can work for face-to-face, blended, and online courses.

**Bright Idea**

The one-minute paper can consist of asking students to respond to a few simple questions such as, What was the most important idea you learned in this session? What questions for you remain unanswered? What is the muddiest point for you in the content? or How could I help you learn this better? Having students write their answer on a half-sheet of paper and hand it to you as they leave the classroom or creating a quiz or discussion question online gives them an opportunity to share where they are in learning the material. Anonymity may help you get greater genuine responses from students who may be afraid to admit what they don't know or what they are unclear about, so ensuring anonymity is usually preferred either online or on paper with no names. If the students know each other well, use a discussion question so they can discuss and clarify it with one another. —**Zala Fashant**

### *Creating Your Own Course Assessments*

Using the statements we have created in course assessments at our institutions can assist you in developing a formative evaluation for your students to measure course quality. The scale measuring students' responses is the Likert type: *strongly agree, agree, disagree, strongly disagree.* Notice there are just four choices, which forces students away from the noncommittal neutral response, which will not help you make any course improvements. Typical statements for students to indicate their agreement or not include the following:

- The Getting Started information was helpful as I started the course.
- The Description and Purpose of the Course was clear to me.
- Having the technical requirements needed for this course was helpful.
- The instructor provided ways for me to learn more about my instructor and classmates.
- The course outcomes were written so I could understand them.
- The design of the course demonstrated how the outcomes and learning activities were aligned.
- I understood how the learning goals and the learning activities were connected.
- It was clear to me that the exams and other learning assessments were tied to the course outcomes.
- Instructions for assignments and assessments were clearly communicated.
- A variety of learning activities and assessments allowed me to demonstrate what I learned.
- The course activities and assessments helped me engage in my learning.
- I was able to track my learning progress regularly.
- My instructor was interested in my learning progress in the course.

- The content in this course provided a variety of resources to learn from.
- The content resources reflected multiple viewpoints (i.e., different cultures, levels of experience, gender, etc.).
- The content was current and properly cited so I can learn more from the sources.
- The course design had a variety of Web links so I can access the campus information I need to support my learning when I need help.

Your institution may require a standard summative student course survey evaluation that may or may not use some of these statements to assess your course's quality. You may have noted that responding to all these statements would probably take more time than you have to give in one survey. You could break them up into a few each week to give you timely feedback. Asking all of them in each course, at once, or in weekly segments can give you feedback to measure course improvement over time. Or you can include only the items you want feedback on once you know which items have scored high in past evaluations.

## Feedback Improves Course Quality

The information you learn from feedback can help you make course design improvements to avoid similar challenges in the future. Getting this valuable feedback from students will help you write clearer directions and instructions for assignments and assessments. You may decide to teach the content in a different way or in a new order. Perhaps you need to add more introductory information to set up the new content. You may also realize you need to give students more practice in using the information through group discussions or by using a think-pair-share activity where students first think of the answer individually, then discuss it with a partner, and then finally respond out loud to the class. You can set up the same experience by developing talking groups in the course shell discussions.

## Measuring Quality After You Teach Your Course

Once you have had the opportunity to reflect on the feedback from your colleagues who have reviewed your course; made course corrections by using what students have shared informally through CATs and LATs, discussions, and formative assessments; and examined the success your students are demonstrating in mastering the course outcomes by completing learning activities and assessments, it is time to consider moving to a formal means of measuring course quality by using diagnostic tools.

### *Institutional Course Evaluations*

As previously discussed, using student-completed course surveys and evaluations are a valuable way to obtain feedback about your course. Many faculty appreciate this feedback as a way to improve their courses, and they use this information to help write clearer directions, improve assignments to make them even more meaningful, and get additional ideas on what students valued in the course. Deans appreciate this information from students to help determine what kinds of professional development the institution could provide to assist faculty. If your institution has a professional development committee, having a dean participate in it is helpful. Feedback shouldn't be feared. It is a great way to do your job better by delivering quality instruction to help with student retention. None of us wants to be getting in the way of our students' success. Your institution may have prescribed course surveys that you must administer during the course, and many wait until the end of the semester to provide the assessments.

### *Self-Assessing Your Course Design*

As you design your course, consider the following for providing learning pathways to help your students succeed. The ideas presented here develop clearer course navigation and communication to help your students succeed in your course. We have developed the following set of rubrics to help you measure your own course shell's quality using the best course design practices, no matter the delivery method. In the course design, faculty should provide the following components of quality. See Table 9.1 for details to help you assess your course design quality overview.

Providing a Getting Started section in your course helps students by guiding them through the content so it doesn't appear overwhelming. Pointing to where to start in the course shell menu and in your syllabus will direct them to a course navigation pathway.

The purpose of the course is a great place to share your big dream. Why should students benefit from this course? What do you want them to achieve? Include previous courses and knowledge students need to be successful.

The technological requirements tells students what hardware, software, and skills are needed for the course. If your institution has a page on its website that offers this information, providing the link to that is good, but sharing how to download the technology and what a student's computer needs to have in your course and syllabus is even more helpful.

Building course community engages students by making them feel welcome, gets them off to a great start, and helps them complete the course. Faculty can share a teaching philosophy, purpose for the course, the big dream, and some personal profile information using text or video. Having students introduce themselves by sharing some personal information and what they hope to obtain and achieve in the course gives them a great chance to network with one another. See Table 9.2 for details to help you assess your course design quality learning outcomes and alignment.

The learning outcomes should be measurable and clearly written in language students understand, and the outcomes need to match the level of the course. Verbs for introductory courses are used for more basic concepts and should reflect higher level thinking for more advanced courses.

Learning activities should be aligned with course outcomes and prepare students for assessments to measure the achievement of outcomes and completion of activities.

This alignment could be presented in a crosswalk table in your syllabus and learning managment system (LMS) so students understand the relationships. A crosswalk table is a valuable way to demonstrate relationships and acts as a pathway that bridges topics from varying categories. Developing this crosswalk table to show course outcomes, unit objectives, assignments, and assessments can be placed in the syllabus and the course shell. We also recommend posting this crosswalk relationship to show what students are learning in each unit, as shown in Fink's (2013) three-column table (Table 2.5).

Learning activities should be aligned with course outcomes and prepare students for assessments to measure the achievement of outcomes and completion of activities. This alignment is presented in a crosswalk table (Table 8.2) for students to understand the relationships and are identified throughout course units, assignments, and assessments in the syllabus and the course shell. This is shown in Fink's (2013) three-column table (Table 2.5). See Table 9.3 for details to help you assess your course design quality in the areas of assignments, activities, and assessments.

Detailed descriptions of assignments and assessments clarify your expectations to students by explaining grading, learner participation, resources and materials, checklists and rubrics, time lines and due dates, and how all student work equates to the final grade.

Sequencing activities that build on one another and providing a variety of course activities gives students several ways to demonstrate their mastery of learning. Knowing that students learn differently, the design includes different learning styles and perhaps customizable ways for students to show what they have learned to use in their career.

Engaging students in doing something is the best way they can learn. Active learning opportunities include discussions, hands-on activities, presentations, and demonstrations, all workplace-based activities that provide real-world experience to prepare them for their careers.

Students can monitor their progress throughout the course. Access to grades and faculty feedback is critical to learning and course completion. Students should see this progress weekly as three tests and a final paper over a semester don't provide this ability to monitor progress. See Table 9.4 for details to help you assess the quality of your course's instructional and content materials.

Course content should support the outcomes and represent a variety of perspectives including a diverse and inclusive set of viewpoints. Choosing a variety of materials helps keep students engaged and interested as they see role models from a variety of backgrounds. Content is identified as required and optional for additional learning.

Content should be current with proper citations and sources. Textbooks, readings, and videos should be recent. Be intentional with your materials. Use something older if you tell students your reason for doing so, and match your content to current industry and professional organizational standards.

Develop a variety of learning materials that comply with the Americans with Disabilities Act (ADA; 1990) to ensure that your course shell, readings, videos, and

**TABLE 9.1**
**Course Quality Rubric: Course Overview**

| *Criteria Checklist* | *Score* | *Excellent (4 points for each criteria)* | *Very Good (3 points for each criteria)* | *Developing (2 points for each criteria)* | *Opportunity (1–0 points for each criteria)* |
|---|---|---|---|---|---|
| Course overview | | Total Point Range 16–14 | Total Point Range 13–10 | Total Point Range 9–6 | Total Point Range 5–0 |
| Getting started in the course | | Complete instructions for getting started and how to maneuver in the course are provided in the course design and the syllabus. | Complete instructions for getting started and how to maneuver in the course are provided in the course design or the syllabus. | Instructions for getting started and how to maneuver in the course are provided but are not complete or are unclear. | Instructions for getting started and how to maneuver in the course are missing or incomplete. |
| Clearly stated purpose or description of the course | | A clear, detailed purpose or description of the course is provided, which includes a listing of previous knowledge and skill needed in the course, institutional or course policies, schedule of assignments, grading, attendance, confidentiality, and learner behavior. | A clear purpose or description of the course is provided, which includes many of the following: a listing of previous knowledge and skill needed in the course, institutional or course policies, schedule of assignments, grading, attendance, confidentiality, and learner behavior. | A clear purpose or description of the course is provided, which includes only three or four of the following: listing of previous knowledge and skill needed in the course, institutional or course policies, schedule of assignments, grading, attendance, confidentiality, and learner behavior. | A purpose or description of the course is not provided or only includes one or two of the following: listing of previous knowledge and skill needed in the course, institutional or course policies, schedule of assignments, grading, attendance, confidentiality, and learner behavior. |

| | | | | | |
|---|---|---|---|---|---|
| Technological requirements | | All the technological requirements (hardware and learner skills) are stated, and all the links are provided to get assistance. | Most of the technological requirements (hardware and learner skills) are stated, and many of the links are provided to get assistance. | Some of the technological requirements (hardware and learner skills) are stated, and some of the links are provided to get assistance. | Technological requirements (hardware and learner skills) or links for technology assistance are missing. |
| Building course community | | The design includes all of the following: instructor welcome and self-introductory video or audio discussing teaching philosophy, past teaching experience, course expectations and hopes, and personal information, and an opportunity for students to do the same is provided. | The design includes most of the following: instructor welcome and self-introductory video or audio discussing teaching philosophy, past teaching experience, course expectations and hopes, and personal information, and an opportunity for students to do the same is provided. | The design includes some of the following: Instructor welcome and self-introductory video or audio discussing teaching philosophy, past teaching experience, course expectations and hopes, and personal information, and an opportunity for students to do the same is not provided. | The design lacks portions of the following: Instructor welcome and self-introductory video or audio discussing teaching philosophy, past teaching experience, course expectations and hopes, and personal information, and an opportunity for students to do the same is not provided. |

*Note*. This rubric provides a means to assess course overview criteria.

**TABLE 9.2**

**Course Quality Rubric: Learning Outcomes**

| *Criteria Checklist* | *Score* | *Excellent (4 points for each criterion)* | *Very Good (3 points for each criterion)* | *Developing (2 points for each criterion)* | *Opportunity (1–0 points for each criterion)* |
|---|---|---|---|---|---|
| Learning outcomes (competencies) | | Total Point Range 12–11 | Total Point Range 10–8 | Total Point Range 7–5 | Total Point Range 4–0 |
| Measurable, clear, and written to an appropriate level for the course introductory versus advanced | | The learning outcomes and competencies are measurable, stated clearly so students can understand them, and written at an appropriate level for the course. The design includes unit or weekly objectives written in the same manner. | The learning outcomes and competencies are measurable, stated clearly so students can understand them, and written at an appropriate level for the course. | The learning outcomes and competencies lack one of the following: are measurable, stated clearly so students can understand them, and written at an appropriate level for the course. | The learning outcomes and competencies lack two or more of the following: are measurable, stated clearly so students can understand them, and written at an appropriate level for the course. |
| Align with learning activities | | The learning outcomes and competencies align with the learning activities and are communicated to students by showing the alignment relationship in the design of the course by stating them in the course units and as a part of each activity or assignment. | The learning outcomes and competencies align with the learning activities and are communicated to students by showing the alignment relationship in the design of the course by stating them in the course units. | The learning outcomes and competencies align with the learning activities and are communicated to students. | The learning outcomes and competencies are not aligned with the learning activities or are not communicated to students. |
| Align with assessments | | The learning outcomes and competencies align with the assessments and are communicated to students by showing the alignment relationship in the design of the course by stating them in the course units and as a part of each activity or assignment. | The learning outcomes and competencies align with the assessments and are communicated to students by showing the alignment relationship in the design of the course by stating them in the course units. | The learning outcomes and competencies align with the assessments and are communicated to students. | The learning outcomes and competencies are not aligned with the assessments or are not communicated to students. |

*Note.* This rubric provides a means to assess course overview criteria.

**TABLE 9.3**

**Course Quality Rubric: Assignments, Activities, and Assessment**

| *Criteria Checklist* | *Score* | *Excellent (4 points for each criteria)* | *Very Good (3 points for each criteria)* | *Developing (2 points for each criteria)* | *Opportunity (1–0 points for each criteria)* |
|---|---|---|---|---|---|
| Assignments, activities, and assessment | | Total Point Range 16–14 | Total Point Range 13–10 | Total Point Range 9–6 | Total Point Range 5–0 |
| Expectations and measurement | | A clear, detailed description of assignment and assessment expectations is provided including all of the following and more: grading, learner participation, resources and materials, checklist and rubric, due dates, and the relationship to the final grade. | A clear, detailed description of assignment and assessment expectations is provided including all of the following: grading, learner participation, resources and materials, checklist and rubric, due dates, and the relationship to the final grade. | A clear, detailed description of assignment and assessment expectations is provided including some of the following: grading, learner participation, resources and materials, checklist and rubric, due dates, and the relationship to the final grade. | The design lacks clear descriptions of assignment and assessment expectations by not including many of the following: grading, learner participation, resources and materials, checklist and rubric, due dates, and the relationship to the final grade. |
| Sequenced and varied | | The design of the course sequences the level of the learning assignments, activities, assessments, and provides five or more ways for students to demonstrate a level of mastery. Activities are designed to provide significant learning. | The design of the course sequences the level of the learning assignments, activities, and assessments, and provides three or four more ways for students to demonstrate a level of mastery. Activities are designed to provide significant learning. | The design of the course sequences the level of the learning assignments, activities, and assessments, and provides a couple of ways for students to demonstrate a level of mastery. Activities are designed to provide significant learning. | The design of the course fails to sequence the level of the learning assignments, activities, and assessments, and/or provides only one way for students to demonstrate a level of mastery. |
| Engaged and active learning | | Active learning to engage students is embedded throughout the entire course. | Active learning to engage students is embedded in this course. | There is some active learning to engage students in this course. | There is little active learning to engage students in this course. |
| Ability to track learning progress | | The course design provides eight or more opportunities to measure and monitor learning progress. | The course design provides six or seven opportunities to measure and monitor learning progress. | The course design provides four or five opportunities to measure and monitor learning progress. | The course design provides three or fewer opportunities to measure and monitor learning progress. |

*Note*. This rubric provides a means to assess course overview criteria.

handouts are accessible for all learners. Talk with staff in your accessibility office on campus to help you with resources.

Provide learner support in a Need Help? tab in the course menu bar. Explain to students where they need to go on campus and whom to contact to get help with technological requirements, library resources, and learning accommodations.

By adding these elements, you will help your students navigate your course and build welcoming, engaging, and inclusive learning environments.

### *Self-Assessment Scorecard*

A rubric to assess course quality has been designed by the State University of New York (n.d.) for reviewing and improving the instructional design and accessibility of online courses based on online best practices. With 50 integrated instructional design and accessibility standards, the rubric can be used to identify and target aspects of online courses for improvement. Many of the rubric's criteria are useful for designing face-to-face and blended courses as well. The rubric's categories include course overview and information, course technology and tools, design and layout, content and activities, interaction, assessment, and feedback.

### *Peer-Assessing Your Course Design*

There are many standards for assessing course design that have been developed by institutions and international organizations. Your institution may have a set of design templates to use in creating your courses. We don't want to discourage using the institution-developed resources, but we encourage using an additional established set of criteria to help your course meet quality standards to benefit students.

Using the expertise of peer evaluators who have been trained to analyze courses for improvement is the next stop on the pathway to measuring course quality. Quality Matters (QM; 2018b) offers peer mentoring for faculty through a framework of design principles to ensure quality in their courses. Even though QM developed criteria primarily for online courses, the design elements apply well to course shells for face-to-face and blended courses. Faculty have the opportunity to learn more about the design layout that QM provides to get their courses peer evaluated and certified as having reached QM standards.

QM's (2018c) rubric assesses the best practices for student-centered course design because "when online courses are well-designed, organizations are more likely to see an increase in student engagement, learning, and overall satisfaction" (para. 3). In addition,

> QM Rubrics and Standards were created to help course developers, teachers, faculty, entire organizations, and—most importantly—students. The General Standards and Specific Review Standards in each Rubric are intended to guide you through the development, evaluation, and improvement of your online and blended courses. . . . Meeting these quality expectations at or above the 85% level is key to certify the quality of courses. (para. 1)

One of the advantages of using this organization is that the standards were developed by researching the literature on best practices in online learning. The standards are peer-reviewed about every three years by the users to maintain quality and reflect changes in literature. The QM (2018a) higher education rubric evaluates the following general standards:

- Course overview and introduction
- Learning objectives (competencies)
- Assessment and measurement
- Instructional materials
- Course activities and learning interaction
- Course technology
- Learner support
- Accessibility and usability

The QM rubric assesses the concept of alignment. Each of the rubric's criteria provides detailed annotations with examples and explanations to meet the standard. This level of detail helps you develop the best design to achieve the 85% threshold for certification.

Most QM reviews involve a team of three faculty consisting of an external reviewer, a subject matter expert reviewer from your discipline, and the master reviewer chair. Each team member provides feedback about how you did or didn't meet the criteria. They also provide you with ideas on how to meet the criteria and with enhanced ideas that can help you improve your course. Team members have seen many courses from across the country and can share strategies for delivering similar content to students across a variety of disciplines. In getting your course reviewed, you benefit from these ideas and from supportive faculty who want to see you succeed. There is a fee for courses to be formally reviewed.

In our work as directors of centers for teaching and learning we have coached many instructors in measuring the quality of their courses. After having courses evaluated and having done the reviewing as evaluators, we have designed faculty development workshops on our own campuses. The training and mentorship has provided an opportunity for rich conversations about course design and developed a safe learning environment for faculty to share their ideas openly about how to develop quality in their courses. Faculty who have one of their courses successfully reviewed are able to apply what they have learned from the review team to their other courses. Once they have a quality course, they usually aren't satisfied until they see that quality in all their courses, and they want to pass along that knowledge to their colleagues. In a way, it is a bit addictive; the wave of improvement is contagious. Other faculty want to learn how to develop stronger courses so they also can provide significant learning.

Apply the strategies from this chapter for test-driving and making course corrections from student feedback through CATs, LATs, and course evaluations

**TABLE 9.4**

**Instructional Content and Materials Rubric**

| *Criteria Checklist* | *Score* | *Excellent (4 points for each criterion)* | *Very Good (3 points for each criterion)* | *Developing (2 points for each criterion)* | *Opportunity (1 point for each criterion)* |
|---|---|---|---|---|---|
| Instructional content and materials | | 16–14 | 13–10 | 9–6 | 5–4 |
| Content support | | Course content selected richly supports the outcomes/competencies.<br>A detailed description is provided for learners on how to use the materials.<br>A distinction is made between the required materials and optional materials. | Course content selected strongly supports the outcomes/competencies.<br>A description is provided for learners on how to use the materials.<br>A distinction is made between the required materials and optional materials. | Course content selected supports the outcomes/competencies.<br>A description is provided for learners on how to use the materials.<br>Additional content for extended learning is not provided. | Course design lacks either of the following:<br>Course content selected supports the outcomes/competencies.<br>A description is provided for learners on how to use the materials. |
| Current and cited | | The learning content is current and proper citations are provided. | The learning content is fairly current and proper citations are provided. | The learning content is a few years old (yet still accurate) and proper citations are provided. | The learning content needs updating with current information or practices and proper citations are not provided. |

| | | | | | |
|---|---|---|---|---|---|
| Variety and ADA compliant | | The design includes a variety of learning content (6 or more formats throughout the course) and each meets ADA requirements for all learners. Links to accessibility services and to technologies are provided. | The design includes a variety of learning content (4–5 or more formats throughout the course) and each meets ADA requirements for all learners. Links to accessibility services and to technologies are provided. | The design includes a variety of learning content (2–3 formats throughout the course) and each meets ADA requirements for all learners. Links to accessibility services and to technologies may or may not be provided. | The design uses one format of learning content and uses formats that do not meet ADA requirements for all learners. Links to accessibility services and to technologies are missing. |
| Learner support | | The design of the course provides an extensive list of links and information to access institutional learning support and technology support. Links are provided in the menu of the course in a separate Need Help? section and in the syllabus. | The design of the course provides a complete list of links and information to access institutional learning support and technology support. Links are provided in the menu of the course in a separate Need Help? section or in the syllabus. | The design of the course provides many of the links and information to access institutional learning support and technology support. Links are provided in the menu of the course or in the syllabus. | The design of the course does not provide links and information to access institutional learning support and technological support. |

*Note*. This table provides a means to assess instructional content and materials.

sprinkled throughout the semester. Start a discussion with other faculty development staff on your campus as you apply the rubrics provided here when you examine your course. If you have more support, we recommend using a peer-assessment process to submit your course to a team of reviewers who can guide you to meet the highest standards. Determine if your campus has a review process and funding for such an endeavor, either continuous improvement or faculty development funds. Using these strategies will provide you with many opportunities to assess the quality of your courses.

## Reflect on This Chapter

Now that you have completed reading this chapter and thinking about the content as it applies to your work, please reflect on the following questions:

- What could your course design do to help your students succeed that you aren't currently implementing?
- What strategies do you currently use to measure the quality of your course?
- How do you currently gather feedback from students about your course?
- Which strategies in this chapter would you use to help you decide the quality of your course?

**Jot Your Thoughts**

## Action Checklist

Use Checklist 9.1 to apply the chapter content to your practice and help you identify the steps for implementing these ideas in your teaching.

**CHECKLIST 9.1** Assessing Course Quality Action Checklist

| ✓ | **Develop Opportunities to Assess Course Quality** |
|---|---|
| ❑ | Analyzed the informal ways to measure the students' course experience. |
| ❑ | Test-drove course design with trusted colleagues or former students. |
| ❑ | Integrated feedback received in student completed formal course survey evaluations. |

(*Continues*)

**CHECKLIST 9.1** *(Continued)*

| | |
|---|---|
| ❑ | Developed information course surveys to dig deeper at specific areas for improvement. |
| ❑ | Analyzed CATs to determine which ones can be integrated into a course to provide feedback. |

| ✓ | **Create Educative Assessment** |
|---|---|
| ❑ | Developed opportunities for forward-looking assessments. |
| ❑ | Designed student self-assessment opportunities. |
| ❑ | Created rubrics to communicate criteria and standards to learners. |
| ❑ | Integrated the FIDeLity (Fink, 2013) strategy in course design to provide feedback to students. |
| ❑ | Analyzed comments made in course feedback to glean ideas to improve course design. |

| ✓ | **Peer-Assessed Course Quality** |
|---|---|
| ❑ | Researched organizations such as QM (2018a) to learn more about design standards. |
| ❑ | Identified campus resources and staff to learn more about quality review participation. |
| ❑ | Teamed with a colleague mentor to help assess course design quality. |

| ✓ | **Self-Assessed Course Quality** |
|---|---|
| ❑ | Applied rubrics to assess course design elements: course overview, learning outcomes, assessments and assignments, and instructional content and materials. |
| ❑ | Downloaded the suggested chapter resources to assess the design of your course. |

# 10

# ASSESSING YOUR PROGRAM AND INSTITUTION

## Points to Ponder

Chapter 10 illustrates the importance of course design in the assessment pathway from student assessment to the assessments of courses, departments and programs, and institutions. In thinking about integrating the elements of your course design, consider the following questions to examine your prior knowledge:

- What assessments does your program or department use to measure the effectiveness of a curriculum for its graduates to be hired?
- What benefits could an advisory committee provide for your program or department?
- What national credentialing or accreditation standards does your program or department support?
- How does your institution benefit from continuous improvement?
- What roles do faculty play in your institution's assessment framework?

**Jot Your Thoughts**

There were 2 similar institutions not far from each another in the same system. Each offered curricula in more than 40 career and technical programs as well as a general education curriculum. Administrators of each institution were working on projects for review by the accreditation body. The difference was the process these 2 institutions used to conduct their continuous improvement initiatives in preparation for their reviews and on-campus visits.

The first institution coordinated the efforts of faculty, staff, and administrators to develop teams to lead the collection and integration of data into telling the story of the institution. Team meetings consisted of trying to understand what each team's part of the report needed and to identify the data and personnel that would best help to tell this story. For a couple of months the team interviewed campus staff, pored over data, and wrote its section of the accreditation report. Team members discussed what they found and reported that even though it was a lot of work, they better understood how the institution worked.

The second institution relied on a more centralized model for preparing and writing the report. The academic vice president instructed the director of quality initiatives to collect data and deliver the report. Much of the work was done with little communication with the institution's internal audience. Save-the-date information for the accrediting visit was sent to participating campus faculty and staff, and even less was communicated about the report. The academic vice president grew nervous about how much the campus participants really knew about the information that was in the report, which was turned in on the day of the deadline to the evaluation body. Most of the institution's faculty and staff were in the dark about what was in the report, and little was communicated with them once the results were known.

The institution that involved its faculty, staff, and administration was much more prepared for its accreditation visit. During the interviews conducted by the accreditation team with campus faculty and staff, many more people who had played a role in gathering the data and writing the report understood how aspects of the institution worked and how processes were integrated. They better understood the big picture because they saw how the pieces fit together, and they were invested in the outcomes and realized they had something at stake in this evaluation. It took a lot of work to coordinate efforts and get everyone to participate in the process. In the end, everyone took pride in the institution's results and understood that they were invested in making future changes. They saw themselves as an institution of we, ours, us.

At the other institution, the academic vice president, who led a very small team of data collectors and writers, was nervous about how the faculty and staff interviews with the accreditation team would go. They didn't play much of a role in the production of the report and weren't as prepared for the interviews. They didn't understand the big picture, and offered more opinions than facts. Faculty, staff, and administrators considered that the report belonged to the academic vice president and was a report card on the effectiveness of her leadership. The rest of the institution wasn't as invested in the results of the report because it played such a small role in the development. They were an institution with a philosophy of you, hers, not me.

Both institutions gathered information and wrote their story. Both got results on their strengths and challenges. Both needed to start working on making the improvements. Which institution do you think was in a better place to do so?

## The Big Picture of Assessment

In chapter 8 and chapter 9 we discuss student assessment and course quality assessment; however, assessments go beyond measuring the quality of student and course performance. A broader assessment of quality is necessary to measure the attainment of program or department and institution outcomes and goals. Therefore, it is critical to analyze how your course relates to the curriculum of the program or department, and how these varying levels align with the institution's mission helps to complete the overall picture.

## A Framework for Institutional Assessment: Micro to Macro

The following is a framework for institutional assessment:

- Unit or weekly assessments: formative measure of learning activities objectives
- Course outcomes assessment: uses formative and summative means to measure course outcomes through assignments and assessments
- Course survey assessment: a summative measure of course and delivery quality
- Program or department assessment: usually a summative measure of program or department quality
- Institutional assessment: a summative measure of the institution's ability to meet its mission goals

The smallest assessment, which should occur with the most frequency, is the unit or weekly formative assessment measuring objectives in a course. This is followed by formative and summative assessments that measure course outcomes through learning activities and course assessments. Our discussion in this chapter focuses on the elements of program or departmental assessment and institutional assessment. Depending on the number of years of teaching as an adjunct or in a full-time tenured position and their participation in a variety of campus experiences, faculty may be less familiar with this portion of an institution's assessment plan and process. The assessments of programs and departments and the institution occur less frequently and are at times in part handled by others in the administration who may or may not include faculty regularly. It is important however, for faculty to know that the mission, vision, and values of the institution are embedded in the course design to ensure these are being adhered to and are reflected throughout the micro- to macro-assessment pathway.

## Necessity of Institutional Assessments

According to Mentkowski and Associates (2000),

> Probing the elements of a curriculum in relation to learning outcomes and elaborating them through learner attributions can provide observations about which relationships drive and sustain learning, one basis for inferring the potentially transferable curricular elements for fostering learning that lasts. The perspectives of learners—as students and alumnae—are a critical point of entry to elaborate curriculum elements. In pointing to the powerful and sustaining elements in the curriculum that account for learner outcomes, these perspectives serve a similar role. (p. 310)

Some faculty think of assessment as something the administration does or that happens mysteriously behind the scenes. Assessment is often the forgotten part of many processes and is the furthest thing from many people's mind until they need to do it.

It may feel like a chore unless it is woven into the institution's practice as an ongoing process of continuous improvement. What do you say you are doing in your course, and how will you measure that you are doing it? The same question needs to be asked at the program or departmental and institutional levels. We send graduates to workplaces saying they are qualified, after charging them large amounts of money, some of it taxpayers' money, for their degrees. There is a greater call for accountability today. How do we know our graduates are qualified unless we also measure the quality of programs, departments, and institutions?

We need to assess our institutions for multiple reasons. At all levels, verifying that we are doing what we say we are doing through assessment is a critical mission of the institution. Let's consider our external and internal stakeholders. The external stakeholders consist of federal and state government departments with laws, rules, and guidelines for grants, student loans, and funding, such as the Carl D. Perkins Career and Education Act (2006). Other external stakeholders are the accreditation organizations for programs, departments, and institutions (see Figure 10.1). In Minnesota for example, the Minnesota State Board of Trustees governs all public colleges and universities except the University of Minnesota, which has its own governing body. Additional external stakeholders may include unions, program and department advisory boards, certification boards, discipline-specific organizations, taxpayers, and alumni. All these groups will be interested in an institution's ability to excel in the areas of curriculum development, student transferability, tuition costs, job placement, and graduations rates.

Internal stakeholders consist of students, alumni, faculty, administration, and staff. Groups of these stakeholders also are a part of the internal focus of institutional assessment and consist of programs and departments, academic affairs and curricula, student affairs and student support, shared governing, and resources. Assessment of the effectiveness of each of these internal organizations and data are collected by institutional research personnel. Faculty are at the center of the assessment process because they assess courses and programs in collaboration with feedback from employers that hire graduates and report on the level of proficiency students demonstrate in the workplace. This collaborative feedback isn't something that institutional research can analyze as easily as graduation and program or department completion rates. Faculty listen to feedback about employer needs and make adjustments to

**Figure 10.1** Stakeholder audiences.

| External | Internal |
|---|---|
| Federal and state government<br>Accreditation organization<br>Board of trustees<br>Unions<br>Advisory boards, employers<br>Discipline organizations<br>Taxpayers and funders<br>Alumni | Students and student organizations<br>Faculty<br>Administration<br>Staff<br>Programs and departments<br>Academic affairs<br>Student affairs<br>Shared governance<br>Resources |

update their curriculum, course design, and teaching methods to meet the workforce trends and innovations. This is why faculty are pivotal in an institution's assessment process. Documenting the needs for change is something all faculty need to be proficient in so changes can be blended into the process, and when the time comes for accreditation, this information can be shared.

The assessment process can run better when institution administrators show their employees the complexity and interrelatedness of all the levels of assessments. To illustrate the complexity of the myriad parts of an institution's integrated assessment plan, imagine a 1,000-piece jigsaw puzzle where employees get a section of puzzle pieces to put together but don't have the box cover to see the finished puzzle. An even more difficult aspect of assessment is that the parts don't remain constant; assessment is a measure of objects in motion. Most organizations need to freeze the model and evaluate the picture they see at a given moment. Doing this without the faculty's full understanding of their role in the importance of overall accountability and organizational excellence is a barrier to obtaining quality results.

## Where the Institution Should Start

The following steps in getting started are applicable at all levels of an institutional assessment program to measure course, program or department, and institutional quality:

- Create an institutional effectiveness assessment task force. For courses, this could be done with faculty who teach multiple sections of the same course.
- Examine the institution's mission statement. Are courses and programs or departments aligned with the mission statement?
- Design an institutional (course, program, department) plan or model to guide the assessment program. At the course level, you have done this by aligning course outcomes with learning activities and assessments. At the program level, show how the curriculum (learning activities) matches the program outcomes and determine how the quality is being assessed.
- Determine and prioritize the specific assessments to be undertaken.
- Take an inventory of existing data collection efforts.
- Ask, Is there anything missing? Determine what additional data collection procedures need to be implemented to inform the assessment priorities.
- Prioritize the list. Start small. Determine what will deliver the best data with the least amount of effort. What will be easy to collect and what will require more effort?
- Get started by being flexible, adaptive, and prepared to change.
- Prepare to share the results of assessments publicly using the best means available to communicate them to stakeholders.
- Keep in mind that the primary emphasis in assessment is on continuous improvement of teaching, learning, and services to students (Banta, 2004).

## Faculty Role in Assessment

As you read this chapter, reflect on your understanding of the responsibility you have in the larger picture of assessment. Of course you evaluate course assignments and assessments. You may track attendance or participation in your course, and it is hoped that you understand your role in the drop, fail, and withdrawal rates to work on improving course success and completion. However, as an active participant in the process, you have a larger role in understanding and advancing the assessment plan of your institution. Your responsibilities may include the following:

- Creating and collecting data at the course and program level
- Assessing your program through a review process
- Participating in developing course and program assessments that demonstrate institutional outcomes
- Developing your skills as an expert in assessment, one of your most important roles, to be sure you are delivering what you say you are teaching

In weaving your course assessments with program assessments, you show how your individual work can team with that of your colleagues to demonstrate the achievement of program outcomes, which can align with institutional outcomes. To help you better understand the process, we dig deeper into each of these components in the ways programs or departments and institutions conduct assessment. Figure 10.2 contains possible elements used in many programs and departments assessments.

**Figure 10.2** Program or department assessment types.

## Advisory Boards

One of the most rewarding experiences for program or department faculty is working with advisory boards. The structure of these groups is flexible, which means there isn't one way to create an advisory board. However, we recommend the creation of a more formal versus ad hoc structure for the board to conduct its work successfully. The following template may stimulate your thinking about developing an advisory board.

### *Why Have Advisory Boards?*

The purpose of advisory boards or committees is to establish and maintain partnerships with business and industry leaders, faculty, students, and college staff related to the program or department. Advisory boards are a means to learn industry trends, communicate institutional needs, and share general enrollment information on students and assessment data. A discussion of assessment results can be insightful as you build a relationship with possible employers of program graduates. These advisers can provide valuable information to help programs close the loop on making curriculum changes based on industry trends and assessment results that will benefit students (Banta, 2004).

The term *advisory* is important. The boards are meant to guide and provide advice and direction. They are not meant to dictate. Meeting with advisory boards allows your program or department to gain a market perspective. Most advisory boards have a set of bylaws that provide a necessary structure on items like membership, voting, purpose, and so on. Without bylaws, the framework can easily change as the group changes membership or as memory fades over time on what was initially established.

### *Who Serves on the Advisory Board?*

The following people are generally considered for membership on advisory boards:

- Program or department faculty and student representatives, current and alumni
- Business and industry leaders including those in your community who hire your graduates
- Career placement staff
- Representatives (faculty and business leaders) from related programs or departments
- Two chairpeople such as a dean or faculty member from the institution and a business or industry leader and an external vice chair in case the external chair isn't able to attend a meeting

### *When Do You Meet?*

Most advisory boards meet once or twice a year depending on the nature of the work during the academic year. The following items are usually on the agenda:

- Curriculum improvements
- Successes of and challenges to the program including courses
- Equipment and software improvements
- Skills necessary for graduates to land entry-level or higher level positions
- Skill gaps and skill enhancements
- Establishing internships and additional partnerships
- Hearing student learning and internship experiences and graduate testimonials
- Analyzing employment placement data
- Analyzing trends in the discipline and field

### *Meeting Framework Ideas*

Many programs and departments schedule their meetings on campus because it is always a good idea for members of the community to see the institution's facilities. Perhaps the next meeting could be hosted by one of your business partners so you can tour that member's facilities. This works well if there aren't competing businesses serving on your board.

Also, pay for parking for your off-campus attendees, and provide refreshments. Send a meeting reminder to participants a month before the meeting, and create an action agenda to send out a week prior to the meeting. The cochairs develop the agenda for the meeting a couple of weeks in advance.

**Bright Idea**

When planning for an advisory board meeting, create a form to use as an agenda action to send to members before the meeting. This form should also have a place for action items and names of those responsible for leading completion of action items. This will help you monitor progress between meetings and prepare the next meeting's agenda items to follow up on old or continuing business. **—Zala Fashant**

## Capstone Portfolio Assessment

Some experiences in your institution can help measure quality on many levels of assessment. One such learning activity is a capstone experience that demonstrates achievement at the course, program or departmental, and institutional levels. Capstone projects go beyond writing research papers, completing unit assignments, and taking tests. Using this approach for a high-level summative assessment on students' demonstration of learning throughout the program allows faculty to show the proficiency of teaching and learning that occurs and provide evidence for employers to see the abilities of students that build the institution's reputation.

Capstone portfolios provide a multidimensional opportunity to assess outcomes on many levels through a mega-assessment activity. As you may already know from your own experience, a capstone assessment allows students to demonstrate skills learned throughout the curriculum of a program or department and from cross-department opportunities. This comprehensive, or super summative, assessment provides you with the opportunity to measure students' mastery of competencies, determine the effectiveness of the program curriculum to produce successful graduates for the workplace, and link performance to community and industry stakeholders for employment and for the program's or department's reputation.

Portfolio and capstone events have many forms; however, seldom do administrators of programs, departments, or institutions take the opportunity to truly analyze and benefit from the results (see Zubizarreta, 2009). Capstone portfolio assessments can measure outcomes on the course, program or department, and institutional levels. Furthermore, this measurement can produce a wealth of useful information for the students, program, and institution in addition to feedback necessary for data-driven improvements.

Multilevel aspects of the capstone portfolio assessment include

- guided student and faculty self-assessment;
- student peer-to-peer assessment;
- program assessment, including curriculum analysis;
- professional business, industry pathways assessment; and
- institutional assessment.

An example of a super summative assessment is a robust graphic and Web design portfolio capstone showcase where students produce portfolios of Web and print material, and the capstone showcase exhibition of portfolio artifacts demonstrates the quality of their learning. In this case, outcomes are measured on all the levels in the preceding list. The faculty of this design program developed a model portfolio capstone course, resulting in an exhibition for students to plan and execute in the last semester of the program. During this two-year program, students learn the elements of design in graphic and Web design. They are working on a degree in either graphic design or Web design, but a majority of them are enrolled in both programs. The capstone, or summative portfolio, showcases the skills students need for employment in design agencies or to set out on their own. So how is this organized?

Students are provided with a structure in two courses: Portfolio and Show Preparation and Career Planning. During these courses, which take place in the final semester, students are provided with leadership experiences as they determine the theme of the portfolio show, develop and implement the marketing strategies, invite participation from contacts in industry, and manage the portfolio development and showcase setup and operation. During this three-day event, institution faculty and staff, professional business and industry partners, and families and friends are invited to participate in a variety of activities. The activities include student-produced exhibits of print and Web materials similar to a science fair, student oral presentations to evaluators and visitors, and professional presentations by industry leaders and alumni. Because of its success, this process has been expanded to include other School of Design and the Arts programs, such as photography and apparel technologies. Design teams of faculty and top students working together across programs have expanded the event to a week-long succession of shows. These collaborative teams are tasked with planning and implementing final events in the areas of design, production, branding and marketing, public relations, advertising, funding, project management, and art gallery and show exhibit design. Program faculty, peers, and professionals all provide formative and summative assessment feedback at various stages in this showcase.

Guided student self-assessment is conducted weekly throughout the process of creating the showcase. Students gain knowledge, make guided decisions through critique and research, implement change by perfecting their work, and create a focused final presentation. During this self-assessment, each student develops a professional mission statement. A checklist of possible artifacts such as Web pages, marketing materials, packaging, posters, advertisement layouts, business cards, and other print material is presented by the students. The student and faculty member evaluate and rank them to determine what to include in the showcase that best suits the kind of employment the student wants to pursue. During the portfolio and show preparation course, students individually and as a class are asked to assess their contributions to their project and to their teams in planning and implementing the final portfolio show events. Students also assess their own work and the artifacts that best reflect the skills they want to demonstrate as they prepare to meet with industry employers who will visit the showcase and identify students to possibly interview. Faculty from four-year institutions also attend the showcase to meet with students who are interested in continuing their education.

Students develop targeted marketing themes for their body of work and can use aspects of their course preparation as talking points while industry professionals assess their work during the showcase exhibit. These discussions provide a way for students to obtain feedback on their portfolio and have conversations with other students and professionals. A faculty-produced assessment rubric helps students prepare by practicing their communication skills and developing confidence. Each portfolio requires intentionally chosen artifacts to best represent the audience that assesses the students' work per the criteria of the rubric.

Student peer-to-peer assessment occurs as students prepare their portfolio's artifacts (in this case, graphic or Web design). This level of assessment is often done with students only during an open classroom critique session, with little documentation or recommendations. By taking this practice to a higher level and making it a more formalized assessment, students can gain a deeper appreciation for assessment from thoughtful written and verbal critiques of their peers. Each student's choice of a final creative project undergoes a rigorous written peer review by three other students.

The peer review consists of five examples of what they liked and why, followed by five examples of what they would fix with possible solutions for what they did not like. Students learn to work collaboratively and use others' feedback to determine which pieces will be displayed in their final portfolio. Students also gain personal skills in assessment by learning to provide meaningful critiques of their peers' work. They develop and improve their skills at providing professional feedback to one another as they discuss their work, a skill they need to master to meet workplace expectations.

Program assessment including curriculum analysis is also examined during the production of portfolios and the capstone shows in which portfolio artifacts demonstrate the quality of the programs' curricular outcomes. The targeted analysis of a program's curriculum reaps an abundance of information, from answering basic questions to exploring deeper evolutionary changes in curriculum development to demonstrated success. This process allows advisory board members, people in business and industry, and alumni to develop partnerships by engaging in conversations and submitting evaluations about the overall creative quality of the show. This goes far beyond the existing advisory board; this range of professionals provides deeper and ongoing feedback to be analyzed and acted on. The showcase offers the opportunity for discussions between faculty and industry leaders with the goal of the program to grow and remain at the forefront of industry trends in knowledge, equipment, hardware and software, and process and product improvement, and provide insights to course and curriculum improvements. It also offers opportunities to identify what wasn't demonstrated and may be added in the future.

Professional business or industry assessments benefit students and faculty. The collaborative interaction among stakeholders, faculty, and students helps everyone reach a deeper understanding of industry needs. All industries have expectations, and the creative industry is no different. Business owners expect graduates to have a baseline of current knowledge, but more often they are also looking for those innovative and higher level thinkers, who go beyond the expected skill knowledge and provide a fresh perspective. A program or department is only as strong as the graduates it produces. People from industry or educational institutions look deeply at portfolios that demonstrate a broad range of creativity, planning, and implementation; these are evolutionary and living documents. Each portfolio must be deliberate and directed at its audience as people from each business or industry are looking for a variety of evidence of knowledge and skill sets. It is not uncommon for a creative, a student in the program, to develop several focused portfolios. Much like a résumé or curriculum vitae, portfolios need to be developed in consideration of their purpose, that is to obtain employment specific to a business type or to move on to more advanced educational opportunities. Programs or departments educate students for successful careers in the workplace. Faculty and programs stand to gain an advantage by remaining current in knowing where an industry or profession is heading as well as becoming the leaders of change through thoughtful and sustainable plans for improvements.

Institutional assessment should also use the portfolio assessments. Institutions require program and curriculum assessment at many levels, yet they typically ignore shows and portfolios as a reportable source. Because the capstone portfolio provides assessment of the student's work, the curriculum, and program, it can be a very useful addition to the body of evidence of student learning, program currency, and internal program integrity. Knowing that a program or department is assessing itself in what it provides, whether through an accredited program evaluation or simply a thoughtful multilevel portfolio evaluation, helps to strengthen an institution. Strong programs and departments that properly model assessment on many levels and have integrated their student learning outcomes into program outcomes that link to institutional outcomes demonstrate understanding and practice to accrediting agencies and to college leaders.

This type of multilevel assessment activity provides faculty and program administrators with the opportunity to be invited for membership on professional organizational and industry boards by being recognized as educational leaders. These relationships provide wonderful opportunities that reinforce all the assessments mentioned earlier. Faculty who participate in professional organizations or visit industry partner facilities learn from other professionals, faculty, and industry to increase their knowledge, skills, and processes and bring them back to campus to develop newer best practices to benefit students.

For program or department evaluations, capstone course projects allow students to demonstrate the course and program outcomes that meet national standards and competencies in an industry or a discipline. This demonstration of program outcome mastery is necessary for the program and institutional accreditation. Even if you don't have program accreditation for your discipline, we strongly recommended researching discipline competencies that should be covered in your program's evaluation.

There are two commonly used ways for faculty to effectively measure these competencies in program evaluation. The first is measuring all of a program's competencies in all courses in its curriculum. The second is to determine the individual competencies that are best measured in specific courses. Knowing there are differing levels of competencies, the latter approach may be a better fit. Assigning program courses to each competency where students already need to demonstrate mastery for course assessments provides a way to measure both student learning and program effectiveness with the same assessment. Using the approach accomplishes the task of assessment and provides students with the greatest amount of time for learning and application of the content.

Institutional outcome assessment can happen in a similar way. Some institutions have developed autonomous assessments that take a portion of the course time. Others have identified required courses where practice for the outcome is provided, and the same assessment in each of these courses is used to standardize results. The latter is an interesting way to show how the outcome is assessed in a variety of learning activities and can provide some best practices for programs and departments to learn from one another.

**Bright Idea**

Capstone projects are a way to bring stakeholders together. This is not only an effective motivator for your students to perform in a real-world situation but also a great way for the greater community of employers, institutional faculty and staff, prospective students, and parents to see excellence demonstrated in a showcase of your program or department. Performing arts students showcase their talent through concerts, plays, recitals, and exhibits. Consider how these benefit the learning community as you consider designing your own capstone. The extra effort pays off through recruitment, networking, and employment for your students. —**Zala Fashant**

## Program or Department Review Process

Administrators of every program or department should develop a review process to identify strengths, challenges, and opportunities. During this process you have the opportunity to reexamine your program outcomes and curriculum upgrades, identify trends and opportunities, consider staffing, match program assessments to institutional assessments, develop new internships, determine how external partners can assist in this assessment of your program, and analyze program data to improve the student experience. Consider the following:

- What is the review process for your program or department?
- How often does your assessment process occur?
- Is it best to use a comprehensive process every few years or a continuous process where you review certain areas each year?

This review may occur during meetings or may be assigned as work to be completed during additional meetings that focus only on the review.

Using your advisory board to discuss some of this information and gathering their responses during meeting minutes will help you prepare for your review process. We recommend designing questions to send ahead of time to determine trends and opportunities. Ask advisory board members for recommendations about and donations of equipment they use. Ask them to commit to internship opportunities in a face-to-face meeting to provide enhanced experiences for your students. The members can also write testimonials about the quality they see in the program or department and the quality of your graduates in the workplace.

**Bright Idea**

Much like a personal portfolio, collect materials for program or department review throughout the year. Assign personnel to lead the preparation of materials. Use your monthly program or department meetings to discuss and plan for the collection process. Embedding this review process makes the work less daunting as you accomplish a little at a time throughout the year rather than making it a monumental project to be completed all at once. —**Zala Fashant**

## External Funding Assessments

As you obtain external funding through grants, donations, and government programs, an assessment plan to meet the outcomes for the work is critical to report success to the funding body. The assessments you use for this work shouldn't be add-ons to the assessments you have in place. Consider embedding them in your total assessment plan. It is hoped you were prudent in acquiring funding to help you achieve your current program or department goals or planned expansion of goals rather than short-term supplemental funding that doesn't fit into a longer term plan. Combining assessments so you don't take time away from teaching and students' learning is critical to measure what you need to determine outcome achievement. The process of combining and embedding will help you refine your assessment process and instruments because you develop a broader sense of evaluation.

**Bright Idea**

Developing assessments prior to applying for grants is the first step in understanding what you need to accomplish, helps you sell the quality of your grant proposal, and increases your chance of receiving the funding. First, bring your assessment specialist into the conversation early to help you design the required assessment. Second, create the assessments for this grant like you would in course design. Once you have your grant project outcomes, design the assessments. Doing so will help eliminate confusion throughout the grant and clarifies the purpose of the grant for everyone involved. You would be surprised how many times this is not done and how difficult it is to develop assessments when you are in the middle of the grant. —**Zala Fashant**

## Program and Department Accreditation

This level of assessment is critical to bridge your course assessments to the institutional assessments because it helps pave the way to institutional assessment. In other words, having assessment structures in place are what agencies expect in renewing an institution's accreditation. Your program or department may or may not have these assessments as a part of your work, so it is important for you to discuss the kinds of program or department assessments that will require your participation.

At the program or department level, you may be accredited by a national organization that has developed standards to demonstrate competence. Program or department accreditation is not institutional accreditation. Several different accrediting bodies will be involved with different programs or departments during accreditation review. All the feedback can affect the success of an institutional accreditation and serve to improve individual courses. Knowledge of the expectations for accreditation is helpful in determining your course's situational factors.

### *Why Is Accreditation Important?*

Until you have gone through your program or department's accreditation yourself, you may not fully understand the process. The purpose of accreditation is for the program or department to be recognized for the level of quality it delivers based on a set of professional organization standards or industry competencies. It shows you provide students with quality experiences that meet rigorous criteria and provide value. The willingness to achieve accreditation demonstrates your commitment to continuous improvement. You show you are willing to reflect through self-study and have peer evaluators analyze your program or department to identify strengths and opportunities and provide the feedback necessary to grow.

Accreditation not only assists you in program or department improvement but also serves students and other stakeholders. Students will benefit by obtaining approval for their degrees and credit transfers by other institutions. Employers know your graduates have achieved a level of rigor that is established by national standards and industry competencies. Accreditation also ensures a level of continuity across programs, cultures, and nations, making your program or department a quality educational destination with the reputation necessary for recruiting students and delivering in-demand graduates to the workplace.

### *What Does the Process Look Like?*

Starting with the premise that each accrediting organization will have its own established process, we can provide a general picture of the elements that many of them use to measure the quality of a program or department.

Administrators of each program or department will prepare for the process by beginning with self-reflection and evaluation. A site-visit questionnaire will ask the program or department staff to gather data to work with a liaison or mentor. The purpose for gathering these data is the basis for self-study, which is based on the professional standards or industry competencies. The documentation you need to provide usually includes data about the number of students and their licensure pass rates. Completion or graduation rates may be used if licensure isn't necessary. These data shows that the program or department sufficiently meets accreditation criteria.

The accreditation portfolio will tell the story. Program or department information, student enrollment statistics, faculty credentials, and curriculum offerings will be included to paint an overall picture. Some accrediting agencies will use well-established criteria examples provided from the Baldrige excellence framework (Baldridge Performance Excellence Program, 2019), total quality management (American Society for Quality, 2019), and International Organization for Standardization (n.d.) standards.

Most of the accreditation processes include a site visit involving a team of two or three peer evaluators who come to the campus and meet with the department faculty. They also interview administration and staff so they can learn more about the support of the dean or vice president of academic affairs, institutional researcher, academic advisers, and financial aid staff. The evaluators will use these interviews to compare to the data provided in the portfolio to prepare their final report.

The final report will name the strengths of the program, opportunities for improvement, and the final decision for accreditation. Most programs and departments don't lose their accreditation without an opportunity to improve to meet the required criteria. Campus teams of faculty and administration will continue to submit reports to show how they are making the improvements recommended. Time lines are established for plans and progress reports until the next reaccreditation visit 5 to 10 years later.

## Skills Assessments

Agencies and professional organizations external to the program or department may require students to complete a skill assessment to measure the program's success in delivering the curriculum to result in employment. The Carl D. Perkins Career and Education Act (2006) requires all programs that offer an award (certificate or degree) to assess students' technical and workplace skills for accountability to receive funding. These assessments need to be reliable and aligned with industry-recognized standards, credentials, and competencies. The assessment instruments are developed by third-party vendors and often chosen by faculty to best measure the students' level of proficiency based on the institution's curriculum. Departments outside technical education may provide opportunities for students to take national credentialing or certification assessments in a similar manner.

Knowing the assessments your program or department uses is another part of the role you play in making sure your students will succeed in them. Designing activities and assessments for your courses and seeing how the effective design of your program's curriculum is key to this success and leads to accreditation at the program, department, and institutional levels. These assessments will also help you improve the curriculum, course design, and instructional methods. It will also help students see how their daily learning ties to the workplace, helping their transition from school to work. According to Maki (2017),

> Key to a continuous commitment to students' equitable academic program toward achieving a high-quality degree is developing a real-time reporting system that enables internal stakeholders to see continuously how undergraduates are progressing. (p. 79)

Some programs and departments have developed dashboards on their websites that show updated information on students' progress for internal and external audiences. This practice is a way to transparently communicate the broad picture of the program or department.

**Bright Idea**

Developing a comprehensive program or department assessment plan with corresponding rubrics to measure achievement levels ensures intentionality has been established. However, are similar templates applied to programs and departments that aren't accredited? We recommend for institutions to develop a process to set similar standards that provide faculty with an opportunity to identify areas for improvement and showcase the strengths of their programs and departments. —**Zala Fashant**

As you develop program or department assessment plans, demonstrate the alignment of program outcomes, elements, and assessments much like you would in integrated course design. This integrated program design provides the crosswalk necessary for internal and external stakeholders to see the work you have done in the architecture of your review process. This crosswalk is similar to the document shared for aligning course assessments and learning activities (Table 8.2). In this case, course outcomes and assessments are aligned with program or department and institutional outcomes and assessments. This should be applied to all programs for sustainability and serve as a substantial artifact for the institutional accreditation process. See Bresciani Ludvik (2019) for samples of alignment tables from various institutions.

**Jot Your Thoughts**

## Institutional Assessment

Institutional assessment uses much of what is gained from the program or department assessments and has a format similar to the one discussed in the Program and Department Assessment section. As we stated earlier, unless an institution is transparent, many faculty haven't been exposed to this level of assessment. As this is the highest and most comprehensive level of assessment, let's examine what faculty should know about how it takes place on your campus. See Figure 10.3 for elements used in many institutional accreditation assessments.

## Institutional Advisory Boards

Much like program or department advisory boards, institutions have similar boards to guide the direction of their mission, vision, and values. The focus may be more on the role the institution plays in the community than the pathway to student employment. Presidents establish advisory boards with community members, politicians, funders and foundation personnel, alumni, and others to gain perspective on how the institution can best serve and benefit from its standing in

**Figure 10.3** Institutional assessment types.

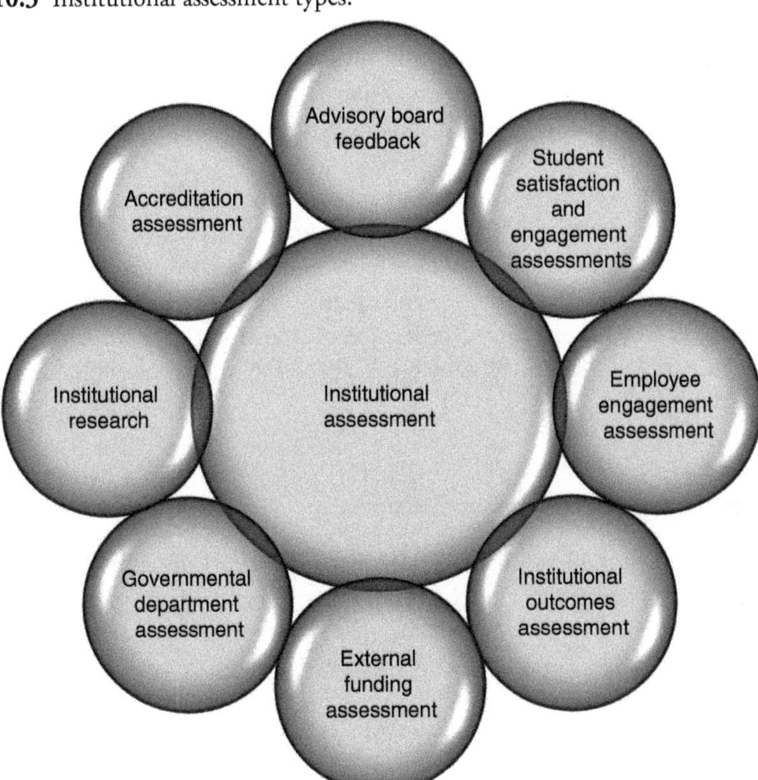

the community. This feedback from its members will have an impact on the direction of the institution and a smaller impact on its day-to-day operation. The support of this board at your institution can help during the accreditation process.

**Bright Idea**

Using your institution's advisory board to review your accreditation renewal submission provides immense feedback to improve your document. Often outside audiences have insight on items we are too close to in our daily work. Board members can offer testimonials for the impact of the work your institution provides to the community. Involving them also helps them better understand the work the institution does. —**Zala Fashant**

## Student Satisfaction and Engagement Assessments

Part of the accreditation process requires a survey of students' opinions. The data from these surveys provide a valuable clue to the direction of the institutions and ought to be considered in the design of the academic master plan (AMP). As students are the major clients of the institution, their experience needs to be considered in planning. Two examples of common survey tools are the Community College Survey of Student Engagement (2019) and the National Survey of Student Engagement (2019). These surveys publish results that are shared with the institution's administration and compared to all participants in cumulative results. These data provide a picture of how your institution compares to the general opinions of students nationally.

It would be helpful to obtain your institution's results because knowing the perceptions of your students will help you with your course design. This will also help you better understand why your institution is taking steps to improve the learning climate and experiences for students on campus. You can also use these results to support students with what they need in their learning to improve student satisfaction and engagement at a micro level, which can also serve to improve your own course's student survey results.

## Employee Engagement Assessments

Your institution's human resources department has probably chosen an employee engagement assessment tool, and the results of this survey help to guide the staff's work to improve the overall work climate. The assessment may provide insight on your work environment specifically. We suggest contacting your human resources department for the results of the previous assessment. Because administrators of institutions and employee committees need time to process the results of an assessment and implement plans to analyze the successes and address the challenges, assessments are not often conducted annually.

**Bright Idea**

The employee engagement assessment can also provide some ideas for questions you may want to ask your students as you assess your own classroom or course learning environment. Read through the assessment and apply what interests you in the students' perspectives in the design of your own course quality evaluations. —**Zala Fashant**

## Institutional Outcomes Assessment Framework

Many institutions have assessment plans to measure the success of their learning outcomes. You may be familiar with measuring your course outcomes through assessments, but there are also assessments at the program or department level that are designed to measure goals and outcomes. Each program or department may assign goals to be measured in particular courses. For instance, a more foundational outcome may be measured in one or two 100-level courses all students are required to take. Obviously, elective courses aren't used because you won't have the broad numbers you get in core curricular courses. More advanced program or department outcomes are measured in higher level courses and perhaps the capstone course that are required for all students in the major.

The tools for this type of program or department assessment are usually created by faculty, and knowledge of developing assessments is an excellent skill. Keep in mind that most faculty didn't receive much training in developing assessments even though it is an important part of the job. It is critical to ensure that faculty are teaching and, more important, that students are learning what was intended. Assessment is a bit like peeling an onion. There are layers and layers of assessment, and the more you learn, the more you think about. Learning more about assessment is a great goal to include in your professional development plan, and many campuses have faculty development centers and assessment coordinators who offer training to groups or individual mentoring.

Most institutions also measure the learning outcomes they have established for accreditation by developing a tool to measure individual outcomes for all full- and part-time students. Developing and administering this assessment is complex. The upside is that all students take the same assessment, making the results comparable. The downside is that students who are in automotive programs, theater arts, and mathematics have a variety of experiences, so taking the same online or paper-and-pencil assessment may provide a larger range of results. This will require a deeper analysis in order to make improvements.

Another way to assess institution-wide learning outcomes is using a breadth of assessments designed to measure the outcomes. Programs and departments align their courses to meet particular learning outcomes to be sure that all institutional outcomes are measured in enough courses with adequate enrollments and with a pool of students large enough to demonstrate proficiency. For example, if the institution has an oral and written communication learning outcome, then it makes sense for students taking communication and English courses to take the assessment. Other disciplines that require in-depth writing assignments or major oral presentations such as a business capstone project, could also be used in assessing this outcome. A rubric to assess a variety of courses has to be developed to have a standard expectation for multiple assessors.

For example, English department faculty could use the rubric to read assignments, grade them individually, and discuss how each met the criteria to determine a norm prior to reading the assignments in the institution-wide assessment. They could also participate on assessment teams for other disciplines to help them find norms and teach other faculty how to apply the rubric.

Students could show their mastery of outcomes through hands-on demonstrations, paper/pencil activities, construction of physical projects, oral presentations, and written assignments. Providing rubrics to standardize the measurement of achievement through the variety of assessment types will assist in the data collection as they are individually tailored to the types of programs offered. Comparing these rubrics will provide a better picture for standardizing levels of excellence across the institution. For example, a student in a technical program can design a website, a manufactured object, a dress, an art project, a 3D printed artifact, or a spreadsheet that demonstrates an institutional learning outcome. In biology the design and completion of an experiment would demonstrate a learning outcome, and an English composition can do the same as well as a mapping project in geography. Each is a different assignment, but each could demonstrate that the student has meet the same outcome or competency.

## External Funding Assessments

We noted earlier that there are times where an entire institution receives external funding for an initiative that is not tied to a specific department. So a special type of assessment may need to be developed, and the measurement and achievement of the initiative's outcomes may be included in the institution's accreditation portfolio.

## Governmental Department Program Assessments

Your institution is required to report a variety of results that federal and state governments are monitoring. Student loans, degree completion, tuition and course costs, and graduation rates are all of interest to agencies that provide funding to components of an institution.

## Institutional Research

Your campus should have a person or department whose duty it is to collect all of the data that is used to report out on the results of institution assessments. This person or assessment coordinator can help to design assessments for all the initiatives to meet requirements of reporting to stakeholders. This is a critical role for your institution so knowing who or which department is responsible will be beneficial to you. As your program or department explores external funding, or is designing an initiative that is unique, having this person involved is important from the beginning. Often this person will provide great insight on the front end to help you rather than digging through the difficulties once they appear. Your dean is a valuable contact for you to learn how to access this information and how to work with this person. Your program or department might even invite this person to a meeting to build a relationship.

## Institutional Accreditation

Have your ever wondered why institutions are accredited? Some people think some schools are better than others, and some schools have been accused of being diploma mills. How do prospective students know which institution to attend unless there is some standard for comparison?

Boards or administrative agencies of professional disciplines in your state have websites that list the licensure requirements for degrees, diplomas, or certificate. Your institution is linked to a regional accreditation organization and is assigned a staff liaison from that organization who will work with you directly. Your institution also has a designated person (liaison officer) who works directly with the accreditation organization. Which accrediting organization oversees your institution? Who is the person who leads the accreditation process for your institution?

The following are some tips to help you understand your institution's process:

- Talk with the person on your campus who leads the accreditation process.
- Find out who your regional accreditation organization is, and search for additional information online.
- Read your institution's report from the last visit, looking at strengths and opportunities.
- Identify ways you can support current plans (technology, assessment, academic, accreditation, etc.).
- Find the time line for your next accreditation visit and where you are located in the cycle.

## Academic Master Plans

Which came first—the AMP or the institutional assessments? At this point in the history of your institution, the two are probably deeply integrated. If you haven't already done so, you should locate and read your institution's AMP. Every few years, academic vice presidents and leadership teams of deans and possibly faculty redevelop or refine this plan to guide the academic improvement work over the next few years. As a frontline member of the academic team in delivering curriculum to students, you need to make sure this guide helps your work.

Why have an AMP? The most obvious reason is to identify the academic mission for the institution, which is the road map of all academic work and helps everyone deliver the mission's components, focus on the work, and not get waylaid by other distractions demanding time and energy. The AMP communicates agreed-on strategies to achieve the mission so that everyone, including other integrated areas of the institution, are able to align with the plan in their own planning process. The AMP also drives the continuous improvement projects and processes for the institution. If not addressed in the AMP, many of the improvements won't take place because they get lost in the day-to-day work.

A well-written AMP should include the reasons for making decisions about

- curriculum development,
- investment and allocation of resources,
- student success initiatives and support,
- budget,
- facility planning,
- staffing,
- shared governance agreements and flexibility in making improvements as necessary,
- assessment of outcomes at all levels,
- communication with internal and external audiences,
- marketing competitiveness, value, and telling the story, and
- action.

The AMP is often the cornerstone in planning all other master plans on campus. For instance, a technology master plan will consist of the elements needed to deliver the outcomes in the AMP. Technology will be needed to support computer and academic learning labs, Wi-Fi connectivity, software updates, and more to make the AMP successful. A technology master plan must include other nonacademic equipment and software for areas like security and staffing and business needs. Obviously, a robust AMP is critical to the overall success of your institution.

In summary, one the greatest benefits of assessing courses, programs and departments, and institutions is to set the future direction of all institutional learning. This isn't just for the students as curriculum changes are made to better meet ever changing real-world workplace experiences and expectations. It also establishes professional development offerings to better align faculty and staff knowledge and skills with the direction of the institution to meet its mission and vision to achieve its prioritized values, making lifelong learners of the employees as well as the students. According to Senge (2006),

> Learning organizations are where people continually expand their capacity to create the results they truly desire, where new and expansive patterns of thinking are nurtured, where collective aspiration is set free, and where people are continually learning to see the whole together. The basic rationale for such organizations is that in situations of rapid change, only those that are flexible, adaptive, and productive will excel. For this to happen, it is argued, organizations need to discover how to tap people's commitment and capacity to learn at all levels. (p. 3)

**Bright Idea**

One of the things we have noticed is that very few institutions have an assessment master plan showing how all the levels of assessment are related. Most assessments are developed in isolation for the immediate need of the outcomes they are designed to measure. Consequently, master plans for all outcomes haven't been developed, which makes it difficult to understand these relationships. You aren't alone in your confusion. Getting to know the institutional researcher and assessment coordinator on your campus is a step toward understanding how assessments are developed and how you play a role in developing assessments at the course, program or department, and institutional levels. —**Zala Fashant**

## Reflect on This Chapter

Now that you have completed reading this chapter and thinking about the content as it applies to your work, please reflect on the following questions:

- Do you have a copy of and have you read your institution's AMP? Have you discussed the AMP with your dean and shared governance committee representative? How does the AMP affect the way you teach? Do you have any responsibilities to make sure that the AMP is achieved?
- How have you aligned your course, program or department, and institutional assessments? In what ways do you communicate how your course outcomes align with program or department outcomes? How does your institution measure its learning outcomes?
- What benefits does an advisory board bring to your program or department? If you don't currently have one, who might make excellent internal (faculty, staff, students) and external (business and industry partners and other educational partners) members?
- Have you seen your institution's continuous improvement accreditation report? What areas of strength have been recognized? What challenges were presented for improvement? Are there areas of improvement that you can work on to help the institution?

**Jot Your Thoughts**

## Action Checklist

Use Checklist 10.1 to apply the chapter content to your practice and help you identify the steps for implementing these ideas in your teaching.

**CHECKLIST 10.1** Assessing Your Program and Institution Action Checklist

| ✓ | **Program or Department Assessment** |
|---|---|
| ❑ | Identified the types of program or department assessment currently used. |
| ❑ | Learned the history of campus advisory boards. |
| ❑ | Considered a portfolio assessment as a super summative assessment for courses and programs. |
| ❑ | Examined the latest program or department review of outcomes or the curriculum. |
| ❑ | Identified current external funding outcomes and assessments. |
| ❑ | Learned program or department accreditation process. |
| ❑ | Analyzed how skills assessments currently play a role in program or department assessment. |

| ✓ | **Institutional Assessment** |
|---|---|
| ❑ | Read the institution's AMP. |
| ❑ | Read the results of student satisfaction and employee engagement surveys. |
| ❑ | Identified the process for measuring institutional goals and outcomes. |
| ❑ | Met with institutional researcher to learn the process to request data. |
| ❑ | Read the institution's accreditation portfolio report. |

# PART FOUR

# REFLECTING

# 11

## REFLECTING ON YOUR TEACHING

### Points to Ponder

Chapter 11 discusses how reflection on your teaching plays an essential role in course redesign. In thinking about designing the courses you teach, consider the following questions to examine your prior knowledge:

- Why do you think reflecting on your teaching is a helpful practice?
- What kinds of evidence of your work would you include in the reflection of your teaching?
- When should you collect the items you would want to include in a teaching portfolio?
- How could you use the reflection of your teaching to develop a portfolio of your work?

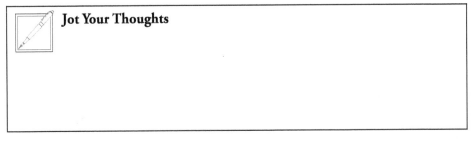

Sometimes we find that our assumptions about what is important to learn or how best to deliver instruction is rooted in our experience as experts in a discipline instead of viewed from the learner's perspective, as illustrated in the following vignette.

> As a young instructor and recent graduate with a PhD in music education, Stewart inherited a preexisting music appreciation course, which was a general education offering for all students. Enrollment averaged about 150 to 200 students per semester, and he was asked to teach the infamous 3-hour night class.

Stewart was hoping to share his love of classical music with his students. Even though some music faculty hinted this was the punishment course assigned to new faculty, he was happy to take it on. After all, what if he could ignite the curiosity of these students to learn more about the music they did not often listen to? Many of his colleagues were stuck in the teacher paradigm, that is, they taught the way they enjoyed teaching without getting student feedback about how well they were learning and whether the teaching strategies were effective. He followed the practice of his colleagues, lecturing and assessing through a multiple choice midterm and final exam. "I had so many students to teach what else could I do?" he asked.

He used the previous instructor's text, which had 1 chapter for each of the 10 weeks of the term, and he began writing 50-minute lectures for each class that included recordings of musical examples. He made sure that every historical period and nearly every composer known to him was covered, even if it meant some were only discussed for 1 or 2 minutes. Beethoven got 10 minutes, Mozart 5 minutes, and Vivaldi 1 minute.

As the midterm exam approached, nervous students started to pepper him with questions such as, How many questions will there be? Are they multiple choice? Will questions come from the text or just your lectures? He designed a 100-question multiple-choice test, and the scores were shockingly poor. One-fourth of the class got 60%. When he told other faculty about this, they said, "Don't worry, students just don't care about classical music" or "Good for you, we need to ferret out the strong and weak students; some just don't study like they used to." He wanted to believe the poor scores were the fault of the students but wondered if something else was going on.

As they got closer to the final exam, students began to ask if the final exam would be all inclusive or on only the material covered after midterm. What students were really asking was, Do we need to remember everything for the final exam, or can we dump stuff from before the midterm to make room for the second half of the course?

After consulting his colleagues, he decided to make the final exam an all-inclusive 100-question multiple-choice test. Knowing this, students began asking how they could do extra credit work to improve their grades. After all, he had decided to use high-stakes grading with only two 100-question tests as the only learning assessments.

The day of the final, a young man approached Stewart on the recital hall stage after completing his exam and instead of putting it on the pile, he handed it to Stewart personally. The student looked him in the eye and said, "Thank you for teaching this course; now I know why I hate classical music." Needless to say, Stewart was very disappointed with the way things turned out with his first music appreciation course.

His interest in teaching and excitement to have an impact on so many undergraduate students was not matched by his ability to create the kind of course that leads to significant learning. Reflecting on that first year, he realized he taught the way he was taught. He was thinking of each student as a mini music major who needed to learn all the facts that he had learned about music. He had not thought much about goals for a general music course at the college level, nor had he thought about how to put students in the best environment to learn. He liked lecturing, so he lectured. He had two exams that could be graded by a machine, making it easier for him. He said, "All I had to do was create the exam and put the scores in my grade book. After all, I had so many students to deal with, what else could I do?"

During the summer Stewart reflected on teaching this course and the pain he was in after hearing he had clarified for at least one student why he hated classical music. Many students in the class had the same feeling as the young man who had the courage to tell him to his face. Stewart realized major changes were needed, and most of them had to do with him. He had assumed that

- most students enjoyed all kinds of music, including classical;
- telling stories about music and showing off his vast knowledge would be enjoyable for students;
- students would listen to what he said and be able to remember every word for an exam as his main goal was for them to learn as many facts about music and prove they knew these facts by spitting them out in the two exams; and
- if they had all the facts, they would then develop an appreciation for and the joy of listening to music they never much cared for before taking the course.

To help students learn, he had to stop listening to his colleagues and listen more to the students. On the first day of the next term he asked them about their interest in classical music and was amazed to find out that nearly all of them not only had little interest but also said they actually hated classical music. Some said they were forced to take music lessons and they finally caused enough problems for their parents that they were allowed to quit. Only a small minority found any use for classical music.

Armed with valuable student feedback, Stewart reflected on what he wanted for students to gain from the course. He wanted to show them why the course could be important and how to enjoy many types of music, rather than just learning facts about music. He realized that the major pedagogical challenge was to find ways to develop a deeper understanding and enjoyment of classical music.

Luckily for him, the new movie *Star Wars* hit the theaters, and the composer of the movie's music, John Williams, was making a big splash with his bold scores filled with loud brass and percussion and romantic themes and melodies. Stewart went to see the movie, and looking back on that night, he knew that this was the beginning of his journey to be the best teacher he could be. He quickly realized the composer had borrowed ideas from romantic composers such as Holst, Strauss, Mahler, and Bruckner. Although these same composers were not held in high esteem by the students, the theater audience was absolutely transfixed by the music.

Stewart was on to something powerful and perhaps game changing so he purchased the *Star Wars* video for the class to watch on the recital hall's large-screen TV with its excellent sound system. He started class not by lecturing but by playing the beginning of the movie. As the music began, he could see the excitement of the students. It immediately captured their interest. They could not believe their good fortune to be able to listen to music they loved instead of listening to their professor drone on about how the issues of the Middle Ages related to music. He asked, "How many of you enjoy listening to this music?" All the students in the hall raised their hand high. Then he asked, "What kind of music would you call this soundtrack?" The students were silent for what seemed like two to three minutes. The lack of response made him nervous. Perhaps his idea was not going to work as planned. Finally, a student from the back row yelled out, "I do believe that is classical music!"

With that he started to ask all sorts of questions. He dropped the questions about the history of music, full of facts and dates, and instead got the students to think about how they felt about the music and its purpose. The students were engaged. He pointed out that they seemed to enjoy this classical music even though most had said that they hated classical music when asked earlier. He then played some excerpts from other similar classical music: portions of Holst's *The Planets*, a Mahler symphony, and a Bruckner symphony. The class was on a roll, with more students participating in the discussion.

At the end of the *Star Wars* lesson, a student raised her hand, asking, "Can we listen to *West Side Story* next week?" In an instant Stewart realized he was on to something very powerful, and he could create a unit of study around *West Side Story*'s composer, Leonard Bernstein, the conductor of the New York Philharmonic Orchestra.

Nearly three decades later he realized he had stumbled across the meaning of significant learning. Through trial and many errors, he had realized that his goals for the students, memorizing facts and dates, were not significant to their lives. He developed student-centered course outcomes and created class activities and assessments where learners performed their own compositions and actively analyzed musical recordings. Stewart's big dream was for students to develop confidence in their ability to listen to all kinds of music, understand why others sometimes cared about music they did not particularly enjoy, and ultimately move them to explore other kinds of music than what they already knew and valued.

## Perspective Through Reflective Lenses

If we, as educators, don't look back on how we have taught, we will to continue to teach in the same way. Just as we try to close the loop by using formative and summative assessments of learning, we also need to consider reflecting on our teaching as part of a circular process. We are hired to contribute to a department, a program, and a college or university, and as often as possible, we should examine our work as instructors. This doesn't happen by chance or when we get some free time in our schedule. Time to reflect needs to be an intentional practice, much like taking time to assess learning in our courses.

Some institutions have formalized a structure for developing faculty portfolios, evaluating performance, matriculating through promotion and tenure processes, and recognizing exemplary contributions. Other campuses are less formal. In either case, you should find out what your institution expects of you, learn the acceptable methods of documenting your teaching and other contributions, and get started immediately. Visit your dean or chair, center for teaching and learning, and other experienced faculty for assistance in learning the process.

Brookfield (2017) offers a series of four lenses to use to think about our teaching: autobiographical, student, colleagues, and theoretical.

The first lens is an autobiographical lens, which involves looking back at your teaching with a critical eye:

- What is your impression of how things are going in your classes?
- What would you like to improve?
- What is working well, and what you would plan to continue?

- Do you reflect on how well class sessions go?
- Do you make written notes about how you might improve a particular activity, lesson, lab, test, or set of materials?

In Stewart's case, he asked himself all these questions to redesign his course and improve his teaching so that it provided significant learning. He quit teaching at students and started delivering learning to students.

The second lens focuses on the students' perspective. Getting student feedback in the form of surveys, short reflective feedback sessions by students as described in chapter 9, and anecdotal evidence such as letters and thank-you notes are all examples of students providing information on your teaching. Always be thinking about what additional feedback you can get from your students.

Stewart heard some painful feedback from one particular student at the end of the first course he taught and wondered how many other students felt the same. He asked students about their attitudes toward classical music and began working with students where they were as they entered the course, not where he thought they should be. Taking their suggestions, he tailored the course to their needs and interests and allowed them to have a voice in their learning. He realized that this course was going to be a journey for them and that through their engagement he could reach many more students to achieve the course outcomes and his big dream of his them appreciating other forms of music.

Our colleagues provide us with the third lens; your program or department chair who observes you, a mentor, or a member of your teaching team can all help you gain perspective. Using a protocol for peer observation and a follow-up structured conversation on a predetermined, essential question have been found to encourage productive reflection on teaching (Daniels, Pirayoff, & Bessant, 2013). Many colleges have peer observation protocols that are part of a formal evaluation, but you can ask colleagues to observe your teaching at any time. The more observational feedback you receive, the more you develop multiple perspectives on your teaching.

Stewart learned that he needed to be selective when seeking advice from colleagues. Finding colleagues who are forward thinking and supportive of innovation in teaching and learning will help your professional growth. It doesn't mean you have to discount those who teach differently from you. You may still value what they are doing for their courses as you determine what you need for your own. Teaching isn't a herd-mentality activity. It is a science and art that provides opportunities to design learning for students at their level as they move from novice to expert. This requires your ability to be flexible and work with colleagues who will support your growth.

The fourth lens is the theoretical lens. Research-based literature helps you know you are using best practices, solid techniques that have proven to be effective, and other data that keep you current in your discipline and in teaching and learning. Ask yourself the following:

- How do you keep current in your discipline and teaching methods?
- How could you blend your professional development time to learn from discipline-related professional organizations and teaching and learning professional organizations?
- What campus resources are available for you to learn individually and with colleagues?
- Which regional or national conferences are you currently participating in?

At the end of Stewart's reflection and the application of his new approaches to teaching and learning, he eventually discovered a framework, Fink's (2013) taxonomy of significant learning that made sense for his experiences. Because many of our colleagues have shared their practices through scholarly publications, finding a framework to help you develop your own philosophy of practice has become easier as you link your experiences to the research-based literature.

Organizing your work using all four lenses will help you become reflective so that you can show your best self to your superiors, your colleagues, and your students as you develop your professional portfolio, which we discuss later in this chapter. Using each of these four lenses will help you gain experiences and artifacts to demonstrate a well-rounded set of professional experiences.

**Jot Your Thoughts**

## Reflecting on Your Professional Practices

As you get to a place in your professional growth where you develop confidence in your teaching, and you begin to see success in your students' learning, it is time to become intentional as you more deeply reflect on your work. In Figure 11.1 you can see how new ideas are implemented. Although you could begin anywhere in this cycle, reflecting on your teaching and student learning is a helpful starting place. Your teaching and your students' learning are important to consider. Find literature on teaching that pertains to your conclusions after reflection. As you plan your next teaching term, use the ideas you have read about in your classes. When you finish activities or courses, assess the effectiveness of the methods—during and after the course so you have a chance to adjust your methods immediately if necessary. Finally, share what you have learned with colleagues. The experience of sharing can generate new ideas for you to reflect on, and the cycle continues.

**Figure 11.1** Reflection of practice cycle.

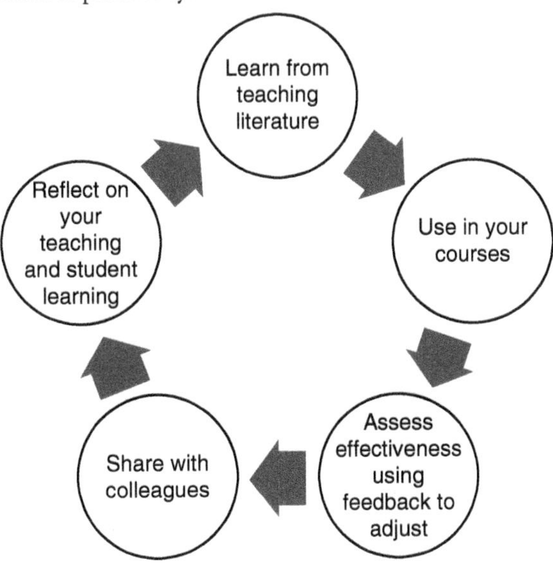


*Note*. This diagram illustrates Fink's cycle of reflection as a way grow in teaching practice. From "The Joy and Responsibility of Teaching Well," by S. Ross, 2014, keynote address at a faculty development workshop, February 2014, Truman State University, Kirksville, MO.

A faculty member can learn first from reading the teaching literature and from leaders at a teaching and learning conference. By reading more, faculty can apply what they learn to practice in their course. Using these concepts with students provides an opportunity to see them in action and assess their effectiveness to help students learn. Assessing this effectiveness provides feedback from students to make adjustments in the next round of implementation. As the ideas are perfected, faculty can share the success with other colleagues on campus and perhaps present them to other professionals in workshops at conferences. With reflection, faculty gain a broader perspective of their work, which usually leads to wanting to learn more through a deeper dive into what they have implemented or into new concepts and ideas.

Using the cycle in Figure 11.1 increases the rate of improvement in your teaching and, subsequently, student learning. In Figure 11.2 you can see an illustration of how the combination of learning on your own, sharing with colleagues, and using teaching literature increases the quality of teaching.

Using the reflection of practice cycle in Figure 11.1 in your teaching will provide you with a variety of material to document improvement in the quality of your work. This is critical in defining who you are as a professional as you work toward tenure, apply for new positions in your career, and are recognized for your achievements. Most faculty wait too long to start this process because they spend their time trying to grow early in their career. We recommend not waiting—begin the documentation process while you are building the foundation of your career.

**Figure 11.2** Increasing rate of improvement by combining reflection strategies.

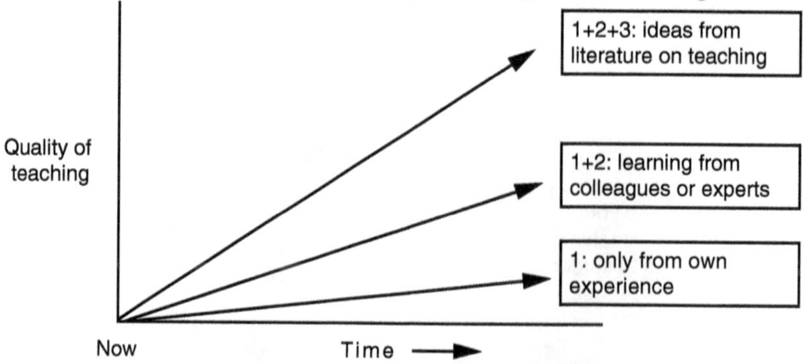

*Note.* At the starting point (Now) this graph shows that the quality of teaching improves over time as reflection strategies are scaffolded, starting with one's own experience, combined with learning from colleagues or experts and adding ideas from literature on teaching. From "The Joy and Responsibility of Teaching Well," by S. Ross, 2014, keynote address at a faculty development workshop, February 2014, Truman State University, Kirksville, MO.

## Reflective Practice Is Good for Higher Education

Just as you became an expert in your discipline by reading, problem-solving, discussing, analyzing, and taking directions from your professors and advisers, as a professional it is important to stay current and relevant by reflecting on your practice on a regular basis. Ashwin and colleagues (2015) encourage us to begin by considering our identity as teachers, our students and how they learn, and the very foundations of effective teaching. Having a strong orientation to reflective practice is as important as having a strong background in your own discipline (Ashwin et al., 2015). You can create a systematic approach to reflecting on your teaching by creating a portfolio to demonstrate your practices. A portfolio, like your curriculum vitae, is a living document that changes as you progress in your career. We offer the following steps to guide you as you begin the process of creating your portfolio.

## Documenting Your Teaching

So much happens during a semester that at the end it is difficult to remember how the semester even started. Many of us are so busy taking care of the needs of students and requests by the administration that we seldom make time to document the quality work we are doing. If you wait until the end of the semester to keep track of the great things you do during the semester in teaching and working with students, it is easy to lose track of some of your best work. If you don't schedule the time, you won't make the time. For this reason it is important to document your teaching by collecting student experiences and conversations, personal reflections and triumphs, committee and program and department work, and professional development activities.

We have found the biggest obstacle to having evidence of your work is keeping records. Who has time to do that? You do. It isn't as difficult as it first seems if you set up a methodology. We offer the following suggestions to help you choose artifacts as evidence of your professional work (see also Seldin, 2010).

- Recordkeeping
  - Start with a binder, drawer, box, or computer file to put artifacts in during the semester. Some faculty are great about organizing weekly, and others will wait for a break in the semester or the semester's end.
  - Place artifacts in this safe place when you come back from a professional development event. Include your reflections on what you intend to do with what you learned.
  - Keep a journal during committee meetings to organize your thoughts and contributions.
  - Scan paper documents and take some pictures with your phone's camera of events, colleagues, and artifacts you can't keep, such as an award that you helped your institution achieve or a sample of exemplary student work.
- Archiving
  - Do it right away, don't wait until you have time because you will never have time. It is a goal you need to attend to.
  - Schedule time on your calendar for archiving, maybe the first of the month or at the end of the semester after you submit your grades. Develop a system of reminders to make the time such as calendar reminders or a monthly to-do list reminder.
- Professional Portfolios
  - Developing a professional portfolio is much more than a scrapbook collection of what you have done. It provides you, your dean, program or department, institution, and professional organizations with career evidence.
  - The artifacts you collect are a reflection on the quality work you have exhibited over time and shows your growth and mastery of teaching in your discipline.
  - The portfolio experience is more meaningful when faculty write narratives about the experiences that describe what they did and learned in their professional growth. Discuss the impact of what you did, what you learned, and how it affected other learning for yourself and your students.
  - Ask your dean or chair if there is an excellent example of a portfolio. Seeing one a colleague has developed can inspire the development of your own portfolio.

Portfolios can be created electronically or in binder form. We are not making recommendations on which format to use, but we suggest you start collecting evidence immediately (Bernstein & Burnett, 2006). The reason most faculty think of this as such a monumental chore is that it is much like the room in your home where things go to gather dust or the junk drawer in the kitchen. Although this can seem more like a chore, it needs to be added to your end-of-semester duties like completing grades, writing letters of recommendation, checking on book orders in book stores, and prepping for next semester. If this seems daunting, focus on a single course each term instead of trying to broadly consider all your courses.

When you examine the list of artifacts collected throughout the semester, you can determine the best times of the semester or year to integrate your new artifacts into the established portfolio. It is easier to do this a little at a time than to tackle the whole project at once.

## What Should You Start Collecting to Build Your Portfolio?

Your portfolio should include a set of general artifacts about your professional work; it can include archives about individual courses you have taught and designed. We suggest including the following:

- A philosophy of teaching statement, the anchor of your work, is usually three to five pages and is a common practice for faculty at colleges and universities. Reflecting on your philosophy helps you identify your core of teaching. This document is your brand and mission statement to share with your students on the syllabus and in your course (Harrington & Thomas, 2018).
- Your current curriculum vitae or résumé should be updated every year; it is an archive of your work responsibilities and professional development participation.
- Teaching strategies and materials in your course design should include the content you developed; how you developed and delivered this content; its impact on students; any increase in the completion rate of your courses, programs, certificates, or degrees based on your innovation; an explanation of why you teach a particular course the way you do or why a course is important to offer in your department's curriculum (Hutchings, 1998); any curriculum advancements you have made in your courses; and how you improved your teaching and course content based on partnerships and external experiences.
- Content expertise and professional growth should show how you have distinguished your work in your discipline, changes you have made based on your experiences in the classroom and through professional development, your story as an educator, how you participated in teaching and learning activities on your campus and through conferences and workshops, and what conferences you have attended and presentations you have made.
- Service describes how you have served your program or department and institution. What innovations have you helped provide for your students? Are you participating in community and professional organizations that link to your work? What advances have you brought to your discipline?

- Assessment includes your contribution to advance program or department quality assessment. How do you know your students are completing courses and degrees at a higher rate? What evidence do you have that more students have met higher standards or completed a greater number of competencies than in the past? How are you measuring the improvement your work is having with student learning?

**Bright Idea**

Keep in mind that your portfolio should follow the same guidelines as a research project. Be sure to use proper citations and respect copyright and privacy rules. With electronic portfolios you can provide links to collaborative projects and conferences to provide additional information. —**Zala Fashant**

## Portfolio Artifacts to Collect for Tenure and Promotion

The following personal, course, and program or department information should be included:

- Updated curriculum vitae
- Course survey evaluations
- Letters and e-mails from students, alumni, and administration
- Assessment tools you developed and administered
- Institutional data about your program or department
- Classroom observation forms
- Self-evaluation activities
- Performance evaluations
- Samples of student work, with permission
- Books, texts, or course materials you have written
- Research projects you have conducted
- Professional reflection materials
- Awards and certificates from institutions and community and professional organizations
- Internship development
- Team-teaching courses and projects with a colleague
- Curriculum development projects and course revisions
- Course descriptions and responsibilities

Include all events you have led or participated in on and off campus. Examples include the following:

- Campus activities you participated in, such as student success days, open houses, professional organizations, advisory boards, and community meetings
- Campus activities you planned and helped to implement

Service to your institution includes the following:

- Committee initiatives, agendas, and charters
- Service to the institution examples
- Accreditation activities

Professional development activities includes the following:

- Conference and workshop programs
- Conference presentations and session evaluations results
- Professional development plans
- Advanced degree completion materials
- Teaching and learning professional development opportunities
- Evidence of improving your practice

Partnerships should also be in your portfolio. Examples include the following:

- Letters, e-mails, and testimonials from collaborative partners
- Partnerships you developed with community and business organizations

**Bright Idea**

Don't keep everything you collect in your portfolio. Fine art museums don't try to hang every painting they own. Continue to refine your collection. Think of your portfolio as an exhibit of your best work. You want samples of quality. Eventually, most faculty will have more than what they need, so learn to be selective: quality versus quantity. —**Zala Fashant**

## Performance Evaluations

Your institution will have a regular cycle of performance evaluations, which may consist of classroom observations, written work, a professional development plan, and course success data and is often provided in a new faculty orientation or meeting with your dean. Find out when you will be evaluated so you are prepared. Most new faculty are evaluated more frequently to determine progress toward promotion and tenure.

Performance evaluations are a great opportunity for you to grow by getting feedback about your teaching and institutional work. There are times when we can fear feedback as we don't like to hear bad things about ourselves. Instead of fearing this process, use it as an opportunity to improve so you do your best.

One of the things we have learned as faculty developers and supervisors is that employees react to performance evaluations in two ways. The first way is they learn from their strengths and weaknesses, working on the latter to turn them into strengths.

The second way is they hide from weaknesses in the hope that they aren't discovered. Most of us would agree that it is better to meet the weaknesses head-on. This is a great time to employ a growth mind-set (Dweck, 2006) as discussed in chapter 4. Although your weaknesses may be evident to others, such as your dean, students, and colleagues, acknowledging your efforts to improve is more important than worrying what others think of you. If you approach your weaknesses by thinking, "I haven't got it yet," you will have a more positive approach to improving. Modeling this growth mind-set in your teaching sends the message to your students that everyone can learn from mistakes and do better, including you. Your colleagues and supervisors will also not dwell on your weaknesses if they see that you are deliberately working to up your game (Dweck, 2006).

Being honest with yourself is important. If you are serious about being your best, you can't worry about how others will see you. Identify ways you want to improve and act on it, for example,

- ask for help from your campus teaching and learning center and participate in the programs provided as they are trained to assist you and will do so without judgment,
- talk with your trusted colleagues about how they have dealt with challenges,
- take advantage of peer-mentoring program with trusted colleagues and talk with your dean or chair for recommendations, and
- attend campus workshops on teaching and learning topics to improve your practice.

Reflect on what you have learned and how you have implemented the ideas for your portfolio.

**Bright Idea**

You may invite colleagues to observe your teaching. Don't be hesitant to invite your dean or department chair to visit when your students give oral presentations, conduct experiments, work in pairs, or do some other active tasks. Even if the visitor stays for only 15 minutes, your work with students will be remembered. Be sure to explain to your students why the visitor is in your classroom. The visitor is there to provide feedback to you, or to see quality work the students are doing, not to evaluate students. —**Zala Fashant**

Our experience is that students enjoy seeing the dean or chair visit the classroom. They enjoy seeing that the administration cares about the learning taking place in the classroom. This also works well in an online course where the instructor shows the dean or chair the quality of the work in the course shell. You could post any congratulatory notes from the administrator in the LMS's Announcements or News section.

When preparing for your formal evaluation, gather the required information according to your institution's process. There will be forms to complete, usually an observation of your teaching, evaluation feedback form, and a follow-up meeting. Some campuses allow faculty to choose from options for the evaluation; for example, a colleague conducts a peer observation and fills out a report. You may be able to select which supervisor will conduct your evaluation, in which case it is good to learn about the team of supervisors so you can make an informed choice. We recommend asking your supervisor to observe you for the first couple of times so you build a relationship with the person who will be recommending you for tenure. Faculty in an online course can grant permission for their supervisor to enter the course to observe how the faculty member presents the course and observe his or her pedagogy.

The evaluation process will include a follow-up meeting with your dean or chair to discuss their observations, but it will also include questions about your teaching relative to the goals of your department or program and to the college's goals. Be prepared to answer questions like the following:

- How does your teaching support or further the goals of your program or department?
- How do you stay current in your discipline and apply best practices in your teaching?
- What are your career goals?
- How do you use the information gathered on student evaluations to improve your teaching?
- What are three things you would like to improve in the next semester? What are three things you are most proud of in your current teaching?
- How have you collaborated with members of your department or program?
- How would you like to become involved in the wider college community?

Be careful not to overextend yourself in your early teaching. Investigate any committee opportunities to understand the politics and effectiveness of its work.

You don't get many one-on-one meetings during the year with your dean or chair, so take this opportunity to discuss questions you have about institutional practices to learn more about how you can be successful in your work, such as the following:

- Ask about professional development opportunities and how you can participate. How are conferences fees funded?
- What advice does your dean or chair have for you in how you are progressing in your work?
- What does the dean or chair think the greatest challenges are for the institution and your program or department during the next year?

This a chance for you to show your commitment to the institution, so blend the feedback into your practice.

## The Benefits of Creating a Portfolio

Documenting your work reinforces and exhibits the great work you do and your professional and personal growth. Reflection is a great learning opportunity, and by developing a portfolio you will enhance your thinking about teaching by taking stock in what you are doing and giving yourself room to dream about the direction you next want to go. Portfolios can be a process to reach new levels of teaching and of learning more about yourself.

Portfolios showcase your work and growth as a professional. There are times when your institution or a professional organization may want to support your work through grants or awards. Having this documentation archive helps the process tremendously as you will have this portion ready for the application.

Your teaching is an amazing journey and should be archived. Looking through your portfolio is a great way to reenergize and re-create the professional you are. The collection can be rewarding as it provides a wonderful way to recall all the experiences you have had.

**Bright Idea**

Look at your colleagues' portfolios so you don't develop your own in isolation. Your dean or chair may offer suggestions from some of the best examples to help you. Many of your colleagues will consider it a compliment to be asked to share their portfolios. Looking at other exemplary portfolios will help you develop an excellent one of your own. —**Zala Fashant**

## Reflect on This Chapter

Now that you have completed reading this chapter and thinking about the content as it applies to your work, please reflect on the following questions:

- What practice do you implement or want to implement in reflecting about your teaching?
- How have you already started to archive evidence of your work?
- Why do you think reflecting on your teaching is a helpful practice?
- How will you use the reflection of your teaching and portfolio of your work?

**Jot Your Thoughts**

## Action Checklist

Use Checklist 11.1 to apply the chapter content to your practice and help you identify the steps for implementing these ideas in your teaching.

**CHECKLIST 11.1** Reflecting on Your Teaching Action Checklist

| ✓ | **Brookfield's Four Lenses for Reflective Teaching** |
|---|---|
| ❑ | Determined how to document the autobiographical lens. |
| ❑ | Determined how to document the students' lens. |
| ❑ | Determined how to document the colleagues' lens. |
| ❑ | Determined how to document the theoretical lens. |
| ❑ | Considered how to implement the reflection of practice cycle. |
| ❑ | Designed a plan to combine strategies to increase the rate of teaching improvement. |

| ✓ | **Artifact Collection Process** |
|---|---|
| ❑ | Chosen either a box, drawer, computer folder, or some other method to collect teaching artifacts. |
| ❑ | Deposited teaching artifacts using a predetermined schedule. |
| ❑ | Established time after this semester to organize and assess the artifact collection. |

| ✓ | **Teaching Philosophy and Curriculum Vitae** |
|---|---|
| ❑ | Located or updated or written a personal philosophy of teaching. |
| ❑ | Checked that curriculum vitae is current and determined a time to update it regularly. |

| ✓ | **Professional Development** |
|---|---|
| ❑ | Identified or joined a professional association in this discipline, for teaching, or both. |
| ❑ | Selected one or two professional development activities to participate in this year. |
| ❑ | Created a professional development plan to set goals and assess professional growth. |
| ❑ | Shared the professional development plan with supervisor. |

| ✓ | **Performance Review** |
|---|---|
| ❑ | Identified when the next performance review will occur. |
| ❑ | Reflected on the questions asked during such a performance review. |
| ❑ | Gathered documentation of teaching, including observations, prior to review. |

# 12

# LEARNING HOW TO LEARN

## Advancing Your Professional Development

### Points to Ponder

Chapter 12 brings us full circle in course design as you plan for your own practice to remain current with the latest content advancement and the development of teaching skills to then redesign your courses. In thinking about designing the courses you teach, consider the following questions to examine your prior knowledge:

- Although you are an expert in your academic discipline, what formal preparation do you have in teaching and learning?
- How could a mentor be helpful to you on your campus?
- What resources do you wish you could access to improve your teaching?
- What professional development opportunities do you currently participate in?

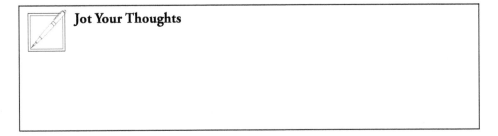

The phone rang at the Center for Teaching and Learning, and the leader noted the caller ID and picked it up, saying, "Hi Todd, what's up?"

"Linda, I just had the worst thing happen!"

"Sounds serious," Linda replied, noting Todd's fast breathing and panicked voice. "Want me to stop by?"

"Do I ever!" Todd gasped.

A second-year instructor in a new technical program, Todd had just experienced something none of us ever wants: Every single student in one of his classes failed the midterm exam. Starting a new program had been quite a challenge for Todd. His field was a new one, and no educational materials were available; practitioners had simply learned on the job. Now that credentials were becoming more valued in his industry, certification programs were just emerging in technical colleges. The only material he had available was a manual designed for experienced practitioners. It was difficult and written for technicians who already had background knowledge and experience. His students struggled to understand it, so Todd spent a lot of time trying to make it simpler and easier to follow. He also had no colleagues with which to collaborate. He was a one-man department, and there were no other programs of its kind in his state. He had never had academic training in his field, nor in the study of teaching and learning. Todd wrote his own exams, based on the manual and his own understanding of what students needed to know. Clearly, this time he guessed wrong.

Todd and Linda had a first meeting on the day he discovered that all his students had failed his midterm exam. Linda reassured him that he would not be fired for this and helped him calm down. Then they developed a plan.

Linda met with Todd's class, without Todd, to debrief the students on their exam experience. The students were asked to give feedback on the exam and also on the teaching and learning that led up to it. It was a type of informal midterm evaluation but with a specific focus: the exam. Students were unhappy about the exam, but to Todd's surprise they were not unhappy with his teaching or even with him. They worried the exam would cause their grades to suffer, but offered several suggestions to mitigate its effect on their grades.

Todd and Linda discussed the results of the students' feedback session, and he decided to give the exam again but this time have students work in pairs and use their course materials to find the answers. The test really was too hard, but by making it an open book exam and a collaborative endeavor, the students actually did learn the material, and he was able to use that second exam in his grading instead of the first one.

The next semester Todd joined a teaching circle on exam writing. He learned other techniques, such as scaffolding, to help his students deal with an especially difficult textbook, which in his case was a technical manual for practitioners. He developed a study guide to help his students manage the textbook, posing the important questions that students needed to focus on. This reduced his students' feelings of being overwhelmed and also clued them in to the key points for each chapter. Todd had learned how to bridge the gap between challenging materials from the field and novice students in his program. He rethought what he wanted his students to take from this course and how it would better prepare them for the workplace. He wrote and shared his big dream with his students so they understood what he wanted for them to take away from his course.

## Learning How to Learn

It isn't by accident that this chapter's title is taken from Fink's (2013) taxonomy. Faculty know better than anyone that learning never stops. As in every job, knowledge, skills, and practice change to respond to the variations in the needs of students and society. Some of your learning will help you keep current, and some will help you advance or innovate. As with your students, a deep foundation will help you progress faster and further. This chapter is intended to help you plan for this change so you can keep learning.

Most of us who contributed to this book have run teaching and learning centers at the college, university, or systemwide level. We have worked closely with faculty and administration to design programs to facilitate campus teaching and learning needs. Beyond that, we have helped with strategic planning of faculty development and campus initiatives as well as stayed active in professional educational organizations. This chapter is designed to provide you with the options you have for learning about teaching and learning, developing as an educator, and seeking on-campus and off-campus opportunities for professional development.

## Campus Faculty Development

Many campuses have professional development centers for faculty; however, it is important to be aware that centers go by various titles. Examples include the following:

- Center for Teaching and Learning (CTL)
- Center for Excellence in Teaching and Learning
- Center for Teaching Excellence
- Center for Faculty Development
- Center for Faculty Development and Instructional Design
- Teaching Resource Center

These centers were originally developed to help faculty with instructional technology, but their purpose has broadened considerably (Lieberman, 2018). You might find such a center housed in the technology department, although it also might be under the jurisdiction of your chief academic officer (vice president or provost). Your center might be an actual geographic location, or it might be *floating* and reserve a room somewhere on campus when needed. It could be staffed by an instructional designer (although usually that implies technology) or a faculty colleague on reassignment or permanently assigned to the center.

The mission of the centers is ever changing. Many started by designing workshops to help faculty learn more about elements of teaching and learning. However, on most campuses, the mission has expanded to develop greater expertise beyond delivering instruction to meeting mission initiatives for the institution such as improving retention. The centers can be a great way for faculty and administrators to collaborate in designing solutions for continuous improvement.

CTLs offer many services to faculty who would like to learn more about teaching and learning, create cross-discipline discussions and collaborations, try innovative approaches to their teaching, and experiment with new formats of teaching or use of technology. Sometimes they offer ongoing activities, such as teaching circles, book clubs, new faculty seminars, promotion and tenure planning, and so on.

Often the leaders of your CTL are senior faculty who have knowledge of the institutional goals and initiatives, are trusted by faculty and administrators, and have demonstrated teaching success of their own. These mid- to later-career faculty have developed the expertise necessary to mentor newer faculty in areas of teaching and learning, institutional knowledge and mission, multilevel assessment, community and business partnerships, and professional development planning for individuals. They may also help to organize campus professional development days, developing programming or selecting outside speakers or workshop facilitators.

Whether your campus has a CTL or not, the following are aspects of faculty development and will help you expand your skills in teaching.

### *Networking With Other Faculty*

One of the greatest opportunities you have is meeting faculty from other disciplines on your campus and faculty in your discipline from other institutions through professional events and conferences. Knowing that you can find common practices in teaching and learn about the common challenges that all faculty have working with students helps you realize that you have allies going through similar experiences.

Joining other faculty at lunch or meeting for a beverage can you get you started. The next time you might each bring another colleague to join the group. One of the campuses we worked with borrowed the title of the book *Stone Soup* (Brown, 1975) for the following activity. For those of you who don't know the *Stone Soup* story, some soldiers came into a town and asked the townfolk to each contribute one thing to the soup. Even without a chef, the soup, which had contributions from all the villagers, was delicious, and everyone shared a great meal. For those of you who don't have a CTL to help organize networking, you can build your own soup of faculty experiences through informal networking, and you might find other faculty on campus who enjoy some of the same hobbies or activities as you. Just as we promote building a community of student learners, forming a network of faculty across the campus strengthens the institution and provides you with a sense of belonging in what may feel like an overwhelming and isolating environment.

A more formal method for networking with colleagues is to create a faculty learning community (Cox & Richlin, 2004). These sometimes serve a cohort group, such as new faculty, and other times provide a mixed faculty group with an opportunity to explore a topic of interest, much like teaching circles (discussed later in this chapter).

A different model is the formative mentoring community that Felten, Bauman, Kheriaty, and Taylor (2013) and others have promoted. This approach is formal in its organization of members but very informal in terms of its day-to-day structure, conversations, and goals. The purpose of formative mentoring communities is to build trust among faculty colleagues, mentor each other, and explore the meaning of the work they do.

### *New Faculty Seminars and Programming*

If you are new at your college, ask if there is a CTL and if any of its offerings are directed at first-year, junior, or part-time faculty. If you can participate, you will gain valuable information and tips, as well as meet other new faculty. Your own department or program will certainly help you, but a CTL's primary mission is to help you acclimate and develop your teaching skills. If there is no formal offering, consider maintaining contact with the new faculty you meet in orientation (or onboarding) meetings. This group can be a great transition group and, in some cases, an opportunity to stay connected across disciplines for the duration of your tenure. Some campuses offer new faculty seminars that focus on topics many faculty experience in the first few semesters. Your campus may have a new faculty handbook to guide you through things like where and how to make copies or to how to connect with resource staff who can help with student support and challenges. We have more information for new faculty on our website (https://encoreprodev.com/book) in the bonus chapter called "Making a Strong Start on Your Campus."

## Peer Consulting or Observations

As you will be formally evaluated during your first year, seek colleagues who might observe your classes informally or even meet with you to discuss your teaching. If you have a CTL, this is a typical service offered. For this activity, seeking the advice of a more senior member of your department would be an excellent starting place. You may also ask a trusted colleague you met during new faculty orientation or other networking events to observe each other's classes.

### *Teaching Circles and Workshops*

A teaching circle (or sometimes called a learning circle) consists of a voluntary group of faculty who would like to work on a topical short-term project and get together with colleagues to discuss, cross-pollinate, and support each other. Typically, they are one semester or one term in length. Examples of teaching circle topics are critical thinking, rubric creation, syllabus development, test writing, creating writing assignments, equity, active learning, gaming, or collaborative learning. Each participant chooses a small doable project related to the topic and presents it to the group at the end of the term. Often shorter workshops or brown-bag lunch sessions are held on similar topics. Teaching circles and workshops are productive, energizing opportunities that will improve you as a teacher. Your college or university may have a formal structure for these types of activities, but if it doesn't, you can look for willing participants and do this informally.

### *Book Clubs*

Faculty book clubs are just like regular book clubs but usually without the wine. One book per semester or year is chosen by the campus CTL leaders, and faculty are encouraged to read it and join a conversation. Several books might be suggested, and individuals may join the group reading a title they are interested in. Books are usually on the topics of teaching, learning, communicating, assessment, mindfulness (or other health-related topics), working with subsets of students (e.g., cultural awareness or students on the autism spectrum), and so on. If your campus does not offer this, there is nothing stopping you from finding a good book and sending an invitation to your colleagues to join a conversation about it. Book clubs don't need many members, perhaps just you and another colleague can meet over coffee. Your program or department faculty may choose a book to read and discuss it as a way to address a challenge in a continuous improvement plan.

### *Academic Advising*

Faculty play a huge role in helping students complete their program, not only in teaching but also in academic advising. Students look to faculty for advice in completing their program on time, employment opportunities, or transferring to another institution to continue their learning. You know which electives may help students develop skills for the workplace. As a mentor during advising sessions, you have an opportunity to promote student leadership in taking control over what they can do to learn how to learn. As a mentor you encourage your mentees to take the lead in identifying their needs and working on a plan toward reaching their goals. Your department chair or program dean can help familiarize you with the formal advising structure. Your colleagues can help you lead students through the academic pathway and provide you with some of the best practices and tell you about campus resources or professional development opportunities to help you learn more about how to be an effective adviser.

## Balancing Professional and Personal Life

Early in your career you may spend most of the hours of your week prepping, teaching, and grading. Learning more about how you can deliver significant learning to students efficiently will help you find a balance between work and your personal life. Integrated course design allows you to spend a greater amount of your time working directly with students. Many of the lessons you learn in designing your course and teaching actually help you design your free time as well. Having the confidence of knowing that your course is designed well allows you to teach well with more time to develop healthy boundaries and know when it is time to focus on other aspects of your life. Students will provide constant work for you, so it is important to not only have systems in place to meet their needs but also give you time to accomplish your personal goals. A non-teaching life is critical for your own growth and sustainability. Other faculty can help you learn the importance of reenergizing yourself with personal endeavors.

## Mentoring Program

If there is a mentoring program at your institution, consider taking advantage of it, even if you are not new to teaching but may be new to the campus. It is helpful to have a mentor outside your department or program because they don't have any leverage over you, and thus it is safe to confide in them. Some campuses also assign new faculty to an inside-department mentor as well because that person will understand the intricacies of the department, the details of the tenure process, and the culture of the group. It is important for department administrators to convey that they are welcoming and that they want to include all their faculty in decision-making (Phillips & Dennison, 2015). Many new faculty appreciate having both kinds of mentors as they begin a new position.

Setting up mentors for new or junior faculty is a relatively common practice in higher education (Mullen, 2012; Phillips & Dennison, 2015). As Phillips and Dennison (2015) point out, it costs an institution money to conduct a search, so it is worth the effort to offer support for new faculty to enhance retention. Mentoring is a multipurpose program in an institution serving practical interests, such as retention of faculty, advancing professional learning, and socialization into a particular milieu, and humanistic interests, such as increasing the diversity of college faculty, supporting early-career professionals, and building relationships among faculty (Hargreaves & Fullan, 2000; Mullen, 2012).

Mentees should enter a mentoring relationship with several goals that can be discussed early in the process. Perhaps you are considering your contributions to your discipline, your big dream as a teacher, or how you will find "community in your work" (Mullen, 2012, p. 22). We have also noted in our own mentoring relationships that new faculty are often overwhelmed with the details of particular institutional quirks such as how to add or drop students from courses, learn the learning management system (LMS), order books and materials, and answer students' questions in advising. Therefore, mentees should prioritize their topics for the mentor meetings so that urgent questions can be answered but with planned time for meatier discussions.

Ideally, mentors have maturity, a wealth of knowledge, the ability to communicate, an empathetic nature, the ability to frame good questions, and a tradition of successful teaching. Phillips and Dennison's (2015) characteristics of effective mentors are the following:

- Good listener
- Organizational skills
- Willingness to promote others
- Ability to support
- Ability to challenge
- Reliability
- Collaborative skills
- Insightful (p. 29)

Mentors can help identify where mentees are in their growth and where they might want to go. Mentors share what they know, to help mentees navigate through the politics, processes, and bureaucracy. It helps if mentors are good storytellers and can see the value of a mentorship project playing a significant role in a faculty member's life.

The mentoring participants typically begin with introductory activities to break the ice and build the relationship. A discussion of the goals and action plans can cover details like the meeting framework, timing, and who is responsible for creating a session agenda. Mentors may need to start this conversation based on the experience of the mentee; however, for the mentee's own development, this can be the role of the mentee. It is critical to maintain a professional relationship, keeping discussions confidential.

Take time to celebrate short-term wins and benchmark the progress you are making. This relationship needn't be senior versus junior, as each can learn from one another. In our experiences, mentors often comment how much they learn in the process. Phillips and Dennison (2015) report that departments with formal mentoring programs help create a culture "in which everyone is viewed as being both a learner and teacher/supporter of others" (p. 27).

Table 12.1 contains some of the roles for mentors and mentees and their responsibilities together.

## Learning How to Continue Learning

Your professional development activities help you learn how to keep learning. A faculty member has a lifelong set of skills and strategies for learning. Faculty need to master teaching delivery, course design, writing, implementing and assessing outcomes (course integration), classroom management, advising, discipline-specific advancements, and program or department and institutional continuous improvement leading to accreditation.

Your learning isn't going to stop at the borders of your campus. This book's Additional Reading and Resources section contains links to national and international teaching and learning organizations. Your own discipline probably has a professional organization that may provide resources and perhaps annual conferences. You may be able to use professional development funds from your institution to pay for membership and conference opportunities to help you keep up with the latest information you need to keep your courses and practices current.

**TABLE 12.1**
**Mentor and Mentee Roles and Responsibilities**

| *Mentors* | *Mentees* | *Together* |
|---|---|---|
| • Deliver expertise<br>• Share strategies<br>• Listen, then speak<br>• Display and develop wisdom<br>• Model excellence<br>• Inspire<br>• Frame confidence<br>• Demonstrate empathy<br>• Offer storytelling<br>• Praise | • Ask questions<br>• Identify weaknesses<br>• Establish agenda<br>• Run the meeting<br>• Be open to new ideas and ways of doing things<br>• Be willing to risk<br>• Develop skills<br>• Apply concepts<br>• Increase self-branding | • Trust and connect<br>• Prepare to meet<br>• Develop and discuss outcomes<br>• Be willing to learn<br>• Display integrity<br>• Be accountable<br>• Lead<br>• Take notes<br>• Assess progress<br>• Enjoy the experience |

### *Professional Development Plan*

Consider making a professional development plan even if your institution does not require one. The plan helps you think through the needs of your professional development and helps you communicate your career direction to your dean or chair. You may not have enough money or time to attend several conferences a year, so analyze them and prioritize your needs. Your supervisor's approval of your plan may help you secure funding for these conferences. We suggest creating a three-year plan as portions of your plan may take more than a year to implement. We also suggest meeting with your dean or chair annually to discuss the progress you are making in meeting your plan's outcomes. A plan can also include ideas you have for a sabbatical, help you secure the sabbatical, and help your administration plan for it. Again, check to see what is required by your institution.

### *Reflecting on Your Teaching and Career*

Your institution may provide learning opportunities to help you reflect on your teaching, how to manage your teaching load, your professional responsibilities to the institution, and the long-term sustainability of your career. Many institutions will require you to follow guidelines for preparing for tenure and promotion (see chapter 11 for reflection strategies).

## Reflect on This Chapter

As college or university faculty, your main emphasis in your education has been to become an expert in your field. You may have spent years gaining experience, certifications, and degrees to arrive at this point. As a teacher you may be far less prepared. The skills of teaching and knowledge about how to facilitate learning are just as important as your disciplinary expertise. Have you ever had a professor who was impossible to understand or who doled out information and expected you to learn as if by magic? We all have, unfortunately. That is why it is so important for you to pay close attention to the learning that is occurring or not occurring in your courses. Seek ways to improve your ability to reach students, facilitate their learning, and develop into the well-rounded professional that you can be.

Now that you have completed reading this chapter and thinking about the content as it applies to your work, please reflect on the following questions.

- How might you connect to your professional development campus resources?
- What kinds of professional development activities appeal to you?
- How could a mentor be helpful to you in your teaching and learning development?
- What process does your campus use to support professional development?
- What might you include in your professional development plan?

**Jot Your Thoughts**

## Action Checklist

Checklist 12.1 serves as a way for you to apply the chapter content to your practice and helps you identify the steps for implementing these ideas in your teaching.

**CHECKLIST 12.1** Learning How to Learn Action Checklist

| ✓ | **Campus Resources** |
|---|---|
| ❑ | Identified the resources on my campus for professional development in teaching. |
| ❑ | Identified a few colleagues to go to for informal or formal advice. |
| ❑ | Chose at least one type of campus-based professional development activity to pursue (book club, teaching circle, mentor, etc.). |

| ✓ | **Creating a Professional Development Plan** |
|---|---|
| ❑ | Created a draft personal development plan in the faculty evaluation process. |
| ❑ | Included on-campus (if available) and off-campus resources in my plan to improve teaching practice. |
| ❑ | Discussed with the department chair (or other designated person) how to access funding to attend professional development activities. |

| ✓ | **Current Professional Development Activities** |
|---|---|
| ❑ | Created a list of current professional development memberships and ongoing activities in this discipline and for teaching improvement. |
| ❑ | Updated curriculum vitae with these memberships and activities. |

| ✓ | **My Wish List** |
|---|---|
| ❑ | Created a list of professional development activities to explore. Shared this list with supervisor and added it to the professional development plan. |

# EPILOGUE

Our goal for this book is to provide you with a wealth of ideas to help you design courses that provide significant learning. Starting with Fink's (2013) framework in faculty workshops on our campuses and all over the world, we realized that faculty want to share their big dreams with their students. In our experience, we have seen what aligning the learning outcomes with the assessments and activities can do for student success. Faculty have told us hundreds of stories about how using this process has ignited their teaching and professional development.

We also recognized that our teaching demands greater communication, deeper understanding of the learning process, accessibility for all learners, and integrating technologies that enhance learning. Increased accountability requires designers of courses, programs or departments, and institutions to demonstrate the highest standards that confirm that we do what we say we are doing. Saying it is easy, doing it and proving it requires work. We want you to think about your work and all your accomplishments as a way to reflect on your best practices and feel pride in your work. Finally, we want you to consider how you, a person who has been a successful learner, continue to model excellence in learning for your students and colleagues through lifelong learning.

We hope you have enjoyed this journey and that you can learn from our practice and that of the many faculty and thousands of professionals we have worked with. As we told you in the preface, you are not alone. All educators go through the same steps in learning to teach and in developing significant learning. We hope this book can assist you in reaching your goals as a successful faculty member by changing the lives of your students and by achieving your mission and the mission of your institution.

# APPENDIX A

# INITIAL DESIGN PHASE OF INTEGRATED COURSE DESIGN

## Designing Courses That Promote Significant Learning

If professors want to create courses in which students have significant learning experiences, they need to design that quality into their courses. How can they do that? By following the five basic steps of the instructional design process:

### *Step 1. Give Careful Consideration to a Variety of Situational Factors*

What is the special instructional challenge of this particular course?
What is expected of the course by students? By the department, the institution, the profession, society at large?
How does this course fit into the larger curricular context?
Use the backward design process. This process starts at the end of the learning process and works back toward the beginning.
Use information about the situational factors (Step 1) as you make the following key decisions.

### *Step 2. Learning Goals*

What do you want students to learn by the end of the course that will still be with them several years later?

Think expansively, beyond understand and remember kinds of learning.
Suggestion: Use the taxonomy of significant learning as a framework.

### *Step 3. Feedback and Assessment Procedures*

What will the students have to do to demonstrate that they have achieved the learning goals (as identified in Step 2)?

Think about what you can do that will help students learn, as well as give you a basis for issuing a course grade.
Suggestion: Consider ideas of educative assessment.

*Note.* Appendix A is from Fink (2005). Used with permission.

### *Step 4. Teaching and Learning Activities*

What would have to happen during the course for students to do well on the feedback and assessment activities?

### *Step 5. Think Creatively of Ways of Involving Students That Will Support Your More Expansive Learning Goals*

Suggestion: Use active learning activities, especially those related to rich learning experiences in which students achieve several kinds of significant learning simultaneously.
In-depth reflective dialogue opportunities encourage students to think and reflect on what they are learning, how they are learning, and the significance of what they are learning.
Suggestion: Assemble these activities into an effective instructional strategy, such as an interdependent sequence of learning activities, and a coherent course structure.
Make sure that the key components are all integrated.
Check to ensure that the key components (Steps 1–4) are all consistent with, and support, each other.

# APPENDIX B

# KNOWING YOUR STUDENTS

Your classes are made up of a range of students in terms of experience, skill, motivation, and background knowledge. Many students who enter college underprepared are very successful once they receive the academic and student support they need to bridge any gaps they have. Others continue to struggle with academic demands. Your job is not to diagnose them, try to discourage them from continuing their educations, or abandon the integrity of your course by lowering standards; it is to assist them with learning strategies that work in your discipline, be clear in explanations of content, and be open to questions.

The definition of *developmental education* is well summarized here.

> Developmental programs at institutions of higher education encompass a variety of courses and services that are conducted to provide assistance to individuals who have been denied regular admission to the institution because of failure to meet specified admission and placement requirements or because of predicted risk in meeting the requirements of college-level courses. These services focus primarily on skills in reading, writing, mathematics, and study and test-taking strategies, as well as personal adjustment and other affective variables that are critical to success in the college curriculum. (Tomlinson, 1989, p. 5)

## Who Are Developmental Students?

Students in the developmental education (DE) curriculum are usually new to college. They are often nontraditional, first generation, older, and people of color (National Center for Education Statistics, 2014). They may also be immigrant students who are still learning English. They are the least familiar with the college setting, expectations of time and level of work, and have few role models to assist them (Jimenez, Sargrad, Morales, & Thompson, 2016; Xianglei & Simone, 2016). Many have had bad experiences in schooling and may be anxious about testing and other assessments. They may have a fixed mind-set about their skills ("I'm really bad at math"; Dweck, 2006). They may not really have ever honed an academic skill, although it does help to try to connect honing any skill to academic work so students can feel that they are capable. If you are new to teaching students in the developmental curriculum, you may notice some of the following characteristics:

- Many DE students lack confidence in academic settings. They have low expectations, and they often attribute any success or failure to outside forces, for example, "My teacher hates me," or "I just got so lucky on that test." They don't have much experience seeing themselves as the actor in success or failure, and their locus of control is external. Furthermore, this lack of confidence may be accompanied by fear, even panic. Faculty must be prepared for dealing with this affective side of learning.

- Some students in the highest DE course may be resentful. They may think they don't need it. Does your department offer some alternative placement procedure, or an option to retake the placement test?
- Most students in the lower DE courses know they need help and are happy to get it, even if they have low expectations because of their mind-set.
- English language learners may also be placed in developmental courses because they are still learning English, especially academic English. They may be well educated in their home countries or not educated much at all. International students in the United States on a student visa usually are well prepared academically. Refugee students may have interrupted educations because of their displacement. Other immigrants range from being conversant in English but lacking in literacy skills to being fully bilingual in all areas. It is helpful for you to find out what your students' backgrounds are so you don't make incorrect assumptions about their skills and experiences.

There may be preparatory college success courses they can take (free or for credit) that will help them get used to the learning environment and expectations. To assist students who need more direct help or who seem to be missing the point, the instructor could do the following:

- Be very explicit about how the course works. Tell and show students how you expect them to use the syllabus. Is it a guide to be used throughout the semester and to be referred to during the class and in the course design? Does it have dates, deadlines, and such in it? Model your use of the syllabus clearly in class. The same goes for any other tool you expect them to use.
- When giving a writing assignment, put the instructions in writing in the course shell. Make sure the assignment instructions explain its purpose, how it will be evaluated, how much it counts toward the grade (if appropriate), suggested steps to follow, and all protocols you prefer (how many pages, font size and type, etc.). We've had students turn in work on five-by-nine-inch notebook paper, not realizing that they were expected to use eight-and-a-half-by-eleven-inch paper. Do not assume your students are familiar with college course requirements.
- Provide a rubric to communicate the expectations, laying out all the criteria with specific details that will demonstrate how they can achieve the highest level. You can also use an exercise with a sample assignment to get them to understand how to use a rubric to assess their own work before they submit it for your grading feedback.

- In general, try to give positive and negative feedback so that when students are doing things correctly, they get recognized positively and know to continue in that vein. Using the sandwich technique for feedback helps students. Start with a positive, discuss areas for improvement, and end with a positive. This helps to motivate students to complete additional assignments. Inexperienced students may not know that saying nothing is usually tacit approval. Give praise, but make sure it is not empty praise. Make praise specifically descriptive so they know what exactly they did well.

How can you help students navigate your course readings? You can do the following:

- College reading assignments are often much longer than anything your students have ever seen. For DE students, the sheer volume of reading is their first hurdle. You can help by assigning a lengthy reading in separate assignments, breaking the piece or chapter into logical sections. You can do this more overtly at the beginning of the semester, and then give your students explicit instructions on how to do it for themselves later. For example, if there are clear headings and sections, can you find a good place for them to stop and reflect on a cluster of related topics before moving on to the rest of the chapter?
- If you were going to read the material, how would you approach it? Would you read the summary first? Look at discussion questions at the end? Page through it slowly, looking at the headings to get a sense of where it's going? Share your strategies with your students. This is part of disciplinary literacy building. How do people in your field read?
- Do you take notes when you read material in your discipline or write on the text in some way? Use sticky notes? Share this with your students. Even show them what you do, and let them use it as a template. How do you cluster related ideas together in your notes (or your thinking)? How can you tell that ideas are related, opposing, supporting, or irrelevant? Can you explain those different ways of understanding to your students?

How can you assist students with the new vocabulary? There are several challenges with vocabulary in college, for example:

- New terms—words students have never heard or seen before—are the backbone of learning the fundamentals of a discipline. These are the words often in boldface or italic type and usually defined in the text. Student know they are supposed to memorize these words and their definitions because that is the kind of testing they have seen most often. Never mind that in college students might be expected to know and understand those terms and even show a deeper knowledge by analyzing information.
- Familiar words that have new, specialized meanings in the discipline. *Supply and demand. Table. Group. Insane.* DE students, as well as English language

learners, have less flexibility with language, and they sometimes don't realize the significance of a familiar word with a new meaning. It's like they just don't see it. If instructors are explicit about those words too, it will help students learn them.

- College instructors tend to assume that students have a college-level vocabulary, whatever that means. Some instructors even pepper their lectures with sophisticated language that sails over the students' heads. We recommend for you to check periodically that your students are actually understanding what you say, either with a classroom assessment technique (discussed in chapters 4 and 5) or by allowing time for questions. You certainly don't have to talk down to your students to make every effort to be clear. This will help any English language learners you happen to have in class as well as the developmental students.

How can you help students who have learning challenges succeed in college? There are no easy answers to this question, as learning issues are extremely idiosyncratic, but you could to the following:

- Don't say to a student, "I think you must have a learning disability." Stick to the facts of a situation, "I think you are having trouble keeping up with the readings, managing test taking, learning the vocabulary, and so on." You are not the diagnostician in this matter.
- Don't discuss a student's challenges in any place where someone else might hear. Offer to meet in your office or other private place to talk.
- Don't change the rules for a disabled student. Your accessibility services department will suggest appropriate accommodations. Meet with someone from that office as soon as possible.
- Don't get hung up with the actual diagnosis, whether it might be dyslexia, dyscalculia, a nonverbal learning disorder, or autism spectrum disorder. Instead, simply ask the student who has told you about a disability, "How do you think this affects you in my class?" That will get the conversation going and provide ideas for modifications or accommodations that may help.
- Don't talk with others about particular students, and this is true of any student, disabled or not. Confidentiality is of the utmost importance in the college setting. The general rule of thumb is to talk with a colleague about a student only if you have an educationally necessary reason to do so, and keep your conversation relevant to that topic.
- Do read any notifications you receive from your accessibility services department about what accommodations they are suggesting. You may need some lead time to honor them, and you must honor them. It's the law. A student might need extended testing time, and you must figure out how to provide that within the constraints of your college. Some colleges have testing centers or private testing rooms that the student can reserve. Your job is to

get the test where it needs to be so the student can take it about the same time as the class does. The student's job is to communicate with the testing center about reserving a room according to your time frame. Students must learn to advocate for themselves in college. This is much different from the K–12 experience in which the child's teachers and parents make individual education plans and teachers follow the plan generated by adults on behalf of the student.
- Do extend the same expectations to your learning-challenged students. With appropriate accommodations, most will be able to find ways to succeed.
- Do ask for assistance. You may certainly talk with other faculty about general ways to be helpful to students with diagnosed conditions. Your accessibility services department may also have good suggestions.
- See chapter 6 for more information about making your course accessible.

How can you make numerical content in nonmath classes easier to understand? The following are some tips:

- Many students may have difficulty gaining meaning from the type of numerical content that appears in social sciences, for example. They may not be expected to actually do mathematical calculations, but they will be expected to make sense of graphs, tables, trends, and other numerical material. Also, it is not uncommon to see statements like, "Although 1 in 5 Americans loves fish, another 30% hate seafood." Switching between a fractional statement and a percentage statement is not easy for many students. They may not have any idea which group is larger and could miss an easy test question as a result. You can point out these discrepancies and just take a moment to put them in parallel form (or ask your students to do so) if they are important to the course.
- Inexperience in mathematics affects student learning in so many ways. Understanding a graph (a positive correlation or a negative correlation, economic trends, a graph showing variance) is a common way to show conclusions for complex relationships in many disciplines. If your discipline does use mathematical notations or graphs of any kind, this is part of the disciplinary literacy skill set that you should overtly teach your students. Don't assume they already know how to read this type of material, nor that they can pick out the salient points that are particular to the subject.

How can you help students do better on tests? You can do the following:

- If you give multiple-choice and true-or-false exams, you probably notice that some students perform poorly even when you observe that in class they seem to be understanding the concepts. This is frustrating to faculty and demoralizing for students. They usually come to the conclusion that they don't test well.

- Realize that taking a multiple-choice or a true-or-false test is a separate and distinct skill that has nothing to do with one's knowledge of the material. It relies on very careful and accurate reading, the use of logic, and an understanding of how these test items are constructed—three things that many students have never received instruction on or practiced in a low-risk environment.
- It's too large a subject for this book, but there are good resources for improving test taking. Visit www.howtostudy.com for more information. Your students could learn many good techniques from it, and so can you.
- Try giving some practice tests in class on a regular basis. This will give your students clues on how you write test items (if you use a test bank, use examples from it for consistency), and it will be a low-threat opportunity for them to discuss with other students not just the answers but why they are the answers. That last part is the most important part because it reinforces the concepts and the thinking, rather than memorizing arbitrary facts. Chapters 4, 5, and 8 offer many other suggestions for low-risk assessments of learning.
- At-risk students often benefit from establishing a relationship with faculty. This doesn't mean friendship, but it does help them if you remember their names and chat with them before or after class a bit and in other ways let them know that you know who they are. It matters to them that you appear to care. It can cause them to place your course higher on their priorities list if they feel their progress matters to you. There is a caveat: Some students may feel that your relationship will lead to you giving them better grades. You need to separate the two and be sure to evaluate work on clear criteria so it does not appear to be subjective. Use a rubric, for example.
- Be careful how you use language. Remember, these students have often had painful experiences in school. If they do poorly, don't assume they didn't study. Instead, acknowledge that it looks like they're having trouble with X concepts, offer to meet with them to try to figure out how you can help clear it up, and also offer to talk with them about the kind of studying that you know works, whatever that is. Do not just tell them to study harder. Do not just tell them to read the chapter again. These are completely unhelpful, and they may not help the student's learning challenge.

Seek to understand what they think they need help with rather than telling them what they should do. Let students explain what works and doesn't work for them. This technique helps them learn how to learn as well as become a good self-advocate.

- Some instructors find it useful to collect best practices from their most successful students to share with the class each term. Getting a sense of how much time the best students take to study, how they organize their notes or materials, how they think about preparing for a test, what they actually *do* to prepare for a test (e.g., make outlines, flashcards, teach it to a classmate) are all very specific and helpful ways to assist all students, not just the at-risk ones. If you can post or make a copy of some samples of student notes or flashcards to show your next term's students, they can be used as models.

- Other faculty have created an assignment for students to write a letter for course success, which is a great reflective assignment for students completing the course by offering advice for the next students entering the class. New students can read the letters and have small-group discussions to get the best ideas of all the letters. New students can then write a pledge letter or contract to themselves to follow throughout the semester.

**Jot Your Thoughts**

# APPENDIX C

# STANDARD SYLLABUS DESIGN AND CONTENT

## Standard Syllabus Content

As you construct your course syllabus, we suggest including the following elements that we used in the courses we taught. The following content headers were created through a faculty-administration collaboration we participated in to standardize syllabi at one of our institutions. Many of our faculty were participating in Quality Matters (QM) course assessments so we integrated these standards for all courses.

### *Opening*

- Program name
- Course prefix and number
- Name of course
- Course schedule identifier and course section
- Number of credit hours
- Semester or dates if partial semester
- Course delivery format (e.g., face-to-face, blended, online)

### *Contact Information*

- Instructor name
- E-mail address (institution issued), phone
- Office hours (day and times, arranged by appointment or through e-mail), purpose of office hours in a first-year class or on a commuter campus
- Office location and directions for online students

### *Course Information*

- Description (as stated in the current course catalog, prerequisites or corequisites that can be copied and pasted from official course outlines)
- Course learning outcomes or objectives (copy and paste from course outline)
- Course requirements and grading policies (QM standard)
    - Best practices may include listing assessment types (e.g., quizzes, exams, journals, observations, performances, etc.); if class participation and attendance are factored in, explain how these are evaluated, weighting of assessments, and grading scale to be used

  - Discuss the timing of returned feedback on student-submitted assignments
- Reference to institution's learner outcomes and values if appropriate
  - Highlight those that will be addressed in your course. This is an opportunity for you to share a crosswalk document to show how your course outcomes relate to the institution's learner outcomes
  - Alert students that they may be asked to participate in program or department or institutional assessment activities as a part of the course
- Course instruction schedule
  - The scheduled hours of instruction include __ hours for each lecture credit
  - Log in to the learning management system (LMS) daily and check the course shell for news
  - This course meets (days, times, campus location).
  - Semester or summer class officially begins on _____ and ends on _____.
  - Course cancellation notification delivery information

### *Course Materials*

- Texts and references including ISBNs (QM standard)
- Tools and supplies including software (QM standard)

### *Campus Emergency Notification*

- Inform students how they will be alerted in case of a campus emergency, an excellent place to provide a link to information on the institution's website

### *Last Day to Withdraw From a Course*

- Information on when and how students may drop or withdraw a course or a link to the drop and add policies on the institution's website are recommended

### *Required Technology Skills (QM Standard)*

- In addition to basic computer knowledge, list the technology proficiencies must students have to be successful

### *Required Technical Access (QM Standard)*

- Create a list of the technical access requirements students need to be successful including, computer system, word processing version, Web browser, active institution student e-mail account, USB storage device, and so on
- Provide access to help for technical questions including website information, help desk e-mail and phone with the days and hours of operation

### *About the Course*

- You may decide to talk more personally about the course. This is a place you could share your big dream (Fink, 2013) about what you want students to achieve by taking your course. You could share your philosophy of teaching in this section

### *Student Handbook and Calendar*

- Provide the website links to where to access the student handbook and calendar so students have information on student conduct, transferring credits, testing out, tuition and fees, grade point average determination, emergency closing, and the school calendar.

### *Academic Integrity*

- This information is also usually found on the institution's website. Provide a link to access this information to support your policies about a learning environment of trust, honesty, and fairness. These policies are to be followed by students, faculty, staff, and administration.
- Portions of the policy, as they pertain to your course, could be discussed in your syllabus. Concerns such as students completing their own work, cheating, and plagiarism need to be addressed. Discuss what will happen to grades for assignments and assessments if policies aren't respected.

### *Attendance*

- Expectations of attendance and course participation have probably been established at your institution. Post this policy so if you are required to withdraw a student from your course they know the reason and expectation up front.
- Copy and paste the institution's policy in your syllabus. This is also important because if a student doesn't attend class, financial aid may not be distributed fully or may be adjusted accordingly.

### *Netiquette (QM Standard)*

- Creating an online community relies on integrity and kindness to colleagues much like the work students will be doing after graduation. To develop this community, students need to adhere to a set of rules (netiquette). Examples can be found at www.albion.com/netiquette/corerules.html.

### *E-Mail Communication*

- Provide the pathway to activating the student e-mail account. Remind students to check their e-mail every couple of days. You can also communicate when you will be responding to e-mails so, for example, students will know if you will be replying over the weekend or not.

### *Support Services (QM Standard)*

- Library information: link to library website, locations, staff contact
- Learning resources center: link to website, locations, contact information, details on the types of tutoring and academic support offered

- Student computer labs: link to website information, operation hours, locations
- Academic advising: link to website information and staff contacts
- Veteran services: coordinator contact information and location
- Accessibility services: director contact information, link to website information and location
- Counseling services: link to personal counseling website with staff contact information
- Career development and placement services: link to website information with contact information
- Note: information on both veterans and accessibility services are included to address federal compliance issues required by some accreditation agencies

### *Academic Difficulty (QM Standard)*

- Provide a set of opportunities for students to get assistance including
    - Appointment with instructor before or after class or during office hours
    - Tutoring help by visiting the learning resources center (link)
    - Meeting with faculty adviser or staff academic adviser

### *Weekly Course Schedule*

- This schedule of units, content, outcomes, and deadlines doesn't need to be a part of your syllabus. It is a document that you can send to students with the syllabus in an e-mail. It can also be placed in the LMS course shell and handed out the first day of class. Some faculty choose to include it with their syllabus, which makes a lengthy, yet comprehensive document.
- Some faculty give a partial schedule, perhaps for the first four weeks and then will have another schedule for the next month, and so forth. This allows some flexibility in the event of class cancellations or some other change. It also is less daunting for students to see just part of the semester at one time.

# APPENDIX D

# AUTOMATED MESSAGING EXAMPLES

Automated messaging tools like the learning management system (LMS) D2L Brightspace's Intelligent Agents or Blackboard's Notifications can be an effective way to deliver reminders to students automatically, while you use less of your teaching time to monitor progress. We discuss these in chapter 3 and provide specific examples here to help you design automated messages in your LMS.

## Welcome to the Course

This automated message will be sent to each student on entering the course.

> Hello [Student's Name],
>
> I see that you have accessed the [Name of] online course. I hope you are as excited as I am for this learning opportunity. My name is [Name] and I am your instructor for this course.
>
> To achieve the course outcomes, it is important that you keep up with the schedule of the course activities. Please read the course syllabus and schedule in [LMS] carefully.
>
> If you have questions or concerns, please contact me through my e-mail at [instructor e-mail]. Remote office hours are available online via webinar by scheduling an appointment.

## No Course Access During the First Week

This automated message will send an e-mail to the students with a copy to the instructor to remind them the semester has started and they will fall behind if they don't get started right away.

> Hello [Student Name],
>
> The first week of the semester is completed. I see that you have not yet accessed the [Name of] online course. I'm concerned about your participation. It is imperative for you to get started with the class activities. If you need assistance, please contact me immediately so I can help you.

## Chapter 1 Completed

This automated message will send an e-mail to the student with a copy to the instructor to assure them they have completed all the required chapter 1 activities for the course.

> Congratulations [Student Name]!
>
> You have completed all of the required activities for chapter 1 [Course Name].
>
> Congratulations on a good start for this course. You should now proceed to the chapter 2 content module and begin work on that now. There are a couple of deadlines next week. I look forward to your continued good work.

# APPENDIX E

# RUBRIC EXAMPLES FOR STUDENT LEARNING ACTIVITIES

The following three rubrics are samples for you to examine, use, adapt, or take ideas from. They differ in terms of the number of levels of proficiency and scope. One is used for a large capstone project, and two are used for single assignments. We hope they help you devise rubrics that will be useful in your assessments. Visit www.kumc.edu/Documents/mph/CapstoneReportRubric.pdf for an additional rubric you may find useful for capstone courses or projects.

## *Research Portfolio Rubric*

The Research Portfolio Rubric (see Tables E.1, E.2, and E.3) is intended to assess an entire portfolio of research but could be adapted to assess students' research projects and papers.

**TABLE E.1**
**Research Portfolio Rubric**

| **Requirement** | **Insufficient** *(D/F level work)* | **Basic** *(C level work)* | **Proficient** *(B level work)* | **Advanced** *(A level work)* |
|---|---|---|---|---|
| *The student specified the dimensions of the topic appropriately.*<br>• *Clearly states the focused topic.*<br>• *Developed an appropriate working thesis.*<br>• *Took appropriate steps to narrow and focus the topic.* | Topic has an imprecise or unclear focus. The focus needs to be narrowed or clarified.<br><br>Thesis statement does not clearly state a focused topic, lacks precision. Thesis statement does not clearly lay out the main ideas and issues.<br><br>Research questions are too broad or vague and do not adequately focus the topic. | Topic has a discernable focus but lacks precision.<br><br>Thesis statement addresses the topic but needs more precise focus and precision. There is an argument, but it needs to be more clearly stated.<br><br>Research questions address the topic but need more focus and precision. | Clear focus on the topic, which is adequately precise.<br><br>Thesis statement that is clear and focused and adequately precise. The argument is adequately stated and precise.<br><br>Clear, focused, and adequately precise research questions. | Very clear focus that is precise, appropriately narrow, and well-articulated.<br><br>Thesis statement that is very well focused and concise. The argument is clear, focused, and well stated.<br><br>Very clear, concise, and well-focused research questions. |
| **(TOTAL POINTS)** | **(POINT RANGE)** | **(POINT RANGE)** | **(POINT RANGE)** | **(POINT RANGE)** |

| | | | | |
|---|---|---|---|---|
| | Research process is not clearly stated or is confused in its application. | Research process is articulated but needs more focus and clarity. | Clear research process that adequately takes account of the issues related to the topic. | A clear, concise, and well-focused research process that takes into account all the relevant issues related to the topic. |
| | Research process does not adequately take account of the topic focus and is much too broad in application. | Basic search techniques are adequately applied but no or little demonstration of advanced search strategies, or errors are made in the application of search techniques. | Clear use of basic and advanced search techniques. Minor errors in application of search techniques, or lack of connection in search strategies across library resources. | Used basic and advanced search techniques very well and has applied the search techniques consistently well across all the library resources. |
| | Consistent mistakes are made in applying basic search techniques. Confusion related to application of search terms and search techniques. | Keywords, keyword phrases, and/or subject headings used in searching relate to the research focus. | Many useful keywords, keyword phrases, and/or subject headings that clearly relate to the research focus. | Very useful keywords and subject headings that clearly relate to the research focus. |
| | Keywords, keyword phrases, and/or subject headings were not useful for the topic focus. Misapplication of keywords and subject headings. Shows a lack of understanding of what subject headings are and how they are to be used. | Keywords and subject headings may be too broad or need to be combined to be effective. | Indication that the keywords and subject headings have been combined in useful ways to help focus searching. | Used keywords that located specific sub-aspects of the topic, or located sub-headings and connected them appropriately with main subject headings. |
| | **(POINT RANGE)** | **(POINT RANGE)** | **(POINT RANGE)** | **(POINT RANGE)** |

*(Continues)*

**Table E.1** (*Continued*)

| **Requirement** | **Insufficient** (*D/F level work*) | **Basic** (*C level work*) | **Proficient** (*B level work*) | **Advanced** (*A level work*) |
|---|---|---|---|---|
| *The student selected resources that were appropriate for the topic and demonstrated how each resource supported specific aspects of the topic focus.* | Most resources selected were not appropriate for supporting the topic focus. Little to no consistency in the selected resources and the research topic focus. | Most of the resources selected are appropriate for the topic. | All of the resources selected are appropriate for the topic. | All of the resources selected are very well focused on the topic or specific sub-aspects of the topic. |
| | Little or no demonstration of the appropriateness of resources for topic relevance, or confusion related to resource relevance. | Demonstration of the appropriateness of resources for topic relevance is adequate for most resources. | Demonstration of the appropriateness of resources is well documented and clearly stated. Good level of detail provided concerning relevance of resources to thesis statement, research questions, and topic focus. | Demonstration of the appropriateness of resources is very well documented with in-depth analysis of each resource. Clear and detailed explanation of how each resource supports the thesis statement, research questions, and the various aspects of the topic focus. |
| **(TOTAL POINTS)** | **(POINT RANGE)** | **(POINT RANGE)** | **(POINT RANGE)** | **(POINT RANGE)** |

| *The student evaluated each resource according to specific evaluation criteria. The student provided clear and specific evaluations.* | Little or no evidence of evaluation of the resources. Attempts at evaluation were not based on any criteria but were mere assertions of credibility without evidence to support claims. | Clear evidence of evaluation of most of the resources, but evaluation lacks depth. | Clear evaluation of resources based upon specific criteria of authority, reliability, and bias. | Strong and in-depth evaluation of all resources based upon specific criteria. Clear understanding of the bias, authority, reliability, and credentials of the author, publisher, or website sponsor. |
|---|---|---|---|---|
| **(TOTAL POINTS)** | **(POINT RANGE)** | **(POINT RANGE)** | **(POINT RANGE)** | **(POINT RANGE)** |

*Note.* This rubric may be used to assess a research project. From "Research Portfolio Rubric," by the Communications Assessment Project, 2006, Minneapolis, MN: Minneapolis Community and Technical College. Copyright 2006 by Minneapolis Community & Technical College. Used with permission.

**TABLE E.2**
**Rubric for Homework Assignment**

Student Name ______________________________

Assignment Title________________ Points: 10______________Your score: ____________

| *Grading Criteria* | *Needs Work* | *College Level* |
|---|---|---|
| 1. Following Directions<br><br>*1 point* | 1.1 You have omitted some part of the directions<br>1.2 You didn't answer the question that was asked<br>1.3 Didn't use your own words<br>1.4 Didn't write 3 sentences as required | You followed all parts of the directions.<br>You answered the question that was asked<br>In your own words<br>In 3 sentences |
| 2. Applying the concept<br><br>*3 points* | 2.1 You used an incorrect/ inaccurate example<br>2.2 You have mixed up some concepts<br>2.3 You gave an unrelated example | Your example was correct/ accurate and is appropriately related to the concept |
| 3. Demonstrating main idea level understanding of the concept<br><br>*3 points* | 3.1 You didn't represent the key points of the concept<br>3.2 You showed confusion about the concept | You represented the key points clearly |
| 4. Demonstrating depth of understanding<br><br>*3 points* | 4.1 Your statements were too general; you didn't included enough detail or show the evidence<br>4.2 You have a lot of details, but didn't make the point clear | Your answer showed enough details to support the main ideas and you were succinct (not too long or wordy) |

From *Rubric Project*, by D. Skogstrom, 2006, Minneapolis, MN: Minneapolis Community and Technical College. 

**TABLE E.3**
**Rubric for a Writing Assignment**

## Writing Evaluation Guide

Student Name______________________________
Case Study #______________________________
Semester ____________________
**Components of Assessment summary:**
**Assessment Summary**
**Diagnosis**
**Recommendations**
**6 Dimensions**

| *Evaluation Area* | *Below College Level Proficiency* | *At College Level Proficiency* |
|---|---|---|
| **Context (50%)** | • Missing components of assessment summary as outlined in assignment | • Addresses all components of assessment summary as outlined in assignment |
| **Style and Organization (15%)** | • Uses judgmental terms to describe information<br>• Uses nonclinical terminology to refer to subject<br>• Refers to client by name<br>• Uses or includes only some of the proper headings | • Uses nonjudgmental terms to describe information<br>• Uses clinical terminology to refer to subject<br>• Never refers to client in body of assessment by name<br>• Uses and includes all the proper headings |
| **Process (20%)** | • Did not attend/participate in classroom group assessment<br>• Work does not appear to be done independently<br>• Work is late | • Attended/participated in classroom group assessment<br>• Work is clearly done independently<br>• Work is on time |
| **Grammar and Mechanics (15%)** | • Frequent misspelled words<br>• Frequent grammar errors that confuse the reader<br>• Not type written<br>• Uses no quotes | • No misspelled words<br>• Minor grammar errors not leading to reader confusion<br>• Type written<br>• Uses quotes appropriately |

TOTAL:_____

*Note.* From *Rubric Project*, by B. McDougal, 2006, Minneapolis, MN: Minneapolis Community and Technical College. 

# GLOSSARY

**Accessibility or disability services.** The unit on a college campus designated to determine reasonable accommodations for disabled students, provide other services to designated students, and advise faculty on meeting federal disability requirements.

**Accessible, accessibility.** Your course and its materials are able to be used fully by all students.

**Accommodations.** Assistance or changes to an assignment or exam or other instructional or living condition so a student can fully participate in college despite having a disability.

**Advance organizer.** Visual organizers of information used to show a framework for the concepts and ideas. They are often charts or tables, but can be drawings, diagrams, concept maps, or other graphics.

**Applications, Apps.** Software you can download to a smartphone or tablet.

**Authentic activities and assessments.** *Authentic* refers to student-produced work that relies on the student's experiences and thoughts. Authentic work focuses on original thoughts by students as well as real-world applications.

**Blended, hybrid.** Courses that deliver content and provides activities in a combination of a face-to-face classroom and online instruction.

**Capstone projects.** Final projects, presentations, or other demonstrations that can be learning activities and summative assessments. Most often these are used as opportunities for students to demonstrate the mastery of course or program outcomes and are scheduled at the end of the course.

**Center for teaching and learning.** A place or service providing faculty development about teaching to promote significant learning for students.

**Classroom management system.** Computer software that allows you to control the students' individual computer monitors in a lab to see presentations up close and stay on task with your instruction until it is time for them to practice individually.

**Close the loop.** Means that you have considered all the aspects of teaching (course design).

**Course outcome**. Learning goals of a course that identify the desired skills and behaviors from all six domains of Fink's (2013) taxonomy of significant learning.

**Course shell**. The course structure in a learning management system that hosts content and requires logging in, or the course that can be used for online, blended, and face-to-face delivery.

**Crosswalk tables**. Crosswalk tables are a valuable way to demonstrate relationships and the pathway that bridges topics from varying categories. An example of this would be showing the alignment of how course outcomes match learning activities that prepare students for the assessments to measure the outcomes.

**Developmental education**. Programming that serves students who are underprepared for college course work but have been admitted or conditionally admitted to a college.

**Disciplinary literacy**. The specialized ways of thinking, seeking knowledge, reading, writing, speaking, and problem-solving that make each discipline unique.

**Distributed learning**. Reading, practicing, doing problems, retrieving, or quizzing over several separate study periods, rather than a cram session.

**Effortful retrieval**. Retrieving learned information to write about it, summarize it, draw a concept map of it, and so on. Quizzing with immediate feedback and making corrections is also an effortful retrieval activity. These promote deeper learning than simply choosing a correct answer on a multiple-choice test.

**Integrated course design**. Creating a course with the components of learning goals, teaching and learning activities, and feedback and assessment, and includes consideration of situational factors and big dreams.

**Interleaved practice**. Mixing up practice by doing different types of learning in one or more study sessions.

**Learning management system**. The platform that hosts course information and tools to facilitate communication, presentation, and reporting.

**Learning outcome**. The learning goal of a course or subpart of a course that identifies the desired skills and behaviors from all six areas of Fink's (2013) taxonomy of significant learning; used interchangeably in this book with *course outcome*.

**Open Educational Resources**. Educational materials that are in the public domain or introduced with an open license. They are free and may be adapted as needed for use.

**Portfolios**. A type of capstone project, either electronic or physical, that shows progress over time, culminating work, or best show quality work at the end of a course or program. Usually used as a means to provide summative assessment and follows the students as a demonstration of outcomes and proficiency for employment.

**Professional portfolio**. Consists of professional work outside teaching such as an artist, photographer, welder, chef, and so forth.

**Program**. Generic term referring to a computer program.

**Rubric**. A tool (usually a table) that displays the expectations of and the criteria used to grade assignments and assessments. Each criterion has an annotation to explain the level of quality.

**Scaffolding**. Activities built on skills previously taught and learned.

**Software**. Free or purchased programs and applications downloaded on your computer.

**Student learning outcomes**. Development, formative and summative student assessments, learning activities, and course assessments whereby you reflect with a purpose to improve on an ongoing basis.

**Super summative assessment**. Three or more summative measures of a level of outcomes or multiple levels of courses during one assessment activity.

**Teaching portfolio**. A documentation of your teaching experiences, may include course descriptions, student work samples, and materials you developed.

**Technology**. Any device, program, or other tool used for learning.

**Universal design**. Creating physical spaces and intellectual environments such as classes that are accessible to all.

# OUTCOMES

Each chapter in this book is based on a set of outcomes for use by administrators of institutions faculty teaching seminars or certificates.

## Chapter 1. Preparing for Your Course Design

We hope that by the end of the chapter you will be able to

- analyze the differences between Fink's (2013) and Bloom's revised taxonomy (Anderson, 2001) as they guide outcomes for course design,
- identify the situational factors that affect your course design,
- choose the greatest pedagogical challenges to be addressed at the beginning of the course, and
- analyze your characteristics and those of your learners.

## Chapter 2. Integrating Your Course Design

We hope that by the end of the chapter you will be able to

- identify the key elements of Fink's (2013) integrated course design principles and process (foundational knowledge domain of Fink's [2013] taxonomy);
- analyze the standards for evaluating course design established by self- and peer-reviewed rubrics (application level of Fink's [2013] taxonomy);
- develop engaging learning activities and assessments for your courses (application domain of Fink's [2013] taxonomy);
- align course learning outcomes, activities, and assessments through integrated course design (integration domain of Fink's [2013] taxonomy);
- reflect on the effect your integrated designed course has on your ability to improve your teaching (human dimension–self domain of Fink's [2013] taxonomy);
- include a variety of best practices from other colleagues, experts, and resources while designing your courses (human dimension–other domain of Fink's [2013] taxonomy);
- express the value of significant learning course design for students (caring domain of Fink's [2013] taxonomy); and
- select items from a course design checklist for future use (learning how to learn domain of Fink's [2013] taxonomy).

## Chapter 3. Communicating in Your Course

We hope that by the end of the chapter you will be able to

- use two-way communication to help the learning process,
- apply community-building strategies to your courses, and
- develop a communication plan for your courses.

## Chapter 4. Creating a Learning Framework

We hope that by the end of the chapter you will be able to

- link the learning process and the characteristics of simple to complex learning to research-based learning activities;
- model research-based study strategies to help students learn how to learn material at higher levels and develop skills they will need in the future;
- select content, materials, and activities to reflect the strengths and prior experiences and motivate a diversity of students; and
- plan scaffolded, low-stakes authentic tasks and assignments with frequent supportive feedback to build skills and confidence to meet high expectations.

## Chapter 5. Developing Learning Activities and Techniques

We hope that by the end of the chapter you will be able to

- select activities to best fit your class needs and connect each activity you choose to a student learning outcome (or sub-outcome),
- create a plan for minimizing lecture or presentation time and increasing active learning, and
- devise a method for awarding points or some other grade to some in-class activities.

## Chapter 6. Making Your Course Accessible

We hope that by the end of the chapter you will be able to

- describe the differences between accessibility and accommodations;
- identify the elements of accessible courses;
- determine the role faculty, students, and institutions play in developing reasonable accommodations; and
- identify ways you can improve the accessibility of your course materials.

## Chapter 7. Integrating Learning Technologies

We hope that by the end of the chapter you will be able to

- analyze course technology needs;
- integrate technology to improve your teaching and student learning,
- develop a course technology plan; and
- align technology with learning outcomes, activities, and assessments.

## Chapter 8. Assessing Student Learning

We hope that by the end of the chapter you will be able to

- distinguish between testing and assessment,
- use student learning outcomes to create assessment activities,
- develop appropriate scoring guides or rubrics to use in assessment, and
- plan for assessment improvement after reflecting on current assessment use.

## Chapter 9. Assessing Course Quality

We hope that by the end of the chapter you will be able to

- analyze your course outcomes and competencies,
- align course assessments with learning outcomes and activities,
- use feedback strategies to improve your courses,
- examine several strategies for measuring the quality of your courses, and
- assess your courses using rubrics with quality course design principles.

## Chapter 10. Assessing Your Program and Institution

We hope that by the end of the chapter you will be able to

- identify institutional level assessments including program and department,
- examine institutional goals and outcomes,
- analyze continuous improvement strategies,
- recognize the reason for national accreditation and industry credentialing standards, and
- develop program and department advisory committees.

## Chapter 11. Reflecting on Your Teaching

We hope that by the end of the chapter you will be able to

- identify the components of a teaching portfolio,
- analyze ways you can reflect on your teaching,
- collect evidence of your work necessary for a teaching portfolio,
- develop a plan for you to obtain assistance in your teaching, and
- create ways to get feedback from your teaching.

## Chapter 12. Learning How to Learn

We hope that by the end of the chapter you will be able to

- identify the resources at your campus for professional development in teaching,
- select external professional organizations to advance your teaching and your work in your discipline, and
- create a plan for professional development in teaching and learning, either using campus resources or outside professional groups.

# ADDITIONAL READINGS AND RESOURCES

## Chapter 1

Fink, L. D., & Fink, A. K. (Eds.). (2009). Designing courses for significant learning: voices of experience. *New Directions for Teaching and Learning*, 119.

## Chapter 2

Fink, L. D. (2013). *Creating significant learning experiences.* San Francisco, CA: Jossey-Bass.

Freeman, S., Eddy, S. L., McDonough, M., Smith, M. K., Okoroafor, N., Jordt, H., & Wenderoth, M. P. (2014). *Active learning boosts performance in STEM courses.* Proceedings of the National Academy of Sciences June 2014. Retrieved from https://www.pnas.org/content/111/23/8410

Kober, N.. (2015). *Reaching students: What research says about effective instruction in undergraduate science and engineering.* Washington, DC: The National Academies Press.

National Academies of Sciences, Engineering, and Medicine. (2016). *Barriers and opportunities for 2-year and 4-year stem degrees: Systemic change to support students' diverse pathways.* Washington, DC: The National Academies Press.

National Academies of Sciences, Engineering, and Medicine. (2018). *The integration of the humanities and arts with sciences, engineering, and medicine in higher education: Branches from the same tree.* Washington, DC: The National Academies Press.

Using Steam to Power Your Course Design https://encoreprodev.com/book

## Chapter 3

Gannon, K. (n.d.). *How to create a syllabus: Advice guide.* Retrieved from https://www.chronicle.com/interactives/advice-syllabus

Howard, J. (2015). *Discussion in the college classroom.* San Francisco, CA: Wiley.

Moosavian, S. A. Z. N. (2016, June). *Employing technology in providing an interactive, visual "big picture" for macroeconomics: A major step forward towards the Web-based, interactive, and graphic syllabus.* Paper presented at the American Economic Association Conference on Teaching and Research in Economic Education, Atlanta, GA.

Richards, S. L. (2001). *The interactive syllabus: A resource-based, constructivist approach to learning.* Retrieved from https://library.educause.edu/~/media/files/library/2001/1/edu01108-pdf.pdf

University of Cincinnati. (n.d.). *Rubric for assessing your teaching syllabus.* Retrieved from https://www.uc.edu/content/dam/uc/cetl/docs/Rubric for Assessing Your Teaching Syllabus.pdf

## Chapter 4

Bresciani Ludvik, M. J. (Ed.). (2016). *The neuroscience of learning and development.* Sterling, VA: Stylus.

Campus Compact. (2003). *Introduction to service learning toolkit* (2nd ed.). Boston, MA: Author.

Doyle, T., & Zakrajsek, T. (2019). *The new science of learning* (2nd ed.) Sterling, VA: Stylus.

*Guided inquiry learning*. Retrieved from https://serc.carleton.edu/sp/library/pogil/index.html

*5 advantages and disadvantages of problem-based learning (PBL) + activity design steps.* (n.d.). Retrieved from https://www.prodigygame.com/blog/wp-content/uploads/Downloadable-Guide-Problem-Based-Learning-Activity-Design-Steps.pdf

Hockenbury, D., & Hockenbury, S. (2013) *Discovering psychology* (6th ed.). New York, NY: Worth.

Pedagogy in Action. (2019). *Problem-based learning.* Retrieved from https://www.niu.edu/facdev/_pdf/guide/strategies/problem_based_learning.pdf

Smilkstein, R. (2011). *We're born to learn* (2nd ed.). Thousand Oaks, CA: Corwin Press.

Team Based Learning. Retrieved from http://www.teambasedlearning.org/

University Teaching and Learning Center. (n.d.). *Classroom assessment techniques (CATs).* Retrieved from https://library.gwu.edu/utlc/teaching/classroom-assessment-techniques-cats

Vanderbilt University Center for Teaching. (2019). *What is service learning or community engagement?* Retrieved from https://cft.vanderbilt.edu/guides-sub-pages/teaching-through-community-engagement/

Wolfe, P. (2001) *Brain matters: Translating research into classroom practice.* Alexandria, VA: Association for Supervision and Curriculum Development.

## Chapter 5

Bain, K. (2012). *What the best college teachers do* (2nd ed.) Cambridge, MA: Harvard University Press.

Bransford, J. D., Brown, A. L., & Cocking, R. R. (Eds.) (1999). *How people learn: Brain, mind, experience, and school.* Washington DC: National Academies Press.

Brookfield, S. D. (2015). *The skillful teacher: On technique, trust, and responsiveness in the classroom* (3rd ed.). San Francisco, CA: Jossey-Bass.

How to Study, https://www.howtostudy.org

## Chapter 6

American Psychological Association. (2019). *Reasonable accommodations explained.* Retrieved from http://www.apa.org/pi/disability/dart/toolkit-three.aspx

Cielo24, https://cielo24.com/ (Caption and transcription services, fee based)

Do-It, https://www.washington.edu/doit/ (General resource on accessibility, universal design, and access to communities of practice)

Dragon Naturally Speaking, https://nuance_dragon_naturallyspeaking.en.downloadastro.com/ (Text-to-speech software, your institution may have the professional version license)

D2L MOOC Session, https://weba11ymooc.wordpress.com/ (Web accessibility)

Minnesota Information Technology Services Office of Accessibility, https://mn.gov/mnit/about-mnit/accessibility/ (How to make documents, maps, meetings, multimedia, and Web and apps accessible)

Morgan, A. (2016, January 25). *Accessibility as a civil right.* Retrieved from https://er.educause.edu/articles/2016/1/accessibility-as-a-civil-right

Portland Community College. (2019). *Instructional support: Creating accessible content.* https://www.pcc.edu/instructional-support/accessibility/

Rev, https://www.rev.com/ (Transcription and caption service. Fee based)

3Play Media, https://www.3playmedia.com/ (Transcription and caption service, fee based)

United Spinal Association. (2019). *Introduction to disability etiquette.* Retrieved from https://www.unitedspinal.org/disability-etiquette/#Introduction

WebAIM, https://webaim.org/ (Training for creating accessible materials)

## Chapter 7

Collaborative, Organized, Online Learning Table 7.2. This is a collected list of technology tools.

Educause. (2019). *Horizon Report preview 2019.* Retrieved from https://library.educause.edu/resources/2019/2/horizon-report-preview-2019

Luckin, R. (2018). *Enhancing learning and teaching with technology.* Sterling, VA: Stylus.

University of Minnesota Open Textbook (2018). Retrieved from https://open.umn.edu/opentextbooks/

## Chapter 8

Brookhart, S. (2013). *How to create and use rubrics for formative assessment and grading.* Alexandria, VA: Association for Supervision and Curriculum Development.

Capstone Report Rubric. http://www.kumc.edu/Documents/mph/CapstoneReportRubric.pdf

Collegiate Learning Assessment, www.cic.org/projects_services/coops/cla.asp

North Carolina State University. (2013). *Internet resources for higher education outcomes assessment.* Retrieved from https://2014.accreditation.ncsu.edu/pages/2.5/Internet%20Resources%20for%20Higher%20Education%20Outcomes%20Assessment.pdf

## Chapter 9

ECampus Essentials, https://ecampus.oregonstate.edu/faculty/courses/Ecampus_Essentials.pdf

Open SUNY Course Quality Review, http://oscqr.org/

OSCQR Scorecard, https://s3.amazonaws.com/scorecard-private-uploads/OSCQR+version+3.1.pdf

University of Cincinnati. (n.d.). *Rubric for assessing your teaching syllabus.* Retrieved from https://www.uc.edu/content/dam/uc/cetl/docs/Rubric for Assessing Your Teaching Syllabus.pdf

## Chapter 10

Accrediting Commission for Community and Junior Colleges, www.accjc.org

Council for Higher Education Accreditation, www.chea.org

Higher Learning Commission, www.hlcommission.org

Middle States Commission on Higher Education, www.msche.org

New England Commission of Higher Education, cihe.neasc.org

Southern Association of Colleges and Schools Commission on Colleges, www.sacscoc.org

WASC Senior College and University Commission, www.wscuc.org

## Chapter 11

Russell, T., & Mundy, H. (2005). *Teachers and teaching: From classroom to reflection.* Bristol, PA: Taylor & Francis.

Sorcinelli, M. D., & Mues, F. (2000). *Preparing a teaching portfolio.* Retrieved from http://works.bepress.com/marydeane_sorcinelli/2/.

Vanderbilt University. (n.d.). *Center for teaching and learning teaching guides: Teaching portfolios.* Retrieved from https://cft.vanderbilt.edu/guides-sub-pages/teaching-portfolios/

## Chapter 12

Educause, https://www.educause.edu/

Lilly Conferences, https://www.lillyconferences-ca.com/about

Professional and Organizational Development Network, https://podnetwork.org/

North American Council for Staff, Program, and Organization Development, https://www.ncspod.org/

# REFERENCES


Ambrose, S. A., Bridges, M. W., DiPietro, M., Lovett, M. C., & Norman, M. K. (2010). *How learning works: 7 research-based principles for smart teaching.* San Francisco, CA: Wiley.

American Psychological Association. (2019). *Reasonable accommodations explained.* Retrieved from https://www.apa.org/pi/disability/dart/toolkit-three

American Society for Quality. (2019). *Total quality management.* Retrieved from https://asq.org/quality-resources/total-quality-management

Americans with Disabilities Act of 1990, Pub. L. No. 101-336, 104 Stat. 328 (1990).

Anderson, L. W., Krathwohl, D. R. (Eds.). (2001). *A taxonomy for learning, teaching, and assessing: A revision of bloom's taxonomy of educational objectives.* New York, NY: Longman.

Angelo, T. A. & Cross, K. P. (1993). *Classroom assessment techniques: A handbook for college teachers* (2nd ed.) San Francisco, CA: Jossey-Bass.

Ashwin, P., Boud, D., Coate, K., Hallett, F., Keane, E.; Krause, K-L., . . . Tooher, M. (2015). *Reflective teaching in higher education.* London, UK: Bloomsbury.

Assess. (n.d.). In *Merriam-Webster's online dictionary* (11th ed.). Retrieved from https://www.merriam-webster.com/dictionary/assess

Association of American Colleges & Universities. (2019). *Value rubrics.* Retrieved from https://www.aacu.org/value-rubrics

Astin, A. W., Banta, T. W., Cross, K. P., El-Khawas, E., Ewell, P, T., Hutchings, Pat, . . . Wright, B. D. (1993). Principles of good practice for assessing student learning. *Leadership Abstracts, 6*(4), 1–3.

Ausubel, D. P. (1960). The use of advance organizers in the learning and retention of meaningful verbal material. *Journal of Educational Psychology, 51*, 267–272. Retrieved from http://dx.doi.org/10.1037/h0046669

Bain, K. (2004). *What the best college teachers do.* Cambridge, MA: Harvard University Press.

Baldridge Performance Excellence Program. (2019). *Baldridge excellence framework.* Retrieved from https://baldrigefoundation.org/

Banta, T. (Ed.). (2004). *Community college assessment: Assessment update collections.* San Francisco, CA: Jossey-Bass.

Banta, T. W., & Associates. (2002). *Building a scholarship of assessment.* San Francisco, CA: Jossey-Bass.

Barkley, E., & Major, C. (2016a). *LAT quick reference guide.* Retrieved from http://www.designlearning.org/wp-content/uploads/2016/11/LAT-Quick-Reference.docx

Barkley, E., & Major, C. (2016b). *Learning assessment techniques.* San Francisco, CA: Jossey-Bass.

Beckem, J. M., II, & Watkins, M. (2012). Bringing life to learning: Immersive experiential learning simulations for online and blended courses. *Journal of Asynchronous Learning Networks, 16*(5), 61–70.

Bergmann, J., & Sams, A. (2012). *Flip your classroom: Reach every student in every class every day.* Washington, DC: International Society for Technology in Education.

Bernstein, D., & Burnett, A. N. (2006). *Making teaching and learning visible: Course portfolios and the peer review of teaching.* Boston, MA: Anker.

Bloom, B. S., Engelhart, M. D., Furst, E. J., Hill, W. H., & Krathwohl, D. R. (1956). Taxonomy of educational objectives: The classification of educational goals. New York, NY: David McKay.

Boser, U. (2017). *What do people know about excellent teaching and learning?* Retrieved from https://www.americanprogress.org/issues/education-k-12/reports/2017/03/14/427984/people-know-excellent-teaching-learning/

Brame, C. (2016). *Active learning.* Retrieved from https://cft.vanderbilt.edu/active-learning/

Brame, C. J. (2015). *Effective educational videos.* Retrieved from http://cft.vanderbilt.edu/guides-sub-pages/effective-educational-videos/

Bransford, J. D., Brown, A. L., & Cocking, R. R. (Eds.) (1999). *How people learn: Brain, mind, experience, and school.* Washington DC: National Academies Press.

Bresciani Ludvik, M. (Ed.) (2016). *The neuroscience of learning and development.* Sterling, VA: Stylus.

Bresciani Ludvik, M. (2019). *Outcomes based program review.* Sterling, VA: Stylus.

Brookfield, S. D. (1986). *Understanding and facilitating adult learning.* San Francisco, CA: Jossey-Bass.

Brookfield, S. D. (2017). *Becoming a critically reflective teacher* (2nd ed.). San Francisco: Jossey-Bass.

Brookfield, S. D., & Preskill, S. (2005). *Discussion as a way of teaching* (2nd ed.). San Francisco, CA: Jossey-Bass.

Brookfield, S. D., & Preskill, S. (2016). *The discussion book.* San Francisco, CA: Jossey-Bass.

Brown, M. (1975). *Stone soup: An old tale retold.* New York, NY: Atheneum Books.

Brown, P., Roediger, H., & McDaniel, M. (2014). *Make it stick: The science of successful learning.* Cambridge, MA: Harvard University Press.

Burgstahler, S. (Ed.). (2015). *Universal design in higher education* (2nd ed.). Cambridge, MA: Harvard Education Press.

Cambridge, D. (2010). *E-portfolios for lifelong learning and assessment.* San Francisco, CA: Jossey-Bass.

Canada, M. (2013). The syllabus: A place to engage students' egos. *New Directions in Teaching and Learning,* 135, 37–42. Retrieved from https://doi.org/10.1002/tl.20062

Carl D. Perkins Career and Education Act, Pub. Law 109-270, 20 U.S.C. 2301 et seq. (2006).

Carrington, A. (2015). *The padagogy wheel V. 4.1.* Retrieved from https://designingoutcomes.com/assets/PadWheelV4/PadWheel_Poster_V4.pdf

Center for Applied Special Technology. (n.d.). *Legal obligations for accessibility.* Retrieved from http://udloncampus.cast.org/page/policy_legal#.WuDKV5ch200[

Center for Applied Special Technology. (2019). *The UD guidelines.* Retrieved from http://udlguidelines.cast.org

*Centre international d'études pédagogique.* (2018). *Test de connaissance du français.* Retrieved from http://www.ciep.fr/en/tcf

Chickering, A. W. & Gamson, Z. F. (1987) Seven principles for good practice in undergraduate education. *American Association of Higher Education Bulletin, 39*(7), 3–7.

College Board. (2019). *Trends in higher education: Average estimated undergraduate budgets, 2018–19.* Retrieved from https://trends.collegeboard.org/college-pricing/figures-tables/average-estimated-undergraduate-budgets-2018-19

Community College Survey of Student Engagement. (2019). *Why CCSSE?* Retrieved from http://www.ccsse.org/.

Coombs, N. (2010). *Making online teaching accessible: Inclusive course design for students with disabilities.* San Francisco, CA: Jossey-Bass.

Council for Aid to Education. (2019). *Collegiate learning assessment.* Retrieved from https://cae.org/flagship-assessments-cla-cwra/cla/

Cowie, A. (1936). *Educational problems at Yale College in the eighteenth century.* New Haven, CN: Yale University Press.

Cox, M. & Richlin, L. (2004). Building faculty learning communities. *New Directions for Teaching and Learning,* 97, 1–4.

Creative Commons. (n.d.). *About the licenses.* Retrieved from https://creativecommons.org/licenses/

Cross, K. P. (1998, July/August). Why learning communities? Why now? *About Campus,* 4–11.

Crowe, A., Dirks, C., & Wenderoth, M. (2008). *Biology in bloom: Implementing Bloom's taxonomy to enhance student learning in biology.* Bethesda, MD: CBE Life Sciences Education.

Curriculum. (n.d.). In *Merriam-Webster's online dictionary* (11th ed.). Retrieved from https://www.merriam-webster.com/dictionary/curriculum

Daniels, E., Pirayoff, R., & Bessant, S. (2013). Using peer observation and collaboration to improve teaching practices. *Universal Journal of Educational Research, 1,* 269–274.

Davis, B. (2009). *Tools for teaching* (2nd ed.). San Francisco, CA: Jossey-Bass.

De Gale, S., & Boisselle, L. (2015). The effect of POGIL on academic performance and academic confidence. *Science Education International, 26*(1), 56–79.

Dehn, R. (2003). Is technology contributing to academic dishonesty? *Journal of Physician Assistant Education, 14,* 190–192.

Diamond, R. (2008). *Designing and assessing courses and curricula* (3rd ed.). San Francisco, CA: Jossey-Bass.

Doyle, T., & Zakrajsek, T. (2019). *The new science of learning.* Sterling, VA: Stylus.

Duch, B. J., Groh, S. E., Allen, D. E. (2001a). *Team-based learning: A transformative use of small groups in college teaching.* Sterling, VA: Stylus.

Duch, B. J., Groh, S. E., Allen, D. E. (2001b). Why problem-based learning? A case study of institutional change in undergraduate education. In B. Duch, S. Groh, & D. Allen (Eds.), *The power of problem-based learning* (pp. 3–11). Sterling, VA: Stylus.

Dunlosky, J., Rawson, K. A., Marsh, E. J., Nathan, M. J., & Willingham, D. T. (2013). Improving students' learning with effective learning techniques: Promising directions from cognitive and educational psychology. *Psychological Science in the Public Interest, 14,* 4–58.

Dunn, D. S., McCarthy, M. A., Baker, S. C., & Halonen, J. S. (2010). *Using quality benchmarks for assessing and developing undergraduate programs.* San Francisco, CA: Jossey-Bass.

Dweck, C. (2006). *Mindset: The new psychology of success.* New York, NY: Ballantine.

Educational Testing Service. (2019a). *ETS graduate record examinations.* Retrieved from https://www.ets.org/gre

Educational Testing Service. (2019b). *ETS professional assessment for beginning teachers.* Retrieved from https://www.ets.org/praxis

Educational Testing Service. (2019c). *ETS proficiency profile.* Retrieved from https://www.ets.org/proficiencyprofile/about

Educational Testing Service. (2019d). *Test of English as a foreign language*. Retrieved from https://www.ets.org/toefl

Educause. (2019). *Horizon Report preview 2019*. Retrieved from https://library.educause.edu/resources/2019/2/horizon-report-preview-2019

Epstein. (n.d.). *What is the IT-AF?* Retrieved from http://www.epsteineducation.com/home/about/

Ernst, D. (2015). "Open Textbooks: Let Us Begin." Keynote address at US MoodleMoot conference, 2015.

Eynon, B., & Gambino, L. M. (2017). *High-impact ePortfolio practice*. Sterling, VA: Stylus.

Federal Communications Commission. (2018). *Closed captioning on television*. Retrieved from https://www.fcc.gov/consumers/guides/closed-captioning-television

Felder, R., Bullard, L., & Raubenheimer, D. (2008, June). *Effects of active learning on student performance and retention*. Paper presented at the Annual Conference of the American Society for Engineering Education. Pittsburgh, PA.

Felten, P., Bauman, H-D. L., Kheriaty, A., & Taylor, E. (2013). *Transformative conversations: A guide to mentoring communities among colleagues in higher education*. San Francisco, CA: Jossey-Bass.

Fink, L. D. (2003). *Creating significant learning experiences* [revised and updated]. San Francisco, CA: Jossey-Bass.

Fink, L. D. (2005). A Self-Directed Guide to Designing Courses for Significant Learning. Retrieved from https://www.deefinkandassociates.com/GuidetoCourseDesignAug05.pdf.

Fink, D. L. (2011). *A self-directed guide to designing courses for significant learning*. Retrieved from http://www.bu.edu/sph/files/2011/06/selfdirected1.pdf

Fink, L. D. (2013). *Creating significant learning experiences*. (Revised and updated). San Francisco, CA: Jossey-Bass.

Fink, L. Dee (2018a). *Situational factors to consider*. Retrieved from http://www.designlearning.org/wp-content/uploads/2010/03/Situational-Factors-to-Consider-When-Designing-a-Course.pdf

Fink, L. D. (2018b). *Three-column table*. Retrieved from http://www.designlearning.org/wp-content/uploads/2010/04/3-column-table-blank-2-pp.doc

Fornaciari, C. J., & Dean, K. L. (2014). The 21st century syllabus: From pedagogy to andragogy. *Journal of Management Education*, 38, 701–723. doi:10.1177/1052562913504763.

Gabriel, K. F. (2018). *Creating the path to success in the classroom: Teaching to close the graduation gap for minority, first-generation, and academically unprepared students*. Sterling, VA: Stylus.

Gannon, K. (n.d.). *How to create a syllabus: Advice guide*. Retrieved from https://www.chronicle.com/interactives/advice-syllabus

Gray, C. (2017). *Podcasting in education: What are the benefits?* Retrieved from https://www.thepodcasthost.com/niche-case-study/podcasting-in-education/

Guo, P. J., Kim, J., & Robin, R. (2014, March 4–5). *How video production affects student engagement: an empirical study of MOOC videos*. Presentation at Learning at Scale 2014 Conference of the First Association of Computer Machinery Conference on Learning at Scale, New York, NY.

Hargreaves, A., & Fullan, M. (2000). Mentoring in the new millennium, *Theory Into Practice*, *39*, 50–56. doi:10.1207/s15430421tip3901_8

Harrington, C. & Thomas, M. (2018). *Designing a motivational syllabus: Creating a learning path for student engagement*. Sterling, VA: Stylus.

Haugnes, N., Holmgren, H., & Springborg, M. (2018). *Meaningful grading: A guide for faculty in the arts.* Morgantown: West Virginia University Press.

Heffernan, K. (2001). *Fundamentals of service-learning course construction.* Boston, MA: Campus Compact.

Heller, R. (2018). *All about adolescent literacy.* Retrieved from http://www.adlit.org/adlit_101/improving_literacy_instruction_in_your_school/vocabulary/

Herman, J., Aschbacher, P., & Winters, L. (1992). *A practical guide to alternative assessment.* Alexandria, VA: Association for Supervision and Curriculum Development.

Herman, J., & Nilson, L. B. (2018). *Creating engaging discussions.* Sterling, VA: Stylus.

History on the Net. (n.d.). *World War II Timeline.* Retrieved from https://www.historyonthenet.com/world-war-two-timeline-2/

Hockenbury, D., & Hockenbury, S. (2013). *Discovering psychology,* (6th ed.). New York, NY: Worth.

Howard, J. (2015). *Discussion in the college classroom.* San Francisco, CA: Wiley.

Hutchings, P. (1998). *The course portfolio: How faculty can examine their teaching to advance practice and improve student learning. the teaching initiatives.* Washington, DC: American Association for Higher Education.

Insight Assessment. (2019). *California Critical Thinking Test.* Retrieved from https://www.insightassessment.com/Products/Products-Summary/Critical-Thinking-Skills-Tests/California-Critical-Thinking-Skills-Test-CCTST

International Organization for Standardization. (n.d.). *ISO 9000.* Retrieved from https://www.iso.org/standards.html

Iowa State University Center for Excellence in Learning and Teaching. (2019). *Classroom assessment techniques: Quick strategies.* Retrieved from http://www.celt.iastate.edu/teaching/assessment-and-evaluation/classroom-assessment-techniques-quick-strategies-to-check-student-learning-in-class

Jacoby, B. (2014). *Service learning essentials: Questions, answers, and lessons learned.* San Francisco, CA: Jossey-Bass.

Jankowski, N. A., Timmer, J. D., Kinzie, J., & Kuh, G. D. (2018, January). *Assessment that matters: Trending toward practices that document authentic student learning.* Urbana: University of Illinois and Indiana University, National Institute for Learning Outcomes Assessment.

Jimenez, L., Sargrad, S., Morales, J., & Thompson, M. (2016). *Remedial education: The cost of catching up.* Retrieved from https://www.americanprogress.org/issues/education-k-12/reports/2016/09/28/144000/remedial-education/

Kamenetz, A. (2015). *The test: Why our schools are obsessed with standardized testing—but you don't have to be.* New York, NY: PublicAffairs.

King, A. (1993). From sage on the stage to guide on the side. *College Teaching, 41*(1), 30–35.

Krathwohl, D. R. (2002). A revision of Bloom's taxonomy: An overview. *Theory Into Practice, 41,* 212–218.

Kuh, G, D., Ikenberry, S. O., Jankowski, N. A., Cain, T. R., Ewell, P. T.; Hutchings, P., & Kinzie, J. (2015). *Using evidence of student learning to improve higher education.* San Francisco, CA: Jossey-Bass.

Kuh, G., Kinzie, J., Shuh, J., Whitt, E., & Associates. (2005). *Student success in college: Creating conditions that matter.* San Francisco, CA: Jossey-Bass.

Larkin, J. H., & Simon, H. A. (1987). Why a diagram is (sometimes) worth ten thousand words. *Cognitive Science, 11,* 65–100. doi:10.1111/j.1551-6708.1987.tb00863.x

Lecture. (n.d.). In *Merriam-Webster's online dictionary*, 11th ed. Retrieved from https://www.merriam-webster.com/dictionary/lecture

Lee, V. S. (Ed.). (2004). *Teaching and learning through inquiry: A guidebook for institutions and instructors.* Sterling, VA: Stylus.

Lewis, S. E., & Lewis, J. E. (2005). Departing from lectures: An evaluation of a peer-led guided inquiry alternative. *Journal of Chemical Education, 82,* 135–139.

Lial, M., & Hestwood, Diana L. (2018). *Prealgebra* (6th ed.). Boston, MA: Pearson.

Lieberman, M. (2018, February 28). Centers of the pedagogical universe. *Inside Higher Education.* Retrieved from https://www.insidehighered.com/digital-learning/article/2018/02/28/centers-teaching-and-learning-serve-hub-improving-teaching

Lowman, J. (1995). *Mastering the technique of teaching* (2nd ed.). San Francisco, CA: Jossey-Bass.

Luckin, R. (2018). *Enhancing learning and teaching with technology.* Sterling, VA: Stylus.

Lyman, F. (1981). The responsive classroom discussion. In A. S. Anderson (Ed.), *Mainstreaming digest* (pp. 109–113). College Park, MD: University of Maryland College of Education.

Maguire, E. A., Woollett, K., & Spiers, H. J. (2006). London taxi drivers and bus drivers: A structural MRI neuropsychological analysis. *Hippocampus, 16,* 1091–1101.

Maki, P. (2010). *Assessing for learning: Building a sustainable commitment across the institution* (2nd ed.) Sterling, VA: Stylus.

Maki, P. (2017). *Real-time student assessment: Meeting the imperative for improved time to degree, closing the opportunity gap, and assuring student competencies for 21st-century needs.* Sterling, VA: Stylus.

McDonald, B. (2012). Portfolio assessment: Direct from the classroom. *Assessment & Evaluation in Higher Education, 37,* 335–347.

McDougal, B. (2006). *Rubric project.* Minneapolis, MN: Minneapolis Community and Technical College.

McGuire, S. Y. (2015). *Teach students how to learn: Strategies you can incorporate into any course to improve student metacognition, study skills, and motivation.* Sterling, VA: Stylus.

McKeachie, W. J. (2014). *Teaching tips* (14th ed.) Boston, MA: Houghton-Mifflin.

Mentkowski, M., & Associates. (2000). *Learning that lasts: Integrating learning, development, and performance in college and beyond.* San Francisco, CA: Jossey-Bass.

Microsoft. (2019). *Get your document's readability and level statistics.* Retrieved from https://support.office.com/en-us/article/Test-your-document-s-readability-85b4969e-e80a-4777-8dd3-f7fc3c8b3fd2

Middendorf, J., & Shopkow, L. (2018). *Overcoming student learning bottlenecks: Decode the critical thinking of your discipline.* Sterling, VA: Stylus.

Miller, G. A. (1956). The magical number seven, plus or minus two: Some limits on our capacity for processing information. *Psychological Review, 63,* 81–97.

Minneapolis Community and Technical College, Information Literacy Department Rubric, 2006.

Minnesota Information Technology Accessibility. (n.d.). Retrieved from https://mn.gov/mnit/about-mnit/accessibility/

Mintu Wimsatt, A., Kernek, C., & Lozada, H. R. (2010). Netiquette: Make it part of your syllabus. *MERLOT Journal of Online Learning and Teaching,* 6, 264–267.

Mueller, P. A. & Oppenheimer, D. M. (2014). The pen is mightier than the keyboard: Advantages of longhand over laptop note taking. *Psychological Science, 25,* 1159–1168.

Mullen, C. A. (2012). Mentoring: An overview. In S. J. Fletcher & C. A. Mullen, *Sage handbook of mentoring and coaching in education,* 13. London, UK: Sage.

National Center for Education Statistics. (2014). *Percentage of first-year undergraduate students who reported taking remedial education courses, by selected student and institution characteristics 2003–04, 2007–08, and 2011–12.* Retrieved from https://nces.ed.gov/programs/digest/d15/tables/dt15_311.40.asp.

National Institute for Learning Outcomes Assessment. (2018). *Uses of assessment data for all schools.* Retrieved from http://www.learningoutcomeassessment.org/documents/NILOA%20Presentation%20for%20RosEvaluation.pdf

National Survey of Student Engagement. (2019). *Registration for NSSE and FSSE 2020 is now open!* Retrieved from http://nsse.indiana.edu/

Nilson, L. B. (2007). *The graphic syllabus and the outcomes map: Communicating your course.* San Francisco, CA: Jossey-Bass.

Nilson, L. B., & Goodson, L. A. (2017). *Online teaching at its best: Merging instructional design with teaching and learning research.* San Francisco, CA: Jossey-Bass.

Oakley, B. (2014). *A mind for numbers: How to excel at math and science (even if you flunked algebra).* New York, NY: Penguin.

O'Brien, G., Millis, B. J., & Cohen, M. W. (2008). *The course syllabus: A learning-centered approach* (2nd ed.). San Francisco, CA: Jossey-Bass.

OER Commons. (2019). *Explore. Create. Collaborate.* Retrieved from https://www.oercommons.org/

Ormrod, J. E. (2017). *How we think and learn: Theoretical perspectives and practical implications.* New York, NY: Cambridge University Press.

Palmer, M. S., Bach, D. J., & Streifer, A. C. (2014). Measuring the promise: A learning–focused syllabus rubric. *To Improve the Academy, 33(1),* 14–36.

Palomba, C. A., & Banta, T. W. (Eds.). (2001). *Assessing student competence in accredited disciplines.* Sterling, VA: Stylus.

Pantelidis, V. S. (2017). Reasons to use virtual reality in education and training courses and a model to determine when to use virtual reality [Special issue]. *Themes in Science and Technology Education, 10*(2), 59–70.

Pascarella, E., & Terenzini, P. (1991). *How college affects students: Findings and insights from twenty years of research.* San Francisco, CA: Jossey-Bass.

Paymar, J. (2012). Speak like a leader. *Forbes.* Retrieved from https://www.forbes.com/sites/jimpaymar/2012/02/02/speak-like-a-leader/#d5b783a71443

Pearson. (n.d.). *Evolution of developmental education.* Retrieved from https://www.pearsoned.com/wp-content/uploads/584H072-EvolutionOfDevEd_infographic_new.pdf

Pew Research Center (May 25, 2017). *Factank.* Retrieved from https://www.pewresearch.org/fact-tank/2017/05/25/a-third-of-americans-live-in-a-household-with-three-or-more-smartphones/

Pew Research Center. (2018). *Mobile fact sheet.* Retrieved from https://www.pewinternet.org/fact-sheet/mobile/

Phillips, S. L., & Dennison, S. T. (2015). *Faculty mentoring: A practical manual for mentors, mentees, administrators, and faculty developers.* Sterling, VA: Stylus.

Prensky, M. (2001). Digital natives, digital immigrants. *On the Horizon, 9*(5), 1–6.

Quality Matters (2018a). Course design rubric standards. Retrieved from https://www.qualitymatters.org/qa-resources/rubric-standards/higher-ed-rubric

Quality Matters (2018b). *Helping you deliver on your online promise.* Retrieved from https://www.qualitymatters.org/

Quality Matters (2018c). *QM rubrics and standards.* Retrieved from https://www.qualitymatters.org/qa-resources/rubric-standards.

Rawitsch, D., Heinemann, B., & Dillenbeger, P. (1971). *The Oregon trail* [Computer game]. Minneapolis: Minnesota Educational Computing Consortium.

Rehabilitation Act of 1973, *Pub. L. 93-112.* 29 U.S.C. §701 (1973).

Section 504 of the Rehabilitation Act of 1973, *Pub. L. 93-112.* 29 U.S.C. §794d (1973).

Section 508 of the Rehabilitation Act of 1973, as amended, 29 U.S.C. §794d (1998).

Research Portfolio Rubric. (2006). *Rubric project.* Minneapolis, MN: Minneapolis Community and Technical College..

Respondus Test Bank Network. (2019). *Thousands of ready-to-use publisher test banks.* Retrieved from https://www.respondus.com/products/testbank/index.shtml

Reynolds, C., & Patton, J. (2014). *Leveraging the ePortfolio for integrative learning.* Sterling, VA: Stylus.

Richards, S. L. (2001). *The interactive syllabus: A resource-based, constructivist approach to learning.* Retrieved from https://library.educause.edu/resources/2001/1/the-interactive-syllabus-a-resourcebased-constructivist-approach-to-learning

Schwartz, D., Tsang, J. M. & Blair, K. P. (2016). *The ABC's of how we learn: 26 scientifically proven approaches, how they work, and when to use them.* New York, NY: Norton.

Seale, J. K. (2014). *E-learning and disability in higher education: Accessibility research and practice* (2nd ed.). New York, NY: Routledge.

Seldin, P. (2010). *The teaching portfolio: A practical guide to improved performance and promotion/tenure decisions* (4th ed.). San Francisco, CA: Jossey-Bass.

Şen, Ş., Yilmaz, A., & Geban, Ö. (2015). The effects of process oriented guided inquiry learning environment on students' self-regulated learning skills. *Problems of Education in the 21st Century, 66,* 54–65.

Senge, P. M. (2006). *The fifth discipline: The art and practice of the learning organization.* New York, NY: Random House.

Shanahan, T. (2017, March 15). Disciplinary literacy: The basics [Web log post]. Retrieved from http://shanahanonliteracy.com/blog/disciplinary-literacy-the-basics#sthash.3R9pCTl0.dpbs

Shea, V. (2004). *Netiquette.* San Francisco, CA: Albion.

Silberman, M. (1996). *Active learning: 101 strategies to teach any subject.* Boston, MA: Allyn & Bacon.

Silva, E. (2008). *Measuring skills for the 21st century.* Washington, DC: Education Sector.

Silverthorn, D. (2015). *Human physiology: An integrated approach* (7th ed.). Boston, MA: Pearson.

Skogstrom, D. (2006). *Rubric project.* Minneapolis, MN: Minneapolis Community and Technical College.

Smilkstein, R. (2011). *We're born to learn* (2nd ed.).Thousand Oaks, CA: Corwin Press.

Smith, R. (2016). *Conquering the content: A blueprint for online course design and development.* San Francisco, CA: Jossey-Bass.

Spanish Diplomas. (2019). *2019 DELE exams, deadlines and exam dates: Spanish diplomas.* Retrieved from https://www.dele.org/

State University of New York. (n.d.). *Open SUNY course quality review rubric.* Retrieved from http://oscqr.org/

Stevens, D., & Levi, A. (2012). *Introduction to rubrics* (2nd ed.). Sterling, VA. Stylus.

Strait, J. R., & Lima, M. (2009). *The future of service learning: New solutions for sustaining and improving practice.* Sterling, VA: Stylus.

Sweet, C., Blythe, H., & Carpenter, R. (2017). Teaching for deep learning. *NEA Advocate, 33*(4), 12–*15.*

Sweller, J. (1988). Cognitive load during problem solving: Effects on learning. *Cognitive Science, 12*, 257–285. Retrieved from https://doi.org/10.1207/s15516709cog1202_4

Teach Learn Online. (2018). Retrieved from https://www.howtostudy.org.

Thompson, B. (2007). The syllabus as a communication document: Constructing and presenting the syllabus. *Communication Education,* 56(1), 54–71. doi:10.1080/03634520601011575

Tinto, V., Russo, P., & Stephanie, K. (1994). Students who interact with their teachers develop a support network and are more likely to persist in classes. *Community College Journal*, 64(4), 18–22.

Tobin, T. J., & Behling, K. T. (2018). *Reach everyone, teach everyone: Universal design for learning in higher education.* Morgantown: West Virginia University Press.

Tomlinson, L. M. (1989). *Postsecondary developmental programs: A traditional agenda with new imperatives.* Retrieved from ERIC database. (ED316076)

University of Cincinnati. (n.d.) *Rubric for assessing your teaching syllabus.* Retrieved from https://www.uc.edu/content/dam/uc/cetl/docs/Rubric%20for%20Assessing%20Your%20Teaching%20Syllabus.pdf

U.S. Department of Education. (2013). *Resolution agreement: South Carolina Technical College System OCR compliance review number 11-11-6002.* Retrieved from https://www2.ed.gov/about/offices/list/ocr/docs/investigations/11116002-b.html

Vella, J. (2002). *Learning to listen; learning to teach.* San Francisco, CA: Jossey-Bass.

Walvoord, B. E., & Anderson, V. J. (1998). *Effective grading* (2nd ed.). San Francisco, CA: Jossey-Bass.

Walvoord, B. E., & Banta, T. W. (2010). *Assessment clear and simple: A practical guide for institutions, departments, and general education* (2nd ed.). San Francisco, CA: Wiley.

Ward, A. F., Duke, K., Gneezy, A., & Bos, M. W. (2018). Brain drain: The mere presence of one's own smartphone reduces available cognitive capacity. *Journal of the Association for Consumer Research, 2*(2), 140–154.

WebAIM. (n.d.). *Web accessibility in mind.* Retrieved from https://webaim.org/

Whyte, W. H. (1950, September). Is anybody listening? *Fortune*, p. 174.

Wiggins, G., & McTighe, J. (2005). *Understanding by design.* Alexandria, VA: Association for Supervision and Curriculum Development.

Wilson, R. C. (1986). Improving faculty teaching: Effective use of student evaluations and consultants. *Journal of Higher Education* 57, 196–211.

Wolfe, P. (2001). *Brain matters: Translating research into classroom practice.* Alexandria, VA: Association for Supervision and Curriculum Development.

Woollett, K., & Maguire, E. (2011). Acquiring "the knowledge" of London's layout drives structural brain changes. *Current Biology, 21*, 2109–2114.

Xianglei, C., & Simone, S. (2016). *Remedial coursetaking at U.S. public 2- and 4-year institutions: Scope, experience, and outcomes.* Retrieved from https://nces.ed.gov/pubs2016/2016405.pdf

Yin, R. K. (2012). *Applications of case study research.* Thousand Oaks, CA: Sage.

Yin, R. K. (2018). *Case study research and applications: Design and methods* (6th ed.). Thousand Oaks, CA: Sage.

Zubizarreta, J. (2009). *The learning portfolio: Reflective practice for improving student learning* (2nd ed.). Bolton, MA: Anker.

# ABOUT THE AUTHORS

## Zala Fashant

As a faculty member, faculty developer, dean, and course design coach, Fashant understands how course design plays a major role in student success and retention. He has seen firsthand the importance in designing an environment where every student grows and succeeds. Working with faculty through L. Dee Fink, he has shared these course design strategies nationally in workshops and online courses.

Fashant's big dream is to help faculty have an impact on their students by identifying and sharing their own big dreams in courses that prepare students for success in the classroom and workplace. Fashant has taught face-to-face, blended, and online courses for 30 years in K–12, college, and university settings and presented at many national conferences and faculty development workshops about using course communication to increase student engagement. He has seen the positive effects when faculty engage their students at the very start and throughout a course by two-way communication, which allows and encourages all students to be included in learning.

Fashant has helped faculty design quality assessments that lead to improved teaching and learning. As a dean, he used his departments' assessments to promote each program's goals and performance. He has taught college faculty in online credentialing courses for course design and assessment techniques and has developed assessment tools to measure institutional learner outcomes.

Fashant has evaluated faculty courses as a Quality Matters (QM) peer reviewer. As a dean he evaluated faculty teaching performance through observation and student feedback of courses. He teamed with faculty on professional development committees to promote course design review for more than 200 faculty on two campuses to improve the ways all courses were designed and approved.

As a dean working closely with faculty in liberal arts and career and technical education programs, Fashant has had the opportunity to design strategic plans for institutional outcome assessment, academic and technology master plans, program accreditation, and institutional accreditation. He understands the integration of elements and the need to coordinate courses to institutional assessment into a comprehensive plan.

As assistant director of the Minnesota State Colleges and University's Center for Teaching and Learning, he worked with colleagues in the Office of the Chancellor to develop a system-level portfolio submission for the Board of Trustees Excellence in Teaching Awards, and as a college dean nominated several of his faculty to receive this award.

Fashant developed campus- and system-level faculty development programming for more than 20 years for thousands of college and university faculty in conferences, campus workshops, and webinars. He has made more than 25 highly rated presentations at international conferences on teaching and learning.

### Stewart Ross

As a faculty member, faculty developer, course design coach, and workshop presenter, Ross, professor emeritus of music, Minnesota State University, Mankato, understands how course design plays a major role in student success and retention. As the Center for Excellence in Teaching and Learning founding director at Minnesota State Mankato, Ross provided professional development opportunities through a faculty teaching certificate for which he received an honorable mention award from the Professional and Organizational Development Network. He shared his experiences directly with his colleagues in his role as a member of the leaders' network of the Minnesota State Center for Teaching and Learning.

Ross knows the importance of designing an environment where every student grows and succeeds. Working with faculty in more than 160 workshops and online courses through L. Dee Fink, he has shared his expertise in course design strategies internationally. Some of his experiences with faculty are included in this book as well as some of his journey in improving his own teaching.

Ross developed campus- and system-level faculty development programming for more than 10 years for thousands of college and university faculty. His highly rated presentations at international conferences on teaching and learning have reached hundreds of faculty worldwide. Ross's big dream is to help faculty have an impact on their students by identifying and sharing their own big dreams and creating courses that motivate students to learn.

### Linda Russell

Russell honed her teaching skills as a developmental educator, teaching high school, junior high school, and college reading and English classes. This experience provides a unique perspective on how students make the transition from K–12 to higher education. She also co-coordinated the learning center at her community college for 16 years. Over the years of working closely with nontraditional learners and underprepared learners, she has gained considerable knowledge about best practices for working with at-risk students. As many of those students eventually matriculate into the regular college curriculum, it is imperative for all faculty to become skilled at working to improve the success of all types of students.

Russell served as the Center for Teaching and Learning campus leader conducting many in-class assessments, consultations, and presentations on various topics related to effective learning and teaching. She also created workshops to develop new faculty portfolios as a part of campus faculty performance evaluation. Russell helped faculty design course assessments that led to improved teaching and learning experiences. As a faculty member, she participated in several department-related assessments, which led to curriculum changes and improvements over the years. Russell has shared her expertise in highly rated presentations at international conferences on teaching and learning.

As a member and past board member of the Minnesota Association for Developmental Education and the College Reading and Learning Association, Russell has experience at the state and national levels of professional development leadership. She has been awarded the Minnesota State Board of Trustees Outstanding Educator Award, the College Reading and Learning Association Distinguished Teaching Award, and the Minnesota Association for Developmental Education Service Award. Russell is a contributor to two developmental mathematics textbooks.

## Karen LaPlant

LaPlant has designed courses and taught in face-to-face, blended, and online formats for 30 years. She has taught business and IT, Web design, and information media and is a National Occupational Competency Testing Institute subject matter expert for Business Information Processing. Her work in her institution's Center for Teaching and Learning as a campus leader has affected the quality of courses and learning for thousands of students. She has presented at many national conferences and professional development workshops for faculty and administrators in course communication, integrating technology, classrooms of the future, and accessibility of course materials to increase student engagement. She worked on the Minnesota State Captioning Project to develop a tool kit of resources for institutions considering video captioning. She has served as conference planner at regional and local conferences and served as a Minnesota Learning Commons Advisory Board member.

LaPlant has evaluated faculty courses for years as a QM peer reviewer. She also served as a master reviewer for a team of peer reviewers, managing the course review process from beginning to end and coaching faculty in obtaining certification for their. As the long-time chair of her institutional professional development committee and QM campus coordinator, LaPlant promoted course design review for more than 200 faculty on two campuses and secured funding to obtain certification for more than 50 courses. She chaired the campus curriculum committee and developed a course approval system to help faculty streamline the process of getting courses approved. She developed a syllabus template providing all courses with the campus information required by the QM standards. And, as an Accreditation Council for Business Schools and Programs accreditation site evaluator team member she has seen firsthand the improvement that can occur at an institution when faculty measure their courses for quality.

## Jake Jacobson

As a campus Center for Teaching and Learning leader working closely with faculty in liberal arts and career and technical education programs, Jacobson understands how program or departmental and institutional assessment play a major role in student success and retention. As program chair of Minneapolis College's School of Design and the Arts, as well as a faculty in graphics design, Web and interactive media, and art history, he has been a leading developer of a creative portfolio show and other events that focus on students, college program development, and industry needs. He has designed workshops for faculty on teaching and learning and cohosted one of the largest faculty development conferences in the country on his campus and served as member of a systemwide planning committee.

Jacobson has shared his experience in presentations at local, state, and national conferences on faculty development and on the use of Adobe software. Through his membership in the Professional Organizational Development Network, Jacobson has had opportunities to present and to learn from others in the field. Additionally, he is the museum director and curator of the Virtual Museum of Education Iconics at the University of Minnesota.

Jacobson has had the opportunity to design strategic plans for institutional accreditation and been integral in the preparation of the campus reports, including designing the accreditation report for Minneapolis College. He understands the need to coordinate program advisory committee input to develop course offerings in curriculum development and how student and faculty evaluation plays a role in improving course and program quality.

## Sheri Hutchinson

Hutchinson has presented on the topic of accessibility at campus workshops and national conferences. She designed and wrote a systemwide train the trainer guide that serves as a model for many institutions to begin the task of teaching faculty and staff about using the accessibility checker in Microsoft Office 2010. She recently worked on the Minnesota State Captioning Project to develop a tool kit of resources for institution administrators who are considering the video captioning process. She has seen the positive impact on students when faculty design their courses for accessibility so all learners can be successful.

Hutchinson's work as a campus director of online learning has allowed her to share her expertise on the topics of integrating technology and classrooms of the future at national and regional conferences. She has also worked to assist students who need help to read course materials through text-to-speech technology. She has assisted in the success faculty have had as they design their courses to integrate technology, which facilitates learning and allows all students to be actively engaged.

Hutchinson has taught computer science programming and computer information systems courses, and served as an academic program director for the Minnesota

State system. She has provided assessment leadership at Minneapolis College and is a QM master peer reviewer. Additionally, she has developed nine online textbooks and learning management system user manuals and served as an educational development manager for ReadSpeaker Text to Speech in the learning management system and created development courses for ReadSpeaker World Wide for use by educational institutions. She is a certified scrum master in software development project management.

# INDEX

*Assessment and Accreditation Education books from Stylus Publishing*

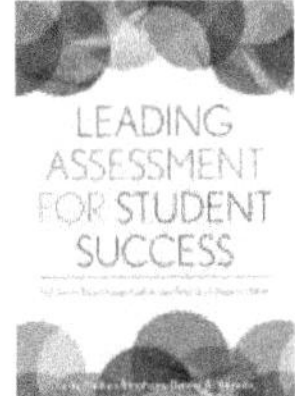


**Leading Assessment for Student Success**
*Ten Tenets That Change Culture and Practice in Student Affairs*
Edited by Rosie Phillips Bingham, Daniel Bureau, and Amber Garrison Duncan
Foreword by Marilee J. Bresciani Ludvik

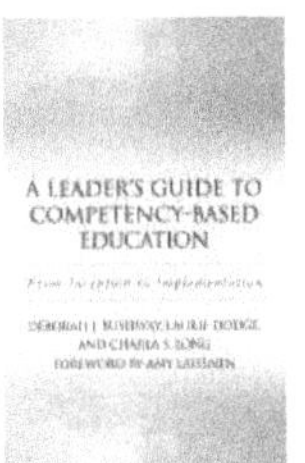


**A Leader's Guide to Competency-Based Education**
*From Inception to Implementation*
Deborah J. Bushway, Laurie Dodge, and Charla S. Long
Foreword by Amy Laitinen

**Enhancing Assessment in Higher Education**
*Putting Psychometrics to Work*
Edited by Tammie Cumming and M. David Miller
Foreword by Michael J. Kolen

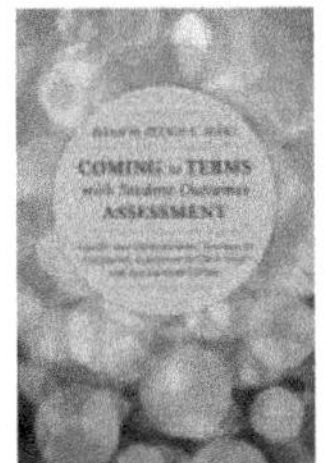

**Coming to Terms with Student Outcomes Assessment**
*Faculty and Administrators' Journeys to Integrating Assessment in Their Work and Institutional Culture*
*Edited by Peggy L. Maki*

**Assessing for Learning**
***Edition 2***
*Building a Sustainable Commitment Across the Institution*
*Peggy L. Maki*

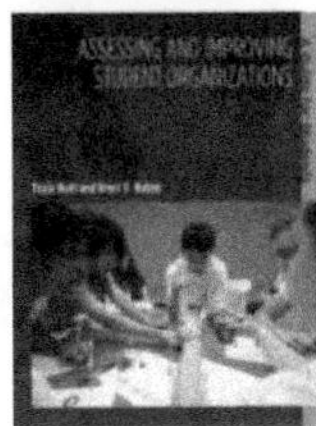

**Assessing and Improving Student Organizations**
*A Guide for Students*
Brent D. Ruben and Tricia Nolfi

*Community College books from Stylus Publishing*

**Alternative Pathways to the Baccalaureate**
*Do Community Colleges Offer a Viable Solution to the Nation's Knowledge Deficit?*
Edited by Nancy Remington and Ronald Remington
Foreword by Carol D'Amico

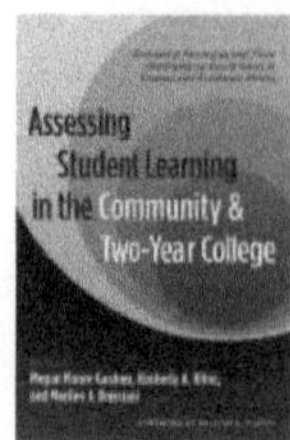

**Assessing Student Learning in the Community and Two-Year College**
*Successful Strategies and Tools Developed by Practitioners in Student and Academic Affairs*
Edited by Megan Moore Gardner, Kimberly A. Kline and Marilee J. Bresciani Ludvik

**The Community College Baccalaureate**
*Emerging Trends and Policy Issues*
Edited by Deborah L. Floyd, Michael L. Skolnik and Kenneth P. Walker

**Community College Leadership**
*A Multidimensional Model for Leading Change*
Pamela L. Eddy
Foreword by George R. Boggs

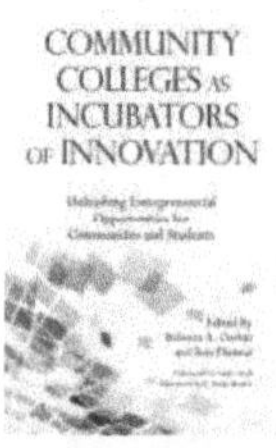

**Community Colleges as Incubators of Innovation**
*Unleashing Entrepreneurial Opportunities for Communities and Students*
Edited by Rebecca A. Corbin and Ron Thomas
Foreword by Andy Stoll, Afterword by J. Noah Brown

**Developing Faculty Learning Communities at Two-Year Colleges**
*Collaborative Models to Improve Teaching and Learning*
*Z Nicolazzo*
Foreword by Kristen A. Renn

*Faculty Development books from Stylus Publishing*

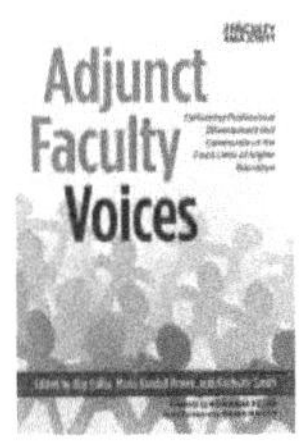

**Adjunct Faculty Voices**
*Cultivating Professional Development and Community at the Front Lines of Higher Education*
Edited by Roy Fuller, Marie Kendall Brown and Kimberly Smith
Foreword by Adrianna Kezar

**Advancing the Culture of Teaching on Campus**
*How a Teaching Center Can Make a Difference*
Edited by Constance Cook and Matthew Kaplan
Foreword by Lester P. Monts

**Faculty Development in the Age of Evidence**
*Current Practices, Future Imperatives*
Andrea L. Beach, Mary Deane Sorcinelli, Ann E. Austin and Jaclyn K. Rivard

**Faculty Mentoring**
*A Practical Manual for Mentors, Mentees, Administrators, and Faculty Developers*
Susan L. Phillips and Susan T. Dennison
Foreword by Milton D. Cox

**The Prudent Professor**
*Planning and Saving for a Worry-Free Retirement from Academe*
Edwin M. Bridges and Brian D. Bridges

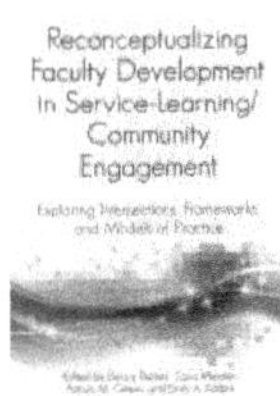

**Reconceptualizing Faculty Development in Service-Learning/Community Engagement**
*Exploring Intersections, Frameworks, andModels of Practice*
Edited by Becca Berkey, Cara Meixner, Patrick M. Green and Emily Eddins Rountree
Foreword by L. Dee Fink

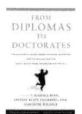

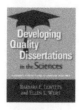

*Leadership & Administration books from Stylus Publishing*

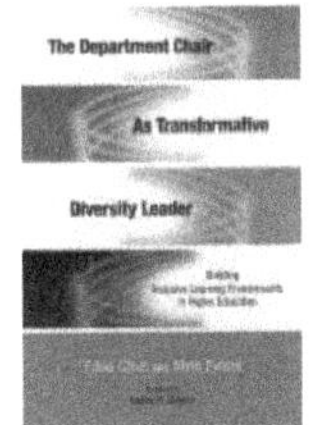


**The Department Chair as Transformative Diversity Leader**
*Building Inclusive Learning Environments in Higher Education*
*Edna Chun and Alvin Evans*
*Foreword by Walter H. Gmelch*

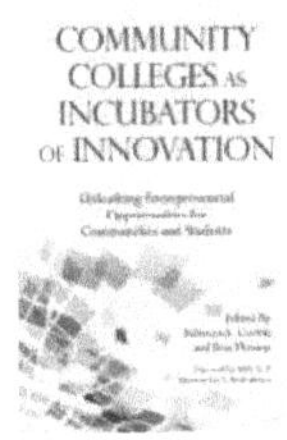


**Community Colleges as Incubators of Innovation**
*Unleashing Entrepreneurial Opportunities for Communities and Students*
Edited by Rebecca A. Corbin and Ron Thomas
Foreword by Andy Stoll, Afterword by J. Noah Brown

**Contingent Academic Labor**
*Evaluating Conditions to Improve Student Outcomes*
Daniel B. Davis
Foreword by Adrianna Kezar

**Community College Leadership**
*A Multidimensional Model for Leading Change*
Pamela L. Eddy
Foreword by George R. Boggs

**College in the Crosshairs**
*An Administrative Perspective on Prevention of Gun Violence*
Edited by Brandi Hephner LaBanc and Brian O. Hemphill
Foreword by Kevin Kruger and Cindi Love

**Building the Field of Higher Education Engagement**
*Foundational Ideas and Future Directions*
Edited by Lorilee R. Sandmann and Diann O. Jones

*Online & Distance Learning books from Stylus Publishing*

**Discussion-Based Online Teaching To Enhance Student Learning Second Edition**
*Theory, Practice and Assessment*
*Tisha Bender*

**Social Media for Active Learning**
*Engaging Students in Meaningful Networked Knowledge Activities*
Vanessa Dennen

**High-Impact Practices in Online Education**
*Research and Best Practices*
Edited by Kathryn E. Linder and Chrysanthemum Mattison Hayes
Foreword by Kelvin Thompson

**The Productive Online and Offline Professor**
*A Practical Guide*
Bonni Stachowiak
Foreword by Robert Talbert

**Jump-Start Your Online Classroom**
*Mastering Five Challenges in Five Days*
David S. Stein and Constance E. Wanstreet

**eService-Learning**
*Creating Experiential Learning and Civic Engagement Through Online and Hybrid Courses*
Edited by Jean R. Strait and Katherine Nordyke
Foreword by Andrew Furco

*Scholarship of Teaching and Learning books from Stylus Publishing*

**Engaging in the Scholarship of Teaching and Learning**
*A Guide to the Process, and How to Develop a Project from Start to Finish*
Cathy Bishop-Clark and Beth Dietz-Uhler
Foreword by Craig E. Nelson

**Engaging Student Voices in the Study of Teaching and Learning**
Edited by Carmen Werder and Megan M. Otis
Foreword by Pat Hutchings and Mary Taylor Huber

**Exploring Signature Pedagogies**
*Approaches to Teaching Disciplinary Habits of Mind*
Edited by Regan A. R. Gurung, Nancy L. Chick and Aeron Haynie
Foreword by Anthony A. Ciccone

**A Guide to Building Education Partnerships**
*Navigating Diverse Cultural Contexts to Turn Challenge into Promise*
Matthew T. Hora and Susan B. Millar
Foreword by Judith A. Ramaley

**SoTL in Action**
*Illuminating Critical Moments of Practice*
Edited by Nancy L. Chick
Foreword by James Rhem

**Teachers As Mentors**
*Models for Promoting Achievement with Disadvantaged and Underrepresented Students by Creating Community*
*Aram Ayalon*
Foreword by Deborah W. Meier

*Student Affairs books from Stylus Publishing*

**Developing Effective Student Peer Mentoring Programs**
*A Practitioner's Guide to Program Design, Delivery, Evaluation, and Training*
*Peter J. Collier*
Foreword by Nora Dominguez

**The First Generation College Experience**
*Implications for Campus Practice, and Strategies for Improving Persistence and Success*
*Jeff Davis*

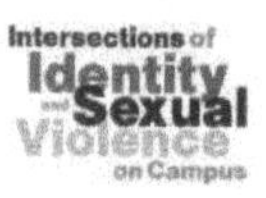


**Intersections of Identity and Sexual Violence on Campus**
*Centering Minoritized Students' Experiences*
Edited by Jessica C. Harris and Chris Linder
Foreword by Wagatwe Wanjuki

**A Guide to Becoming a Scholarly Practitioner in Student Affairs**
Lisa J. Hatfield and Vicki L. Wise
Foreword by Kevin Kruger

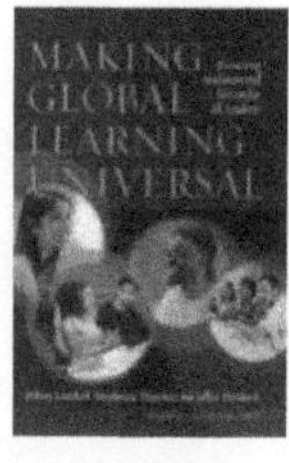


**Making Global Learning Universal**
*Promoting Inclusion and Success for All Students*
Hilary Landorf, Stephanie Doscher, and Jaffus Hardrick
Foreword by Caryn McTighe Musil

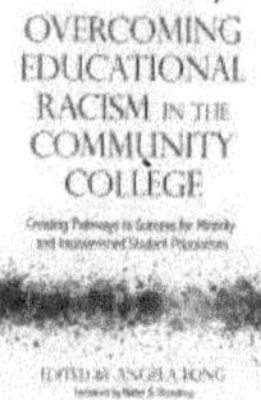


**Overcoming Educational Racism in the Community College**
*Creating Pathways to Success for Minority and Impoverished Student Populations*
*Edited by Angela Long*
*Foreword by Walter G. Bumphus*

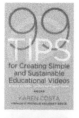

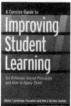

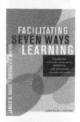